# Comparative Government

# Comparative Government

## AN INTRODUCTION

J. BLONDEL

European University Institute
Florence

## SECOND EDITION

 PRENTICE HALL
HARVESTER WHEATSHEAF

LONDON   NEW YORK   TORONTO   SYDNEY   TOKYO   SINGAPORE
MADRID   MEXICO CITY   MUNICH

First published 1995 by
Prentice Hall/Harvester Wheatsheaf
Campus 400, Maylands Avenue
Hemel Hempstead
Hertfordshire, HP2 7EZ
A division of
Simon & Schuster International Group

Typeset in 10/12pt Sabon
by PPS Limited, Amesbury, Wiltshire

Printed and bound in Great Britain
at the University Press, Cambridge

---

Library of Congress Cataloging in Publication Data

---

Blondel, Jean, 1929–
    Comparative government : an introduction / J. Blondel. — 2nd ed.
      p.   cm.
    Includes bibliographical references and index.
    ISBN 0–13–433905–3
    1. Comparative government.    I. Title.
  JF51.B5615   1995
  320.3—dc20                      94–41757
                                        CIP

---

British Library Cataloguing in Publication Data

---

A catalogue record for this book is available from
the British Library

ISBN 0–13–433905–3

---

1  2  3  4  5     99  98  97  96  95

# Contents

# Preface to the first edition

In the course of the last few decades, the study of comparative government has had a tempestuous journey. First, it moved in the 1960s from a constitutional and legalistic approach to one in which grand taxonomies were elaborated. The idea began to prevail that government formed a 'system' and that the various institutions which were part of this system were related to each other in terms of the 'functions' which they fulfilled. Comparative government had also to be concerned with the newly created developing countries, in which the traditional social base of tribes and ethnic groups was associated with 'modernizing' single parties and 'charismatic' leaders. Grand taxonomies seemed necessary: these alone appeared able to take new countries into account, alongside liberal democracies and dictatorships.

Yet, these hopes proved illusory: taxonomies were static and descriptive, while what seemed to be needed were dynamic and explanatory theories. In the late 1960s and early 1970s, it appeared necessary, therefore, to use different approaches, which would link political life to underlying social and economic forces at both national and international levels: models based on analyses of developmental factors and on international dependency seemed to provide the answer, at a time when Western liberal democracies were increasingly challenged for perpetuating their control over the countries of the 'South' instead of offering help to solve the problems at hand.

'Developmental' approaches came to be criticized in turn, however, for the explanations which they offered seemed too general and indeed simplistic. Thus, in the 1980s, comparative government has partly returned to its original focus on political institutions and on the state, though in a more sophisticated and more realistic manner. The turbulent period during which constitutionalism, systems analysis, and grand developmental theories had been successively adopted and strongly criticized helped to deepen the analysis; meanwhile, there is a calmer and more mature recognition that studies need to remain close to the structures of government. This new maturity is also the result of the accumulation of data on all countries which has taken place over the last decades, as these have helped to build a more complex picture of political life than had been the case earlier.

This volume is thus written at a time when comparative government aims at being a genuinely cross-national study of the institutions of government and of the interconnections between these institutions. What the models of the 1960s and 1970s made abundantly clear was that comparative government had to be general, but that it had also to be grounded in a concrete picture of individual cases. Thus, as I wrote twenty years ago in an earlier version of a work which had the same aim as this volume, comparative government must consider both 'the general conditions which lead to the development of political systems and the more detailed factors which account for the characteristics of political structures, whether groups, parties, governments, assemblies, or bureaucracies' (*Introduction to Comparative Government* (1969), p. x). This was indeed the purpose of comparative government at its origin, at the time when Aristotle wrote his *Politics*. This is what it is recognized to be once more, in a period in which changes in many countries, and indeed the collapse of apparently strong regimes in the Communist world, show in a striking manner the part which institutions can play in shaping the character of political systems.

It has been particularly pleasant for me to return to a general reflection on comparative government at this point: I am therefore especially grateful to Philip Cross, of Philip Allan, for having given me the opportunity to undertake this task as well as for having helped and encouraged me while this work was being prepared. I wish also to thank my students of the European University Institute in Florence, who gave me numerous occasions to discuss many sections of this text. I am most grateful to Professor J. Schwarze, also of the European University Institute, for his comments on two of the chapters which relate to constitutions. I owe a special debt to Maureen Lechleitner, who put on the computer draft chapters, tables, and bibliography. Finally, I wish to thank Tess for the unfailing support she gave me while this book was being written. I know that, with their help, I have prepared a markedly better volume than would otherwise have been the case: I only hope that this work will be of use in leading to further developments in the systematic study of comparative government.

J.B.
Florence, Italy
1990

# Preface to the second edition

This is a substantially revised version of the text which appeared in 1990. The basic structure of the work remains the same; it is manifest that the framework of the volume, which was initiated in the earlier Weidenfeld version, is increasingly adopted by comparative government scholars as the only formula which can help to describe in a systematic manner the characteristics of contemporary government.

The present volume introduces two types of modification. First, in terms of substance, changes have naturally been introduced, where appropriate and in particular in the section on parties, to take into account the massive developments which have taken place, not just in the Communist area, but throughout the world, as a result of the collapse of communism in Eastern Europe and of the apparent total victory of liberal democracy. Second, in terms of presentation, this new edition contains summaries and other inserts which will make developments easier to follow.

I wish to thank particularly Clare Grist, of Simon and Schuster International, for the interest she has consistently shown in this work and for the most valuable advice she gave me throughout the preparation of this new edition. I also wish to thank my students and colleagues at the European University Institute for the stimulus they gave me as I discussed, sometimes unknown to them, various sections of this work. I wish above all to thank my wife for the patience which she displayed as I was, often painstakingly, revising my earlier text.

J.B.
Florence, Italy
September 1994

# List of tables and figures

## Tables

## Figures

**Part I**

# General framework and concepts

# 1

# The importance and scope of comparative government

## Introduction

This book studies the politics of governments on a comparative basis. Although the words 'politics' and 'politicians' are typically associated with governments, and especially with national governments, there is also politics in groups of all kinds, such as trade unions, businesses and even churches. This book, however, concentrates on *governmental politics* because governments are very powerful and are seen to be very powerful, even in the most liberal countries and even where they do not run the economy. They have great financial resources, their decisions have the authority of the law, and the coercion of physical punishment is at their disposal. In countries large or small, the actions of our own government and the actions of the governments of the great powers will shape our destiny.

The political life of governments is studied here on a comparative basis. This is because only if this approach is adopted can one hope to discover trends and thus achieve a satisfactory understanding of the broad characteristics underlying governmental politics. Many among the great 'classical' writers of political science, from Aristotle onwards, have studied governmental politics in a comparative framework.

The fact that governmental politics is important and needs to be studied is not really controversial, even if some might shy away from such a study on the grounds that the ways of politicians are impenetrable or, on the contrary, too closely associated with personal interests. What may be more controversial, however, is the idea that the study should be undertaken on a comparative basis. We need therefore to spend a little time, at the outset, in examining the reasons why such a framework is the only truly satisfactory way of approaching the study of governmental politics, before considering what is the scope and the object of the study.

# Benefits of comparative study

## The study of government on a country basis is hampered by the small number of cases

Governmental politics needs to be studied comparatively, in the first place, because studies undertaken on a single-country basis often do not provide enough cases for firm conclusions to be drawn. This is not so true in other fields of learning, either because one can conduct experiments or because the same phenomena occur frequently. It is in the main by observing series of identical or at least similar phenomena that we learn about our environment. This is, for instance, how scientists began to grasp the main characteristics of the physical world and some aspects of social life. Moreover, even where the same phenomenon tended to occur often, it took a very long time to distinguish spurious relationships from genuine interconnections: for instance, it was only after much reflection that the phenomenon of gravitation among physical bodies was discovered, both on earth and in the universe in general. A further long period had to elapse before a second type of regularity, the statistical regularity, began to be discovered in the biological and the social sciences. These regularities were discovered only because of the existence of large numbers of happenings of the same class. Such repetitiveness does occur in some aspects of governmental politics, to be sure, but this is rare: an example is the field of voting behaviour, where a better understanding has been achieved largely because millions of electors cast their ballots in national elections.

In most aspects of the study of governments, on the other hand, there are few instances of the same phenomenon. To begin with, there is in each country only one president, one prime minister, one national cabinet. In some countries there is only one party, but even where there is more than one, the number of these parties is always small. There is sometimes no national legislature at all, but when such a legislature exists, there is only one. It is sometimes possible to increase the number of cases, by looking at local governments or by examining a number of presidents, prime ministers or cabinets over time. However, such a step, first, may not always be possible or advisable and, second, means in effect undertaking comparisons.

One can certainly undertake comparisons by looking at events in one country over time, but the more obvious way to undertake comparisons is to compare governments across countries. Such an approach seems in general more advisable because it enables us to discover how governments behave at the same moment, without having to control for the possible effect that one event may have on a subsequent one. If we are to look for regularities in governmental politics, cross-national comparisons, especially now that there are well over 150 countries in the world, provide the opportunity to obtain a substantial, if still not truly large, universe of observations, and thus to establish some general trends.

## Inevitability of the comparative approach

Comparison not only constitutes a better means of studying governmental politics; in reality, comparison is embedded in the very way in which we discuss governmental politics. One can therefore claim with justification that comparison is inevitable. Deep down, any judgement passed on the workings of a particular government or of a particular institution of government is based on an underlying notion, however vague, of the way in which similar governments or similar institutions of government work in other circumstances. It may be possible, in theory, to 'invent' all the workings of governments: indeed, we may think that we do so when we discuss 'ideal' types of government, such as parliamentary or presidential systems. In practice, however, such abstractions are based on impressions and on ideas to which we have come by learning gradually about a variety of real-world situations.

This is why we can justifiably claim that proposals suggesting amendments to existing sets of arrangements, and even proposals which put forward fundamental changes, are built on implicit comparisons. One good example is that of electoral change: the case for altering the electoral system of a country is based on conclusions drawn from the workings of other electoral systems. The reform of legislatures provides another example: debates on reforming parliament in a given country – for instance, by introducing 'question time' or increasing the power of committees – are fuelled by views about the way such arrangements operate in other countries.

We must therefore recognize that there is comparison everywhere, even if it is hidden or implicit. Since this is the case, it is better to be explicit and therefore, when studying governmental politics, to undertake it quite openly on a comparative basis.

## Inevitability of the comparative approach

The value of comparative government has none the less been questioned. It has been challenged on the ground that it is often undertaken in an unsatisfactory or even superficial manner (Macridis, 1955: 7–12). This was truer in the past, but the criticism remains in part justified. If we are to compare, we must do so in detail and systematically, and not only in a general manner. For instance, we should not merely describe successively the institutions of a number of countries and claim that such a description constitutes a comparison; we must examine jointly the characteristics of these institutions and see in what specific ways they are similar or different.

One of the reasons why true cross-national comparisons have taken place only slowly is the accidental fact that the number of scholars in the field was until recently very small, while the data are often rendered difficult to collect as a result of prohibitions: many aspects of the life of governments are regarded as state secrets, for instance. So, while it is true that Aristotle did begin to compare the constitutions of the Greek cities in a systematic manner in his *Politics*, in reality only in the twentieth century has the study truly taken shape, and even then in a relatively modest manner until the 1960s, especially outside the United States (Blondel, 1981: 162–87). Naturally, therefore, the information which has been amassed remains limited, and genuine comparisons are consequently difficult to undertake.

Yet there is a second criticism, which is more fundamental: it is, in a nutshell, that no two countries are similar enough to be compared, essentially because their history is different. It is pointed out that cabinets or legislatures, parties or groups, are all sufficiently different from one country to the next to make it impossible to obtain truly comparable cases. According to this view, the *cultural idiosyncrasies* of each country are such that they condemn comparative analyses to superficiality, if not to grave misunderstandings. Governmental politics in each country at each point in time is thus regarded as being the result of traditions which are so deep rooted that the only thing that can be done is to describe and analyze each case separately. To proceed from the assumption that institutions can easily be compared leads, so the argument goes, to making unwarranted links and to drawing unwarranted general conclusions (Mayer, 1972: 67–81, 273–81; Ragin, 1987: 34–68; Badie, 1989: 344–51).

## Comparisons as the root of analysis

The argument has force: historical traditions do fashion in a particular way the governmental life of each country. Yet the argument has limitations too, since as we have seen, comparisons are always made, implicitly or explicitly. Indeed, they are made even by those who eschew comparisons because the categories and constructs which all have to use are by definition general, and thus in essence comparative. It is not possible to refer to such institutions as cabinets, legislatures, parties, etc. without being comparative. One may think that one is concerned with a particular country only, but in reality, the underlying concepts are inherently comparative as they apply to institutions which exist in many, if not all, countries. Since we cannot discuss governmental politics in a country without the help of these concepts, and since these concepts make sense only if they apply to other countries as well, the comparative approach is embedded in all our analyses.

## General nature of study of government

Going further, the implication of the existence of general concepts is that the study of government has also to be general. Comparative government should not merely concentrate on the examination of a relatively small number of countries or a small number of institutions. It should relate to all governments, even if, in practice, there are limitations because our knowledge remains insufficient.

## The comparative approach improves significantly our understanding of governments

We could merely argue that comparative government should be general because the concepts which we use are general, but there is more. An explicit and general comparative

## BOX 1.1
## Comparative government and the emergence of new nations

The growth of comparative government has in many ways coincided and been associated with the emergence of new nations across the world. In 1945, at the end of the Second World War, there were approximately 70 independent states, almost all of which were in Europe and the Americas, Latin America being the only part of the developing world in which the struggle for independence had led to the setting up of new states out of colonies, following the US example, in the early part of the nineteenth century.

Some new states were created in eastern Europe in the late nineteenth century and after the First World War out of the break up of the Turkish and Austro-Hungarian empires, but the main push towards independence occurred from the late 1940s to the late 1960s, a period during which the number of independent states doubled. These were mostly set up in south and south-east Asia, the Middle East and north Africa, and Africa south of the Sahara. After a lull during which only a small number of island states became independent, primarily in the Pacific and in the Caribbean, a further wave of independent states occurred in the late 1980s as a result of the break-up of the Soviet Union and of Yugoslavia. There were thus in the mid-1990s over 170 states. Most of them have small to very small populations, except two giants (China and India, each of which have about one thousand million people) and a small number of very populated states (the United States, Indonesia, Brazil, Russia, Japan, Bangladesh, Pakistan and Nigeria) which have between over 250 million and somewhat over 100 million people.

The emergence of new countries has markedly affected the character of comparative government. Not surprisingly, it was previously essentially a European and North American field of study. It has increasingly been concerned with the developing world. In the process, it has become more complex, and efforts have usually been made to overcome the difficulties posed by world-wide comparisons.

approach improves our global understanding of governmental life, as, through comparisons, we are able to have a better vision of what can be described as the overall 'landscape' of politics across the world. We can then discover more easily the extent to which the characteristics which we find in a particular government are unusual or, on the contrary, rather common. Comments about the effect of electoral systems, for instance, have become appreciably more sophisticated as political scientists have looked at these effects in a general manner. Comments about the duration of the tenure in office of leaders or of cabinet members have become more precise and therefore more valid as they have come to be made on the basis of world-wide comparisons. This is, indeed, how general and particular go together, and how the problem of 'cultural idiosyncrasies' can be overcome. Far from being antithetical to the study of individual governments or institutions, general comparative studies provide a framework, an irreplaceable framework, which indicates in which directions studies of individual governments or institutions can most profitably go (Hague *et al.*, 1993: 23–37).

## The scope of the study of comparative government

If the approach is to be comparative, what then is the scope of comparative government? This scope gradually broadened as the nature of the web which constitutes government became better perceived. In the nineteenth century, the study of government was generally regarded as coextensive with the study of constitutional arrangements. The events of the eighteenth century, the American and French Revolutions in particular, themselves resulting in large part from the example of the English Revolution of the previous century, seemed to suggest two conclusions. The first was that absolutism was a thing of the past; the second was that societies would henceforth be governed on the basis of the rule of law and of constitutional principles. This meant that it was no more necessary for political scientists to study absolutist governments than it was necessary for economists to study barter economies. Constitutions were then viewed as the core of the analysis of government; political scientists became constitutional lawyers.

This view has gradually come to be regarded as narrow both in terms of geography and in terms of the workings of modern government. The operations of governments could not be confined to the provisions of constitutions; extra-constitutional bodies, such as political parties, started to play a large part in the political life of many nations in the nineteenth century. Moreover, far from spreading over the whole globe, constitutionalism seemed for a long time to be restricted primarily to a limited 'Atlantic area'. Even if there has been an expansion of constitutional government during the 1980s, there is still considerable doubt as to how far or how deep constitutionalism has taken root.

### Comparative government as the study of the political system

Comparative government could therefore no longer be restricted to the study of constitutional arrangements. Indeed, already before the Second World War, the search for a broader framework had begun – a framework which would be broader even than the notion of the state, since the goal was to make it possible to study all governments and all aspects of governmental politics on a comparative basis. The framework would have to make it possible to study authoritarian regimes, of which there had always been many and which had in several cases become harsher in the twentieth century, not in order to justify these systems, but in order to analyze their workings. Moreover, comparative government needed also to be able to cover institutions or organizations such as parties and groups, which, even in constitutional regimes, did not form part, strictly speaking, of the constitutional process or even of the state apparatus.

---

## BOX 1.2
## Constitutionalism, behaviourism and neo-institutionalism in comparative government

The main emphasis in the study of comparative government has been significantly modified in the course of the twentieth century. One can distinguish three phases:

- The *constitutionalist phase*, up to approximately the Second World War. Constitutions had been gradually introduced in Europe and Latin America. They were viewed as characterizing 'modern' political systems even if they were sometimes seriously distorted.

- The *behavioural phase*, primarily during the 1940s, 1950s and 1960s. Behaviourism was first successful in the study of national politics, particularly in the United States. It was based on the recognition that what was essential was to study what took place in reality, not what was stated formally (see Dahl, 1963). The approach was naturally applied to comparative government, where many constitutions were not applied and dictatorships often prevailed. Yet behaviourism could not be used in the study of comparative government without a new framework: this was what the concept of political system was to provide.

- The *neo-institutionalist phase*, which began in the 1970s with the recognition that not everything could be understood by studying behaviour. Structures were essential. Critics of behaviourism stressed that one needed in particular to 'bring the state back in' (Skocpol in Evans *et al.*, 1985) and, together with the state, a whole range of institutions. The result is a more balanced approach and a more complex analysis which takes into account institutions and behaviour, constitutions and practices. This renders comparative government better able to account for the considerable variations which exist in the contemporary world.

---

Such a broad framework was gradually elaborated. It was to be based on the recognition that, everywhere, governments constitute a system – a *political system* or, perhaps more accurately, a *governmental system*. Governments form a system because they are engaged in an activity in which a substantial number of elements are interconnected, in a process through which policies are initiated, developed and implemented (Easton, 1953: 96–100).

The scope of comparative government is thus the combined study of the elements in the society which form such a political system. These elements include bodies established by constitutions, such as presidencies, cabinets and legislatures; but they also include parties, groups (to the extent that these participate in governmental politics), bureaucracies and courts. Thus political systems are both similar and different in two ways. First, many elements of these systems are the same, but not all of them: some exist in some political systems and not in others. Second, the way in which these elements are combined or interconnected vary from one system to another.

## Institutions in the political system

The elements of the political system, such as those which we mentioned earlier – legislatures, parties and groups – can be described under the generic terms of 'institutions', 'organizations' or 'structures'. The political system operates essentially through and by institutions; they are in effect the pieces of the machinery.

There has been substantial controversy about the role of institutions. They have sometimes been regarded as less important than the actors within them. It has been felt that what should be studied is not so much institutions as behaviour. This view was a reaction against an analysis of institutions that was based primarily on the formal examination of their powers, instead of also encompassing what actually happened in the institutions – that is, the behaviour of the actors within them.

Such a distinction between institutional and behavioural analysis is not realistic, however, and is no longer regarded as such. On the contrary, both aspects need to be jointly examined. A more balanced view of the scope of comparative government has therefore emerged which takes into account both the importance of institutions and the way in which these institutions are shaped by the behaviour of actors. This more balanced view has been embodied in the idea of the *new institutionalism*, which developed from the second half of the 1980s (March and Olsen, 1984: 734–49; 1989).

Such a combined analysis is essential. On the one hand, the analysis of government must not be concerned exclusively, or even primarily, with formal powers and rules, but with what actually takes place; on the other hand, institutions are crucial in that they structure the way in which governments operate. Behaviour occurs within the context of institutions: these are the means by which governmental processes occur and which shape behaviour.

## The role of societal values and norms

Comparative government has also to be concerned with societal values or norms because these are, directly or indirectly, at the origin of both institutions and behaviour. For instance, parliaments are set up because there is a desire to introduce the representative principle: this is a societal value. Parties are established because their founding fathers wish to put forward viewpoints or defend interests: these, too, are societal values. Institutions are products – even if in a complex and often roundabout manner – of societal values. Comparative government therefore needs to examine the values which underlie the development of institutions in different political systems.

## Political development

Institutions do not remain static in any political system. On the contrary, they are established and grow; they also decay and even disappear. This is often the result of changes in societal values, but may also be the result of what might be regarded as 'institutional fatigue'. The study of institutional change is therefore naturally a key aspect of the study of comparative government. It has to be conducted in combination with the study of changes in behavioural patterns within these institutions, and of changes in the values on which the institutions are based. The study of the dynamics of political systems is typically referred to, perhaps optimistically, as being the study of *political development* (or, as was said in the past, in an even more optimistic vein, the study of political 'progress').

## Support, authority, legitimacy and coercion

The institutions of the political system and the political system itself are means by which decisions are taken on behalf and for the society: the question of the relationship between government and society has thus to be addressed if the effectiveness of the political decisions is to be assessed.

This raises the question of support and authority. Some governments have much support and enjoy much authority: they can be regarded as legitimate. Others have little support and have to rely on coercion. How far government can operate with limited support is highly debatable and indeed highly debated, since examples of long-standing dictatorships are numerous. Support, authority, legitimacy and coercion are key elements in building up a realistic picture of the characteristics of political systems.

## The structure of the book

These concepts are the tools which help to appreciate, if not perhaps truly to measure, the way political systems are related to the society. They need to be carefully examined if we are to analyze fully the nature of governmental institutions and the way they combine in the political system.

Part I of this book will therefore be devoted to the following:

- Analysis of the relationship between institutions and the political system.
- Examination of the way in which societal values shape the political system.
- Study of political change and 'development'.
- Discussion of the extent to which governments obtain obedience naturally or need to rely on coercion.

Parts II and III will then look at the role of groups and parties, Part IV at governmental structures in the narrow sense, such as legislatures and cabinets, and Part V at the way decisions are implemented and control is exercised on governments.

# Overview

The study of governmental politics gains markedly by being comparative: indeed, comparisons are embedded in all aspects of the analysis of governments. These comparisons gain by being undertaken in a truly general mould.

The cultural idiosyncrasies of each country must be taken into account, but it is better to do so within the general cross-national context which comparative government can provide.

The political life of governments can be analyzed on a fully comparative basis if we recognize that governments constitute a *political system* in which policies are initiated, develop and are implemented.

The prime objects of study in comparative government are the *institutions, organizations or structures* of the political system, such as groups, parties, legislatures, cabinets, bureaucracies and courts.

Institutions are shaped by the values or norms which prevail in the society.

Political systems change over time, partly as a result of changes in norms, partly as a result of changes in institutional arrangements, and partly as a result of changes in behaviour. The question of political development is thus a crucial aspect of the study of governments.

Governments also need support and authority; they may or may not be *legitimate*; they may have to rely strongly on *coercion*.

These characteristics provide a picture of the life of governments on a comparative basis, and will serve as a guide as the institutions of governments are being studied.

# Further reading

There is naturally a great abundance of texts on the nature of politics. Among those which can be read with great profit are the introductory sections of R.A. Dahl's classic, *Modern Political Analysis* (1963: 4–13), of A. Leftwich, ed., *What is Politics?* (1984: 1–18) and of M. Laver, *Invitation to Politics* (1983: 1–16).

The difficulties and indeed basic inadequacy of comparative analysis have been repeatedly mentioned, especially in the 1950s and 1960s. One often quoted article is that of R.C. Macridis, *The Study of Comparative Government* (1955), in which the parochial and truly 'non-comparative' character of comparative politics was denounced. A more fundamental critique was made in the early 1970s by R.T. Holt and J.E. Turner in an often quoted article on 'The methodology of comparative research', which appeared in the volume of the same title edited by these authors (1970). On the recurrent debate between supporters of general and individual analyses, see in particular L.C. Mayer, *Comparative Political Inquiry* (1972: 67–81, 273–81), M. Dogan and G. Pelassy, *How to Compare Nations* (1984) and C. Ragin, *The Comparative Method* (1987: 34–68). The 'father' of comparative government is unquestionably Aristotle with his *Politics*; the subject was developed again on a systematic basis by the Frenchman Montesquieu (1689–1755), who wrote the *Spirit of Laws* in 1748. The most outstanding modern works on the subject were those of Lord Bryce (*Modern Democracies*, 1891) and of A.L. Lowell (*Governments and Parties in Continental Europe*, 2 vols., 1896). A resumé of the evolution of comparative analysis within political science can be found in my *Discipline of Politics* (1981): chapters 4 and 7).

The conflict between behaviourists and anti-behaviourists which has marked the decades since the 1950s can be examined further in Mayer, *op. cit.* (1972: 67–81) and in M. Landau, *Political Theory and Political Science* (1979. 43–71), see also P. Evans *et al.*, eds., *Bringing the State Back In* (1985). The more recent 'new institutionalism' has been presented in particular by J.G. March and J.P. Olsen, 'The new institutionalism' *Am. Pol. Sc. Rev.* (1984: 734–49) and in the subsequent volume of these authors, *Rediscovering Institutions* (1989).

# 2

# Political systems and the role of institutions

## Introduction

If truly valuable comparative analyses are to be undertaken, a framework is needed to help to detect similarities and differences among governments. It was pointed out in the previous chapter that the concept of the political or governmental system could form the basis of such a framework. This will be the case if it fulfils two requirements: first, it must be applicable to all types of government; second, it must provide a yardstick with which to assess the detailed characteristics of these governments.

Both conditions are equally important. A comparative framework is clearly not satisfactory if it cannot be applied to all governments. Constitutionalism was used as a framework for comparative analyses in the past, as we saw, and for precise comparative analyses. Indeed, the well-known distinction between presidential and parliamentary systems continues to be in use because, for some types of polity, it helps to contrast sharply and specifically the powers of the national executive and of the elected chamber, the legislative assembly or parliament. But constitutionalism cannot provide a general framework for the comparative analysis of governments because it manifestly cannot help to describe regimes which are not based on constitutional principles. On the other hand, the concept of the political system is truly universal, since, as we saw in the previous chapter, it provides a framework within which to analyze the way decisions are initiated, elaborated and implemented in any society. As, in any society, collective decisions must be taken, every society has a political system. Thus the concept of the political system fulfils the first of the two requirements.

The framework must also be detailed enough to enable us to distinguish concretely among the many governments which exist. On this point, the concept of the political system has been less successful: in fact, less successful than the idea of constitutionalism had been. Efforts have been made to refine and develop various aspects of the framework, but these efforts have been criticized. So far, while one may be able to list the components or elements of political systems, the specific nature of the *links* between these components is far from clear.

This chapter will therefore look successively at three questions:

- It will survey the *general characteristics* of the concept of the political system.
- It will explore the nature of the *components* within this system. These are the *institutions or groups* on the basis of which comparisons between political systems can be made.
- It will assess how far these components can be concretely *linked*, and thus help to distinguish among political systems.

# The political system

## The political system viewed as a framework for the 'authoritative allocation of values'

The idea of the political system (as it is being known, although we noted that it would be more accurate to refer to it as the governmental system) stems from the recognition that the purpose of government is to elaborate and implement decisions for the society. These policies may be either positive or negative. To reject a proposal is to undertake a policy; and not to take a decision at all is also to adopt a policy.

This process of decision making has three characteristics:

- It is a process of *allocation*, since there is a distribution of goods to some or all the members of the society.
- It is a process of allocation of *values*, since policies can be spiritual as well as physical: they decide on divorce as well as on taxation. Physical policy making is also concerned with values: a taxation system is based on values, as is a law on abortion or divorce.
- The process is *authoritative*, since the political system needs the obedience or acceptance, natural or contrived, of the members of the society for the implementation of its policies (Easton, 1953: 96–100, 129–41; 1965: 29–33).

If we leave for Chapter 5 the question of whether the government has enough authority to ensure that the values it allocates are accepted – that is to say, to ensure that the laws are obeyed – and if we concentrate on the characteristics of the allocation of these values, two general remarks need to be made. First, the object of governmental activity is *not specified*, because it is (or can be) universal: the political system allocates values; it does not allocate some values rather than others. The political system exists because values have to be allocated (goods and services distributed, spiritual or moral standpoints adopted), not because some values rather than others have to be allocated.

This is what makes the idea of the political system truly general and applicable to any government in any society; constitutionalism, on the other hand, had a more restricted scope, since the values with which it was concerned tended to be liberal. While the emphasis may be on different values in different societies, the *concept* of political system can appropriately be used to analyze all types of polity; it is not dependent on any particular set of values.

Second, the definition which has been given relates to a political (or governmental) *system*: we are defining a set of interconnected activities undertaken by large numbers of agents. This system, as we have already had occasion to note, is composed of elements which may or may not be in accord, but which are at least interdependent, as they would not otherwise be part of a system. These elements are the 'structures' of the system: they are the institutions or groups, which we will consider more closely later in this chapter.

## Why values need to be allocated

Before doing so, however, we need to ask: why is there a political or governmental 'system' at all? Why do we need a mechanism to allocate values in the society? The answer lies in the fact that the number of values which might be allocated is larger than the number of values which can be allocated: that is, there is *scarcity*.

The scarcity may be *physical*, just as, in the economic field, the scarcity of goods creates the necessity for the allocation mechanism called the price system. Indeed, the political system operates in parallel with the economic system, as it provides a mechanism by which some values, including goods and services, are allocated in the polity, but in a manner distinct from the price mechanism. Thus the economic system could be regarded as being part of the political system, since it is dependent on the political system allowing some goods and services to be distributed by means of the price mechanism. This explains why there can be variations over time and space in this respect: some political systems allow more free enterprise than others; some goods and services (in particular, health, education and pensions) may be distributed 'free' (i.e. by governmental decisions) or by the operation of the price mechanism (Laver, 1983: 17–46).

The scarcity which is regulated by the political system is not only physical, however; it is also spiritual and moral. In such cases, we are typically confronted with alternatives among which we have to choose, though there is sometimes scope for compromise. For instance, divorce may or may not be allowed; but it may also be allowed more or less liberally. In such matters (and indeed also with respect to many goods and services, particularly those which the government provides directly, such as roads), the scarcity to which one refers is based on the fact that one cannot decide both to do and not to do. With respect to these goods, which are typically labelled *collective*, a decision has to be taken to provide or not to provide 'on behalf' of the society as a whole (Olson, 1971: 15).

Society needs a governmental system because both goods and services, as well as spiritual and moral values, have to be allocated, and because it is physically or logically impossible to allocate all of them. 'Anarchy', in the etymological sense of absence of government, is an impossibility because of the constraints which limited resources and life in common impose on the society, although some problems can be alleviated by means of decentralization. Yet the question still remains as to why so many values need to be allocated. Values do not 'emerge' spontaneously; they have to be 'presented', as it were, to the political system. It is clear, for instance, that however numerous values may be in a given society, not all possible values will be on the agenda. Thus the question of the value allocation process raises the question of the reason why values emerge and, specifically, of the mechanisms by which some values, rather than others, are being decided on. This leads again to the part played by institutions and groups in structuring the system, and to the phases of the political system during which these structures operate.

## Why the political system and not the state?

Before analyzing these phases, however, we need to examine a preliminary question: is it worth introducing a new concept when another has been in common use for generations, that of the state? Constitutionalism may be regarded as providing a somewhat restricted framework, since it applies to liberal polities only; but the concept of the state seems broader because it has been applied in the past to a wide variety of polities. Indeed, after having lost much of its glamour in the 1950s and 1960s, the concept of the state regained favour among political scientists in the 1970s and 1980s.

The concept of the state can unquestionably be applied more broadly than the concept of constitutionalism. However, it is less appropriate than the concept of the political system as a basis for comparative government analysis for two main reasons. First, the concept of the state is not truly universal. It can be used only with respect to those polities which have organized administrative arrangements. Admittedly, in the contemporary world, polities tend normally to take the form of states, but this is not universal, as for instance during a pre-independence process or when a guerrilla movement occupies a portion of a territory which it claims to be liberating.

Second, the concept of the state is not neutral with respect to the allocation of values. It sets up an administrative hierarchy: groups and other bodies within the state are legally subordinated to it, even if this is often more formal than real. The state also tends to deny, logically from a legal standpoint, if often unrealistically, the existence of the institutions and groups which it does not recognize. This is because the concept of the state was developed primarily by lawyers at the time of the Renaissance in western Europe in order to establish the supremacy of the central government (in effect of kings) over aristocrats, other social groups, and local communities which had attempted to maintain their autonomy. Thus the concept of the state is ideological and therefore normative. Specifically, when it is claimed that the state has a monopoly of (legal) coercion, or has final authority within its territory and is therefore different in kind from any other grouping, these are legal assumptions, not matters which can be empirically tested (Benn and Peters, 1959: 255–68).

Since it is normative, the concept of the state cannot therefore be used as a general framework in order to analyze the characteristics of all types of polity. To be truly general, comparative government must be able to consider types of relationship which do not coincide with the legal definition of the state.

There is a final drawback. The concept of the state does not provide a means of describing the sequence of activities which happen when collective decisions are taken in a polity. This is why we must move beyond the concept of the state and adopt the more general framework of the political system.

## Phases of the political system

In contrast with the concept of the state, the concept of the political system suggests that the authoritative allocation of values goes through a series of phases which stem directly from the fact that the political system is a mechanism by which policies are decided. The very idea of policy making implies the existence of a succession of phases: policies are first *initiated*, then *elaborated* and finally *implemented*. Another way of presenting what the political system achieves is to say that it converts *demands*, which correspond to the initiation phase of policies, into fully fledged *policies*. This description of the political system was first suggested by Easton in his book entitled precisely *The Political System* (1953); it was elaborated subsequently by the same author in a volume published in 1965. Demands constitute the *inputs* into the system; fully fledged policies are the *outputs*; the conversion process takes place in between, in the *black box*. Easton conceived the political system as being analogous to a computer which processes and thereby transforms 'inputs' into 'outputs', while adjusting mechanisms allow for a feedback from the outputs on the input mechanism. The inputs are the pressures of all kinds exercised on the system, which is activated by way of the demands, and which can then elaborate decisions which will become outputs and be presented to the society (Easton, 1953: 96–100; 1965: 29–33; Almond and Coleman, 1960: 5–9).

The idea is appealing because it corresponds to reality in some respects, especially where 'demands' are made by groups and are then taken up by parties, parliaments and cabinets. However, it is an oversimplification. Such an analysis should be viewed more as a limiting case than as a correct representation of the situation in all types of polity, since the political system is not necessarily activated by demands in this clear-cut manner. The situation may be – and often is – appreciably more confused, in that demands may simply not be expressed, and ideas may come from within the most central part of the machine, such as the cabinet or the national leadership. (Easton does recognize this point, but it is appreciably more common, especially in closed political systems, than he allows for; Easton, 1965: 54–6.) Moreover, the political system can modify the conditions under which society operates, and thus 'manipulate' the demands which may be made – for instance, by allowing some groups to exist and not others, or by making 'propaganda' in favour of some policies and against others.

We thus have a sequence of three phases: inputs, black box conversion, and outputs. This sequence was further elaborated by Almond and Coleman (1960), with the suggestion that the input and output phases could in turn be divided (Almond and Coleman, 1960: 33–58; Almond and Powell, 1966: 27–30).

The input phase was described as being composed of two distinct activities: the *articulation of demands*, i.e. an activity which consists in ideas being presented for

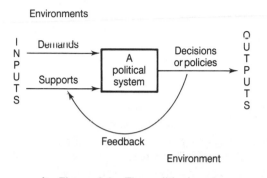

▶ **Figure 2.1**   The political system

discussion and eventual decision; and the *aggregation of demands*, i.e. an activity which consists in bringing these demands together into a package, such as a party programme, in order to diminish problems by reducing inconsistencies.

The output phase was said to correspond to three distinct activities: *rule making* is the most general and is the first aspect of the conversion process; *rule implementation* then details rule making; and *rule adjudication* has to take place when there is a conflict over which of two or more rules is to be applied.

These successive phases were called *functions* by Almond and Coleman, a rather unfortunate expression as it seemed to suggest that the political system had preordained objectives, the term being borrowed from T. Parsons (1951). Whether this term should have been adopted or not, what remains true is that there is a sequence, analytically at least. There is articulation and aggregation of demands; there is rule making, rule implementing and rule adjudicating. While there is a problem in the passage from such an analytical distinction to precise operational criteria, the existence of distinct phases in the policy-making process unquestionably constitutes a characteristic of political life.

## Structures, institutions and groups

So far we referred in a general manner to the terms 'institutions' and 'groups' to describe the components of the political system. We need now to examine these components and see what are their characteristics.

Governmental life has long been conceived in terms of institutions and groups within which actors operate. From Aristotle onwards, theorists have discussed the characteristics of such bodies as executives, elected chambers, such as parliaments or legislative assemblies, 'factions' (in many ways the ancestors of parties), courts and local assemblies; but the analysis of government in terms of a political system led to a reappraisal of both the role and the nature of the institutions. First, since the concept of the political system is based on the idea that politics is viewed as an activity, it may seem that institutions are no longer as important. Second, even if institutions remain key elements, the role of these institutions has to be clarified.

These two points are connected. To say that the main components of the political system are institutions is not inconsistent with the notion that the political system is characterized by its activity: it is merely further stated that political activity cannot be achieved without institutions. To put it more forcefully: without institutions, decisions could not realistically be taken, since the members of the polity would have continuously to be involved and all the members would also have to be prepared to concur in the implementation of these decisions. Such a state of affairs might be regarded as perfect, in that it appears to constitute full democracy; but it can equally be regarded as a predicament resembling the one described as 'nature' in what some pessimistic political theorists, such as Thomas Hobbes in his *Leviathan*, called the 'state of nature'. In practice, even in small polities, some ordering, some 'structuring' of the decision process has to take place if the process of allocation of values is to be undertaken, and if the members of the polity are to abide by the policies elaborated. This is what institutional and group arrangements achieve; this is why these arrangements can be described as the structures of the political system.

## The nature of institutions and groups

What, then, are the fundamental characteristics of the structures of the political system? The most general definition which can be given of them is that they *pattern the relationships* among the individuals belonging to them: those who belong to an institution or group are more related to each other than they would be if they did not belong to that institution or group. To put it differently, an institution or group is a set of relationships: those within the set have links with each other which they would not have if they did not belong to the set.

The fact that an institution or group is a set of relationships has two consequences which are important because they shape the way the political system operates. First, the decisions taken by the group extend normally only to those who are connected to the group and not to others; privileges which those who are connected to the group may receive will not (normally) extend beyond the group. Second, decisions within the institution or group have certain procedural characteristics: for instance, these decisions may or may not be taken democratically. Thus the way decisions are taken in one group will differ at least in part from the way in which decisions are taken in another group.

It is sometimes suggested that members belong to institutions or groups on the basis of a calculus which they make about the costs and benefits of membership, a point which is said to distinguish small groups from large groups, since benefits are clearer in small groups (Olson, 1971: 35–6). This is true in some cases only, however, and principally with respect to associations which have a narrow scope, a point which we shall examine in Chapter 7. In the context of long-standing bodies with which individuals have been connected from early life, or to which they are linked for long periods, the point is less valid, if it is valid at all. It has been said that man is a social animal: human beings are born in groups (their family, their neighbourhood) and they live in groups (the workplace, the churches). Group life is the stuff within which human life is embedded (Truman, 1951; Bentley, 1967).

Thus the national political system must be viewed as composed of a (probably very large) number of institutions or groups to which individuals naturally belong. These institutions or groups are in turn linked to each other in many complex ways in the national political system. They also have ill-defined borders: they often overlap somewhat in membership, as members of the polity frequently belong to a number of groups, and thus have relationships with other individuals who in turn may belong also to a number of groups. These institutions or groups are not necessarily involved in a major way in national politics. Some are, such as political parties, parliaments and legislative assemblies. Others are involved more spasmodically and in some countries more than in others: this is the case, for instance, with trade unions, employers' associations and welfare organizations, but also with ethnic groups or tribal bodies. Finally, some groups are almost not at all involved in political life: this is the case with many social bodies. There is political activity *within* them, of course, but this activity may bear no relationship to national decision making.

An institution or group is involved in the political system if that institution or group participates in the process of allocation of values, since this is the definition of the political system. Some institutions may therefore be part only occasionally, intermittently, or almost not at all of this governmental system; others, however, are continuously involved, often because they have been set up in order to help fashion the national decision-making process: parties and parliaments are two obvious examples.

## Why institutions and groups structure the political system

We need now to return to the original question: why is the political system necessarily structured by institutions or groups? We noted at the outset that decisions would otherwise be difficult to take. It is because this is the case that institutions have existed in the most traditional societies, and that they are continuously set up in contemporary polities. The absence and even the weakness of institutions in the national political system would mean that decisions would at best take an inordinately long time. Institutions and groups establish or maintain in existence procedures of decision making; the most successful ones are perhaps those which are long-standing and are the product of habits which remain unchallenged. For instance, in traditional societies, where tribes tend to be the most important structures, the elders may have rights of decision taking which other members of the tribes do not have. The point is not only that social control is exercised in this way; it is also, and perhaps more importantly, that as a result of this 'structuring', decisions are taken more speedily, since they will not involve the consultation, let alone the agreement, of all the members of the tribe (Huntington, 1968: 8–11).

In this practical sense, institutions and groups can be viewed as established arrangements in which decisions are taken in a certain way, with only relatively few members participating in the decision-making process and even these active participants being subjected to large numbers of restrictions. Whether in a party, in a parliament or in a legislative assembly, or even in the national cabinet, the institution or group may be primarily characterized by the way in which decisions are taken within it.

The fact that institutions or groups are, so to speak, machines to speed up the decision process is particularly important to the political system, since the political system is a mechanism by which values are allocated in the society. In the social context as a whole, it may not be so important that institutions or groups should be able to take decisions speedily – indeed, some social clubs may be concerned only incidentally with the taking of decisions (though there are always at least some decisions to be taken) – but the political system could not operate without institutions or groups drastically speeding up the process by which values are allocated.

Thus one must not underestimate, let alone set aside institutions or groups in the context of the political system. To the extent that, in the 1980s, the 'new institutionalism' stressed the part played by institutions, it did contribute to a more realistic analysis of the political system, after a period during which the 'institutional approach' had come to be regarded as unsatisfactory. Some have been tempted to go even further and claim that institutions in a sense 'make' the decision-making process (Skocpol, 1985: 3–43). This is going too far and the point is in any case controversial: it may be that, in some cases, institutions create the conditions under which decisions are taken, but this cannot be regarded as a general rule and it is not part of the definition of institutions that this should be the case.

What is suggested here, therefore, is that the political system is composed of sets of institutions or groups, some of which are set up by a constitution, many of which are not; these structures form together the framework within which decisions are taken. Only by knowing what these institutions are in a given polity can one understand how the national political system allocates values in that society.


## Links among the structures in the political system


### Comparisons based on institutions

If institutions, organizations and groups – in short, structures – are the components which shape political systems, we need to describe these components precisely to be able to obtain a detailed picture of each political system. To do so, we need to have information about the internal organization of these bodies; but, perhaps more importantly in order to obtain an overall picture, we need to know *what these institutions or groups achieve*: this is what constitutes their link with the political system.

So far, however, this last aspect of the problem has not been truly solved; nor is it likely to be solved satisfactorily in the near future. It is admittedly possible to note in general that some institutions or groups prevail in some polities and others in others. We may thus know that in one country there are tribes, assemblies of chiefs and a royal council; in another, there may be interest groups, such as trade unions and business organizations, a number of parties, a legislature and a council of ministers; in yet another, there may only be one party, while the military may be influential, etc. One can see in this way the beginning of a cross-national process of comparison: different political systems will be characterized by the presence of different institutions forming different overall configurations. Indeed, this is often the way in which political systems are compared, including in everyday language – for instance, in the media.

We need to go further if we wish to make precise comparisons, but serious difficulties then begin to emerge. In theory, we might imagine that we might determine, at each point in time, the *composition* of a political system, in the way one determines the composition of a chemical body: after all, chemical bodies are composed in varying degrees of elements such as oxygen and carbon. But the difference is that chemists can measure with precision the proportions of the various elements which form the molecules, while political scientists cannot do the same with respect to the different structures which 'compose' a political system. Like natural scientists of an earlier period, they can only state that, in a given political system, interest groups such as trade unions are 'more' influential than in another, or that the parliament or congress is 'more' involved in the process of national decision making in one country than in another. The comparisons which are undertaken in the field of government are typically imprecise.

## The value and limits of a functionalist approach

The stumbling block in this respect is constituted by the difficulty of attempting to determine what exactly is being 'achieved' by a given structure. Efforts towards a more precise description of this type have been primarily associated with the idea of *functionalism*, but after a period of some success, these efforts were abandoned as no practical solution was found to undertake the description. Yet, in theory, it seemed that the idea might have been fruitful.

The principle behind functionalism was simple and appealing: it was based on the idea that the best way to describe different configurations of structures and therefore to compare political systems, was to look at the activities of these structures, in each of the configurations. One was then to find out the link between structures by describing the activities which each structure performed. For instance, the activities of parliaments or legislative assemblies vary from country to country, since some are more involved in legislation, and others in the scrutiny of the government. The activities of parties also vary: some are more involved in the preparation of governmental programmes, while others are primarily concerned with the 'mobilization' of the population. The activities of the groups which compose the political system also display marked

## BOX 2.1
## The various approaches to the study of government

Despite its limitations, structural functionalism is the only approach to comparative government which seriously attempted to provide an operational framework on the basis of which to distinguish among political systems. In theory at least, this framework made it possible to relate structures (institutions, groups) to particular functions (operations) such as articulation or rule implementation.

There have been many other approaches, all of which are essentially general models, claiming to be 'explanatory', but on the basis of which it is difficult to locate concretely particular types of system or, on the contrary, more than a few systems. The four main approaches have been as follows:

- The *dependency* approach, largely drawn from Marxism, which suggested that the economic life of countries of the Third World, and consequently their political life, was dependent on the actions of the 'advanced capitalist countries' of the West, and especially of the United States. Given this dependency, these countries had no freedom of manoeuvre in policy terms. Regimes or leaders which attempted to break away from the mould were quickly overthrown: Latin America was mentioned as the typical example of an area under dependency (Wallerstein, 1979).

- The *administrative state* approach, largely based on an analysis of the historical development of a number of European states. It was suggested that state centralization had dynamics of its own and that this led to marked differences between such states and others. France, but also Russia, are mentioned as examples of such developments (Moore, 1966; Skocpol, 1979).

- The *social cleavages* approach, based on a historical study of European countries, which states that countries can be classified according to their social cleavages and to the way these cleavages emerged and were handled by the political system. Thus countries underwent *crises*; it was not indifferent whether a given crisis – for instance, over religion – took place before or after another – for instance, over the relation between centre and periphery (Rokkan, 1970).

- The *culturalist* approach, which views the culture of some, if not all, of the Third World countries as so different from that of western countries that one needs to analyze these cultures side by side, but cannot expect to find a common denominator leading to a comprehensive study of comparative government. The point has been made in particular with respect to Middle Eastern countries, but it can be generalized. Indeed, it can even be generalized to include cultural differences *among* western countries, and thus lead to an almost total denial of comparative government, a point which was referred to in Chapter 1 (Badie, 1989).

differences. If one were able to assess precisely the activities of every structure, one might then be able to describe in some detail the characteristics of each political system

If this were done, one might then also be able to compare in a rigorous manner the various political systems which exist in the world. Let us suppose that it were possible to discover a number of *phases* in the cycle of activities of the political system, and that it were also possible to discover that a given structure is concerned specifically with a particular phase of the political system's activities: one could then ascribe structures to 'moments' in the life of this political system, and thereby solve the problem posed by the links between structures. The method would be truly satisfactory, however, only if we were not constrained to ascribe to each structure, party or parliament – an unchangeable position in the political system: there would have to be flexibility. There would also have to be precision: one would need to be able to assign a particular structure to a given phase of the political system in the case of Country X, but to a different phase in that of Country Y. Yet such an objective seems extremely difficult, if not impossible, to attain, since the 'composition' of each political system could not be assessed with precision. In any case, further important steps were needed to make the scheme truly operational (Almond and Coleman, 1960: 3–64; Almond and Powell, 1966: 27–33; Mayer, 1972: 143–61; Chilcote, 1981: 162–82).

## Functionalism does not provide a means of measuring the activities of structures although it has given a basis for a broad categorization of these activities

These steps were never taken, with the result that the problem of the *link* between the political system and the structures which constitute its elements was not adequately solved. Structural functionalism did not provide a detailed means of categorizing and comparing governments, although it did provide a basis for a broad categorization. As a result, and perhaps too quickly, efforts to render structural functionalism operational were abandoned and the approach was dismissed. Efforts should have been undertaken to make further progress in the original direction, although this should have been on the understanding that progress would be slow. Perhaps because hopes had been too high at the outset, these efforts were never made. It seemed to be believed that a genuinely satisfactory descriptive model could not be obtained from the combination of systems analysis and of structural functionalism: structural functionalism moved in other directions, less descriptive and more normative, to which we shall refer in the next chapter.

## Overview

Comparative government needs a *general framework*, and it needs common elements within this framework. An examination of developments in the field in recent decades shows that two positive steps have taken place.

First, there is indeed a general framework, provided by the concept of the *political system*, which is defined as the mechanism by which values are allocated in the society in an authoritative manner. The concept of the political system is truly *general and neutral*, unlike the concept of constitutionalism (which is highly ideological) and that of the state (which is legalistic and therefore normative).

Second, within the political system the key elements are the *structures, institutions, groups or organisations*. These pattern the behaviour of the actors who operate in these structures and generally facilitate the decision-making process.

While institutions are key elements, their precise activities in each political system cannot be truly 'measured', despite efforts made by functionalists in this direction. A gap thus remains, and it is therefore impossible to ascertain the precise links between structures and the political system.

It is therefore also unrealistic to hope to be able to classify political systems on this basis, at any rate at present. We must therefore turn to values to see how far these can provide the basis for a detailed classification.

## Further reading

The analysis of the political system was first developed by D. Easton in the 1950s and 1960s, in his *Political System* (1953) and his *Systems Analysis of Political Life* (1965). It was adopted and adjusted to the idea of structural functionalism by G.A. Almond and J.S. Coleman, in *The Politics of the Developing Areas* (1960), and by G.A. Almond and G.B. Powell, in *Comparative Politics* (1966). This model became highly popular in the 1960s, only to be strongly rejected in the 1970s. Another framework based on the idea of systems analysis was developed by K. Deutsch in *The Nerves of Government* (1963).

For an examination of the importance and limitations of systems analysis and of structural functionalism in political science, see for instance L.C. Mayer, *Comparative Political Inquiry* (1972: especially 48–66 and 43–61), R.C. Chilcote, *Theories of Comparative Politics* (1981: 145–82), and D. Rustow and K. Erickson, eds., *Comparative Political Dynamics* (1991).

On the more recent role given to institutions, see Evans *et al.*, eds., *Bringing the State Back In* (1985), in particular the introduction by T. Skocpol at pp. 3–43, and J.G. March and J.P. Olsen, *Rediscovering Institutions* (1989).

# 3

# Types of political system

## Introduction

While attempts have been made since the Second World War to compare and classify political systems on the basis of structures – the institutions and the groups which exist in the society – the more traditional way of undertaking these comparisons and classifications has been to refer to some general 'characteristics' of the polity. The characteristic which has been most widely used for this purpose is the distinction between *democracies*, *oligarchies*, and *monarchies*. This distinction was first suggested by Aristotle in his *Politics*; it has been adopted subsequently by large numbers of political theorists – indeed, to the extent of appearing to be for a long period the best means of comparing and classifying political systems.

A general characteristic such as that which suggests that a political system is a democracy, an oligarchy or a monarchy constitutes a *norm* or a *normative principle*. It is a norm in that it defines the way in which the authorities who run the country have decided to organize the political system. In this sense, such a criterion constitutes a value, but a value which is so broad that it affects the political system as a whole. It is a principle of government on the basis of which, or according to which, more detailed values tend to be allocated.

Since such a norm is a general principle, it seems logical that the comparison and classification of political systems should be undertaken by reference to it rather than by reference to institutions and groups, of which there are many and whose precise role is sometimes, if not often, difficult to ascertain. Moreover, to an extent at least, structures – the institutions and the groups – are likely to be shaped by the broad norms of the polity. These structures will be different in a democracy from what they are in an oligarchy or a monarchy. Admittedly, structures can also, especially over time, affect the broad norms of the polity, but the influence which takes place in the other direction is almost certainly more widespread.

There are thus theoretical and practical reasons for adopting as the basis for comparisons and classifications of political systems the broad normative principles which characterize them. Yet this does not mean that the structures should not also be considered: on the contrary, the relationship between the principles on which the polity is based and the institutions and groups which exist in that polity needs to be investigated, since, as we have said, institutions and groups can be expected both to shape the broad norms and even more to be shaped by them.

Finally, we have so far mentioned one normative principle, that which distinguishes democracies from oligarchies and monarchies. We must examine whether other norms also need to be taken into consideration. At least one other norm is in widespread use: the norm of *liberalism*, which is typically linked to democracy in the expression *liberal democracy*. It does therefore seem that, at a minimum, the norm of liberalism must be considered alongside the norm of democracy.

- In the first section of this chapter, we shall explore this question; we shall come to the conclusion that three broad dimensions of norms need to be taken into account in order to define the principles on the basis of which political systems operate. Taken together, these principles define a 'space' within which political systems can be located.
- In the second section, we shall examine where contemporary political systems are located in this normative space. We will see that we can distinguish on this basis five main types of political system.
- In the third section, we shall return to the structures of political systems – the institutions and the groups – and examine which of these structures tend to be found in each of the five main types of political system.

## A framework of norms for distinguishing political systems

Let us thus first identify the normative principles on the basis of which political systems can be distinguished. These principles must fulfil three requirements:

- They must apply to all political systems. This does not mean that all political systems should adopt the same principles, but that an answer must be given in all political systems to the questions posed by these principles. This is why we refer here to normative 'principles' rather than to specific values.
- The framework has to be robust and simple enough to enable us to compare types of political system clearly and easily. This means that the number of principles must remain rather small.
- These principles must jointly provide a comprehensive description of the direction in which political systems are expected to go. It is not sufficient that these principles should exist everywhere; they must also be the only ones which can be found in political systems.

The examples mentioned early in this chapter suggest that, at least in a preliminary manner, a positive answer can be given to the first two of these questions. When we say that a political system is *democratic*, for instance, we say that decisions are taken in a way which conforms with a norm of broad participation of the population and indeed, potentially at least, of the whole population. Such a principle is preferred in this political system to the idea that decisions should be taken by a small élite or by an individual alone. Similarly, a political system is regarded as *liberal* if opinions are allowed to be expressed freely and without interference; another system is regarded as authoritarian if these conditions do not obtain. In both cases, the normative principles constitute means of answering questions which have to be answered in all polities; in both cases, both question and answer seem to be clear.

However, to constitute a truly general framework, the normative principles which we just mentioned must meet the third requirement: they must cover all the norms which characterize political systems. To see whether this requirement is met, we cannot just look at some political systems and see whether the norms which we have discussed so far play a major part: this we have done already and the answer is positive. We will find a general answer only if we return to the definition of political systems and see whether it is possible to deduce from this definition what normative principles can be expected to characterize all political systems.

## The dimensions of norms or broad values in political systems

In Chapter 2, we defined political systems as mechanisms by which values are allocated authoritatively in the society. What needs to be done in order to deduce from this definition what a universal normative framework might be is to determine all the questions which are being addressed when we say that the political system allocates values in an authoritative manner.

This problem seems difficult to solve if we look at the matter generally, but it becomes less complex if we remember that the political system allocates values by means of decisions — indeed, by a huge number of decisions taken by those in charge of the political system. We therefore simply need to discover the set of normative questions which are being addressed when a decision is being taken. Reflection on the characteristics of decisions and of decision processes quickly shows that three, but only three, sets of normative questions are being addressed. These three questions can be summarized in the formula: *who rules, in what way, and for what purpose?*

- The first question is concerned with the numbers and proportions of people participating in the decisions. This question has to be answered, since decisions are obviously taken by some persons and these persons have to be defined.
- The second question is concerned with the means of the decision process. This question has also to be answered in all cases, since decisions are taken in a certain manner. They can be taken more or less 'openly' and after a greater or lesser amount of discussion.
- Finally, decisions all have one (or more) purposes, and these purposes must be known. This, too, is clearly a universal question.

Conversely, these three questions are the only ones which need to be answered when decisions are taken. Once we know who rules, in what way, and for what purpose, we can describe the decision process and, in general, the overall allocation of values which takes place in political systems. Thus all political systems can be classified in terms of the answers given to these three sets of normative questions.

These sets of normative questions have a characteristic in common. All three have a *dimensional character*: they give rise not to dichotomous answers, but to answers which are in the nature of 'more or less'. It is not the case that those who rule are either 'many' or 'a few'; there is a gradation from one extreme to another. The same is true of the means by which decisions are taken: there can be more or less discussion, and more or less openness in the political system. As we shall see shortly, the 'purpose' of decisions can also be regarded as ranging from one extreme to another. Let us therefore examine these three dimensions more closely.

### Who rules? The extent of participation and of democracy

This is probably the easiest dimension to define, visualize and even operationalize. The question refers to the number or, more accurately, to the proportion of persons in the polity who are involved in the political process. What is being examined is both who is entitled to take and who effectively takes the decisions. The answer may be all the members of the polity: the system is then a *democracy*. No polity, of course, even approximates this situation: Rousseau did indeed view full democracy as impossible (Rousseau, *Social Contract*, bk 3, ch. 4). The other extreme is constituted by political systems in which one person only rules (monarchies in the strict sense, or *monocracies*): this, too, is so unlikely as to be considered impossible in a polity of any size. Thus what one finds in the real world are a large number of intermediate positions, which correspond strictly speaking to various types of *oligarchy*.

Given that no case is at either extreme, the content of the concepts of democracy and of monocracy has to be relaxed, in two ways. The first of these concerns numbers or proportions: a political system can be regarded as democratic if *a substantial proportion* of the population is involved in the decision process. Second, since it is difficult to define 'power' by opposition to influence (Dahl, 1963: 32–8), it is necessary to take into account even those actors whose role in the decision-making process is limited or intermittent when one considers real-world 'democracies'.

### Means of government: liberalism versus authoritarianism

The second dimension refers to the way in which the decisions are taken. Are there many, some or no restrictions on the discussion of alternative standpoints with respect to decisions by members of the polity? This raises the question of the extent to which the system is liberal or authoritarian, a question which is obviously critical in order to define the characteristics of a polity. Here, too, the dimension is real: political systems can be more or less liberal, or more or less authoritarian. Moreover, this dimension is analytically distinct from the dimension which ranges from democracy to monocracy: the latter is concerned with the extent of participation, while the former relates to the extent to which the system is 'open'.

### *The purpose and goals of governmental decision making*

So far, we have described the two dimensions of norms which have been typically recognized as crucial in political science literature (Dahl, 1971: 1–32). Yet a third question has to be answered, without which it is not readily possible to categorize decision making in political systems: this dimension relates to the *substantive content* of policies and concentrates on the aims of the decision-makers in introducing policies. Such a question is manifestly essential: it may even be regarded as the most crucial of the three which we are analyzing here, since the content of what is achieved is at stake.

Political scientists have none the less tended to classify political systems without taking into account the dimension of goals. Politics is generally regarded as a 'procedural' activity, concerned with the decision-making *process*, not the substance of decisions. As any policy can be allocated by the political system, it might therefore seem logical to exclude the content of policies when attempting to classify political systems according to their norms.

This view is mistaken. A comprehensive description of political systems does have to take into account the policies which these systems pursue. For instance, two political systems may be authoritarian, but may differ according to the actions they take with respect to property, the social structure or education. There are thus conservative authoritarian regimes and 'progressive' authoritarian regimes. Indeed, these distinctions are recognized in 'ordinary' language: governments, as well as other bodies within the political system, such as parties or the military, tend to be characterized by the extent to which they are conservative or 'progressive' as well as liberal or democratic.

It may seem difficult to define precisely this third dimension. In reality, however, what the question of substance raises in broad terms is a certain vision of the 'good society' (Arblaster and Lukes, 1971). Viewed in this way, the dimension is concerned with decision standpoints which aim at producing *more or less equality* in the society. At one extreme is what might be described as the 'communist utopia' of full equality; at the other is the wholly hierarchical society in which one or very few draw the very large majority of the benefits. The *grounds* for inequality may be diverse: they may be based on inheritance, race, creed, or occupation and class; in fact, they are likely to be based on some combination of these characteristics. There will also be many degrees of equality and inequality. The overall effect is none the less to indicate that all societies can be located at some point on this third dimension of goals or purpose, a dimension which is manifestly distinct from the dimensions of liberalism vs authoritarianism and of democracy vs monocracy.

## Characteristics of the three-dimensional space of norms

Since three dimensions of norms or broad values thus characterize all political systems, these dimensions define a space within which all political systems can be placed. This space has four main characteristics.

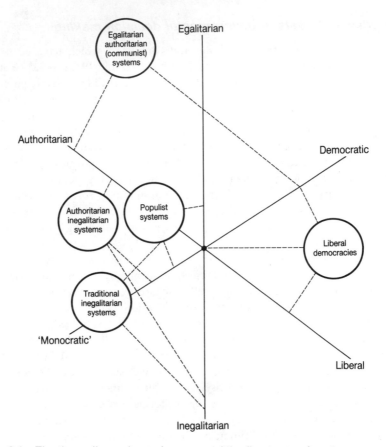

▶ **Figure 3.1**   The three dimensions of norms and the five types of contemporary political systems

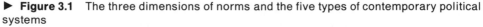

First, the normative principles to which we are referring are those which are expressed in and by the decisions taken in the polity, and not merely by statements of decision-makers about what these principles are. They therefore correspond to the behaviour of the authorities of the political system, and especially of the government and the members of the political élite. Clearly, in any polity, there are dissenters from these prevailing norms; but the views of the dissenters either are repressed or do not have sufficient force. As a result, at any rate at the moment in time at which the observation is made, these views do not translate themselves into the norms of the polity. Over time, however, these views may contribute to a change in the behaviour of the authorities, and thus of the norms of the political system. The existence of these dissenting norms is also likely to contribute significantly to the determination of the position of the political system on the liberal–authoritarian dimension as well as, though perhaps to a lesser extent, to the position of the political system on the other two dimensions.

Second, our current ability to operationalize these norms remains relatively limited. However, it is possible to operationalize them in part, and to a greater extent for some countries than for others. For example, degrees of equality or inequality can be assessed by means of income per head and of the distribution of capital across the population, although other indicators need also to be used, such as the extent to which minorities have equal access to various positions. Degrees of liberalism are typically assessed by the extent to which various freedoms are achieved in the political system, though many of these indicators are likely to be qualitative rather than quantitative. The extent of democracy can, of course, be measured in part by reference to the opportunity given to citizens to participate in the electoral process, but other indicators need also to be taken into account, such as the extent of participation in political parties and in groups which are involved in national decision making. Clearly, the measurement is often based on data which are not wholly reliable, and the weighting to be given to various indicators can give rise to argument. However, it is at least possible – and efforts have already been made – to provide some assessment (Dahl, 1971: 62–104).

Third, these assessments refer to a particular point in time. If a regime changes and is replaced by one which has different goals (more or less liberal, more or less democratic, or more or less egalitarian), the location of the system in the three-dimensional space of norms also changes. While the location of a given political system does not by itself give a dynamic picture, a number of observations made successively can provide the dynamics. It then becomes possible also to see whether there are trends which apply to many regimes, and thus to characterize generally the evolution of political systems.

Fourth, the examination of the evolution of norms over a period can provide a means of assessing the extent to which moves according to one dimension of norms have an effect on moves on another. The three dimensions are analytically distinct, as was pointed out earlier – liberalism is conceptually different from democracy and from egalitarianism – but there are apparent empirical links between positions on the three dimensions. Thus it could be claimed that a move towards liberalism will be followed by a move towards democracy; indeed, this was the evolution of western European countries in the nineteenth century. As a state becomes more liberal, more citizens are able to participate because they are able to express demands, in the first instance, for greater participation. It is also often assumed that changes towards egalitarianism have the effect of reducing, at least to a degree, opportunities for liberalism, as liberty and equality are at times regarded as antithetical. Rapid changes towards greater equality – or, indeed, greater inequality – often lead to protests and tension; this might result in more authoritarianism on the part of the regime and in a curtailment of participation as well.

Overall, therefore, the determination of the position of countries at various points in time with respect to the three dimensions of norms is both a way of characterizing the nature of political systems and a means of understanding the dynamics of these systems on a comparative basis. Our knowledge of these positions and of the evolution of these positions is still vague, despite the fact that we are accustomed to assess many regimes according to two and often all three of these dimensions, as the description of western European countries as liberal democracies and of communist states as

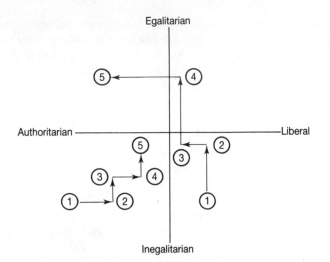

▶ **Figure 3.2**  The relationship between moves according to the liberal–authoritarian dimension and moves according to the inegalitarian–egalitarian dimension

authoritarian regimes indicates. We should therefore at least be able to see in broad terms how contemporary polities can be characterized. This is the matter to which we are coming now.

## The five main types of political system in the world today

The three types of norm which we have described suggest that political systems can be located at an infinity of points in the three-dimensional space determined by the norms. However, there is a tendency for many political systems to adopt similar norms. Admittedly, no two political systems are likely to be placed at exactly the same point in the three-dimensional space; moreover, since even the most stable political system is also likely to vary somewhat in terms of the norms which it embodies, there are small variations in time as well as in space. Nevertheless, the similarities between groups of political systems are more striking than the small differences between those which belong to each group. As a result, one can truly refer to *clusters of political systems*. Two well-known examples of these clusters are, on the one hand, western European countries, which are all described as liberal democracies, although there are substantial variations among them, and, on the other hand, the communist countries which are or were up to 1989 characterized by a high degree of authoritarianism, but were also 'progressive' in their goals.

### Clusters of political systems and their characteristics

These clusters of political systems within the three-dimensional space exist for a number of reasons. Alongside similarity of socioeconomic development, the deliberate imitation of one system by another and the coercion exercised by one system over another play a substantial part. The communist states formed a bloc, and their norms were openly imposed upon them by the Soviet Union after the Second World War; only slowly and in a limited fashion did some differences begin to emerge, especially in Hungary and Poland. Meanwhile, in western Europe, many British institutions and practices were deliberately imitated by other countries.

The adoption of the norms of one country by another goes appreciably beyond western Europe and what used to constitute the communist world. After the Second World War, the influence, first, of colonial countries and, second, of the Soviet Union and China led to the adoption of norms and of institutions in many Third World polities, the imitation being in some cases very close indeed. Since the fall of communism in eastern Europe, there has been a wide degree of uncertainty in many countries about what model to follow, both in eastern Europe itself (including Russia) and in the Third World. On the one hand, there has been a tendency to adopt formally western norms of democracy and liberalism (norms which are often deemed to be implemented by the introduction of a multiparty system); on the other hand, there has often been a maintenance in reality of earlier more authoritarian practices. Meanwhile, rebellions and outright civil war have tended to spread, not just in what were Yugoslavia and the Soviet Union, but in various countries of Africa, in part because of the fragility of the new order which came to be established.

To say that political systems form clusters does not mean that all the polities in the cluster adopt identical norms. There are appreciable normative differences between, for instance, Sweden and Greece, although both countries are generally regarded as belonging to the cluster of liberal democracies. One should thus distinguish between what could be labelled 'macro differences' and 'micro differences' in normative principles, macro differences being those which exist between the clusters, while micro differences are those which exist within each cluster.

Countries do not remain permanently in a given cluster, however, as the evolution of eastern European countries since 1989–90 shows. In a general manner, as a result of coups or revolutions, different norms can characterize the same polities, though the real changes may not always be as large as they appear to be on the surface. Moreover, further coups or counter-revolutions may subsequently lead to the readoption of the normative principles which had been temporarily abandoned.

Moreover, the clusters themselves appear to be, in part at least, time dependent. The emergence and marked decline of communist states showed this to be the case in the twentieth century; so did the emergence of liberal democratic systems in the nineteenth century: there had been very few liberal democracies in the past and these had tended to be small cities. Technical developments (for instance, inventions such as printing in the late fifteenth century and the electrical and electronic media in the twentieth) as well as the spread of education among the population are among the reasons which account for the fact that different clusters of normative principles have tended to spread at different points in time.

## Clusters in the contemporary world

In the world today, there are five clusters of political systems, one of which, that of communist systems, has declined markedly in importance since the late 1980s. These five clusters are constituted by the *liberal democratic*, the *egalitarian-authoritarian*, the *traditional egalitarian*, the *populist* and the *authoritarian-inegalitarian* political systems.

### Liberal democratic political systems

Liberal democratic political systems include the countries of western Europe, North America and Australasia, as well as Japan, Israel, some members of the Commonwealth

---

**BOX 3.1**
**The norms of political systems: past and present**

All political systems, whether of the past or contemporary, can be located in the space defined by the three dimensions of norms – monocracy–democracy, authoritarianism–liberalism, inequality–equality – but the positions occupied in the space have varied over time and will continue to vary. The five positions around which contemporary political systems have been found to be clustered are not those around which past political systems were clustered.

The technical, economic, social and ideological changes which occurred in the nineteenth and twentieth centuries account in large part for the emergence of both liberal democratic systems and authoritarian-egalitarian systems.

Political systems of earlier periods tended to be traditional inegalitarian or authoritarian-inegalitarian. In the first of these two categories fall the strong monarchies in which loyalty to the monarch was widespread; in the second are the continental European seventeenth- and eighteenth-century absolutist monarchies on the French model. There were also a few populist systems in the past, typically emerging when a new leader succeeded in coming to power by force, had a popular following and, at least for a while, needed the support of the population.

Finally, there were occasionally relatively liberal systems in small city-states. These regimes were the ancestors of the liberal-inegalitarian systems which emerged in large countries in the late eighteenth and in the nineteenth centuries, first in Britain and America, and later in several European polities. These regimes did not succeed in remaining liberal inegalitarian for long: pressure for greater popular participation mounted, while demands for greater social equality came to be voiced. Thus the liberal inegalitarian system gave way to the liberal-democratic system which has characterized most western countries, as well as some others, in the twentieth century.

---

and in particular India, and a number of Latin American states, although the latter have tended to be unstable. There are relatively few liberal democracies in Africa, the Middle East and east Asia. Variations have been appreciable, both before the fall of eastern European communism and afterwards. Spain, Portugal and Greece have entered or re-entered the group, while several Latin American countries (Chile being an example) ceased to be liberal democratic, at least for a period, in the 1970s and 1980s. Meanwhile, some of the political systems which ceased to be communist in the late 1980s can be regarded as liberal democracies.

These political systems constitute a cluster with respect to all three dimensions: they tend to be democratic, liberal and, from the point of view of their substantive policies, neither truly egalitarian nor truly inegalitarian. Despite differences among these countries from the point of view of the distribution of incomes and of the social services, the normative principles which are embodied in their systems tend to constitute a compromise between the extremes of full equality and gross inequality. This situation is probably due in part to the liberal democratic formula itself. As groups can express themselves at least with a moderate degree of openness and can compete for support, in particular through elections, an equilibrium tends to be reached at the middle of the dimension of substantive goals. There are, of course, variations on both sides of this half-way position, but these remain small so long as the liberal democratic formula obtains.

## Egalitarian-authoritarian political systems

Communist political systems have tended to be markedly egalitarian, truly authoritarian, but also rather democratic. The countries of this group used to include, beyond the Soviet Union and the eastern European countries, China, North Korea, Mongolia and Vietnam, as well as a number of Third World states such as Cuba, Angola, Mozambique and Ethiopia; a further set of countries, to be found in particular in Africa, has occasionally adopted norms close to those of communist states. The collapse of communism in eastern Europe – in the Soviet Union and the majority, but not all, of the states which used to form the Soviet bloc – led to its collapse in many other polities, in particular in Africa. Meanwhile, communist systems survived in China (which includes one-fifth of the population of the world), in much of east Asia and, for as long as Castro holds power, in Cuba. Admittedly, the economic policies pursued by China since the late 1980s are distant from traditional communist economic policies and are leading the country increasingly towards a populist system, but communist political arrangements remain, and the introduction of capitalism is shaky, conditional and limited to some parts of the country.

The authoritarian character of these political systems is well known and incontrovertible, although there has been in some of them an evolution towards less marked coercion. This evolution may have been the origin of the collapse of the regimes themselves in the late 1980s.

Communist political systems have also been rather egalitarian, even if doubts were often expressed in this respect. The rather negative popular reactions to the social changes which have taken place in Russia and eastern Europe since 1990 are a sufficient indication that the previous regimes were more egalitarian than those which came to replace them. Not only have there not been substantial concentrations of wealth in the hands of individuals in communist states, despite the fact that the power of managers and politicians has tended to compensate in part for the limitations on the economic power of 'capitalists'; but communist states have also been characterized by an extensively developed social security system, which has provided the whole population with a basic equality of provision with respect to education, health and pensions.

Finally, communist states must be regarded as having been democratic. As was pointed out earlier, liberalism and democracy are two analytically distinct concepts, which tend to be associated in the West because of the evolution of western Europe in the nineteenth century. But a political system may be democratic without being liberal, if it gives an opportunity for participation without allowing for appreciable competition. This has typically been the case in communist states, where the party and the other 'mass' organizations ancillary to the party have given large numbers of citizens an opportunity to participate. Moreover, the democratic character of communist societies has to be viewed by comparison with the situation which prevails in other countries, including in the West, where participation, apart from elections, is typically rather small (Verba and Nie, 1972: 25–43; Verba et al., 1978: 1–45).

### Traditional inegalitarian political systems

In the contemporary world at least, there are considerable differences in the norms of the political systems which are neither liberal democratic nor communist. These countries fall into three groups which constitute three clusters in the three-dimensional space of norms. One of these clusters consists of the political systems which have maintained the traditional norms which once prevailed widely across the world, and in western Europe in particular. These countries are 'absolutist', and their head of state, usually a monarch, rules the nation by counting on the loyal support of the large majority of the population; some oligarchical republics have had or still have a similar character. This type of regime is becoming rare, however, mainly because most western European monarchs felt the need to abandon their power in order to remain on the throne, while others were toppled. Thus only in relatively closed or remote areas of the world (the Arabian peninsula, the Himalayas and parts of southern Africa) have traditional inegalitarian regimes remained in existence.

The norms of these systems are 'traditional': they preserve social inequalities and highly oligarchical structures, such as were characteristic of seventeenth- and eighteenth-century Europe. Power and wealth are concentrated in few hands, and moves towards a political opening-up of the society are limited, although many monarchs attempt to ensure the maintenance of their support by introducing at least some of the features of constitutional regimes and by developing the economy. Regimes such as those of the Arabian peninsula, which have been able to disperse substantial resources among the population, have been best able to maintain themselves.

By and large, these regimes are not truly authoritarian, at any rate in the most overt sense. They remain in being on the basis of forms of traditional popular support which will be discussed in Chapter 5. Authoritarianism becomes necessary only when a crisis occurs – that is to say, when an opposition emerges. The regimes may then be toppled (as has occurred to several of them since the Second World War) or different norms may be introduced, rendering the political system populist or authoritarian-inegalitarian.

## Populist political systems

Most of the newly independent states of the 1950s and 1960s, especially in Africa, began as populist regimes, as had some of the South American republics in the early post-independence period. The expression 'populism', used in late nineteenth-century America to refer to movements which wished to help the bulk of the people against political and social bosses, has been applied since the Second World War to those regimes and leaders who, in the newly independent countries of the Third World, attempted to 'modernize' their society – for instance, by reducing tribal influence – while not adopting a Marxist or communist stance (Lipset, 1983: 52–4).

The establishment of a new state typically requires at least some involvement of the population in opposition to a colonial power, and 'traditional' loyalties are usually insufficient. There has to be some participation of at least a large part of the population; there has also to be a degree of group development and of group pluralism. Populist regimes are thus typically born in reaction to traditionalism. Consequently, they tend to be half-way between democracy and monocracy, between egalitarianism and inegalitarianism, and between liberalism and authoritarianism.

These characteristics account in part for the high expectations raised by these regimes at the outset, both within the country and outside; but they account also for their relative instability. A degree of pluralism leads to strong divisions among groups and factions. This may result in a liberal democratic form of government, but only if strong political institutions exist and if social and political tensions remain relatively low, in particular among the minorities, which often have a religious, ethnic or even tribal character. Not surprisingly, this is relatively rare in a newly independent country. Not surprisingly, too, a strong leader is not merely a help, but appears to be a necessity (see Chapter 19); if no such 'charismatic' leader exists, the regime is likely to move rapidly to a different form, and may in particular become authoritarian-inegalitarian.

## Authoritarian-inegalitarian political systems

By and large, authoritarian-inegalitarian political systems emerge as a reaction. They may be a reaction to traditional systems which are no longer able to contain opposition without strong coercion. They may be a reaction to liberal democratic political systems, as was the case in much of southern, central and eastern Europe after the First World War, especially in newly created countries or in those which had been most affected by the war. Fascism and Nazism are the prime examples of such a reaction, but developments of a similar kind occurred in Latin America after the Second World War. Authoritarian-inegalitarian political systems may also be a reaction to populist regimes: there have been examples of such a normative change in Africa, Asia and Latin America, especially from the mid-1960s to the early 1980s. Such a reaction has often, but not always, taken the form of military rule.

These political systems are first and foremost authoritarian: 'normal' political life is reduced to a minimum, and there is even the widespread belief among the authorities that politics can be abolished altogether and replaced by management and administration. Some authoritarian-inegalitarian regimes have had to accept a degree of 'politicization' and set up organizations designed to enrol the population in a 'mass' party, whose primary purpose is to express support for the leader and the regime; consequently, these parties are typically hierarchically structured. There is emphasis on the need to recognize the superiority – indeed, the almost superhuman qualities – of the leader; the concept of democracy is wholly rejected. Society itself is viewed as hierarchical, with everyone having his or her place in a near biologically ordered set of positions. The aim is to construct – or reconstruct – a society in which there is a loyal following.

These political systems are also socially inegalitarian because they have been set up in order to defend a social élite which feels threatened by the growing influence of the 'popular classes', and/or because they are associated with ideas of social as well as political hierarchy. In many cases, there is a longing for a return to what is viewed as the well-organized structure of a past in which everyone had his or her place and in which positions in the hierarchy were not questioned. Such attempts often end in failure, since the effort to remodel the society cannot be pursued for long. The regime is likely to be toppled and replaced by a populist or a liberal democratic system, although the new government may in turn be rather weak and have to give way to another authoritarian-inegalitarian system (or, in some cases, to a communist system).

The norms of the political systems of the contemporary world thus fall into separate clusters, though the sharpness of the differences sometimes becomes blunted as one country moves from one regime to another, or when there is oscillation, as often in Latin America, from one type of norm to another. Whether political systems embody the same norms for long periods or not, however, the patterns which emerge are sufficiently distinct to provide a clear picture of the characteristics of the political systems which belong to each type. It is to a description of these characteristics in political systems that we now turn.

## Institutions and groups in political systems

The norms which political systems embody provide an image of the broad direction in which these systems move, as well as the manner in which decisions are taken. But, as we know, decisions are taken with the help of institutions and groups which form different configurations in different political systems. There are close relationships between the norms of political systems and the structures which prevail in these systems, although these relationships are complex. Some institutions are set up in order to ensure that certain norms are implemented in the polity: in theory at least – but not always in practice – parliaments and parties are set up to provide a means for democratic participation to take place. The relationship may be complex, however, because the role of these institutions may be distorted, as in many authoritarian systems. Moreover, institutions and groups may have an effect on norms when they are well established: tribes may thus maintain the traditional character of a political system. In describing the type of institutions and groups which characterize a given type of political system, one has therefore to consider carefully the part which an institution or group may play in this system, in contrast to the part the same kind of institution or group may play in another type of political system.

## Institutions and groups in liberal democratic political systems

In liberal democratic political systems, the configuration of institutions and groups is based in large part – though not entirely – on constitutional arrangements deliberately designed to implement the norms of the political system. This is particularly the case with parliaments or congresses, but courts, the executive and the bureaucracy are also shaped to a varying degree by the constitution.

Yet, ever since the nineteenth century when earlier constitutions were drafted, liberal and liberal democratic systems have included many institutions not even mentioned in constitutions. The most important of these have been the political parties, but other groups have also played a large part in national decision making. Consequently, even in liberal democratic polities, constitutional structures have often become less influential, or have remained influential only in conjunction with non-constitutional bodies, such as parties. Parliaments and executives tend to be dominated by political parties, both because elections occur on party lines and because day-to-day behaviour takes place on topics and in a manner which correspond to the decisions of the parties (together with the most influential groups). However, of all types of political system, liberal democratic regimes are those where constitutional bodies play the largest part.

The structural configuration of liberal democratic regimes can therefore be described as being based on a number of well-defined arenas (parliaments and executives, but also local and regional parliaments and executives constituting these arenas) in which there are two main levels of actor, the parties and the groups, while the bureaucracy is influential in the wings. The positions of these two types of actor are different. Parties play the main parts and occupy the front of the stage; they typically execute the main movements or recite the main lines. Groups are normally less visible, except when they suddenly irrupt by means of major strikes or demonstrations. Groups tend to be organized for definite purposes (though their aims may be relatively broad, as in the case of trade unions or business organizations); they normally exercise pressure on the parties, although they also endeavour to have direct links with the civil service.

The level of participation in groups and parties is ostensibly high, but in practice it is often small. The mass of the population tends to take a spectator's position, groups and parties being supported from time to time by vigorous clapping or attacked by strong booing. Ties between population and structures are not necessarily much stronger at the local or regional levels. By and large, the 'grass-roots' activities of the national parties and groups directly concern only a minority, although there may be variations from area to area and from time to time. Overall, the system is relatively well ordered, largely as a result of the acceptance of the 'rules of the game' – that is, the characteristics of the constitutional arrangements – by practically all the actors. Where and when this acceptance is less widespread, the probability of the liberal democratic regime being overthrown is high, since there are relatively few means of strong defence of the various arenas and of the actors other than this acceptance.

## Institutions and groups in communist political systems

In egalitarian-authoritarian political systems such as the communist states, the determination of the arenas has typically been less clear, since these regimes have tended to operate on the basis of a deliberate ambiguity. There has been in effect a division between a (political) superstructure and a (political) infrastructure, with two different configurations of institutions.

The *political superstructure* has tended to be constituted by the official organs of the state, most of which have tended to be outwardly similar to those of liberal democratic countries, except for a greater emphasis given to the bureaucratic side of the machinery than in liberal democratic countries. The civil service has not remained 'in the wings', but has been part of the configuration itself. Indeed, at the level of the structure of the state, there has been little, if any, differentiation between administration and politics. This distinction became sharp in liberal democratic countries as political parties wished to control the executive but, by general agreement, did not enter more than to a limited extent in the lower echelons of the administrative hierarchy.

The effectiveness of the organization of the state in communist countries has largely depended on the *political infrastructure*, which has been constituted by the communist party and a host of ancillary bodies, such as trade unions and youth organizations. These bodies suggested directions for action and supervised implementation. Thus the communist party has not had clear and circumscribed areas of activity such as parties tend to have in liberal democratic states. It has been at least as active as parties are in western countries in directing the government, but it has also controlled many aspects of the administrative machine, while maintaining a grip on the 'mass' organizations which it helped to set up.

There have thus been two levels of institutional and group configuration in communist states. The linkage between the two has sometimes been difficult because it has tended to be achieved only by the operation of a number of key individuals at both levels. A further source of difficulty stems from the fact that, below the political infrastructure of the party and the officially recognized groups, a further level, wholly unofficial, of more traditional bodies (ethnic or religious in particular) as well as of more modern (protest) organizations has also existed. These groups – especially ethnic groups – often became very influential in the states which abandoned communism in the 1989–90 period. The party had woven a closely knit web of groups below itself in order to prevent both traditional bodies and more modern organizations from coming to the surface, but it was obviously far from successful in this task. These 'holes' in the domination of groups by the party, which have always been large in some countries (such as Poland, where the Catholic Church proved particularly resilient) are perhaps one of the main reasons which led to the ultimate collapse of communism in eastern Europe and most of the Soviet Union. It is difficult to believe that similar eruptions from the bottom will not gradually spread throughout what remained of the communist world in the mid-1990s.

## Institutions and groups in traditional inegalitarian political systems

Structural configurations in traditional inegalitarian political systems are in sharp contrast with those of liberal democratic and egalitarian-authoritarian systems, since they are in no way the product of deliberate decisions, let alone of imposition on a pre-existing structure. Traditional political systems have the configuration of institutions which among all political systems correspond most closely to the social structure. Indeed, these are the political systems in which the osmosis between politics and society is the most complete because the only elements which count are the traditional groupings and the hierarchical positions which exist within and between these groupings. Thus there is no political arena as such, whether well or ill defined. In particular there are no political parties and there is often even no parliament. The bureaucracy itself is relatively limited, at least in the most traditional of these countries. What characterize these regimes are sets of loyalties of a personal or a group character, which start at the level of small units (in villages or among bands, for instance) and move to that of the tribe and of the chiefs.

This situation has two consequences. First, when the system functions well, groupings are very strong and difficult to shake; their domain is by and large geographically circumscribed and they are likely to resist any encroachments. While liberal democratic polities are based on a permanent competition among groups which have specific activities, traditional inegalitarian systems are based on the principle that there is only one grouping within a particular area – for instance, only one tribe.

The second consequence is at the national level. The various groupings may or may not recognize fully the supremacy of the monarch and of the top political personnel. Admittedly, traditional inegalitarian regimes will be maintained for substantial periods only if some accommodation is achieved between the geographical groupings composing the nation; otherwise, the polity will break up. This is why ex-colonial countries have rarely given rise to traditional inegalitarian political systems: oppositions between geographical groups are typically such that, soon after independence, a different regime has to be introduced.

It is becoming increasingly difficult to maintain a stable equilibrium between monarch and tribal or ethnic groups, in part because every society is subjected to outside influences which undermine traditional groupings, and in part because of the geographical and social mobility of the population. Thus traditional inegalitarian political systems begin to change: institutions such as the bureaucracy and the military become stronger; new groups with specific purposes, such as business organizations and even trade unions, come to play a part. As long as these developments occur on a small scale, the political system can still be described as traditional. When the supremacy of tribal groupings becomes seriously challenged, however, the political system becomes typically populist or authoritarian-inegalitarian.

## Institutions and groups in populist political systems

The structural configuration of populist political systems is hybrid. It is often characterized by a profound opposition between declining traditional groupings and new groups, such as business or trade union organizations, between which uneasy compromises have to be ironed out. This means that, in populist systems, there is not the osmosis between society and political life that occurs in traditional inegalitarian systems. Political structures, and especially parties, are normally set up with the conscious purpose of fostering change in the society. But these parties have naturally to face the difficulties posed by the opposition between the conservative tendencies of traditional groupings and the pressure towards 'modernization' which some of the newer groups, as well as in many cases the bureaucracy and even the army, wish to promote. Parties are therefore often divided between those which represent primarily traditional groupings and those which at least claim to foster and mobilize the demands of the newer groups (though many parties of these countries are characterized by both elements).

This situation of tension has often resolved itself, especially in the 1970s and 1980s, by the (more or less voluntary) merger of political parties and the move towards a single-party system. However, the move has been countered to an extent, especially in Africa, in the early 1990s, by the introduction of multiparty systems; this occurred in large part in order to gain the support of western countries after the fall of communism. Yet the change has been more formal than real in many cases, as some leaders of the old dominant parties continued to control political life on the basis of the same normative principles as in the past.

On the other hand, the single-party systems (or dominant near single-party systems) existing in populist countries have differed markedly from communist single-party systems. The dominant parties in populist regimes usually cannot hold in check the traditional groupings. In Africa, parts of the Middle East and to a lesser extent elsewhere, populist single parties have typically tried to balance the interests of the 'modernizing' groups, including the bureaucracy, with those of tribal or ethnic forces. It does not seem that multiparty systems, where they have been installed, have changed the picture appreciably, except that to some extent ethnic conflicts have come more strongly to the fore. These difficulties explain why these systems have typically been successful only when a popular (or 'charismatic') leader has strengthened the political structures, and the dominant party in particular, by appealing directly to the people. When there are no (or no longer) such leaders, major difficulties occur which are presented, by and large rightly, as indications of the inadequacy of the structural configuration to solve the problems faced by the country. The result is often the emergence of an authoritarian-inegalitarian system.

## Institutions and groups in authoritarian-inegalitarian political systems

Authoritarian-inegalitarian political systems tend to emerge when internal divisions at the level of the institutions cannot be surmounted by compromises. This takes place, as we have seen, when a populist system is confronted with traditional groupings, such as strong tribes, which have been alienated by the regime. But it also takes place when, in a liberal democratic polity, oppositions between parties and between groups are so strong that the government becomes ineffective. The emergence of an authoritarian-inegalitarian political system is then often presented as an alternative to an authoritarian-egalitarian system of the communist variety, although there are in fact very few cases in which communist takeovers have happened in this way. Thus Mussolini, Hitler and Franco claimed that the systems which they installed were the best 'bulwarks' against communist takeovers; and the same argument has been used since the Second World War in many parts of the Third World.

While populist political systems attempt, often unsuccessfully, to build new institutions to counterbalance the influence of traditional groupings, authoritarian-inegalitarian political systems typically try to revive these traditional bodies and to base their strength on the loyalties which these generated in the past. This is, of course, easier to achieve when the authoritarian-inegalitarian political system replaces a traditional system, and in particular when the monarch is the originator of the move. Yet there are difficulties even then, as more modern institutions also emerge, including the bureaucracy. This is why the basis on which authoritarian-inegalitarian systems mainly rely is the military, since this not only provides physical power to control and undermine the opposition, but can help to foster the principles of hierarchy which the regime wishes to maintain. Where a 'mass' organization (a party) is set up – especially in cases when the move is from a liberal democratic to an authoritarian-inegalitarian regime – this is often done on military lines and indeed around the army. However, such parties are created only after the military has been in power for some time, and they help to extend the support for the military beyond the army itself.

Thus, while the configuration of institutions and groups in populist systems is hybrid and leads to serious internal conflicts, the configuration of institutions in authoritarian-inegalitarian political systems is somewhat artificial. Traditional groupings are expected to be the mainstay of the regime, but they are typically too weak. An attempt is made to fill the gap by the army, while the bureaucracy is expected to be concerned with a very large part of the public decision-making process. As a result, the configuration of institutions tends to be divorced from the characteristics of the society. Compulsion has to be strong, unless the leader can maintain the regime by his or her own 'charisma'; but this is rarer than in populist political systems, since there is typically no groundswell of popular feeling supporting the rulers. Not surprisingly, authoritarian-inegalitarian systems face high levels of internal tension and often collapse as a result.

## Overview

Alongside structures – that is, institutions and groups – *normative principles* are key characteristics of political systems: they guide the decisions taken by the actors of these systems.

These normative principles correspond to three dimensions which are summarized by the three questions: *who rules, in what way, and for what purpose?*

These three dimensions form a space in which all political systems are located. In this space, because of imitation and/or imposition, political systems tend to be *clustered* at or around a small number of positions.

In the contemporary world, there have been five such clusters, which are constituted by *liberal democratic, egalitarian-authoritarian, traditional inegalitarian, populist and authoritarian-inegalitarian political systems.*

The configuration of structures varies appreciably from one type of political system to another.

In *liberal democratic* systems, constitutional institutions are prominent; parties and groups also play a very important part, but mostly within the official institutional framework.

*Communist* systems have been characterized by the dominant part played by an all-embracing party and its ancillary organizations trying to control – eventually mostly without success – the more traditional groups, especially those of an ethnic character.

*Third World countries* have typically been divided into the other three types of political system, though some of them, especially in the Commonwealth and in Latin America, have been liberal democratic, while a few have been communist.

*Traditional inegalitarian* systems are primarily based on tribes and have few if any political institutions as such: social groups are the political groupings.

In *populist* systems, attempts have been made to modernize the society and in particular to reduce the role of tribes and ethnic groups, often by using single-party systems. This has been far from generally successful, even with charismatic leaders.

*Authoritarian-inegalitarian* systems have attempted, on the other hand, to return to the past. They have used coercion widely, and the military has often been prominent. Again the result has often been limited, even with charismatic leaders.

Some of these systems thus experience *substantial tensions*, and the configuration of institutions and groups reflects these tensions more than it overcomes them. As these tensions are in large part the result of the oppositions which exist in the contemporary world between loyalties based on tradition and pressures for social change, the question of 'development' in political systems is central to the current character and evolution of these systems. This is the question to which we turn in the next chapter.

## Further reading

It was common practice until the nineteenth century to classify political systems according to the scheme put forward by Aristotle, *The Politics*, book 3, chapter 7. Meanwhile, Locke, in the

*Second Treatise on Government* (1690), and Montesquieu, in the *Spirit of Laws* (1748), elaborated a constitutional classification out of which emerged the current distinction between parliamentary and presidential systems. Rousseau's classification, in the *Social Contract* (1762), was based, like that of Hobbes in *Leviathan*, on a behavioural distinction among regimes. These classifications are discussed by D.V. Verney in *The Analysis of Political Systems* (1959: 17–93). Types of approach to the 'good society' can be found in A. Arblaster and S. Lukes, eds., *The Good Society* (1971).

The most systematic attempt at defining and operationalizing liberal democracy has been given by R.A. Dahl in *Polyarchy* (1971). There have been many other attempts at characterizing polities on the basis of their political and socioeconomic characteristics. See in particular K. Janda, *Political Parties: A Cross-National Survey* (1980) and C.L. Taylor and D.A. Jodice, *World Handbook of Social and Political Indicators* (3rd edn, 1983). On participation, see S. Verba and N.H. Nie, *Participation in America* (1972) and S. Verba, N.H. Nie, and Jae-on Kim, eds., *Participation and Political Equality* (1978).

The works describing the characteristics of regimes in the various regions of the globe are, of course, extremely numerous. A selected list of studies specifically devoted to one or a number of countries can be found in the bibliography at the end of this volume.

# 4
# Political development

## Introduction

The problems posed by changes of norms and by the dynamics of political systems, to which we alluded in Chapter 3, lead directly to a further question, that of the *direction* of these changes. What is at stake is the matter of political 'improvement' (or decline), of political 'progress' (or regress). If there is to be change, it is obviously important to know whether such a change will lead to a 'better' society. Political theory has always been concerned with such questions: as a matter of fact, the main aim of writers such as Hobbes, Locke, Rousseau and Marx was to contrast what they deemed to be the unsatisfactory conditions of politics around them with the 'improvements' which would result from the implementation of the blueprints which they proposed.

The period following the Second World War has been especially characterized by a concern for political progress – typically under the expression of *political development*. There were three main reasons for this renewed concern. The first was the aftermath of the events of the interwar period. The period of relative optimism characterizing the nineteenth and early twentieth centuries was followed by intense pessimism when dictatorships prevailed in Europe. Then the victory of the democracies in 1945 seemed to open a new era for political progress, the United Nations being the symbol of this optimism. Second, there was the emergence of 'new' countries, especially in the 1950s and 1960s, most of which were born from the rejection of colonialism and from the concomitant desire to make a fresh start, as had been the case in the United States in the late eighteenth century (Lipset, 1963). Third, and at the same time, improvements in what came to be known as the Third World seemed to imply profound economic and social changes in agriculture, industry, education, health and welfare. Such changes came to be regarded as economic and social 'development'; a parallel improvement or development seemed necessary in the political sphere. Indeed, development was viewed as a comprehensive process which should not be divided into compartments: improvements in one aspect of the society – political, social or economic – depended on improvements in all the others.

Large numbers of social scientists, and of political scientists among them, therefore came to study development (Blondel, 1981: 90–102; Chilcote, 1981: 271–346). But it soon became clear that political development was difficult to circumscribe and to define. L.W. Pye found no fewer than ten different bases for political development in the literature, ranging from mass mobilization to the operation of the state, and from the politics of industrial societies to stable and orderly change. Although he then proceeded to look for a comprehensive 'syndrome' in order to bring these approaches under a common umbrella, it seemed rather worrying for the intellectual solidity of the concept that there should be so many views about what it entailed (Finkle and Gable, 1966: 83–118; Pye, 1966: 31–48; Jackson and Stein, 1971: 19–111). There appeared to be a major contradiction between practical requirements and the logic of the analysis: while everyone wished to improve society, including its political aspects, it seemed difficult to agree as to what 'improving politics' could entail. There was a conceptual impasse on a topic which was a top priority both for practitioners and for the public at large.

Before concluding that there is, indeed, no hope of coming to an acceptable single definition, we need to examine this impasse somewhat more closely.

- In the first section of this chapter, we shall survey the points which raise *controversy* or lead to *differences in approach*. We will see that both normative principles and structures are key components in the determination of political development.
- In the second section, we will elaborate the *part played by structures* – institutions and groups – in the context of political development.
- The third section will be devoted to the *role of normative principles*.

## The concept of political development

### Many definitions

Why, then, does the concept of political development raise difficulties? Let us start from what it aims to cover: it is concerned with progress, which means change in a 'positive' direction. Change can be described, although there may be problems about its measurement. What causes difficulty is the assessment of what is 'positive' or 'negative' change, as such an assessment depends on having previously determined what makes 'good politics': one cannot speak of political development without having a conception of the 'good society' (Arblaster and Lukes, 1971). The real difficulty arises at this point: it is not so much that it is difficult to define what the good society is; it is that it seems impossible to find a definition to which all will agree. The appreciation of whether a society is good or not, and whether a change is an improvement or not, is a value judgement: what is the good society for one individual may not be the good society for another. Witness the controversies which have raged between 'democrats' and supporters of a 'hierarchical society', or between 'levellers' and those who believe that inequalities are not merely inevitable but indeed just. This explains why political theorists have searched relentlessly for the good society: every political theorist is entitled to renew the search without being bound by the conclusions of others.

If this is the case, should one simply refuse to give a general definition of political development? This is impractical, since society exists and political activity takes place in the society. Whether we define political development or not, society will have to do it; there will be goals and there will be images of what constitutes a good society. There is thus an *existential* need for an operational definition of political progress and development, which is valid at least for the immediate future and for a given society. Political theorists are not just entitled to continue to search for a solution: they have to do so, because society needs to have some practical notion of what political progress entails.

Let us therefore see, following Pye, what kinds of definition have been given of political development, and whether we can at least discover some relatively firm elements. These definitions fall into three distinct categories:

- The first relates political development to *social and economic development* by suggesting that political development is concerned with the politics of industrial societies or with a 'multidimensional process of social change'.
- A second group is concerned with what might be called *the organization of the political system*, by referring to nation building and to administrative structures.
- The third links development to *political values*, such as mass mobilization, the relationship between mobilization and power, and the movement towards democracy (Pye, 1966: 45–8).

## Political development and socioeconomic development

Definitions of the first group, which relate political development to social and economic development, are simple, but seem rather unrewarding. They are simple in that they assume that we know what social and economic development is. In the 1960s and the early 1970s at least, social scientists believed that they did; they even thought that few measurement problems existed, since economic development could be assessed by such means as levels and distributions of incomes and extent of industrialization, while social development could be traced through levels of educational and social services, all of which seemed eminently measurable and were indeed measured by many UN agencies engaged in collecting and publishing the relevant data. On the other hand, political development was obviously more difficult to grasp *per se*. It was not clear what data would have to be collected. But as political activity consists in taking decisions, its effect could be apprehended by policy outputs: that is, precisely by economic and social outputs. One might then conclude that there was political development where one could trace the existence of economic and social development.

This approach is unrewarding, however. Quite apart from making it difficult to perceive the autonomy of politics, it makes it impossible to assess the part played by what may be called political 'bottlenecks', such as corruption, inefficient or wasteful bureaucratic procedures, or the sheer inability of politicians to take decisions speedily. Conversely, it is impossible to discover the political conditions which could favour

---

**BOX 4.1**
## The idea of social and political progress

The idea of social and political progress is relatively recent in human societies. Its real take-off was in the middle of the eighteenth century with the publication of the *Encyclopedia*. Admittedly, in Ancient Rome and Renaissance Italy, to concentrate on Europe, the idea that there might be progress in human societies was sometimes put forward, but the bulk of the population continued to live on the basis of 'ancestral traditions'.

From the second half of the eighteenth century, however, the belief that societies might progress gained ground. The industrial revolution seemed to justify this belief: changes in modes of living, in the West at least, between, say, 1780 and 1880 were such that it seemed difficult not to believe in progress. The idea of social progress became closely linked to technical and economic change. The great exhibitions of the second half of the nineteenth century, from that of 1851 in London onwards, were monuments to the idea that humankind was moving to a better future.

Social progress became translated into political progress. The ideas of liberty and democracy had existed for a long time, but more as symbols or 'utopias', as the sixteenth-century English thinker, Thomas More, had said. These utopias seemed on the verge of becoming reality, if not in Europe, since the French Revolution had turned sour and the 1848 Revolutions had been defeated, but in America, where many were able to implement their 'progressive' ideas and where, in general, the political system was, since the presidency of Jackson in the 1830s, 'democratic'. Old Europe itself was in turn to adopt gradually some of the ideas of the New World.

But how much political progress has truly taken place? The dictatorships of the twentieth century in Italy, Germany, Spain, eastern Europe, Russia, and later China and other communist and non-communist Third World states have shown that whatever political progress there might have been could quickly be erased. The very idea of progress has come to be questioned in the process. Is humankind truly capable of progress on the political front, or is there only cyclical change? Are we so diverse in our views that we shall never be able to work together towards a common idea of political progress?

---

economic and social progress. A place has therefore to be made for political development as such alongside and independently from development in the other spheres.

## Political development as the organization of the political system

The second group of definitions relates to what might be regarded as a 'minimalist' view of politics. These are the approaches which relate political development to the activity of the state, and to the efficiency of administrative processes. Even if it is difficult to describe with precision, let alone quantify, bureaucratic efficiency, it seems at least possible to point to specific examples suggesting that 'progress' in society depends on 'progress' in the administrative sphere. Yet it is hard to see why one should single out the state structure and the bureaucracy as the only elements on which political development should depend. Political decision making results from the activities taking place within all political structures, including groups, parties, parliaments, executives and bureaucracies: inefficiency in any one of them should therefore result in lack of development. Thus political development would seem to relate generally to the way decisions are taken, from the moment they are conceived to the moment in which they are fully implemented, in and by all these structures (Evans *et al.*, 1985: 3–43).

Yet, while the concept of political development acquires a sounder intellectual base as a result, there are practical and theoretical problems. The practical problems of measurement become immense: for instance, we would have to assess whether a party was 'efficient' or not in promoting a given policy at a given point in time; this entails passing judgements on such matters as the extent to which the population is 'ripe' for the policy, whether it would 'cost' too much in terms of money and energy to undertake such a move, and so on. Comparisons across countries may help to an extent, but the magnitude of the practical problem is obvious. Moreover, theoretical difficulties begin to arise as we move from what was basically an examination of the appropriateness and effectiveness of means to an assessment of goals. Since we have to consider the role of parties, groups, parliaments or executives, we need to look at the grounds on which the decisions were taken; we therefore have to pass judgements on the opportunity of choosing these grounds rather than others. In other words, we move from the realm of means to enter that of norms.

## Political development as the implementation of political values

This is probably the reason why some students of political development opted for a definition of the third type, which takes into account values such as mobilization and democracy. The difficulty, however, is that, as we stated at the outset, such definitions are based on subjective standpoints. While one observer may regard development as based on democracy, another may claim that a hierarchical society would be more 'developed'. It seems, therefore, that we have run full circle: only relatively simple and low-level approaches are relatively objective, but at the cost of apprehending only one aspect of the problem; more comprehensive approaches seem to depend entirely on the personal position of the observer. Nor does a 'syndrome' truly help: the problem of value assessment is not resolved, since values are one element of the analysis.

A different solution therefore has to be found. If values play a major part in the determination of the good society, what must be explored is whether there may not be some common ground below the norms and values which appear to be subjective. Meanwhile, we must also explore the part which all structures (and not merely bureaucracies) play in making more efficient the processes of decision making and implementation. We saw in the previous two chapters that political life was concerned both with structures and with norms: it should not be surprising that political development, if it is to be fully assessed, should be based on particular characteristics of both structures and norms.

## Political development and the role of structures

Political development unquestionably depends, in part at least, on the efficiency of the structures of the political system; what needs to be determined is precisely *what constitutes* structural efficiency. The question has two aspects, absolute and relative: first, we have to see whether we can discover principles enabling us to decide what makes a structure efficient; second, we have to see how far other differences within the society may affect the characteristics which make the whole system more or less efficient.

### What makes a structure efficient?

There are no easy answers to either of these questions; nor has it been possible so far to provide precise guidelines. On the first matter, which concerns the characteristics of structural efficiency at the level of each institution or group, attempts have been made to circumscribe the problem by way of an analysis of the concept of *institutionalization*. Structures are likely to be more efficient if they operate more smoothly, if there are fewer difficulties about the procedures on the basis of which they are run, and if these procedures are clear. The concept of institutionalization attempts to summarize these points. It has been defined by Huntington as 'the process by which organisations and procedures acquire value and stability' (Huntington, 1968: 12). In the detailed analysis which he then conducts, Huntington discovers four dimensions along which institutions can be located, and which can help to determine their degree of institutionalization. Institutions have to be assessed, he states, by the extent to which they are 'adaptable' rather than 'rigid', 'complex' rather than 'simple', 'autonomous' rather than 'subordinated', and 'coherent' rather than 'disunited' (Huntington, 1968: 13–24).

It is arguable whether one should conclude, following Huntington, that the highest possible degree of institutionalization is always to be found at the polar extremes of these four dimensions. There may be a trade-off between the four variables: 'adaptability' may affect the degree of 'coherence'; it is probably better to have some 'disunity' if this means a lower level of 'rigidity'. However, to the extent that the analysis applies to each institution, it provides guidelines which are both theoretically rewarding and practically useful. One can at least have, at the level of each structure, an impression of what constitutes 'progress' or 'development': one can, for instance compare parties, groups or legislatures, and see to what extent, by being better institutionalized, they appear to be more developed (Polsby, 1962: 144–68).

## Efficiency at the level of the whole political system

Difficulties are greater when we come to consider the second and larger problem of structural political development across the polity as a whole. At first, it might seem permissible to assess the overall structural efficiency of a political system by adding up, as it were, the results obtained for the different structures which compose the system. Such an operation would, of course, be extremely long and could in practice be only partial. But even if it were partial, it would at least give an impression of the level of the overall efficiency of the system, were it not for the fact that a high level of institutionalization of each structure may not result in a truly efficient political system. For instance, groups which are highly developed may produce a situation in which demands are so numerous that the system cannot cope (a situation which is typically described as one of *political overload*) (Rose and Peters, 1977). Admittedly, this means that the parliament, the executive or the bureaucracy is not then truly adapted to the characteristics of other structures and of groups in particular. One must go beyond the institutionalization of each structure and consider the interconnections between structures. However, it is difficult to see precisely how these interconnections can be assessed.

As a first element of solution, two criteria have been suggested in the literature: the level of *structural differentiation* and the extent of *structural autonomy* (Almond and Powell, 1966: 306–14). The first criterion bears some similarity with the idea of the division of labour, which, since Durkheim, has been regarded as a characteristic of 'advanced' societies (Durkheim, 1964: 39–49). Empirical evidence does indeed suggest that there is greater differentiation of institutions and groups in the societies which are less traditional. The second criterion is related to one of the dimensions mentioned by Huntington, since, as we have seen, he views 'autonomy' as evidence of institutionalization (Huntington, 1968: 12). It seems permissible to claim that, where there is a large number of autonomous structures, there is at least potential for greater political development.

## Structural differentiation and structural autonomy

Difficulties subsist, however, beyond the fact that the concepts cannot easily be operationalized. It is not axiomatic that there is a linear relationship between structural political development and the two variables which appear to account for it. The existence of an infinite number of highly differentiated and autonomous structures may not make the system of itself more efficient than it would be with a smaller number of structures aggregating within themselves a variety of standpoints and approaches. For instance, in some countries, parties and interest groups are quite independent from each other: this is the case in particular in the United States. In other countries, socialist and Christian parties are related to a series of groups, such as trade unions and co-operatives, etc. It is not clear that the first type of arrangement is by any criterion more 'successful' than the second.

While differentiation and overall autonomy may therefore play a part, the nature and extent of the linkages between structures have to be closely examined. The matter resembles that of centralization, which we shall examine in Chapter 14. It is typically suggested that there are optimum levels of decentralization for each situation, and that these optimum levels are at some distance from full autonomy. The same could and probably should be said with respect to the efficiency of the structural configuration as a whole.

This approach to political development raises a more fundamental problem, however, which ultimately takes us away from the realm of structures and into the realm of norms. We are on safe ground if we describe political development in terms of the efficiency of the structures of the political system. We are still on safe ground if we then look at the way in which all the structures combine to enable society to allocate values in an efficient manner: if we look, so to speak, at the capability of the whole system to take decisions (Almond and Powell, 1966: 190–212). We are on less safe ground if we postulate that this efficiency can be assessed by means of structural differentiation and structural autonomy. Although it seems true that a form of 'division of labour' and some degree of decentralization may lead to greater development, the relationship between these two characteristics and efficiency has to be empirically tested. One can state with certainty that the development of the structures depends on the differentiation and efficiency of these structures only if this is shown to be the case in all societies; indeed, if the relationship exists, it is probably not linear.

This strong empirical connection has not yet been proved, however, a state of affairs which might not be truly serious, were it not for the fact that both differentiation and autonomy are characteristics which appear to be value loaded; they seem to lead to the conclusion that the countries which are most developed politically are liberal democracies. Both these characteristics or properties of structures can be found in countries in which groups are numerous and emerge freely in the society – that is, primarily in western liberal democracies.

## From structural to normative analysis

So long as it is not proved that the capacity of the political system entails the existence of differentiated and autonomous structures, the stress on these characteristics constitutes a value standpoint: we are no longer discussing structural, but normative elements. This is an accusation that has commonly been levelled at this approach to political development, which is why the approach has been regarded as western biased, as well perhaps as somewhat underhand. If we are to suggest that western liberal democracies are the most politically developed polities, it is more honest to state this openly – on the basis of a value judgement – than to claim that political development is based on apparently 'objective' characteristics of structures (Chilcote, 1981: 178–82).

It is therefore better at this point to turn to the examination of the role of norms in political development. This does not mean that we are to regard structures as irrelevant in this context; but it is manifest that structures alone do not provide the whole of the explanation which we are looking for. Quite possibly, political development is related to the efficiency of structures and, overall, to the capacity of these structures to cope with the decisions which the system has to take. This is only a hypothesis, however, and the assessment of the possible effect of the differentiation and autonomy of structures on the political system depends on an empirical analysis. What needs to be shown is that structural differentiation and autonomy increase the capacity of the political system. Any conclusion going beyond this point leads us to consider the part played by norms in political development.

## Political development and the role of norms

The assessment of political development cannot, therefore, be complete unless one considers the part which norms play in defining the goals of the polity. This seems to point to the conclusion that there cannot be a single conception of political development to which all could agree: there will be many views as to what these goals of the polity may be. It does not seem permissible to state that political development *is* 'mass mobilization and participation' or 'the building of democracy', or even 'stability and orderly change', as some have suggested according to Pye's analysis (Pye, 1966: 39–42); nor is it permissible to state categorically that the political development 'syndrome' includes the striving towards 'equality', as Pye suggests (1966: 45–6). We are here in the realm of prescription and we do not seem able – indeed, it is logically unwarranted – to claim that these values *are* the values which all have to recognize as characterizing a 'good' society (Jackson and Stein, 1971: 32–4).

### Value-laden character of political development

Is there no way at all out of this impasse? Have we therefore to say that each society, each individual even, can have a different conception of the 'good', society, and that the concept of political development (at least in so far as it refers to norms) cannot be other than subjective? This conclusion seems at first sight difficult to avoid. It was drawn by many in the 1970s, who noticed, as was just pointed out, that writers of the 1960s had somewhat too easily 'demonstrated' the superiority of liberal democracies. New development theories emerged which suggested that the alleged value of liberal democracies was the product of the exploitation of the Third World by the West. Thus the 'development' of liberal democracies was achieved by maintaining other parts of the world in a form of economic dependency. To this was to be added an ideological dependency by which non-western states were subjected to the repeated claim that the western model of government was politically superior (Chilcote, 1981: 296–312; Hopkins and Wallerstein, 1982: 41–82).

This view connected political development closely to economic power. Meanwhile, supporters of western liberal democracies tended to make the same connection, since they typically claimed – and to an extent showed empirically – that liberal democracy

---

## BOX 4.2
## The inherently subjective character of political development

One vivid example of the subjective character of political development has been the hotly debated matter of the right of members of minority groups – especially religious groups – to adopt practices regarded as regressive by the majority of the population. The matter has been raised in particular in those western countries with a large number of immigrants. Hence the question, once debated in Britain, of whether Sikhs were to be allowed to wear their turbans rather than the cap which was part of the uniform of their job. Hence, more seriously, the question of whether Muslim girls were to be allowed to wear a veil at school throughout lessons and to be dispensed from going to gymnastics classes: this matter aroused a major debate in France in the early 1990s.

What constitutes political development over issues of this kind? Does it consist in allowing any group to adopt the customs which it wishes? Or does it consist in making these groups see that the practices which they follow are 'regressive', since they reduce the freedom of the person concerned? In some cases, these practices have been imposed by force, including by intimidation and even assassination.

The subjective character of political development emerges even more vividly when the conflict is not so much over the values themselves, but over which group should be the one whose values should prevail. Over the matter of wearing the veil, two questions have to be answered. There is, first, the substantive question of whether the nation, the social group or the individual should decide what should be worn. Second, there is the procedural but perhaps even more critical matter of who should take the decision about who will decide. The principle of 'expansion of choice opportunities' seems to suggest that the nation should not intervene. But is there not then the danger that the group will decide, rather than the individual?

---

flourished primarily where living standards were high (Cutright, 1963: 569–82; Lipset, 1983: 27–45). Economic and social development seemed to be the key element; political development was merely a 'superstructure', an inevitable consequence.

Yet, in reality, 'developmentalists' faced serious difficulties with this interpretation of society, for they needed to establish the primacy of political development if they were to break the vicious circle in which they saw Third World societies imprisoned. The way out, somewhat illogically, consisted in emphasizing the normative aspect of development, as if, despite the primacy of the economic 'substructure', societies could none the less decide on the basis of which political norms they were to be organized.

## Socioeconomic development values and goals

Such an approach reinforced the view that there could not be agreement on what constitutes political development, and that one's assessment in the matter depended entirely on one's ideological preferences. Yet it is questionable whether this conclusion is truly warranted.

To begin with, it is worth examining the apparent contrast between the characteristics of social and economic development and those of political development. On the surface, while political development appears to be based on subjective standpoints, social and economic development does not seem to raise quite the same fundamental difficulties, and even appears rather uncontentious. Is it, then, that economic and social development is not based on value judgements? This is not the case: economic and social development may be more easily measurable, in some of its aspects, than political development; but, like political development, it is based on values. For instance, it is neither axiomatic nor logically demonstrable that higher incomes per head are a 'good' thing, let alone that industrialization or the use of sophisticated machinery are 'good' things; nor is it even axiomatic or logically demonstrable that more education or more social services are 'good' things.

These questions are not only debatable, they are to an extent debated. They were often hotly debated in the past, and some of them have come to be discussed, in a renewed manner, since the 1970s and 1980s, as a result both of the increased strength of 'environmentalist ideas' and of the spread of conservative views about the state and the individual. The development of 'green' movements and parties since the 1970s, especially in western liberal democracies, has led to a strong questioning of the worth of economic and even conventional social development. The idea of 'rolling back the state' which characterized the policies of a number of western liberal democracies, such as Britain and the United States, also had the effect of leading to a questioning of the worth of conventional economic and social development. These points are debated because they are, like participation or equality in the context of political development, based on value judgements.

If the concepts of economic and social development depend on value judgements about the 'good society', why do these concepts not encounter the same difficulties as political development? There are two reasons for the difference. The first is somewhat peripheral, but it none the less plays some part: because economic and social development is more easily measurable in many of its aspects, there is in practice less scope for argument as to what, from a concrete point of view, might constitute development. As a matter of fact, the question of the measurement of economic and social development has also tended to be raised increasingly. The comparison of the per capita GNP of diverse countries, for instance, is controversial but the fact that countries can be ranked in terms of incomes per head or of educational attainment, while it is not possible to rank them with respect to the level of institutionalization of parties or parliaments, makes economic and social development *appear* more objective.

Second, and more fundamentally, the norms of economic and social development, though theoretically debatable, are indeed debated only to a limited extent. There is a higher degree of agreement on socioeconomic norms than on political norms. Few believe, let alone state (at any rate at present), that society should not educate its members or take care of the health of its citizens; few believe or state that levels of incomes among the mass of the population should be low. Meanwhile, many believe and indeed state that levels of participation should not be high, or that freedoms should be restricted.

As a matter of fact, it is so manifest that there is a debate on social and economic issues that we have argued that political systems should be differentiated along a dimension of substantive goals, of outputs, as well as along dimensions of liberalism–authoritarianism and of democracy–monocracy. Yet the debate which occurs along the dimension of substantive goals leaves considerable scope for broad agreement as to what might be said to constitute 'basic' social and economic values. Admittedly, there is disagreement on levels of equality with respect to property distribution and, indeed, income distribution. However, aspects of social life, such as those relating to health and to an extent education, as well as (though to a lesser extent) some aspects of economic life, such as the increased use of mechanical power instead of human physical force, are broadly accepted.

## An intersubjective approach to political development

The point here is not to assess the precise extent to which economic and social development is being debated; it is to point out that a lower or narrower amount of disagreement with respect to the goals of economic and social development stems not from a difference in kind with political development, but merely from a difference of degree. It is not that economic and social development can be defined in an objective manner, while political development would depend on subjective assessment: all aspects of development are based on subjective assessments. What makes economic and social development apparently easier to handle is that the level of *intersubjective agreement* is appreciably higher – at least ostensibly (Turner, 1986: 188, 328).

Given that the characteristics of development – of 'progress' – depend on a high level of consensus – of intersubjective agreement – if they are to be acceptable, there is a case for examining whether, as for economic and social development, it might not be possible to find a broad intersubjective base for political development as well. The aim is not to discover a 'syndrome' in which the structural elements of political development would reduce the part played by normative elements; it is to see whether some values are sufficiently broadly held in the political sphere to form a basis for an intersubjective approach to the concept.

It is manifestly impossible to discover such values at the level of ideological standpoints which are widely adopted in specific regimes, such as equality, democracy or 'orderly change' (Pye, 1966: 29-48). These concepts are the object of too many public and private debates. There are, however, some deeper characteristics of politics which might appear to the large majority – if not all – as 'positive'. Hobbes stated a characteristic which seems of this type: the right to defend one's life (Hobbes, 1968: pt I, ch. 14).

Could one not go somewhat further, by being positive rather than negative and, building on Hobbes' premiss, consider as 'inalienable' and universally 'valuable' *the right to strive, the right to achieve*, a view which is perhaps not too far from the right to 'happiness'?

## Political development as the expansion of choice opportunities

Let us go back to the definition of politics. It is the authoritative allocation of values. The question is: whose values? The answer may then be: all the values which exist at a given point in time in the polity. However, the political system cannot take all these values into account, as was pointed out in Chapter 2. There have to be mechanisms limiting the number of values (goods and services, but also attitudes) which the society can process at a given moment. Does it not therefore follow that improvement, progress and development would consist in increases in the number and characteristics of the values accepted by the society? If human beings have a right to achieve and at least to strive, this surely means that a better society is one in which all human beings are better able to achieve and at least to strive. This means that a better society is one in which the 'number' of values allocated is larger.

This conception of development is the one which D.E. Apter proposes in his *Choice and the Politics of Allocation*, where he states that development is the 'expansion of choice opportunities', a notion which pertains particularly to politics (Apter, 1973: 6). Such an approach, though normative, is almost certainly intersubjective because it is likely to carry broad agreement. This does not mean that there cannot be conflicts about the concrete manifestations of these 'choice opportunities'; nor is it claimed that the view that political development is related to the expansion of choice opportunities is universally accepted, especially if we consider the matter historically. However, this approach is likely to produce a sounder basis for intersubjective agreement, and thus to reduce the oppositions which seemed at one point to make it impossible even to discuss political development.

## Overview

The concept of political development raises major theoretical problems. These are unavoidable, given the intrinsically contentious nature of political values. There have therefore been many definitions, which have fallen into three types, associating political development respectively with socioeconomic development, with the structural efficiency of the system in terms of institutions and groups, and with the normative framework of the polity.

The definition relating political development to *socioeconomic development* bypasses the specificity of political life and is therefore not helpful.

The definition relating political development to *structures* such as institutions and groups touches only one aspect of the political life, important though it may be.

The definition relating political development to *norms* seems to suggest that the analysis of this concept has to be wholly subjective. This is admittedly true, but contrary to what is often thought, the concept of socioeconomic development is also subjective.

It is possible to look for an intersubjective definition, however, as is the case with concepts of socioeconomic development. This intersubjective definition of political development can be found in terms of the *expansion of choice opportunities*.

If one proceeds in this manner, the analysis can lead to a markedly more precise view of the concept of political development, and thus contribute significantly to an understanding of the direction of change in modern societies.

## Further reading

The number of studies on development are legion. So are those on political development. For a general presentation of the evolution of the studies, see my *Discipline of Politics* (1981: 90–102). For a detailed examination of theories of development, see R.H. Chilcote, *Theories of Comparative Politics* (1981: 271–346).

The most straightforward general presentation of the problems posed by political development can be found in L.W. Pye, *Aspects of Political Development* (1966). Two other general analyses of the problem can be found in J.L. Finkle and R.W. Gable, ed., *Political Development and Social Change* (1966) and in R.J. Jackson and M.B. Stein, eds., *Issues in Comparative Politics* (1971).

Analyses of specific aspects of the problem can be found in S.P. Huntington, *Political Order in Changing Societies* (1968), especially in the early chapters. The concept of capability has been elaborated and developed in G.A. Almond and G.B. Powell in *Comparative Politics* (1966), especially towards the end of the volume.

On the notion of intersubjective agreement, see in particular J.H. Turner, *The Structure of Sociological Theory* (1986: 188ff. and 328ff.). For a presentation of a more intersubjective concept of political development, see D.E. Apter, *Choice and the Politics of Allocation* (1973), in particular the early chapters.

# 5

# Legitimacy, integration and coercion

## Introduction

It is generally believed that political systems need popular *support* to remain in existence; yet many do remain in existence without being ostensibly accepted by the population. The phenomenon of *coercion* is widespread, and the concept of dictatorship is not among those which have little or no practical application. This apparent contradiction between a recognized 'need' for support and the reality of coercive regimes is one of the major questions which political science and comparative government need to analyze.

Support relates to *legitimacy*, a concept which should be sharply distinguished from legality, though there are connections between the two ideas. Cases abound of legal regimes which are not, or have ceased to be, legitimate because they no longer enjoy support: tsarist Russia at the time of the First World War is an example. There are also regimes which enjoy support without being legal, or at any rate without yet being legalized (for instance, if the previous regime was toppled by a coup). In most situations, however, legality helps to increase legitimacy because many will support the political system for the reason that it is legal.

The type of support which has just been referred to is based on the sentiments of individuals. However, there is another type of support, which stems from the relationship between structures (institutions and groups) and the political system: parties and interest organizations, but also tribal, ethnic and religious bodies ostensibly play a large part, as we shall have occasion to see at greater length in the coming chapters. The support given by institutions and groups determines the extent of *political integration* in a country. This form of support is obviously important, as important as and perhaps more important than the acceptance of the political system by individuals. We therefore need to look both at legitimacy among individuals and at the political integration of institutions and groups, to assess the overall amount of support which a political system enjoys.

A regime which does not have (sufficient) support has to rely on coercion or imposition: such a regime is a *dictatorship*. The history of the world, including the contemporary world, suggests that dictatorships are a widespread feature, and therefore that coercion can be a substitute for support in many circumstances despite the claim (or hope) that dictatorships might not be viable. Putting it differently, although there is apparent discontent among the population in many countries, rebellions are rare and successful rebellions (and revolutions) are even rarer. It took a world war to force the end of some of the European dictatorships, while others have sprung up in various parts of the globe since 1945. Dictatorial government is thus a persistent feature of political life, alongside regimes which have support and rely on consent.

One of the keys to the solution of the apparent contradiction between the need for support and the existence of dictatorships lies in the recognition that these situations, like most of those which we have already encountered, belong to *continuous dimensions* and do not constitute only dichotomies. The extent of individual support for a regime varies; the integration of groups in the political system is more or less pronounced. Conversely, there are manifest differences in the extent to which governments rely on coercion, from that used in mildly repressive regimes to that of full-blown totalitarian states. Consequently, one should not simply state that all these regimes are dictatorships, but view them as being characterized by various degrees of harshness. Meanwhile, overall, regimes also enjoy differing levels of individual support and of integration. Finally, we can assume that there are no political systems at either extreme of these dimensions: that is, political systems where there is no coercion at all or no support at all. If the problem is stated in this manner, it becomes unnecessary to attempt to explain the existence of support and of coercion *per se*; one has merely to account for *variations* in support and coercion on the assumption that in all cases there is always a minimum amount of both support and coercion.

This chapter divides naturally into three sections:

- In the first, we shall examine the concept of individual support or *legitimacy*.
- In the second, we shall analyze *political integration*.
- In the third, we shall look at the reasons why and the manner in which *coercion* takes place, and thus describe the occurrence and forms of *dictatorship*.

## Legitimacy and individual support

The concept of legitimacy is used widely both in the specialist political science literature and in common political parlance. However, it remains relatively ill studied from a formal point of view. Neither its origins, nor its growth and decline (since we said that support varied in extent, legitimacy also varies in extent), nor its effect have so far been systematically analyzed (Ferrero, 1945; Easton, 1965: 278–310; Connolly, 1984). This is probably one of the reasons why exaggerated claims are made about its effect, or more specifically why, since degrees are not measured or even assessed with any accuracy, particular effects of given amounts of legitimacy cannot be related to particular outcomes. As a matter of fact, there have been few attempts so far to operationalize the concept and to attempt to compare regimes in order to examine possible effects of different levels of legitimacy on outcomes (Rogowski, 1974). The analysis that we shall

## BOX 5.1
### Legitimacy and legitimation

It is so often said that regimes need legitimacy that the idea of creating legitimacy artificially has naturally come to the mind of most, if not all, leaders. The process by which an attempt is made to engineer legitimacy artificially is known as *legitimation*.

The crudest way in which legitimation is being fostered is through propaganda. With the development of the mass media, it was at first thought that propaganda could succeed in changing the minds of populations. These views have had to be abandoned gradually. Regimes based on propaganda did fall, and much of the propaganda effort seems to have been pointless. It now seems clear that one cannot legitimize regimes by propaganda alone.

Legitimation is attempted in other ways. With the development of public opinion polling on a large scale, governments are engaged to a major extent in a daily legitimation process, first of the government itself, and, second, in many cases at least, of the political system as well. In the past, leaders had to rely on impressions, often distorted, about the support which they had: they appointed 'spies' who conducted their own private polling to discover popular support. They can now know what the population feels about what they do almost before they have done it. The idea of increasing their support is continuously in their minds, and their actions are often guided by this idea.

Seen in this way, the question of support is turned on its head: support exists because society induces individuals to give support. Legitimation becomes part of the socialization process. Individuals become in a sense the expression of the social forces: the conclusion seems exaggerated, but the debate on the matter goes on.

conduct here will therefore lack the solid empirical base which it should have and which will no doubt eventually be developed.

## What individual support consists of

Legitimacy stems from individual support. Let us therefore start from this support and consider first its most elementary forms. There is support when members of the polity are favourably disposed towards the political system or the government (clearly, support may or may not extend to both, and this has consequences). We shall not attempt to examine here the reasons why someone supports the national political authorities; such an examination would bring us into the realm of individual and group psychology, which is beyond the scope of this work. Let us simply note that support may come from the socialization process and thus from outside pressures as well as from the characteristics of the 'personality' – the whole personality, including its affective and cognitive elements.

## Objects of support

Whatever the origins of the positive view which citizens may have of the regime, its object may vary widely. It may relate in a diffuse manner to the system as a whole (though this does not mean that this support is weak), or it may be directed specifically to a number of measures which the government has taken or has promised to take. Indeed, in practice, especially with reference to the national political system and to the national government, whose range of activities is very large, the support of individuals is likely to be composed of a combination of the two elements – general and specific, vague and precise – but to a varying degree. There will be both some overall system support and some support for individual policies (Easton, 1965: 311–19; Berger and Luckman, 1966: 110–46).

## Variations in levels of support

The existence of a combination of types and objects of support suggests that this support also varies in strength over time, even if gradually and in many cases to a limited extent. The rate of these variations is also likely to differ: where support is for specific policies, for instance, variations may well be more rapid. If this is the case, political systems depending primarily on specific policy support would seem to be vulnerable, since they may be subjected to sudden variations in support. However, this is an unlikely occurrence for national political systems. It is more likely to take place in the context of governments, whose support may depend on the success or failure of some policies, as opinion polls repeatedly show. Support for political systems, on the other hand, is more likely to be based on habits, on love for the country or on the ideological stance which the nation represents. As a result, it is likely to be more stable or, if it changes, to change rather slowly – for instance, as a result of the influence of the environment or of variations in personal life conditions.

Although we thus know impressionistically that changes in support levels occur, the extent and rate of these changes have not so far been measured in the context of political systems. (Lack of support – for instance, in terms of rebellions – has been examined: see Gurr, 1970: 183–92; Jackson and Stein, 1971: 265–84; 347–59; Zimmermann, 1980: 167–237.) Theoretically, such a measurement is not impossible, but in practice, it has not been attempted. We cannot therefore assess at this point how much time it takes for a political system to become more or less popular as a result of variations in the characteristics of the society, or in the attitudes of the members of that society. So long as this is the case, the study of legitimacy will remain rather vague and, as a corollary, conclusions about the amount of legitimacy needed by a political system to remain in existence will remain imprecise.

## Intensity of support

As changes in level of support do take place, it follows that its intensity also varies. Support can thus range from being very active to being wholly passive. Citizens may be inclined to behave positively in favour of the political system; they may, on the other hand, refrain from acting against the authorities and accept what these do as long as they are not personally affected. Given that, except when there is an emergency or a war, citizens are rarely directly asked to act in support of the political system, it is perhaps not surprising that many political systems should be able to function with passive support only.

Indeed, passive support is likely to be the normal way in which the population relates to the political system in those countries in which the state achieves little, does not 'penetrate' markedly in the society, and has few civil servants running its services. This situation describes rather closely traditional countries. In predominantly rural polities, for instance, the impact of the political system on citizens is limited. The state does not penetrate into the provinces because it does not have the resources to post officials widely throughout the country, as well as because of the resistance of the local élites. In such cases, active opposition to the regime will manifest itself only if these local élites wish to do so, a point which relates to the extent of integration and not to individual support. The situation is rather different in developing societies, and in those which have a strong urban and industrial base, since the majority of the population is affected by social services, public works and regular taxation. However, even in these cases, one should not overestimate the extent to which the state touches the daily life of most individuals.

## Legitimacy as the 'sum' of the support of individuals

Support is therefore characterized in many cases by a passive and vague sentiment towards the regime and/or the government. This support has then to be aggregated to provide an impression of the overall level of legitimacy of the political system. Since, as we saw, members of the polity display varying amounts of support – since, specifically, some are intensely positively inclined towards the authorities, others are strongly opposed, and yet others are rather neutral or are passive – the extent of legitimacy enjoyed by the political system is the result of the combination of all these reactions. The strong support of some or even the passive support of many can compensate for the opposition of a few. Thus where positive and passive support exceeds negative reactions, the regime can be said to be relatively legitimate; the greater the difference in favour of positive support, the higher the amount of legitimacy.

## Support and the survival of political systems

In the absence of a precise measurement of these positive and negative reactions to the regime, it is impossible to go further than to state that, in view of the characteristics which we outlined (a relatively slow change where habits are the basis of support, an extensive level of passive support), most regimes probably enjoy a substantial, but not a very high amount of legitimacy. This enables the public authorities to continue in office, especially if they do not make large new demands (which could alter the supportive habits of many), unless changes in the society provoke changes in attitudes among the population. In such cases, the authorities then have to introduce policies designed to satisfy these demands, otherwise support is likely to shrink and the possibility of outright manifestations of discontent, leading perhaps to rebellion, might increase. Such a strategy poses problems, however, as there will also be opposition to these changes. Tension is therefore likely to increase whatever is proposed and the government may have to resort to coercion.

Even in such a situation, however, the erosion of legitimacy may not lead (or lead quickly) to the collapse of the regime, since there may not be a credible alternative. In the last resort, public authorities really need support only when they are directly challenged. Of course, when support declines, such a challenge may emerge, but this is unlikely to occur spontaneously and in particular without a group providing a focus. This is why rebellion, let alone revolution, develops rarely from a 'spontaneous' uprising of the people, but more often from an organized body which was not integrated in the system. What support achieves, when it is strong, is to render the emergence of a strong challenge unlikely; indeed, if some elements voice their opposition, they will find little echo. Even when discontent is large and support very passive, moreover, there will always be at least some delay before consequences are felt: the regime is likely to benefit from the fact that it takes time for discontent to be turned into an effective challenge.

## Political integration

Political systems can thus often survive on passive support as long as there is no focal point around which a challenge might emerge. This means that a crucial element of the equation is constituted by the group configuration. In practice, only groups are in a position to mount a real challenge. They alone are sufficiently strong and durable to gather around them the potential oppositions. Thus conversely, to be safe, a political system requires political integration to be high.

*Political integration* has been defined as a 'pool of commonly accepted norms regarding political behaviour and a commitment to the political behaviour patterns legitimised by these norms' (Ake, 1967: 3). The 'parts' of the political system have to be related to each other in such a way as to make a coherent whole. There must not be bodies which continuously, strongly and over a wide range of issues oppose the actions of the public authorities (Rabushka and Shepsle, 1971: 2–22; Young, 1976: 23–65; Lijphart, 1977: 1-24; Sartori, 1984: 239–63).

### Institutions and groups and political integration

Of course, political integration relates principally to those structures – institutions and groups – which are closely involved in political life. As we saw in Chapter 2, many others are also engaged intermittently in politics, and even these can occasionally play a major part. The only bodies which are wholly excluded from consideration are the purely 'social' clubs; cultural organizations which are ostensibly non-political may be important in supporting or opposing a political system on the contrary.

However, the bodies which are characteristically involved in political life, and which are critical for the assessment of political integration, are the constitutional institutions, including the local authorities, the parties, the large interest groups, such as trade unions and employers' associations, and the organizations promoting or defending a cause – environmental and regional bodies, for instance. In many polities, moreover, the most relevant groups are those which form part of the traditional fabric of society, such as tribes, ethnic groups and religious bodies.

## Levels of political integration and group characteristics

Political integration relates to the extent to which structures – institutions and groups – are tied to the political system. For these ties to be strong, as Ake states, 'norms regarding political behaviour' have to be shared by the structures and by the authorities in charge of the political system. There are admittedly manifest variations in the degree to which these norms are shared: nowhere are all the institutions and groups involved in political activity in full agreement with the norms characterizing the political system. One should therefore refer to political integration as ranging from very high – though never complete – to very low, though probably always above a minimum, since below such a minimum, the polity would disintegrate. As levels of legitimacy, levels of political integration have not so far been measured or even assessed with precision, but there can be no doubt that these levels do exist (Rogowski, 1974: 143–97).

## The strength of institutions and groups

The extent of political integration is also affected by the importance of the institutions or the groups. An occasional conflict between a very large group and the political system can be more serious for that system than the permanent opposition of a very small group, even of a group which is frequently involved in political activity. Thus political integration needs also to be assessed by reference to the 'weight' of institutions and groups in the polity, and indeed by reference to variations in this weight over time. This importance has not so far been measured either, but one can give an impression of its contours, and we shall do this in some detail in the next two chapters. At this point it is sufficient to note that the importance of institutions and groups depends on two elements: the breadth of the problems which they cover, and the nature of their following.

The *breadth of problems* covered by institutions or groups is obviously critical. Those which are concerned with all aspects of the life of an individual, such as tribes in traditional societies, can be expected to play a truly huge part in the determination of the overall level of integration, while the more specialized interest organizations which one finds in industrial societies are likely to have a less determinant role.

The *nature of the following* is also fundamental in determining potential effects on integration: institutions and groups have an impact only if they can count on reliable support from their members. Thus while legitimacy relates to the support which the political system has directly in the population, political integration relates to the support which each group has in that population. Political integration can thus be viewed as 'indirect' legitimacy: it is legitimacy channelled and mediated by the groups. Public authorities are therefore naturally anxious to reduce the part played by institutions and groups in this equation: they obviously prefer to depend primarily on 'direct' legitimacy.

This desire may not be achieved, and can almost never be achieved, because institutions and groups exist and it is not within the power of the public authorities to abolish them altogether, although they may declare them illegal and repress them. Indeed, the stronger their following in the population, the less it is possible for the government to wipe them out: where some institutions and groups have a truly massive support, the government is effectively at their mercy. Thus, so long as these institutions and groups accept the political status quo, the political system is safe; but if one or more among them challenge the public authorities, the latter are in serious danger.

## Leaders of institutions and groups

Given the part played by important institutions and groups, the leaders of these bodies are in a strong position: they may be able to undermine and eventually destroy the political system. However, they can do so only if they can carry their following with them. Leaders of institutions or groups need the support of followers to be able to act, in the same way as leaders of the national political system need the support of the population.

Support within institutions and groups has the same characteristics as support within the political system: it can be more or less diffuse, or more or less specific; it can vary over time; and it can be more or less strong – many members of these structures are likely to be passive supporters, for instance. This means that the leaders are no freer to move in any direction they wish to move in while keeping their support intact than are the national political authorities with respect to the whole population. The freedom of leaders of institutions or groups is particularly restricted when, as Ake states, there is a 'pool of commonly accepted norms' among the population. Political integration is then maintained because the leaders cannot act beyond certain limits without endangering their own status within the institution or group, or even the very existence of the body which they run (Blau, 1964: 168–223).

## Political integration and plural societies

Thus political integration is about the extent to which the leaders of institutions and groups are in broad harmony with the national authorities, or wish to confront these authorities. Not all leaders of institutions or groups can engage in confrontations, but

## BOX 5.2
## The state and plural societies

Plural societies are typically regarded as unmanageable. They seem to lead to civil wars, as has been shown in both the West and the East, the North and the South. An assumption widely believed by social scientists in earlier decades was that the problems posed by plural societies, being essentially due to ethnic or religious conflicts, would gradually disappear, as ethnic and religious beliefs declined. Whether such a view will turn out to be correct over the very long period is impossible to say: it clearly does not seem to be correct over the short- and even mid-term period.

There seem to be only two approaches to the problems posed by plural societies, since the most brutal solution of genocide is clearly not acceptable. The first approach consists in attempting to eliminate the problem by dividing the relevant territory into states whose contours would coincide with those of the ethnic or religious groups concerned. This solution has been tried, in particular after the First World War in eastern Europe, but difficulties have always seemed to resurface because ethnic or religious groups are rarely territorially contiguous. The only way to render this solution viable is therefore to move populations, but except after wars, such a solution is not practical.

Hence the other approach, which consists in accepting that the society is plural and in structuring it accordingly. However, such an approach goes against the principles of state organization, at least as they developed in the West: the state has a territorial structure; there are regions, provinces, towns and villages, all of which have geographical boundaries. The people are therefore not divided according to ethnic, religious or other social groups. Indeed, the western state is often praised because it denies communal distinctions: in the process, however, minorities may be forgotten.

It is therefore difficult to reconcile state and plural society. Decentralization helps to an extent, but only if the bodies which are given greater powers in this way are also territorial. The problem goes deeper: what is at stake is the ability of political systems to handle the problems posed by plural societies. This may mean a different conception of the relationship between state and 'communal groups'.

some can do so in an effective manner. By and large, the leaders of structures in which support is based on traditions are more likely to do so than those who lead institutions or groups whose support depends on instrumental calculations. There is therefore a greater likelihood of institutions and groups being strong and independent if they are old and belong to the fabric of society, as are tribal, ethnic or religious bodies. New bodies, on the other hand, do not normally have enough support to challenge seriously the national authorities; they are also likely to be opposed by older established institutions, or groups which fear to lose their support.

Like individual support, political integration – that is to say, the extent to which institutions and groups are closely linked to the political system – is affected by social and economic conditions. If the society is static (and is relatively insulated from the influence of other polities), the strength of structures in relation to the political system will tend not to change. Thus, where integration was high, it will remain high; and where structures and political system were not in harmony, conflict will remain high. This occurs in *plural societies*, namely those polities where some groups (usually tribal, ethnic or religious) are strongly entrenched and are in permanent confrontation with the national political system and with other structures. These are the situations when rebellions tend to occur: examples can be found in many parts of the world, from Northern Ireland to Uganda and from Cyprus to Sri Lanka (Gurr, 1970: 317–59; Rabushka and Shepsle, 1972: 62–92; Lijphart, 1977: 142–76; Horowitz, 1985: 185–228).

If social conditions are changing, on the other hand – for instance, under the impact of industrialization or of geographical mobility – the relationship between structures and political system will tend to be altered. The extent of political integration will also change, sometimes to the benefit of institutions and groups, sometimes to the benefit of the political system. Support for traditional groups may become eroded and 'national sentiments' may increase; but new bodies may be set up and these may come into conflict with the authorities of the political system. This situation may be exacerbated as a result of the action of neighbouring countries, or of groups which are influential in these countries.

Thus the problems which political integration poses for many regimes are large, and at the limit may be such that the polity breaks up. What is sometimes described as the 'end of empires' is in reality an instance of plural societies no longer being in a position to be held together. Whether with respect to Austro-Hungary after the First World War, to colonial possessions of European countries after the Second World War, or to the Soviet Union and Yugoslavia in the late 1980s, the impact of groups, primarily ethnic, but also religious and even tribal, has been stronger than the support which the political system could muster to retain unity. Not surprisingly, in these circumstances, public authorities are often tempted to oppose the action of institutions or groups by forceful means. Can this be a true solution, and are there limits to the extent of coercion which a regime can impose without endangering its own future?

## Coercive political systems and dictatorships

### The large number of authoritarian political systems

Coercive regimes are widespread: in the contemporary world, probably a majority deserve to be described in this manner, and a substantial minority apply very harsh means indeed. The repeated incidence of coups – military and otherwise – is evidence of the magnitude of the problem, though coups (and revolutions) occur both to install and to topple dictatorial regimes.

The means by which coercive regimes are able to maintain themselves in power are well known: not only are the more sophisticated freedoms, such as those of the press or demonstration, curtailed or abolished, while elections are rigged, postponed or not called at all; but the 'basic' rights of individuals are set aside, and opponents to the government are rounded up, imprisoned or shot. Meanwhile, governmental propaganda dominates the media, thus ensuring that information is restricted to the news which the public authorities wish to broadcast. Indeed, there seems to be almost no limit to the coercive measures which a 'totalitarian' state can adopt, modern technical discoveries having substantially added to the instruments of control and 'education' which were traditionally at the disposal of governments (Friedrich and Brzezinski, 1965; Holmes, 1986: 58–75; 379–401).

## Structural dictatorships

Some societal conditions make it likely, if not altogether inevitable, for dictatorships to emerge. By and large, a dictatorial government is likely to come to power when conflicts among institutions and groups are such that no accommodation can be found because political integration is low. In such circumstances, the dictatorship can be described as *structural*, while a dictatorship is *technical* if it emerges as a result of rivalries between a number of would-be political leaders. In practice, the distinction is not always clear-cut, as many dictatorships have included both personal and societal elements (Duverger, 1961: 21–109).

Structural dictatorships tend to occur when societal divisions are deep, since in such a case, the different segments of the polity are unwilling to agree to compromises. These situations occur primarily during times of profound socioeconomic change: traditional structures lose support, while new groups emerge whose members want to accelerate the pace of change. Tension is often also increased because of the direct or indirect influence of neighbouring countries, as the realization that other societies are doing 'better' economically and socially acts as an incentive for those who wish to bring about change. In such circumstances, deep divisions begin to occur between supporters of different models of society, even where the political system previously enjoyed high levels of support and of group integration. Compromises then become difficult to achieve, and a 'strong' government or regime is therefore often likely to come to power and impose its views. This is why structural dictatorships tend to occur during the 'take-off' stage of the economy.

The dictatorship may be 'progressive' if the forces which wish to accelerate the pace of change are able to coerce the traditional groups – as occurred in Ethiopia in the 1970s and 1980s, for instance. It may be 'conservative' if the converse obtains, as was the case in Chile from 1973 to the end of the 1980s. Indeed, there will often be oscillations between one form of dictatorship and the other, since the costs of organizing an effective dictatorship are often so high that the opposition may find means to topple it within a few years.

Dictatorships are less likely to emerge in stable traditional societies where some large groups predominate. They are also very rare in highly developed societies, since the specialized interest groups and the bodies aimed at promoting causes are too numerous to be able to mount a concerted attack and even to want to mount a concerted attack against the political system. However, even during the take-off stage, countries may not be ruled by a dictatorship if tension in the society remains relatively low. This can occur if the polity was originally well integrated, if the pace of change is relatively slow, and if some political structures bridge the gap between the traditional and the modern elements in the society – for instance, if political parties are able to represent elements of both. This peculiar combination of factors leading to gradual change will be found primarily in homogeneous societies which have had a relatively long history, and whose geographical boundaries have remained unchanged for generations. The cases of Great Britain and Sweden can thus be contrasted to those of France, Germany, Italy and Spain. It is not surprising, however, that most societies, and in particular most newly established polities, should find it difficult to avoid periods of dictatorial rule.

## Difficulties encountered by authoritarian regimes

The fact that dictatorial regimes are often successful only for a period suggests that it is probably not possible for an authoritarian political system to be truly viable, or at least that the conditions under which these dictatorships can be maintained are rather stringent.

First, costs are incurred in order to build and sustain a coercive apparatus. The setting-up of a variety of controls implies that the police and the army are sufficiently large to be able to exercise surveillance over all parts of the country; this is clearly so costly that public authorities can have truly sophisticated means of coercion only in relatively rich countries. In Third World dictatorships, the extent to which there is coercion is therefore often more limited than it seems. In particular, in the rural areas, the amount of obedience extracted from the population varies appreciably. This is why the extent of penetration by the state is a crucial variable: there cannot be a totalitarian government unless there is a high level of state penetration.

Second, an even more serious problem is posed for dictatorships by the need to deploy reliable forces to exercise coercion. If the population is truly antagonistic, public authorities will have to select carefully those who will be in charge of the repressive operation. In some situations, this can be achieved with relative ease – for instance, when opposition is concentrated in a particular tribe, ethnic element or religious body. Members of other groups can be used to force compliance: thus administrators, police officers and even the army may often be sent to different parts of the country in order to ensure greater levels of compliance. But the fact that the regime can count on one element of the population to oppress the others also means that the regime enjoys some support in the population. If there is no support at all, or if there is a tiny amount of support, there is a high probability that the regime will not find – or find for very long – a sufficiently large number of persons on whom it can rely to enforce coercion.

## Setting up parties and movements to control the population

Public authorities can attempt to 'create' support by a combination of personal favours and of 'political education'. This is the rationale behind the creation of 'mass movements', and in the first instance of political parties, in many coercive regimes. Such a development has been particularly widespread in contemporary dictatorships, in part because it is easier to set up these movements as a result of the development of modern communication techniques. Yet it is also costly to build such organizations, and it takes time – often a long time – to ensure that active members are truly reliable. This is why many such organizations exist more on paper than in reality, as has often been the case with single-party systems in Black Africa. It is also why the parties which are truly alive, at least for a period, tend to be those which were set up under special circumstances – for instance, during a protracted war of independence, or with the help of a foreign nation which adds external resources to the coercive effort. This was the case when the might of the Soviet Union sustained communist regimes in eastern Europe.

Coercive machines are thus difficult to build and even more difficult to maintain because they need to be extensive precisely in those countries in which the mass of the population is antagonistic. The efforts made to 'educate' the population away from the traditional groups and from the norms which these groups support are usually unsuccessful. The traditional norms embodied in groups such as tribal, ethnic or religious bodies, which have a strong hold on their members, typically prove stronger. This is why another tactic of the public authorities consists in attempting to bring these structures together rather than in opposing them. The idea is to associate all groups in an effort to 'build the nation'. However, this tactic is also often unsuccessful because traditional bodies may simply not want to work for a truly united nation. In many cases, in post-independence Black Africa, for instance, the government has attempted to foster a policy of reconciliation, but this has not abolished ethnic or tribal conflicts, some of which have escalated into civil war.

Overall, coercion seems unable to overcome the determined opposition of long-standing groups. Even in communist states, despite determined efforts made over very long periods to abolish traditional groups, or at least to reduce their strength markedly, the result has been failure. The collapse of communist regimes brought the traditional groups once more to the fore. It is not surprising that the attempt to reduce the strength of traditional groups should have been even more unsuccessful in Third World countries, where dictatorships have typically lasted for shorter periods, and have had fewer resources at their disposal to control the polity.

## Overview

A crucial prerequisite for the stability of political systems is constituted by the *support* which they enjoy. When support is insufficient, political systems have to depend on *coercion*, or collapse.

The support which is extended to political systems takes two forms. There is direct support from the population, often passive and diffuse, but in part specifically linked to the policies adopted by the public authorities. This type of support is referred to as *legitimacy*.

The other form of support is indirect and takes place through the structures – institutions and groups – which exist in the political system. Those who belong to institutions or groups support these bodies (more or less strongly, more or less passively). The groups (in effect, essentially their leaders) in turn support or do not support the political system. These leaders therefore have considerable power, since they may be able to withdraw support from the political system and extract advantages for the institution or group and for themselves.

A political system in which structures are closely associated to the political system is referred to as having a high degree of *integration*. Societies in which integration is low are *plural societies*.

Both legitimacy and integration can and do vary appreciably over time as a result of changes in attitudes of the population, in outside influences, and in the policies pursued by the public authorities.

*Dictatorships* are regimes which enjoy little support and attempt to maintain themselves by coercion. A low level of support is often the result of changes in the socioeconomic structure; hence, in the contemporary world, the many dictatorships which have been found to exist in countries in the process of development, whether communist, populist or authoritarian-inegalitarian.

While many regimes succeed in maintaining themselves for a while by using coercion, the costs of the coercive apparatus are so large that dictatorships have rarely lasted more than a limited period.

Support and coercion are two components of political life which, although and indeed because they are diametrically opposed, have to be seen in combination. Only in this way can one understand the characteristics and the dynamics of political systems, whatever distaste one may have for dictatorships.

## Further reading

Although the concept of legitimacy has attracted considerable interest for generations, it has so far led to little true systematic analysis. One of the most interesting earlier presentations was that of the historian G. Ferrero, *Principles of Power* (New York edn, 1945). D. Easton examines the effect of legitimacy in *A Systems Analysis of Political Life* (1965). See also W. Connolly, ed., *Legitimacy and the State* (1984). The most systematic attempt at measuring some aspects of legitimacy in the context of divided societies is that of R. Rogowski, *Rational Legitimacy* (1974). For an analysis of support within groups, see P.M. Blau, *Exchange and Power in Social Life* (1964: especially chs. 7 and 8).

There have been more systematic analyses of integration, in part because of the immediacy of the problem in many parts of the world. For a general presentation, see C. Ake, *A Theory of Political Integration* (1967). The concept of integration is also discussed systematically by H. Teune in G. Sartori, ed., *Social Science Concepts* (1984: 239–63).

For an empirical examination of the problems of plural societies, see A. Rabushka and K.A. Shepsle, *Politics in Plural Societies* (1971), C. Young, *The Politics of Cultural Pluralism* (1976), A. Lijphart, *Democracy in Plural Societies* (1977) and D.L. Horowitz, *Ethnic Groups in Conflict* (1985).

Works on dictatorships and on coercion are, of course, numerous. Among the most influential are those of C.J. Friedrich and Z. Brzezinski, *Totalitarian Dictatorship and Autocracy* (1965). See also M. Duverger, *De la dictature* (1961). On communist states see in particular L. Holmes, *Politics in the Communist World* (1986: especially chs. 3 and 15).

**Part II**

# Society and government

# 6

# The social bases of political systems

## Introduction

Political life and socioeconomic life are closely related. Few, if any, students of politics would doubt, for instance, that social and economic conditions are at the origin of many of the major conflicts which come to be reflected on the political plane. If a nation has profound social or economic cleavages based on class, race or religion, these are expected to find their expression in political life. Thus the complexity of the political problems will be to an important extent the consequence of the complexity of the socioeconomic problems.

Difficulties arise, however, when one attempts to give a precise content to the association between socioeconomic and political life, and the more we move away from what can be regarded as straightforward economic matters, the greater these difficulties. This is why, in a sense, the political impact of class – or the relationship between class and politics – is the easiest to assess, even if there are problems. By 'class', one means here socioeconomic distinctions, defined in the broadest sense, including those based on income as well as on occupations, on subjective feelings and on objective characteristics. There are problems of measurement, to be sure. Per capita income, for instance, is far from having the same real meaning when we refer to societies in which cash is not the main basis for the exchange of goods and services among large sections of the population. Subjective elements of social life, such as belief systems and attitudinal characteristics about position in society, are also difficult to measure; their meaning also varies as we move from western countries to the Third World. The concept of 'subjective social class' has been defined, examined and carefully operationalized in the West; the same cannot be said for non-western countries. Overall, since concepts and measurement relating to socioeconomic class, both objective and subjective, are principally western in origin, they tend to fit western countries better, although they begin to be applied widely across the world (Harrop and Miller, 1987: 130–72).

However, it is markedly more difficult to measure the impact of other social factors on political life. In Chapter 5, we began to discover some of the characteristics of *plural societies*. These are the societies which are sharply divided by ethnic, linguistic or religious cleavages. It is manifest that these societies have problems of integration which go well beyond those encountered where the class cleavage alone prevails: indeed, polities such as Britain and more specifically England, where class cleavages are strong but other cleavages have a limited impact, are regarded as being homogeneous. We have therefore to consider the effect of geographical, ethnic and religious cleavages – that is to say, of *communal divisions* – alongside the effect of class on political life.

There is a third type of impact of social conditions on political life, an impact which is even more delicate to analyze because it relates to the effect of history: that is, of traditions – on the minds of populations living in a given area and probably having developed a common ethos. This type of social characteristics, known as *cultural characteristics*, is concerned with the effect of diffuse social norms and with their influence on political behaviour. For instance, it has seemed for a long time that countries characterized by a 'protestant ethic' behaved politically in a different manner from other nations (Weber, 1976). Yet culture, whether social or political, is difficult to ascertain and to measure, since there is no universally accepted view of what its components are. Efforts have none the less been made to circumscribe the concept more closely and see how far, whatever the objective social conditions, the political characteristics of a country are likely to differ as a result of differing cultural conditions.

- In the first section of this chapter, we shall therefore look at the general relationship between socioeconomic conditions and political life. One of the ways in which this relationship has been particularly clear is in the context of the *types of political system* which can be found throughout the world: the spread of liberal democracy is thus seemingly associated with socioeconomic development.
- In the second section, we shall consider the case of *plural societies*: that is, those polities or parts of polities in which the level of integration is low because of the coexistence of a number of broad social groupings which are in profound opposition to each other and to the political system.
- Finally, in the third section, we shall examine the extent to which *cultural characteristics* have an effect on political life. We will see how far these can be measured and distinguished from other socioeconomic characteristics.

## Political systems and socioeconomic structure

The question of the relationship between socioeconomic cleavages and political life has been one of the main areas of research in political sociology. In this context, class has long been given a particular importance, not only by Marx, but by large numbers of authors. In a sense, this analysis originated from the founders of political science, whether Aristotle, Montesquieu or Rousseau, each of whom saw in different ways how social characteristics could affect political life. Empirical analyses of voting behaviour have indeed demonstrated that class has played a significant part in accounting for the way in which the population has divided among the political parties, although that part has not been as large as was once thought, and it appears to have declined in importance, not merely in the United States but in Europe as well (Harrop and Miller, 1987: 182–92). Meanwhile, in western countries, in particular since the 1970s, it seems that new cleavages have begun to emerge, as has been shown by the development of 'green' or ecological parties (Lipset and Rokkan, 1967: 1–64; Inglehart, 1990: 66–103).

## Social prerequisites of liberal democracy

While political sociologists thus endeavoured to look generally at the relationship between broad socioeconomic conditions and political life, more specific analyses were undertaken to see, on a world-wide basis, how far these socioeconomic conditions accounted for the distribution of types of political system, and in particular for the emergence of liberal democracies. At most half of the more than 180 countries of the world – and up to 1990 appreciably less – can be labelled 'liberal democracies', even if one extends the category widely and takes into account the fact that, as was pointed out in Chapter 3, we are confronted here not with a single point in a space, but with clusters allowing for substantial variations. Indeed, the number varies over time, sometimes markedly, as for instance in the early 1990s.

A quick survey of the countries concerned suggests that these are not distributed at random: all the polities which can loosely be described as North Atlantic are liberal democracies, while the proportion of these systems is small in the Middle East and, at least during most periods, in Africa south of the Sahara. Most eastern European states have become – or appear to be becoming – liberal democracies, but they had previously never or very rarely adopted such a type of political system. Latin American and south-east Asian countries belong to the two geographical areas where the proportion of liberal democracies is largest after western Europe and North America, but especially in the Latin American case, there have been substantial variations over time.

On the basis of this preliminary impression, basic socioeconomic conditions seem closely related to types of political system. Per capita income is highest in western Europe and North America: these are the areas where liberal democracies are concentrated; indeed, liberal democracy came first to northern Europe, which was richer earlier than southern Europe. A scattering of other rich countries, such as Australia, New Zealand, Israel and Japan, are also liberal democracies. Yet wealth alone cannot constitute the whole explanation: India has a low per capita GNP and is a liberal democracy; and some Latin American countries, such as Argentina, whose per capita GNP is relatively high, have known authoritarian or populist regimes.

One way of analyzing the matter further consists in abandoning dichotomies. In what was the first study in the field, Lipset divided democracies into two categories only, those of 'stable' and 'unstable' (Lipset, 1960, 2nd edn, 1983: 31–45). Going further, Cutright developed in the early 1960s a ranking scheme which enabled him to note that the fit between liberal democracy and the socioeconomic infrastructure was better if one took into account *degrees of stability* (Cutright, 1963: 569–82; Neubauer, 1967: 1002–9). Yet even a ranking based on the number of years during which a country has been liberal democratic is not sufficient: exceptions such as India, Malaysia, Jamaica and Mauritius remain.

**Table 6.1**   Liberal democracies around the world (among 147 countries in the mid-1980s)

|  | Atlantic | Communist | Middle East and northern Africa | South and south-east Asia | Africa south of Sahara | Latin America | Total |
|---|---|---|---|---|---|---|---|
| Liberal democracies | 23 | 0 | 3 | 8 | 3 | 11 | 48 |
| Non-democracies | 0 | 15 | 19 | 9 | 41 | 15 | 99 |
| Total | 23 | 15 | 22 | 17 | 44 | 26 | 147 |

*Source:* calculated from Vanhanen (1987), 39–42.

One reason given for these 'exceptions', for a period at least, was drawn from what is sometimes described as 'geo-politics'. It was argued, especially in the 1970s, that the presence or absence of liberal democracy was markedly affected by the 'dependency' of the nations concerned. This view was expressed in particular in relation to Latin America, since this was the area where one found most authoritarian-inegalitarian countries that, on economic grounds alone, 'should' have been liberal democracies and yet were (often at least) under military rule. It was claimed that many authoritarian governments (especially of the right) were directly or at least indirectly due to the policies of 'core' countries (i.e. of the United States and western Europe) (Chilcote, 1981: 271–346). However, this view has come to be less widely held since the 1980s, as Latin America entered a (perhaps temporary) period of resurgence of liberal democracy.

## Vanhanen's multivariate approach

The exceptions which can be found suggest that we must move beyond socioeconomic conditions to ethnic or other social distinctions, as well as to political culture. First, however, and in order to be able to assess the nature and extent of the exceptions, we need to be more precise about the strength of the relationship between broad socioeconomic conditions and liberal democracy. This was done in the 1980s by Vanhanen: in a series of studies which appeared between 1979 and 1987, and which ultimately extended to 147 countries, this author took into account not merely per capita GNP, but five further variables – the percentage of urban population, the percentage of non-agricultural population, the number of university students per 10,000 inhabitants, the percentage of the literate population, and the percentage share of family farms in the total area of holdings (Vanhanen, 1989: 104). A sixth variable was also considered, but its operationalization was held to be too soft to allow for a truly precise measurement: this attempted to assess the extent to which non-agricultural resources were decentralized and were in effect controlled by relatively independent groups (Vanhanen, 1989: 106).

The five main variables are aggregated in what is described as an Index of Power Resources, which is then correlated to an Index of (Liberal) Democracy in turn based on two variables, which measure liberalism and democracy by means of the extent of competition and of the level of participation in the polity. In practice, this is done by using as indicators election turnout and the share of the votes cast for different parties. Though these can be regarded as reflecting only in part the richness of the two political variables, they do at least provide a realistic start for an empirical analysis.

Vanhanen finds that per capita GNP does correlate with the combined Index of (Liberal) Democracy (0.555), but he also finds that the correlation is appreciably higher when all the variables are taken into account (0.762). About 70 per cent of the variation in liberal democracy in 147 contemporary states is explained in this way. On the other hand, about 30 per cent of the variation in democratization can be said to be due, among other things, to 'unique historical circumstances', and to 'cultural and national peculiarities' (Vanhanen, 1989: 110). Overall, therefore, 'one explanatory variable, the "Index of Power Resources", seems to explain the major part of variation in political systems from the aspect of democratization' (Vanhanen, 1989: 110).

## Apparent exceptions to the influence of socioeconomic factors

About 30 per cent of the variation in liberal democracy cannot be explained by the factors which Vanhanen uses in his analysis. It is interesting to discover whether some exceptions, at least, can be accounted for by special circumstances. Vanhanen thus examines the case of eighteen countries (out of 147) which do not fit the expected relationship (though a further eight countries of which India is one also constitute exceptions, but are not specifically considered) (Vanhanen, 1989: 115). Four of these eighteen countries have been liberal democratic while they 'should not' have been, and the reverse is true in the other fourteen cases.

The few polities found to be liberal democratic in the early 1980s and yet scoring very low on the Index of Power Resources are Gambia, Papua New Guinea, the Solomon Islands and Uganda. While the first three are very small and may be regarded as having an idiosyncratic political behaviour, Uganda was liberal democratic for only a few years in the early 1980s: the socioeconomic index seemed to predict this political change.

The fourteen countries at the other end of the scale are even more interesting. As Vanhanen points out, 'pressure for democratization has been strong in nearly all of [them]' (Vanhanen, 1989: 116). Four had become liberal democracies by 1987: Argentina, Uruguay, the Philippines and Turkey. There were moves towards liberal democracy in South Korea, Singapore and Panama, while Jamaica rated low on the Index of (Liberal) Democracy because the 1983 parliamentary elections were uncontested by the opposition as an act of protest. This leaves six countries on the threshold: Lebanon, Jordan, Mexico, Poland, Yugoslavia and Chile. Poland became a liberal democracy after 1989; it had been for a long time, with Hungary, the communist country closest to becoming a liberal democracy. Mexico has had a dominant, but not a strict single-party system and has indeed moved since the late 1980s towards a less

---

## BOX 6.1
## Geography and political systems

There has long been a belief that political values and political systems were indirectly but strongly associated with geographical characteristics. It was shown, for instance, in a famous early work of electoral 'geography' that votes for the left and the right were associated with geological differences, as the nature of the soil led to particular types of agriculture and consequently of land tenure, this leading farmers to lean towards the left or towards the right (A. Siegfried, *Tableau politique de la France de l'Ouest*, 1913).

Three geographical characteristics have often been regarded as having an influence on political systems.

The first is *climate*, which, especially in the eighteenth century, has been considered as having a direct influence on human behaviour. Remarks about differences between the political systems of the north and the south of Europe were made by Montesquieu and Madame de Stael. Cold climates were said to be more conducive to liberalism and democracy because there was a greater need to co-operate. There are obvious counter-examples, such as Athens, Republican Rome and some of the Italian Renaissance city-states.

The second characteristic is the *island* nature of the state, island-states having seemingly a greater propensity to adopt liberal values. Evidence for this view stems not just from Britain, but from a substantial number of island-states in the Mediterranean, in the Atlantic (though not Cuba or Santo Domingo), in the Indian Ocean (but not the Seychelles or even Madagascar), and in the Pacific. However, many of these island-states belong to the Commonwealth, and Commonwealth countries tend to be liberal democratic; most of these states are also small, which leads to the third geographical characteristic, size.

*Size* has been associated with liberalism and democracy. It has been suggested that it was because they were city-states that Athens and Rome were relatively liberal (though Sparta was also a city-state and was not liberal); similarly, liberalism and democracy developed in Renaissance Italy in small city-states. Rousseau claimed that France could not be liberal and democratic because it was large. The evidence is mixed. One of the world's two most populous states, India, is a liberal democracy (the other being China); the third most populous state, the United States, is also a liberal democracy; conversely, many small states are or have been dictatorships. Size probably has an influence, although this influence may have diminished with the development of modern media of communication.

---

dominant party system. The civil war in Lebanon made it impossible for the country to function as a liberal democracy, but there was a return to 'normalcy' in the early

1990s. Chile became a liberal democracy again in the late 1980s. Jordan had two free elections in the early 1990s, and a competitive party system began to be established. Thus the only real exception is Yugoslavia, in the sense that it broke up as a country; yet the various successor states have shown in general some degree of pluralism, and at least Slovenia and perhaps Croatia can be described as liberal democracies (Vanhanen, 1992b: 19–35).

The method suggested by Vanhanen thus helps to predict which countries are likely to be liberal democracies (and vice versa); it also identifies exceptions and accounts for a high proportion of them. The tendency for the socioeconomic base of political systems to have a strong influence on the norms of the political system is therefore marked, at any rate with respect to the distinction between systems which are and systems which are not liberal democratic. Since a substantial proportion of the variation remains to be explained, however, we need to turn to the examination of this 'exceptional' part by looking at other explanatory factors: namely, at the presence of strong group divisions in plural societies and at the role of 'culture'.

## Plural societies

The stability of political systems can be markedly impaired by the existence of sharp conflicts of a societal character, and in particular by ethnic, linguistic or religious conflicts (or by a combination of these). While the point was always appreciated for the Third World, the break-up of the Soviet Union and of Yugoslavia in the early 1990s, followed by civil war in parts of what used to form these two countries, has clearly shown that ethnic or linguistic tension is not a thing of the past. Moreover, it became evident that economic conditions were far from being the only factor to be taken into account in the analysis of political conflicts. Yet the events of the early 1990s in eastern Europe constitute only a limited part of what is in reality a world-wide phenomenon.

Indeed, in western Europe, the cases of Northern Ireland and of the Basque Country have loomed prominently as areas of major violent conflict. Divisions in Belgium and Canada are deep, although they have not led to major violence and, so far, the unity of these two countries has been preserved. Elsewhere, civil wars and/or partition have affected countries in which such cleavages are prominent, such as Czechoslovakia, Cyprus, Lebanon, Sri Lanka, Uganda and Nigeria.

The picture is neither simple nor one-sided, however. Ethnic, linguistic or religious cleavages do not lead everywhere and automatically to break-up or even to major conflict. Without even considering the case of Switzerland, nations such as India, Brazil and the United States are based on strong ethnic differences, as are Malaysia and Trinidad and many countries of the Caribbean and Latin America. Yet these polities seem to have absorbed or broadly overcome these differences. In what used to be the Soviet Union, the trend towards a strengthening of the ties among the members of the Community of Independent States is also substantial. Finally, the development of the European Union suggests that the move is not wholly towards division where linguistic and ethnic differences exist. To put it in terms of the analysis of Chapter 5, levels of integration may be sometimes sufficiently high to contain the conflicts resulting from ethnic or linguistic diversity.

## Ethnic and linguistic diversity

Ethnic and linguistic diversity are widespread, although they do not correspond to the divisions which might have been expected. The Index of Ethnic and Linguistic Diversity calculated by Vanhanen on the basis of Kurian shows that, while slightly over a third of the countries can be said to be homogeneous (52 out of 147), a comparable number (53) are intermediate and over a quarter (42) are truly heterogeneous (Kurian, 1984; Vanhanen, 1989: 13). These countries are spread unevenly across the world as Table 6.2 shows.

**Table 6.2**   Ethnic and linguistic homogeneity (1984)

| | Atlantic | Communist | Middle East and northern Africa | South and south-east Asia | Africa south of Sahara | Latin America | Total |
|---|---|---|---|---|---|---|---|
| 80–100% | 14 | 7 | 11 | 4 | 4 | 12 | 52 |
| 60–79% | 4 | 4 | 6 | 2 | 5 | 7 | 28 |
| 40–59% | 5 | 2 | 1 | 7 | 6 | 4 | 25 |
| Under 40% | – | 2 | 2 | 5 | 30 | 3 | 42 |
| Total | 23 | 15 | 20 | 18 | 45 | 26 | 147 |

*Source:* calculated from Vanhanen (1987), 35–9.

What was the communist area, as well as the Atlantic, Middle Eastern and Latin American areas, are relatively homogeneous; they are also the regions in which the proportion of old and established countries is the highest, and where we can therefore expect the mix of linguistic and ethnic groups to be greatest. South and south-east Asia is at an intermediate level, while the proportion of truly ethnically and linguistically divided countries is large in Black Africa. Two-thirds of the highly heterogeneous countries belong to that region, which comprises less than a third of the nations of the world.

However, even in the Atlantic area, the proportion of somewhat divided countries is not insignificant: in five countries, the United States, Canada, Switzerland, Belgium and Spain, linguistic or ethnic cleavages affect large minorities of the population. But the mere listing of these countries shows that the type of division and the political consequences of these divisions are sharply different: while Switzerland and even the United States have been affected only to a limited extent, the foundations of the state have been shaken from time to time in Canada and Belgium; in Spain, the separatist problem has clearly contributed strongly to the weaker democratic traditions of the country.

Conclusions of this type could be drawn for the rest of the world. As a matter of fact, the countries which have been most affected, ostensibly at least, by sharp cleavages are not those where divisions are objectively the largest: for instance, Cyprus, Lebanon and Sri Lanka are in the middle of the range, as are Switzerland and the United States. Thus, not surprisingly, Vanhanen finds the level of the correlation between the ethnic and linguistic cleavage and liberal democracy not to be high. He notes that 'usually requisites of democratisation are slightly better in ethnically homogeneous countries than in ethnically less homogeneous countries', but he further points out that there may also be divisions of power resources which are favourable for democracy, as in Switzerland (Vanhanen, 1989: 14).

## Ethnic and linguistic diversity and level of conflict

The most relevant factor therefore seems to be not the extent of ethnic or linguistic diversity, but the extent to which this diversity is *perceived* by members of the polity as a conflict, and indeed as a conflict without apparent solution. For this to be the case, the society must be plural without being pluralist. As Rabushka and Shepsle point out: 'cultural diversity [is] a necessary condition for a plural society: if a society is plural, then it is culturally diverse. However, nearly every modern society is culturally diverse. Thus, although the existence of well-defined ethnic groups with generally incompatible values constitutes a necessary condition of the plural society, it is not sufficient' (1972: 20).

For a plural society to exist – that is to say, for basic ethnic and linguistic divisions to become the source of major conflict – there has to be a sense that the conflict is *preponderant*: 'Permanent ethnic communities acting cohesively on nearly all political issues determine a plural society and distinguish it from a culturally heterogeneous, non-plural society' (Rabushka and Shepsle, 1972: 20–1). It is therefore not the percentage of ethnically or linguistically diverse groups which *per se* creates the conflict and leads to low integration, but the fact that the 'cultural sections are organized into cohesive political sections' (Rabushka and Shepsle, 1972: 21).

## Cross-cutting cleavages and the level of conflict

The central part played by the perception of the conflict naturally led to an examination of the conditions under which such a perception is likely to occur. A crucial factor is constituted by the distribution of the cleavages among the population: ethnic or linguistic cleavages will have a direct effect on the level of the perception of conflicts if they are *reinforcing* rather than cross-cutting. Indeed, ethnic, linguistic or religious cleavages are not the only ones which can and do give rise to conflict. Class is likely to play a part, although perhaps not as strong as might have been expected; even political opinions can be an important source of division. Yet, in the large majority of cases, these divisions do not produce mutually exclusive groupings. Indeed, as Rae and Taylor state, 'linguistic cleavages, for example, seldom produce mutually exclusive groups, for many individuals may be multi-lingual' (1970: 14). Nor do ethnic groups always do so. In general, if these or any other cleavages cut across other cleavages, the probability is high that no group will be mutually exclusive. Too many belong to more than one.

One can see at this point why Vanhanen might have found the correlation between linguistic or ethnic diversity and democracy to be relatively low. A cleavage is unlikely to lead to major political conflicts where its impact is reduced by the presence of other cleavages. In practice, societies in which there is substantial wealth and where geographical and social mobility is high will not be characterized by the preponderance of only one overwhelming conflict. As Rabushka and Shepsle state: 'In the United States, Italian and Irish highway contractors view themselves as businessmen, not ethnic representatives, in competition' (1972: 21). By and large, the greater the wealth, the greater the level of education, and the greater the decentralization of resources, the more other cleavages will develop and the more these will cross-cut the linguistic, ethnic or religious cleavage.

However, one can also see that the *perception* of the cleavage will vary, and will depend on incidents which may at a given point lead to the predominance of that cleavage; there may also be reinforcement of one cleavage by another. This occurred to a substantial extent in the 1970s in Belgium, when the Flemish majority *felt* deprived linguistically at the very moment it had come to acquire economic superiority. In Northern Ireland, the sense of economic deprivation of the Catholic minority has been combined with the sense of religious diversity. A similar consciousness has been visible in America on the part of the Blacks since the 1960s. Thus, while it is true that in general economic prosperity will lead to the emergence of more cross-cutting cleavages, there may also be periods during which a group, hitherto deprived but unable to voice this deprivation, perceives its deprivation in the context of some uplifting of its economic situation.

Thus potentially plural societies are markedly more numerous than effectively plural societies. The impact of cleavages of a linguistic, tribal, ethnic or religious nature (and indeed of others) has to be viewed in the context of the specific configuration (reinforcing or cross-cutting) of these cleavages in the society.

The existence of major divisions of a linguistic, ethnic or religious character is thus likely to affect appreciably the character of the political system, but these divisions are mediated by the general framework of the socioeconomic basis of the society. Where the nature of the division is sustained or reinforced by the socioeconomic base, the political effect is sharp. The less mobility there is in the society, and the less economic wealth and the social services are spread within that society, the more a linguistic, ethnic or religious cleavage can be predominant. To these conditions has to be added another, which stems from the general character of political and administrative life: a cleavage which is clearly geographically marked is more likely to have a strong political base than one which is not, as representation and policy implementation both tend to take primarily territorial forms. When all these conditions are favourable, the 'sectional' effect of a basic division can be expected to be maximized. The polity may fall to such a low level of integration that even the strongest authoritarian regime may be unable to prevent civil war and ultimately the break-up of the nation (Jackson and Stein, 1971: 265–332).

# Cultural characteristics

The impact of cultural characteristics on political life has long been felt to be large: there are numerous comments on the fact that traditions, for instance, led to major differences in political behaviour among western European countries. There is an immense, though highly impressionistic literature (including of the literary kind), which, over the decades and even centuries, has stressed the fact that political and social behaviour, both national and regional, is markedly affected by the specific conditions in which countries developed. Differences between the north and the south of Europe have fascinated writers from the eighteenth century onwards, such as Montesquieu and Madame de Stael to cite only two of the most prominent. As was suggested earlier, the view has been frequently held that the 'protestant ethic' has been at the root of major differences – ranging from the 'rise of capitalism' (Weber) to the development of liberalism and democracy (Montesquieu, 1949; Stael, 1958–60; Weber, 1976).

## Measurement of cultural characteristics

While these comments have repeatedly been made and seem highly plausible, the effect of 'culture' on politics has escaped precise measurement. It has consequently been difficult to disentangle the part played by 'harder' and more easily recognizable variables, such as those which we just examined, from the less tangible factors which 'culture' encompasses. The difficulty is compounded by the point, which seems both intuitively correct and empirically valid, that economic and social 'indicators' also have an effect on culture. It could therefore be that class, ethnic or religious feelings account ultimately for cultural characteristics.

Both substantive matters and difficulties of measurement explain why cultural elements have often been considered as having only a *residual* character. What has occurred for individual psychological variables has occurred also for national (and regional) cultural factors: as the identification and the measurement of economic and social factors is simpler and seemingly more obvious, these have been given priority. The tendency has spread to consider cultural elements in the same way as individual psychological characteristics: namely, as providing an explanation when no other factor seems to play a part (Greenstein, 1969: 33–62).

This state of affairs began to change in the 1960s as a number of authors, such as G.A. Almond, S. Verba and L.W. Pye, gave prominence to the analysis of political culture (Almond and Verba, 1963; Almond and Verba, 1980; Pye and Verba, 1963). A major study by G. Hofstede, *Culture's Consequences* (1980), then constituted the first systematic attempt at measuring, on a truly world-wide basis, the characteristics of culture. Though it is still not possible to assess precisely the extent to which cultural factors affect, and affect independently, political behaviour, one can at least begin to describe the proportions in which the components of culture are distributed among nations and in groups of nations. Meanwhile, work in the field has also been progressing at the level of individual countries to ascertain the effects of the various components of culture. Variations over time, especially with respect to the extent to which 'post-industrial' values spread among societies, have also come to be explored (Inglehart, 1990: 66–103).

## What is political culture?

What, then, is political culture? The concept is elusive, in large part because it is all-embracing. Hofstede suggests that 'culture is to a human collectivity what personality is to an individual' (Hofstede, 1980: 25). This may not be an altogether helpful remark, since the concept of personality is itself rather elusive (Greenstein, 1969: 2–5). The main problem relates to the time dimension. It may be true that personality is, according to Hofstede (quoting Guilford's work on *Personality*), 'the interactive aggregate of personal characteristics that influence the individual's response to the environment' (Hofstede, 1980: 25), but even if we think we know what this definition covers at a given moment, we are in greater difficulty when we consider the concept over time. No one would deny that personalities 'grow' or decay, and at any rate change, if only somewhat and relatively slowly. As this is the case, the 'response to the environment' will not be identical at different points in time and the reality of personality escapes us. Although psychologists recognize the need for a concept such as personality, since underlying characteristics of individuals seem to exist, change only gradually and in some manner 'synthesize' the various 'traits' of these individuals, the concept is clearly difficult to handle: this undoubtedly played a part in slowing down analyses (Blondel, 1987: 124–36).

A similar conclusion can be drawn about culture. Culture, too, embraces a large number of 'traits' – which have only been identified gradually and whose interrelationships are still somewhat obscure. Culture, as personality, varies over time; but a further complication arises with respect to culture: while one can at least observe an individual and subject him or her to various tests which can help to discover the underlying personality, no such facilities are available with respect to culture. Moreover, comparisons are necessary if we are to determine what is specific about the culture of each country. There are difficulties in these comparisons, however, as there is a risk that one might attribute to individuals characteristics which truly belong to a group, a point which has been analyzed in particular in the context of discussions about the 'ecological fallacy' (Robinson, 1950: 351–7).

## Components of the civic culture

Yet, despite these difficulties, the study of culture has progressed, as efforts have been made to discover the components of culture, the underlying dimensions characterizing these components, and the relationships among these components. The pioneering study of Almond and Verba, *The Civic Culture* (1963), first came to a three-fold distinction suggesting the existence of a *parochial*, a *subject* and a *participant* political culture, by taking into account the three elements of the personality of citizens: namely, cognition, affectivity and evaluation (1963: 20). It was also suggested that there could be mixed situations; thus states such as the Ottoman Empire had a 'parochial-subject' culture, while France, Germany and Italy had a 'subject-participant' culture (1963: 20–5). The study covered five countries, analyzed on the basis of interviews: the United States, Britain, Germany, Italy and Mexico. It succeeded in showing great variations among these countries, despite problems posed by the fact that interviews, especially at the time, could reveal only part of the reality.

This analysis led to the elaboration of dimensions in a subsequent study by Pye and Verba, *Political Culture and Political Development* (1965), which covered ten countries on the basis not of interviews, but of a general survey of political (and especially élite political) behaviour in these countries. The four dimensions which were elicited by these country cases were those of 'national identity', 'identification with one's fellow citizens', 'governmental output' and 'the process of making decisions' (Pye and Verba, 1965: 529–43). An effort was made to bring political beliefs together, especially in the context of change. It was pointed out that there may be various developments: for instance, 'the belief that [the citizen] can participate meaningfully in the governmental decision-making process can replace the belief that he is essentially the subject ... or the participant orientation to government can develop on top of, without replacing, the subject orientation to government' (Pye and Verba, 1965: 543–4).

These distinctions led to studies of change, and in particular to the examination of the reasons why countries (those of Europe in the interwar period and of Latin America since 1945) experienced a breakdown in democracy (Linz and Stepan, 1978). They also led to the examination of changes in value patterns and to the stress on a move from 'materialist' to 'post-materialist' values among western societies from the 1970s (Inglehart, 1990: 66–103). Overall, it was clear that cultural 'development' was a characteristic not merely of 'modernizing' societies, but of societies at all levels of socioeconomic development, and that these values could cut across the divide between highly industrial and 'developing' societies. One of the clearest examples is the fact that Commonwealth countries have many political characteristics in common which contrast with those of non-Commonwealth countries (Blondel, 1987: 311–17).

## 'Culture's consequences'

The contribution made by these studies to the analysis of political culture has therefore been considerable; it helped to circumscribe the concept and to show the directions in which a systematic analysis should go. Meanwhile, the assessment of national culture in general, and indeed its measurement, began to be undertaken in earnest, in particular as a result of the major study by Hofstede. On the basis of the examination of the values of large numbers of respondents in 40 countries, the author was able to discover the existence of four components of culture: 'power distance','uncertainty avoidance', 'individualism' and 'masculinity'. The first of these dimensions relates to inequality and to its acceptance; the second refers to the fact that 'the tolerance for uncertainty varies considerably among people . . . in different countries' (Hofstede, 1980: 153); the third is based on the recognition that 'in some cultures, individualism is seen as a blessing and a source of well-being [while] in others it is seen as alienating' (1980: 213); and the fourth stems from the fact 'that the sex role distribution common in a particular society is transferred by socialisation in families, schools, and peer groups, and through the media' (1980: 261). But these four dimensions were not 'imagined', so to speak, by Hofstede. They form 'a generalised framework that underlies the more apparent and striking facts of cultural relativity' (1980: 313). As a matter of fact, as the author notes, they come close to the 'standard analytic issues' which have been identified in the literature on the 'national character' (Inkeles and Levinson, 1969).

On this basis, Hofstede was able to discover a number of clusters, which were defined as 'culture areas', on a more subtle and systematic basis than had previously been the case (Hofstede, 1980: 333). A variety of clusters were identified, described as Latin (divided into more and less developed), Asian (also divided into more or less developed), Near Eastern, Germanic, Anglo and Nordic.

Apart from many specific differences (and in particular the fact that Nordic countries were found to have, together with the Netherlands, an essentially 'feminine' culture), two major findings emerged which are essential for the analysis of the social bases of political life. The first is the unexpected discovery that cultural divisions were strong in Switzerland and almost non-existent in Belgium: the accommodation between the linguistic groups in Switzerland is thus the result of major cultural differences, while the difficulties experienced by Belgium correspond to a more 'superficial' opposition between linguistic groups. This helps us to understand a large part of the history of centralized Belgium, as well as the continued differentiation between the Netherlands and Flanders. But the finding has more general implications in that it suggests that there is not yet one type of plural society: there are likely to be many different models.

The second main finding relates to the relationship between culture and the socioeconomic variables which we examined earlier in this chapter. The fact that both Latin and Asian countries have to be divided into 'more' and 'less' developed suggests that there is a relationship among and a distinction between the two types of factor. In the case of Latin countries, while both groups score high on power distance and on uncertainty avoidance (in contrast, for instance, to Anglo and Nordic countries), the more developed Latin nations are highly individualistic and have a medium score on masculinity; the less developed Latin countries have a low individualism score and are either very masculine or relatively feminine (but less so than Nordic countries) (Hofstede, 1980: 336). It is not permissible at this point to state categorically that these differences can be linked to socioeconomic development, but they at least appear related to these conditions, while they do not on the contrary appear to influence markedly views on power distance or uncertainty avoidance. Generally speaking, Hofstede finds – and in this his findings come close to those of Inglehart on 'post-materialism' – that economic development has an effect on changes over time: the 'need' for 'dependence', for example, tends to diminish, though this may result in higher conflicts (Hofstede, 1980: 368).

It is thus possible to understand better both the characteristics and the 'consequences' of culture. We are no longer confronted with a vague concept to be used only to explain 'accidents' which socioeconomic indicators do not seem able to account for. By being defined through precise components, which in turn are measured by popular attitudes, culture becomes an integral part of the systematic analysis of the social bases of politics. We may still be unable to quantify the impact of culture on political behaviour, but we are at least able to assess the ways in which its components help to form the bases of political life.

## Overview

It has always been felt that the political characteristics of nations were related to the social and economic conditions within which states developed, but the shape and even more the extent of this influence has long remained mysterious. This is no longer the case: variables have been identified and have begun to be measured with respect to the three main aspects which the relationship between socioeconomic and political characteristics takes.

First, the impact of *basic socioeconomic conditions* – of 'class' in the broadest sense of the word – has been measured in the context of many countries, particularly in the West, and it has been found to be less strong than was anticipated. Basic economic conditions also play a substantial part in accounting for the type of political system which prevails in a country: by and large, liberal democracies are associated with favourable economic conditions, but there are exceptions.

Second, among these exceptions, the existence of *strongly perceived divisions* of an ethnic, linguistic or religious character accounts for the severity of political tensions in countries across the world. However, these divisions have to be perceived and favourable economic conditions tend to reduce the incidence of these divisions.

Third, *culture* plays a substantial part in accounting for political behaviour. It can be described, by analogy, as the 'personality' displayed by a political system – a description which raises questions about the origin and strength of this 'personality'. It has been possible to distinguish among the components of culture and, in this way, to perceive better the intrinsic part it plays: for instance, in giving greater prominence to individualism or, on the contrary, to a need for 'dependence'.

The relationship between society and politics is thus not simple. It is not likely to occur in one direction only: the correlations which exist leave room for two-way influence. But it is at least possible to be definite about the strength of some of the connections. On this basis we can now turn to the part played by structures – institutions and groups – on political life, and look for the relationships between these structures and the political system.

## Further reading

The question of the relationship between socioeconomic cleavages and political systems has given rise to a substantial number of empirical studies, starting with S.M. Lipset, *Political Man* (first published, 1960; reprinted with a new Preface, 1983), followed by P. Cutright, 'National political development', in N.W. Polsby *et al.*, *Politics and Social Life* (1963: 569–82, D. Neubauer, 'Some Conditions of democracy', *Am. Pol. Sc. Rev.* (1967: 1002–9), and others. Probably the more sophisticated analysis is that of T. Vanhanen, 'The level of democratisation related to socio-economic variables in 147 States, 1980–85', *Scand. Pol. Studies* (1989) **12** (2), and T. Vanhanen, ed., *Strategies of Democratisation* (1992).

The characteristics of politics in plural societies have been examined in particular by A.A. Rabushka and K.A. Shepsle, *Politics in Plural Societies* (1971), by A. Lijphart, *Democracy in Plural Societies* (1977), and by D.L. Horowitz, *Ethnic Groups in Conflict* (1985), while D.W. Rae and M. Taylor, *The Analysis of Political Cleavages* (1970) study the effect of cross-cutting cleavages. For a presentation of the historical sequence of cleavage crises in western societies, see S.M. Lipset and S. Rokkan, eds., *Party Systems and Voter Alignments* (1967: 1–64).

The nature of political culture is analyzed systematically by G. Hofstede, *Culture's Consequences* (1980). Earlier studies which began to examine the contours of the problem and provide empirical data are those of G.A. Almond and S. Verba, *The Civic Culture* (1963), of L.W. Pye and S. Verba, eds., *Political Development and Political Culture* (1965), and of G.A. Almond and S. Verba, *The Civic Culture Revisited* (1980). The question of the new 'post-materialist' culture was first analyzed by R. Inglehart in *The Silent Revolution* (1977) and further developed in *Culture Shift in Advanced Industrial Society* (1990). See also 'The changing structures of political cleavages in western society' in R. Dalton *et al.*, *Electoral Change in Advanced Industrial Societies* (1984). On the question of the 'national character', see A. Inkeles and D.J. Levinson, 'National character', *Handbook of Social Psychology*, Vol. 4 (1969).

# 7

# Groups and political systems

## Introduction

In all political systems, groups are a key feature. By groups, we mean here structures of all kinds, formal and informal, linking members of a society. They include the more official and often state-controlled institutions, such as the army. Decisions – the allocation of values – may not always be the result of institution or group activities, but they are very often at least initiated (or blocked) by these bodies. Institutions and groups make demands by exercising pressure, whether these are gentle and peaceful or take the form of protests.

Institutions and groups have another role, however, as important or perhaps more important. At least the strongest and largest among them can genuinely be said to shape the political system: they are its foundation and subsequently sustain it (Castles, 1967). For instance, the characteristics of traditional inegalitarian political systems which we described in Chapter 3 are shaped by tribal groups: these determine the relationships among leaders as well as between leaders and people. The plural societies which we examined in the previous two chapters are plural because they have in their midst strong antagonistic groups of a tribal, ethnic or religious character. In western liberal democracies, too, groups are fundamental elements of the political system. As we shall see in Chapter 9, the more important political parties originated and still often draw part of their support from ethnic, religious or class-based groups. Authoritarian polities have occasionally attempted to bypass, ignore or destroy these: such a tactic has often been to their peril, as we saw in Chapter 5. The collapse of communism in Poland can be directly attributed to the part played by the church; in Yugoslavia and in the Soviet Union, ethnic groups were never truly domesticated by the regime, and they have also contributed to the subsequent explosion (Carrère d'Encausse, 1981).

Thus groups are both pillars of the political systems and instruments by which demands are channelled into these systems. Yet they are not fully and wholly 'in' politics: they are in the society at large and enter politics depending on circumstances (Truman, 1951: 45–65; Blau, 1964: 118–25). Admittedly, some groups are involved so often in public decision making that their activities cannot be distinguished sharply from political activities; but most groups are only involved intermittently in the political process. Comparative government has therefore to be concerned, but to a varying degree, with a very large number of these bodies.

Moreover, groups display major differences in size, organization and modes of action: this means that it has always been difficult to encompass all types of group in a systematic manner in comparative government analyses. In this chapter, we shall therefore concentrate on the main ways in which groups affect political systems, rather than on a description of what these groups are. However, in subsequent chapters, we shall examine the groups which are true *political* institutions, such as parties, legislatures and bureaucracies, and we shall also then look at the specific ways in which these institutions are linked to other groups.

- There have been substantial controversies in political science and among politicians about what is to be regarded as *the 'proper' role of groups* in political life; these controversies have even to an extent affected the part which groups effectively play in different political systems. The first section of this chapter will therefore survey these differing views.
- In the second section, we shall describe the main dimension along which groups can be classified, a dimension which is based on the distinction between *communal* groups at one extreme and *associational* groups at the other.
- We shall then in the third section look at the extent to which different types of political systems can be *characterized* in terms of the more or less communal or associational character of the groups which can be found in these systems.

## Controversies about groups in political life

### Early negative views

Modern political science was profoundly affected by controversies about what the role of groups is and what it should be. Many classical authors of the late eighteenth and early nineteenth centuries regarded groups as representing a semi-feudal past, and as preventing the 'will of the people' from being expressed clearly. They therefore concluded that constitutional states should reduce and even eliminate their influence. This was, for instance, the view of Rousseau and the authors of the *Federalist Papers* (Rousseau, 1973; Hamilton *et al.*, 1981 edn.: Letter X). Interestingly, many leaders of developing countries in the second half of the twentieth century have had the same motivations as eighteenth-century theorists.

These views affected behaviour, and in particular that of constitution-makers. The opposition to groups extended to parties, which were often not recognized either; at best their role was played down. Only heterodox writers at both extremes of the ideological divide – either defenders of the 'old order' or radicals – (and a few acute observers, such as Tocqueville) pointed to the role of groups in the new 'bourgeois' political order, especially business groups. But for mainstream students of politics during much of the nineteenth century, political analysis remained confined to the examination of constitutional bodies.

## Group theory and the optimistic approach to groups

A change began to take place in two ways. First, it became recognized that the constitutional political systems, which by the end of the nineteenth century qualified as liberal democracies, were in reality *pluralistic*: that is to say, that they were based on bodies somewhat autonomous from each other, such as parliaments, parties and economic groups. Second, at the beginning of the twentieth century, in the United States, the general – indeed overwhelming – role of groups began to be recognized. The legislatures of the federal and state governments were sought for favours of various kinds by many bodies, and the behaviour of legislators (and members of the executive branch as well) could not realistically be described unless lobbyists and spokesmen of interests were taken into account (Bryce, 1891: 152). Thus it became clear that the framework of a classical 'constitutional' theory was unsatisfactory: the role of groups had to be taken into account.

This was to be done by Bentley, in 1908, in his *Process of Government*, in which an entirely new approach was developed. Instead of accounting for political developments in terms of the actions of individuals within institutional structures, *group theory*, as this interpretation was to be called, did not merely state that groups were important or even essential; it claimed that groups were the centre of social activity. Individuals were characterized by the group interactions in which they were involved, instead of groups being characterized by their members. Overlapping or cross-cutting membership became a key characteristic accounting for the fact that groups followed different or opposite courses (Bentley, 1967; Truman, 1951: 15–44; Hagan, 1958: 38–51).

The new theory also reassessed the character of old institutions of government, including constitutional bodies, on the basis of the same principles. Institutions came to be regarded as groups, albeit of a special kind; they typically included sub-groups which expressed different points of view and promoted different policies. Thus the political system as a whole could be described in terms of a huge network of interlocking groups and political life could be explained in terms of the shocks resulting from the actions of groups.

Though such an analysis was ostensibly empirical and 'neutral', it also had normative undertones and policy implications. Classical theory was opposed to groups, as these were viewed as splitting the 'general will'. The new theory not only accepted groups as facts, it also suggested that it was best not to interfere with group activity, as society had built-in equilibrium mechanisms by which the defects of the system could be automatically redressed. If, in one field of activity, a group or groups became too vociferous in one policy direction, a group or groups promoting opposite policies would emerge and combat the views of the pre-existing bodies.

There is here an analogy with the theory of competition in economics. The classical theory of the price mechanism suggests that the combined effect of a fall in demand

and a rise in production of goods in short supply will check price increases, and that no state intervention is required; indeed, such an intervention would be harmful. Similarly, the automatic emergence of groups opposed to policies hitherto successfully put forward by other groups would prevent, without any intervention (and, indeed, would prevent better if there were no intervention) decisions from getting out of hand and being contrary to the views of the majority. One can see how, by starting from an opposite standpoint from that of the classical theorists, the views of group theorists could be regarded as 'optimistic'; they suggested that the polity would gain from competition between groups. The new 'will of the people' would emerge from and through group activities and group oppositions.

## Pessimistic neo-corporatism

This normative aspect of group theory came in turn to be questioned, in the same way and indeed for the same reasons as those which had led to the questioning of the classical theory of groups (Weinstein, 1962: 153–224). It was obvious that groups were interfered with everywhere. Some societies were dominated by large groupings or by institutions which were far from allowing competing bodies to emerge. Authoritarian polities controlled groups and institutions drastically, but even liberal polities were not characterized by complete openness. In particular, a kind of collusion among some of the larger groups such as employers' organizations and trade unions seemed, in particular on the continent of Europe and in Scandinavia, to lead to what might be regarded as 'cartel' arrangements. This type of development, which came to be fairly common, especially between the 1960s and the 1980s, was described as *neo-corporatism* (Lehmbruch and Schmitter, 1982: 1–28, 259–79). Where this close association existed, demands could be restricted; even the recognition, if not altogether the creation, of new groups was made difficult. While it might still be the case that, were groups to be truly established and not interfered with, a situation corresponding to that described by group theory might prevail, the reality of both liberal and authoritarian states as well as of relatively egalitarian and of inegalitarian polities seemed to be far distant from the model.

## Interest organizations and movements

Meanwhile, from the late 1960s, it seemed that modern societies could no longer be described accurately unless another form of linkage among citizens was taken into account, that of *social movements*. These were less tightly organized than 'classical' groups, and yet seemed able to promote successfully a variety of policies and have a substantial appeal.

Social movements were given considerable recognition, especially in western Europe and North America, in the context of the demands and even 'revolts' of hitherto somewhat unorganized 'minorities'. The student movement of the late 1960s was one of the first manifestations of this trend; but there were also women's movements, the black movement in the United States, and ecological and environmental movements. Admittedly, such developments were not entirely new – movements of the same kind and with similar aims emerged earlier in the twentieth century and in particular before the First World War – but the 'participatory demands' which were made from the 1960s led to a clearer recognition of the part played by less 'organized' bodies in modern, and especially western, societies. These less organized movements contrasted sharply and seemed to constitute even antidotes to the highly organized interest groups which often appeared to work in collusion with each other and with the government, as in the case of neo-corporatist arrangements (Klandermans *et al.*, 1981: Rucht, 1991).

The difference between the groups and the movements may not be as sharp as it seems, however. As a matter of fact, the expression 'movement' covers a double reality, that of one or more *core groups* and that of the broader area of *support*. The core groups in these movements may possibly have forms of organization which are less tight, less bureaucratic and somewhat more open than 'conventional' interest groups, but this is not necessarily the case. These core bodies must in any case have at least some organization, since otherwise the movement soon loses its strength. Meanwhile, these core groups receive support from among the population, this support being more or less strong and more or less widespread. The expression 'movement' in reality measures more specifically the extent and breadth of the support for the core bodies, rather than assessing the degree of organization of these bodies.

Views about the role of groups in political life have thus markedly altered from the time when constitutional systems emerged in the late eighteenth century. What is now universally recognized is that this role is large, possibly overwhelming; but views continue to differ about the 'value', positive or negative, of groups. The negative judgements of the past are echoed by the modern pessimism of those who emphasize the extent to which major interest groups are in 'collusion' (neo-corporatism), or those who wish to draw a sharp distinction between interest groups in the strict sense (regarded as being rather bureaucratic) and movements (regarded as being more open). The field of group analysis thus remains controversial, the controversies being fuelled by periodic allegations and indeed evidence of corruption among many groups and in many countries.

## The classification of groups and political systems

### The basic classification of groups

The question of the part which groups should play in political systems is obviously important, but it can be addressed only after looking at the effective role of these groups in order to see how far this role needs to be modified. In other words, a *description* of the characteristics of groups is a prerequisite to any judgement being passed about what changes should occur.

There are obviously many ways of describing the part played by groups in political systems. Some are more general than others, however, and we should be concerned here with the most general way in which groups relate to these systems. There cannot be a more general approach 'than one which is based on the reason why groups exist at all: that is to say, not just on their direct and immediate purpose, but on what they represent for those who are close to them. This is the distinction with which we shall be primarily concerned here.

Consequently, we shall focus on the nature of the support given to groups. Whatever groups may wish to achieve, their strength and therefore their impact on the political system will depend on the extent to which they have a broad or narrow, relatively superficial or truly deep, support.

Such a distinction finds its translation in the very nature of the group. There are thus bodies which are highly specialized and are concerned with a specific object: for instance, bodies set up to promote an artistic or cultural activity. There are, on the other hand, groups which have wide concerns, such as churches. The nature of the support is clearly different in these two cases. In the second, the group can be said to embody long-standing and even permanent relationships; in the first, the group exists to promote specific goals.

This distinction does not constitute a dichotomy, but corresponds to the two extreme positions along a dimension. At one extreme are bodies such as families, tribes and ethnic, religious or occupational groups to which members are linked because they happen to have characteristics in common: an accident of birth can thus have life-long implications. These groups exist because they express deep and almost indissoluble 'traits', among those who belong to them. At the other extreme are the bodies which exist in order to achieve some purpose, whether it is to defend a section, promote an idea, make money, or enjoy a game. Those who join such organizations may not always do so only because they wish to achieve the stated purpose of the organization; yet, by and large, the membership is brought and kept together because of the aims. In a sense, groups which express patterns of relationships are based on the past, while those which exist to defend or promote a goal are oriented towards the future. Between these two extremes are large numbers of bodies which promote goals but also create among many of those who belong to them bonds of an affective character.

## Communal and associational groups

Let us call *communal* the groups which embody patterns of relationships, and *associational* those which are constituted in order to pursue a goal, while remembering that, in practice, 'pure' communal and 'pure' associational groups are polar positions on a continuum (Toennies, 1955). To the extent that men and women recognize themselves and/or others as members of a communal group, they recognize themselves and/or others as being 'expressed' – 'represented' would be too precise a term – by the communal group. The bond between member and group is the 'image' which the member has of what he or she is, at least with respect to the human relationships which the communal group embodies. Thus a member of a tribe or a family is linked to the group by the image of the relationship to other members of the tribe or family, by characteristics shared in common, by a common 'heritage'. On the other hand, members of an associational group (again in the most extreme form which this type of grouping can have) are tied to the association and the other members by the aim which is common to all, and by the fact that they are achieving or want to achieve something in common.

## Origins of communal and associational groups

Because of this fundamental difference in the basis of support, communal groups tend to be old; they develop around relationships whose origins may not even easily be traced. New communal groupings may emerge in a political system, admittedly, but this is typically because of waves of immigrants or because of changes in the social structure: for instance, as a result of industrialization, which leads to the arrival of large numbers of workers into the cities. Communal relationships may also develop on the basis of the institutionalization of a political or administrative body, such as the army or the bureaucracy. In such organizations, one can expect an *esprit de corps* to emerge gradually. As a result, feelings of belongingness will develop within the institution, which will give it the characteristic of a communal group. Such bodies can be referred to as *institutional* in contrast to the *customary* groups which arise from more long-standing patterns of social relationships (Almond and Coleman, 1960: 33).

## Transfer of support and legitimacy

New groups and especially new associational groups may be strengthened by another means, however: there can be a *transfer of support* from an already existing group, in particular a traditional communal group. This will often occur in societies where traditional patterns of relationships begin to be eroded because new ones emerge – for instance, among immigrants. Leaders of pre-existing communal groups may attempt to maintain the strength of the groups which they control by setting up subsidiary bodies designed to have a more 'modern' appeal. If they see that the church is no longer successful among the young, for example, church leaders may decide to set up an association catering especially for the interests of that section of the community. A complex relationship develops as a result. On the one hand, the new group helps to increase the support which the church has among the young; on the other, this new organization is 'dependent' on the church – it is likely, for instance, to receive help in kind and cash. The church thus transfers some of its capital of legitimacy to it.

The concept of transfer of support or of legitimacy is crucial for understanding the development of groups. Communal groups, in particular, are able to some extent to control new trends in a society, and stop or retard their independent development. Tribal, ethnic or religious leaders may succeed in keeping within their 'wing' segments of the population which might otherwise have come under the allegiance of counter-bodies. Support or legitimacy transfer can also take place in other ways, however: 'modernizing' rulers may use the support which they have in the tribal or ethnic group from which they originate to foster allegiance for new groups which they attempt to develop.

One can go further, since the effect of transfers of support or legitimacy extends to the political system as a whole. In a traditional society, the state tends to be dominated by 'customary' bodies such as tribes or ethnic groups; indeed, it can be argued that the authority of the state has emerged almost everywhere as a result of a transfer of support or legitimacy from these customary groups. Gradually, however, almost in the same way as any other large group, the state comes to be regarded, at any rate by many, as the embodiment of patterns of relationships; it therefore attracts feelings of loyalty, which translate themselves in terms of nationalism. Some bodies within the state, especially institutional groups such as the army and the bureaucracy, but also other communal groupings and parties, can exploit these feelings or this allegiance to their profit, and in turn obtain allegiance because they appear to represent the state. Thus the transfer of legitimacy may extend downwards to more specialized organizations which are set up to control the population.

This type of development occurs especially in authoritarian polities. Among these, it occurs primarily in those of the populist or 'progressive' variety. In these regimes, trade unions, youth organizations, cultural centres and a host of other associations claimed to be 'voluntary' come into existence with the help of the state in order to promote the goals which state leaders wish to pursue. These feel able in this way to push forward their views better and 'educate' the population, though they are likely to find themselves in opposition to the leaders of traditional customary groups whose way of life and traditions are opposed to these 'modernizing' leaders.

Thus, in many cases, bodies which are ostensibly associations are in reality instruments used by communal groups to defend or establish their influence. Such associations are not independent: they are not true associations, but dependencies of communal groups.

## Political systems and types of group

Let us now relate the types of group to the different types of political system which we described in Chapter 3. Let us begin with the two extreme cases. One is that of the wholly traditional polity, which has *only customary communal* groups, the limiting case being that of a tribal society in which there is only one customary group (a tribe) and where demands are articulated exclusively through that tribe. Such a case is so rare, especially in the contemporary world, as to be regarded as non-existent. The other extreme is equally non-existent: it is that of the *wholly associational polity*, in which communal groups have disappeared and in which demands are formulated and articulated by as many associational groups as there are goals, with full opportunity for any new demand or goal to be translated into the political system through a new association. This might be regarded as the idealized version of the 'perfect' liberal democratic polity.

Let us consider intermediate positions which reflect more accurately the situation in the real world. These intermediate positions correspond to cases in which there are *some and often many groups* and where new groups emerge from time to time. In a near-communal polity, to begin with, new groups can emerge in one of two ways. On the one hand, there can be a *natural* development, when new patterns of relationships emerge; on the other hand, there can be *imposed* development, when dependent organizations are set up. The more dependent bodies are deliberately set up, the more the development can be said to be imposed.

As more dependent organizations emerge, the panorama of groups in the polity becomes more complex. In the process, too, even where there is relatively strong imposition, the polity begins to move to an extent towards associationalism. In part, the dependent organizations start to acquire some independence, while other associations are set up which are not dependent on communal groups, perhaps to fight the dependent associations. Meanwhile, the traditional communal groups see the basis of their support being eroded, and they may come to be supported by the dependent groups which they had created. Thus a church may regain some influence because subsidiary religious associations articulate 'modern' demands. The polity is then going gradually in the associational direction.

However, such a movement may be 'frozen' by authoritarian means. This tends to occur when the national authorities are afraid to see subsidiary organizations acquiring some independence and independent associations being set up. It can happen in political systems in which efforts are made to maintain traditional communal groups; it also happens, and more frequently in the contemporary world, as a result of the impact of communism, in political systems in which efforts are more to impose new norms on the polity. Gradually, in this last case, a large network of dependent organizations is set up in order to ensure control over all aspects of social life and to prevent traditional bodies from continuing to exercise influence. Such a policy has the manifest effect of bringing about conflict.

## Groups and societal demands

We can now assess the extent to which groups can be regarded as articulating demands in a polity. This has been said to be their main role, but this view is often challenged as being one-sided, western-oriented, and providing a rather idealized view of western society (Almond and Coleman, 1960; Easton, 1965). The distinction between communal and associational groups and, among the latter, between dependent and independent associations provides a framework for the answer. A fully associational polity – or, more realistically, one which is primarily associational – is one in which groups do indeed *articulate* demands, since groups have goals and the support which they receive is based on these goals. At the other extreme, there is almost no 'articulation' of demands, in the strict sense, in a communal society: there is a *selection* of points corresponding to what the communal groups are striving towards. Where dependent associations prevail, there is some articulation and some selection: articulation is more marked where dependent associations slowly lose the 'tutelage' of their 'parent' group, while selection prevails where the public authorities maintain in an authoritarian manner a strong hold over the associations – communist polities have provided a clear example of such a strategy.

## The ambiguous nature of associational bodies

Distinctions in the part played by groups suggest three remarks. First, associational groups are ambiguous. In reality, 'pure' associations are almost always limiting cases since, in almost all societies, the groups which are described as 'associational' have in reality a near-associational rather than a pure associational character. This is true of 'dependent' associations of communal groups and of the state. It is also true of 'independent' associations, which typically acquire some loyalty on the part of their members irrespective of, or at any rate beyond, specific goals. Their leaders often consciously act to do so, since leaders of communal groups have greater leeway than leaders of associations. The former are related to supporters on the basis of a broad pattern of relationships, while leaders of associations have authority only in relation to and within the frame of reference of the goal of the group. Thus, naturally, leaders of associations often try to build or develop patterns of interpersonal relationships among their supporters, and to broaden their sphere of activity in this way. This can be seen to be the case in many of the groups which emerge within social movements, such as women's groups, ecological groups and regionalist groups. These bodies are at least in part communal, and their leaders may have a broad scope of action as a result.

## Institutions and communal and associational groups

Second, institutions such as bureaucracies, armies and many churches, occupy intermediate positions between pure communal and pure associational groups. They articulate some demands, but they also select demands. Polities in which these groups prevail can be regarded as transitional, institutions being the means by which some relatively 'modern' demands – for instance, on behalf of underprivileged groups – can be expressed, better at least than by the traditional communal groups. This trend has characterized many developing countries in the 1960s: in the absence of a large number of interest groups, the army and the bureaucracy have constituted channels through which some demands have been expressed. There is still limited articulation, but it is not as limited as where traditional communal groups prevail.

## The persistence of communal bodies

Third, in all societies, communal groups continue to play a substantial part. Neither liberal democracies in general nor western countries in particular are wholly

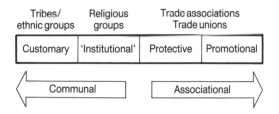

▶ **Figure 7.1**  Communal and associational groups

associational, even in the less 'pure' sense which we just considered. Some communal groupings often remain strong, if not throughout the whole nation, at least among some groups and especially in some regions: in western Europe this is the case, for instance, in the south of Italy, in the Basque country and in Northern Ireland. Not only did communal groups help associational groups to emerge in the past; not only did they help political parties to acquire support, as we shall see in Chapter 9; communal groups have also continued to constitute important elements of political life in their own right, as a result of the direct support which they receive from some sections of the population. Thus all societies are composed of a mix of relatively communal and relatively associational groups, of dependent and less dependent associations. What differs is the mix, not the components.

## Communal and associational groups

### Broad types of communal group

Communal groups, directly or through the dependent associations which they help to create, thus play a major part in most societies. There are substantial differences among communal groups, however, which stem in large part from the fact that some patterns of relationships are more recent or less all-embracing – less fully communal, in reality – than others. The consequences in terms of internal organization and of the extent of the autonomy of dependent associations are important.

Overall, four broad types of communal group have played and continue to play a major part in binding men and women together: they have exercised and continue to exercise a substantial influence on the overall characteristics of political systems. These relationships are tribal or clientelistic; ethnic; religious; and class based.

Tribal or clientelistic organizations can be defined as being either those which link people together by an assumed bond of blood (large families in which fictitious cousinhoods may well be more numerous than real family trees), or those which link natural leaders of a clan or elders to 'clients', an expression borrowed from Ancient Rome, where leaders often had followers defined as their 'clients'. Ethnic relationships associate members by reference to alleged physical characteristics of colour or features.

Religious relationships are organized around beliefs, often in an afterlife. Class relationships are associated with the status of men and women in society and have spread widely in industrial societies, although they have occasionally existed in the past.

*Tribal or clientelistic relationships* constitute the most ancient pattern of relationships. However, some tribal or clientelistic groups developed by means of immigration, as we noted earlier. Moreover, ethnic, religious or even class-based groups can also emerge from pre-existing tribal or clientelistic patterns of relationships. Clan or clientelistic relationships can subsume all the demands in an early stage of socioeconomic development; indeed, very undifferentiated social systems will be characterized by the symbiosis of at least ethnic and religious patterns within a tribal organization. Conversely, tribal or clientelistic groups are least likely and class-based groups are most likely to set up associations with a semi-dependent status. It is therefore through ethnic, religious or class-based patterns of relationships that new communal groups and dependent associations come to exist.

*Ethnic groups* are likely to emerge as a result of immigration, or when the constraints and indeed coercion which were previously imposed on them begin to loosen. The first type of development seems characteristic of the evolution of many western countries, and in particular of the United States, where waves of immigrants changed the character of the basic group structure. The second type has characterized a number of Latin American countries recently, notably those which have a large Indian population.

*Religious groups* can be regarded as more 'modern'. In particular, for generations, they have set up dependent associations, ranging from sports clubs to trade unions. This is particularly true of churches which are hierarchically organized, such as the Catholic Church. These developments tend to occur when the religious body feels threatened by 'anti-clerical' bodies or by competing churches. The dependent organizations which have been set up in this way have often been successful and extended their influence beyond the group of the truly faithful.

*Class-based relationships* developed later, at a point at which many industrial societies had already become somewhat associational and the strength of the clientelistic or religious bodies had substantially declined. Class-based relationships resulted from the start in the setting-up of structured organizations, the trade unions; but communal feelings have continued to play a part. The confraternal and almost religious aspects of early trade unions have often been noted; reverence and loyalty to the organization have been widespread features of these bodies. Indeed, the potential scope of trade union aims is vast: on the one hand, these are created to exercise pressure for concrete demands; but these demands are also aimed at improving the general status of members. As a result, trade unions are genuinely ambiguous: they are half-way between the communal and the associational poles of the dimension. In a sense they are associations, but associations located at some considerable distance from the associational end of the continuum. They are also communal bodies, but they are further away from the communal end of the continuum than religious bodies.

Tribes, ethnic groups, religious bodies and class-based organizations thus both correspond to different levels of socioeconomic development and are characterized by correspondingly different sets of group structures along a continuum. Tribal or clientelist patterns of relationships scarcely give rise to semi-autonomous groupings; nor do ethnic groups typically create dependent associations. Religious and class-based bodies do so, though this is more common in the context of class-based patterns of relationships than among religious bodies; it is also more common among those religious bodies which are centralized and hierarchically structured than among the others.

Moreover, religious or class-based organizations vary markedly in the extent to which they are truly independent from the parent patterns of relationships. Indeed, there are variations over time and from country to country. The Catholic workers' or youth organizations which were created in many European countries in the latter part of the nineteenth century were more dependent on the church organization at the time than they came to be in the second half of the twentieth century; and their dependence remained greater in some countries than in others. Trade unions became more quickly 'associational' in character in some countries than in others, and more in relation to some social groups than in others: miners' unions have typically been characterized by greater 'class loyalties' than the trade of shopworkers; American unions have always been viewed as more 'associational' than European unions; and the extent of class loyalty characterizing European unions has seemingly declined markedly as 'associationalism' appeared to prevail in the minds of many members (Taylor, 1989: 71–95).

Somewhat similar developments occur in imposed political systems which are well structured. The networks of dependent organizations which exist in these systems tend to acquire at least some autonomy over time, since the regime often cannot wholly impede the emergence of demands among the members. This is why this movement is more noticeable in imposed regimes which last for a long period, but these constitute only a minority because many imposed regimes collapse after a few years. Thus populist regimes – in Black Africa, for instance – have been characterized by outbursts of strong autonomous activity on the part of trade unions which were originally truly controlled. In communist states, too, both in eastern Europe (including the Soviet Union) and in China, manifestations of trade union independence have occurred, quite apart from the vast development of the independent trade union 'Solidarity' in Poland in the late 1970s. The dependence of class-based, religious or ethnic groups on 'parent' traditional or institutional bodies thus gradually diminishes even in those cases in which the authorities of the political system do their utmost to maintain their hold on the network of these dependent groups.

## Types of associational development

Communal feelings do not disappear because, conversely, associations are rarely 'pure': their members are rarely linked to the group exclusively through its goal. Thus one can rank associations from the point of view of their 'associationalism'. The most associational groups are those which are organized around a specific activity, such as the defence or promotion of an opinion or a problem, while the least associational are those which protect persons (Finer, 1966: 3–5). Indeed, one can further subdivide the groups which belong to these categories. Bodies which defend points of view or opinions which are wholly acceptable to the national culture are likely to be highly associational. This is because, in such cases, the group will not have to make substantial efforts to gain and retain members: membership will come naturally. Less associational are the groups whose goals are somewhat opposed to generally accepted points of view. Efforts will have to be made to maintain membership and it will therefore be valuable to build patterns of social relationships extending beyond the expressed goals. This is often the case with the social movements which were discussed earlier, such as women's movements, environmental movements and regionalist movements (Klandermans *et al.*, 1981). Less associational still are groups which defend the status and working conditions of persons, especially when these constitute minorities. In such cases, the group will often be – or at any rate was at the origin – a dependent association of a communal group, such as an ethnic, religious or class-based organization.

## Protective and promotional associations

Thus, particularly in countries which have large numbers of relatively independent associations (developed liberal democratic polities, for instance), the distinction between associations protecting persons or classes of persons and associations putting forward opinions is important. The first category, that of *protective groups*, includes a wide variety of bodies, ranging from trade unions and professional associations to trade associations. The second category, that of *promotional groups*, is composed of an equally large variety of bodies ranging from the most 'politicized', such as the social movements, to the most 'social' and politically 'innocuous', such as bridge clubs or angling associations (Finer, 1966: 3–5).

In Western countries, protective associations are typically better established than promotional bodies; they are also more tightly organized and richer. But protective groups also tend to have more general aims than promotional bodies; trade unions, professional or trade associations take up the contentious issues of the moment. Trade unions are the most general, but trade associations and business organizations feel competent to discuss matters of general economic policy, social matters which are related to economic policy, and even in some cases international affairs. On the contrary, promotional bodies are usually concerned with matters pertaining to their own sphere: they typically find it difficult or hazardous to tread outside their original goals, and if they enlarge their sphere of activity, as social movements often try, their following often quickly dwindles. However, the most political of these bodies endeavour to expand their activities and become political parties. We shall see in Chapter 9 to what extent these efforts can be successful without a broad communal base.

Differences among associational bodies are therefore sharp. Where associations are numerous and relatively stronger than communal groups, the sharpness of the differences becomes truly noticeable. It stems from the fact that the legitimacy of associations is limited in scope. If they are truly associational, these bodies cannot call on the support of their membership beyond the goal for which they are created; their leaders will be constrained and their membership is likely to fluctuate. Where communal feelings are strong, on the other hand, truly autonomous associations are unlikely to develop. This is the case whether the system is highly authoritarian or not, since there is simply little scope for 'true' associations to emerge where communal groups tend to cover the main requirements of those who support them.

## Social movements and communal feeling

Communal feelings have thus to be eroded through competition among communal groups and through the emergence of dependent associations, in order for 'pure' associations to have a higher probability to develop. Yet, even in such cases, associ?ations remain fragile if they are concerned solely with a particular issue. This is why, as we have seen, leaders of associations naturally attempt to move away from the truly associational end of the dimension by emphasizing the existence of a way of life behind the associational goals of their group. It is the discovery of this development which has given rise to the suggestion that social movements, rather than interest groups, characterized many of the 'developed' western societies towards the end of the twentieth century. Thus it is remarked that women's movements, ecological movements and regionalist movements are in existence not solely in order to achieve specific, 'instrumental' goals, but in order to present a new blueprint for society within which relationships among members would be different from those which characterize advanced industrial polities. Members are thus brought and kept together as a result of feelings of comradeship which the ideal of a different type of society fosters: new forms of communal groups, rather than new associations, would appear to be developing as a result.

In practice, however, these groups do not appear to have a sufficiently widespread development to justify the conclusion that a new form of communal feeling has emerged. The organizations stemming from or embodying these movements are also typically constrained to adopt specific policy goals which they press on the political system. Although the ideal of the social movement is nurtured and may from time to time, under special circumstances, emerge with great force, it is more common for these organizations to have a real impact with respect to particular objectives which are relatively narrow and do not result in a fundamental questioning of the society.

Many polities have increasingly large numbers of protective and promotional groups of an associational character, while, by and large, communal bodies and even dependent associations are being eroded. The movement is general. In the nineteenth and early twentieth centuries, America and the other Anglo-Saxon countries were the only nations in which associationalism could be said to have taken root. Associationalism then spread across western liberal democracies in the second half of the twentieth century. A similar development is occurring elsewhere even if it is still slow, less carefully monitored and perhaps often difficult to measure.

## BOX 7.1
## Is there a 'new' politics?

One of the major debates about contemporary societies concerns the extent to which they must be regarded as different in character from the societies of only a few decades ago. In the late 1950s, Rokkan and Lipset suggested that there had been four major cleavages in industrial societies: the centre–periphery cleavage, which corresponds to what has been referred to here as territorial or clan-based relationships; the religious cleavage; the class cleavage; and the national cleavage, which is referred to here in terms of the ethnic pattern of relationships. Lipset and Rokkan also suggested that these were the only major cleavages characterizing industrial societies and that, roughly from the first quarter of the twentieth century, cleavages had come to be stabilized.

This view has been challenged both by those who have noted the strength of social movements supporting 'new' issues, and by those who have claimed that societies were moving from a 'materialist' to a 'post-materialist' or 'post-modern' phase. In both cases it is suggested that old cleavages are being eroded, and that the new issues or values might even supersede traditional cleavages.

The argument goes further: it is claimed that new cleavages have different characteristics from older cleavages. Ideas rather than interests have become prominent: new social movements are concerned with causes and with new ways of organizing society.

Are we, then, moving towards a *new politics*? Major changes in political structures and values have taken place in the past: societies were tribal or based on clans; liberal democracies are a relatively recent development. The cleavages which the new issues represent constitute the basis for a new type of society. So far, bodies such as trade unions, ethnic groups, even church-based groups, remain powerful; but many have declined or have somewhat altered their character. Thus the evidence is mixed. The debate over the true impact of the 'new politics', of the 'new issues' and of 'post-materialism' (Inglehart) is therefore likely to continue for many years and perhaps decades.

## Overview

Groups are an essential and ubiquitous feature of all political systems, but they differ markedly in size and in support, and they have a widely different impact.

The role of groups in modern political systems has long been regarded as harmful. Efforts were at first made to deny the part played by groups, and even since this part has been fully recognized, many have continued to be regarded as having a negative effect. The contrast between *interest groups* and *social movements* is often made on these lines, though such a contrast is not truly sustainable.

The key distinction is that between *communal* groups, which represent a way of life, a pattern of relationships, and *associational* groups, which exist to fulfil a goal. In reality, the distinction has to be viewed as being a dimension: most groups have elements of communalism and of associationalism.

Communal groups try to extend their influence, especially when they are in decline or, on the contrary, when they try to impose new norms: they then set up *dependent associations*. Imposed political systems of the populist or communist varieties have to set up many dependent associations, such as trade unions, cultural organizations, youth groups, in order to develop their influence.

There are four types of communal pattern of relationships. These are based on *clan or clientele, ethnic, religious, or class feelings*. The latter two types are those which are most likely to be extended by dependent bodies.

There are two broad types of association, *protective and promotional*. Protective associations defend existing interests and are typically fairly strong: trade unions are a key example. Promotional associations propose goals for the future; their membership typically fluctuates appreciably. Social movements are among the promotional groups which have, or have been regarded as having, the largest importance; as that of other promotional groups, however, their support does fluctuate.

In the contemporary world, patterns of relationships have been eroded, but *feelings of belongingness* still constitute an important element in the development of groups, including associations. Polities seem, therefore, to move towards a middle point, where groups are relatively numerous but limited in scope, rather than to a wholly associational model.

## Further reading

The normative aspects of the role of groups in society and indeed a general critique of group theory, can be found in L. Weinstein, 'The group approach' in H. Storing, ed., *Essays on the Scientific Study of Politics* (1962: 153–224). Classical democratic theory is traditionally represented by the *Social Contract* (1762) by J.J. Rousseau and by Letter X of the *Federalist Papers*. Group theory was first articulated by A.F. Bentley in *The Process of Government* (1967). It was further developed by D. Truman in *The Governmental Process* (1951). On neo-corporatism, see G. Lehmbruch and P.C. Schmitter, eds., *Patterns of Corporatist Policy-Making* (1982).

A systematic mapping of groups has only been undertaken in part. A general overview, though old, can be found in F.G. Castles, *Pressure Groups and Political Culture* (1967). On the distinction between protective and promotional groups in the context of Britain but valid universally, see S.E. Finer, *Anonymous Empire* (1966). On the characteristics of trade unions on a comparative basis, see A.J. Taylor, *Trade Unions and Politics* (1989). On social movements, see B. Klandermans, H. Kriesi and S. Tarrow, eds., *From Structure to Action: Comparing Social Movement Research* (1981) and D. Rucht, ed., *Research on Social Movements: The State of the Art in Europe and the USA* (1991). An analysis of the network of groups in communist states can be found in L. Holmes, *Politics in the Communist World* (1986: 216–29).

For an assessment of the internal life of groups, see P.M. Blau, *Exchange and Power in Social Life* (1964). For a more detailed analysis of the distinction between communal and associational groups, see F. Toennies, *Community and Association* (London edn, 1955).

# 8

# Political communication and the media

## Introduction

In the course of recent decades, the general importance of communication in political life has become fully recognized. In an interesting manner, this recognition has been associated with the analysis of the role of groups: thus 'group theory' can be said to have been at the origin of the study of communication. 'It became clear to Bentley [the originator of group theory] that society and politics were indeed processes and that the central phenomenon of social process was communication' (Nimmo and Sanders, 1981: 49). We have now become fully aware of the fact that no operation of the political system can take place unless each part of the system communicates with the others; more specifically, there are operations in the political system only to the extent that there is communication among the various parts. This is true both within groups – which are communication mechanisms among members – and among groups. Indeed, communication also links the present with the past and the future, so that demands are followed by policies.

Of course, the recognition of the overriding importance of political communication and of communication in general has been triggered by the development of the mass media; it has also to a large extent been set in motion by the belief that these media made it possible for those who controlled them to manipulate opinion and thereby behaviour. 'Assumptions about the political impact of the mass media have played a formative part in guiding the direction of mass communication research ever since its inception' (Gurevitch and Blumler, 1977: 270). It had been originally felt that the opportunities for leaders to influence citizens would be increased to such an extent that the nature of political life would be radically transformed. It was therefore natural that studies should have concentrated on the media; only when these were found to have a more limited influence than had been originally thought did political communication come to be analyzed generally and connected with the universal phenomenon of information (Williams, 1962; Deutsch, 1966; McQuail, 1977: 72–4).

Communication is what gives its dynamics to the political system. It should therefore be studied in the same way as the political system as a whole: namely, in terms of the interpenetration and reciprocal influences between structures and behaviour. Scattered across the political system are complex networks of communication *processes* and of communication *structures*. Depending on levels of development and on the norms of the system, these structures will be more or less specialized, while the growth of engineering techniques of communication has a substantial effect on the development of these specialized structures.

- In this chapter, we shall therefore first look at *the general characteristics of the process of communication*.
- Second, we shall analyze *the nature of the processes and of the structures of communication* in various types of society.
- Third, we shall examine what appear to be *the effects of these structures and processes* on political life in different types of political system.

## Towards a general theory of communication

Let us therefore examine first what communication consists of in general. To do so, let us describe the characteristics of a 'perfect' system of communication and then examine the ways in which the real world differs from such a system, and by doing so reduces the extent to which communication takes place.

### Perfect communication

Communication takes place between two points A and B if there is a *link* between these two points and a *coding–decoding device* at each end. Communication is 'perfect' if the link functions clearly and continuously and if the two coding–decoding machines understand each other fully and are entirely able to perceive what is to be emitted. Similarly, a perfect system of communication between any number of points requires that all the points be related to each other, two by two, by perfect coding–decoding devices, so that anything that happens at any of the points is transmitted fully to all the other points.

### Real-world communication

In a perfect system, there is complete and immediate transmission of all the signals. In the real world, however, the communication process is imperfect in four ways.

First, the machine at each end may only *register a proportion of the signals* which are emitted at the other end, or it may only register these signals to an extent and transform what are continuous variations of intensity into a series of discrete levels.

This is likely to occur because machines are usually adapted to 'perceive' happenings only within a given range or at a given depth.

Second, the machines at each end must be able to 'understand' all that is emitted by the emitting machine, but the translation which takes place through decoding *increases the number of ambiguities* in the communication process. For this not to happen, the machines at both ends would have to be identical (or perfectly matching). This is difficult to obtain even with mass-produced machines; it will not happen with human communication machines, since the 'understanding' of individuals varies in relation to their social background, education, psychology, etc. Thus a signal emitted by A with a certain meaning will often be decoded by B with a different meaning. If A and B are strangers, the danger of misunderstanding and even incomprehension is large. Communication will, of course, be low if A and B know each other's language imperfectly; but even if they know each other's tongue, some aspects of the message will always be lost.

Third, reductions in communication will also result from *imperfections in the link*. For communication to be 'perfect', the link between A and B must be in continuous two-way operation. This is practically impossible: no communication process allows for full simultaneous two-way communication. When A emits to B, B cannot emit to A; B has to interrupt A to communicate his or her information or B in effect ceases to listen to A. In most cases, the situation is worse, since one of A or B may simply not be able to emit at all and may be temporarily or permanently on the receiving side.

Finally, the communication process must be in *continuous operation*, or there must at least be a system (such as a telephone bell) through which A and B may constantly communicate with each other. Real cases, even of two-person relationships, rarely approximate this ideal: A and B will not be able to reach each other in all circumstances.

Thus real-world communication is imperfect because the zone or area of information is limited, either in range or depth; because there is some incompatibility between emission and reception, and misunderstandings or errors in translation occur; because it is not two-way and fully reciprocal; and because it is not continuous. As these types of imperfection can be combined in different ways, the effect can be to compound the problems and thus increase imperfections.

So far, we have considered communication problems arising between two persons only. In the real world, 'imperfections' are further increased because of the numbers of persons involved. A further form of imperfection then arises which results from the existence of *clusters of communication patterns*. As we know, groups privilege relationships among some members of the society (the group members) against others: this means that there will be more communication among some than among others. The measurement of some aspects of these clusters has begun: for instance, by examining amounts of correspondence or the physical movement of persons (Deutsch, 1953; Taylor and Jodice, 1983).

Taken together, all five types of imperfection which we have examined have the effect of reducing real-world communication to being only a minute fraction of what perfect communication could be. It should be noted that the development of the mass media has done little to alter that situation.

## Autonomy, influence and feedback

The fact that real-world communication is 'imperfect' not only means a loss of information on the part of all concerned; it also means that some – those who have information which they are able to withhold or disseminate – can exercise *influence* as a result. Where the information transmitted is not complete, it can be manipulated; where two-way information does not take place, it is possible to ignore reactions, to prevent information from developing laterally, and thus to maintain a situation in which the information which is communicated is one-sided.

Conversely, however, the presence of social clusters or of individual psychological barriers tends to limit the extent to which influence can be exercised. In practice, while leaders (who can be expected to have more information) may sometimes be able to take decisions more easily as a result, since opposition will not have the opportunity to manifest itself fully, they may also be less able to ensure acceptance afterwards, since information on the decision may not have been imparted or may be wrongly imparted. Influence may be increased by imperfections in two-way relationships and the selective sending of messages, but it is decreased by bad 'reception' due to psychological or social characteristics. If it were possible to maximize reception without at the same time increasing two-way relationships, it would be possible to increase the influence of some indefinitely; this cannot be done.

To be able to increase their influence indefinitely, communicators would need to be fully *autonomous*: that is, not subjected in turn to influence. However, influence cannot be exercised by communicators unless they have some knowledge of those to whom they wish to communicate, since the information imparted will have its maximum effect if it is adjusted to those who are receiving it. Those who emit the messages must therefore lose at least some of their autonomy if they wish to exercise influence.

There are even further limitations in autonomy. They result from self-adjusting or *feedback mechanisms*: these automatically tailor the messages to be sent to what can be understood. The emitting body does not even realize the nature and extent of the constraints under which it operates. Information is gathered, processed and sent without the emitting body being able to play any part in the operation.

## Communication processes and the communication media

In contemporary societies, political communication is often regarded as being first and foremost, if not exclusively, confined to the mass media. It is indeed true that the characteristics of the mass media are better described than the use of other aspects of communication. Their relative extension and even their content can be measured and therefore compared, and some aspects of their impact can be assessed fairly precisely. But, restricted to the mass media, the study of communication is partial. The mass media constitute only the most sophisticated technical development of one of the two forms which political communication takes in political systems, *public communication*. Alongside public communication, there is *private communication*, which has always been important in politics, but has also been affected by change under the impact of various technological developments. Indeed, private and public communication constitute strictly speaking the two poles of a dimension, and they are often intermingled in political life. Both need to be given prominence.

## Private communication

The processes of private communication are those in which information is exchanged among persons who have an adequate or at least elementary knowledge of each other. Private communication tends therefore to take place within very small groups and, in particular, in two-person discussions, although it does not need to be face to face. Indeed, not only correspondence, but also telephone conversations have markedly diminished the need for physical proximity in private communication.

Private communication is clearly less 'imperfect' than public communication; yet it is not 'perfect'. For instance, full continuous two-way traffic is theoretically impossible: this is obviously the case when the exchange of information takes place by correspondence. Moreover, although those who exchange information in private communication know each other, there are often problems of interpretation and of assessment of the messages which are being exchanged.

Private communication tends to develop within and along the lines of the group structure of the polity, since it is the group structure which gives rise to the private relationships which are at the root of the communication. Thus one way of detecting patterns of private communications in a political system is to describe the network of groups in that system. For instance, where these tend to have a communal character, private communication will take place both almost exclusively within each of these communal groups and according to the sociopsychological characteristics which have developed within the groups. Where, on the contrary, group patterns tend to be associational, private communications will be less exclusive and more varied, although they may also be more superficial because members of the associations are likely to know each other less well.

## Public communication

Processes of public communication, on the other hand, have always been characterized by a lack of personal knowledge of the members of the 'audience' to which the communication is being addressed. The mass media have extended dramatically the size of these audiences, but the principle by which a signal is emitted without adequate knowledge of the receivers is not new. In political life in particular, this type of communication constitutes a large part of the activities of leaders who have always chaired or addressed public meetings, and often large ones, or sent messages which could be read and passed on to many others.

Public communication is less adequate or more imperfect than private communication for four reasons:

- It maximizes lack of understanding, since it is not known whether the 'language' used will be understood by those who receive the message; thus it is not known either whether the expected effect will occur. This is particularly true when the evidence is not seen by the communicator – a feature which the mass media have obviously increased.
- Public communication minimizes two-way traffic: except for somewhat anomic outbursts and perhaps a limited number of 'questions', those who receive the message cannot participate actively in the communication process.
- Public communication processes cannot be continuous, while private communication relationships can usually be started at the will of each of the communicators.
- They are highly selective, in that the zone or area chosen by the communicator is generally rigidly predetermined (Chaffee et al., 1973: 391–409).

The 'dysfunctional' aspects of public communication are therefore large. They are, of course, counterbalanced by an obvious practical advantage: an individual can address large groups at one moment in time. Since politicians came to deal with large groups as soon as political life started to have an element of popular appeal, public communication developed long before the mass media. But public communication is also less imperfect than private communication in that it can extend beyond specific groups; it can therefore help to break sectionalism. This is not necessarily the case, of course: on the contrary, some leaders may use public communication to promote sectionalism, such as racist views. But public communication *may* be used against sectionalism or as a means of appealing from a narrower to a broader form of sectionalism, to the tribe from the family, the party from the occupational or social group, the nation from the party.

## Communication processes and communication structures

We have hitherto discussed private and public communication in terms of processes, although we have also alluded to the structures through which these processes take place. In the case of private communication, the underlying structures are the very structures of the political system: namely, groups, parties, bureaucracies, governments. *Private communication rarely cuts across these structures.* In the case of public communication, the mass media added a new range of structures, but these act also as constraints on politicians. Newly created mass media can start developing independent tendencies which politicians may not easily control, unless they impose a line to the media. If they do so, some capital of legitimacy has then to be used in order to maintain this control.

Seen in this light, the constraints placed on public communication by the mass media do not appear different in kind from the constraints which earlier forms of public communication and all forms of private communication have also imposed on communication. They chiefly have an impact on selectivity. Public communication is more imperfect than private communication in all aspects, except that it may help to break sectionalism and that it enables political leaders to increase markedly the size of their audience. Political leaders concentrate on these processes of public communication essentially for this reason. The mass media are thus the form of public communication in which the characteristics of public communication are stretched to extremes, and the choice made in favour of large audiences is seen as the counterbalancing factor in the equation.

### Techniques, media and world-wide communication

Two broad points therefore emerge from the analysis of private and public communication: they are both structured; and the structures within which they take form vary with different types of society. The impact of techniques is considerable. This is usually acknowledged in the case of public communication, but the impact of new techniques in the field of private communication is probably equally large, although it may still not be possible to describe this impact with the same degree of precision.

Since techniques play a large part in both aspects of communication, it is tempting to relate levels of communication to levels of socioeconomic development. As a matter of fact, Cutright used an index of communication, relating political development to communication development (both in the private and public senses of the word) and found the association to be high, even though only easily identifiable indicators of communication, such as newsprint and letters, were used (Cutright, 1963: 569–82).

### Political systems and techniques of public communication

To be comprehensive, however, the analysis of political communication should be conducted at three different levels, only one of which is usually considered. There is, first, the level of the *techniques*: one must assess the extent to which various polities use various communication media. The data are generally available: as can be seen in Table 8.1, the residents of countries which are socioeconomically advanced have greater access to the media, although there are interesting differences between parts of the developing world.

### Political systems and structures of communication

The second level is that of the *structures* of the media, within which the processes of private and public communication tend to take place. In this respect, too, socioeconomic development appears to affect both types of communication.

In private communication there will be more barriers, but also perhaps greater depth in societies characterized by communal groups. Patterns of private communication which exist are less imperfect, but both within each group and from group to group, private communication is more narrowly circumscribed. The opening-up of the society and the development of different types of group (including political parties) coincide with a decrease in the 'quality' of private communication.

**Table 8.1**   Spread of the mass media across the world

| Region | Newspapers: daily circulation per 1000 (1973–5) | | Radios per 1000 (1973–5) | | Televisions per 1000 (1972–5) | |
|---|---|---|---|---|---|---|
| | No. of countries | Average | No. of countries | Average | No. of countries | Average |
| Atlantic | 18 | 306 | 23 | 451 | 23 | 267 |
| Eastern Europe and northern Asia | 10 | 222 | 13 | 197 | 14 | 115 |
| Middle East and northern Africa | 11 | 65 | 16 | 183 | 20 | 48 |
| South and south-east Asia | 9 | 97 | 16 | 133 | 20 | 31 |
| Africa south of Sahara | 31 | 15 | 40 | 56 | 44 | 3 |
| Latin America | 17 | 73 | 26 | 216 | 27 | 58 |

*Source:* Compiled from C.L. Taylor and D.A. Jodice, *World Handbook of Political and Social Indicators*, 3rd edn, 1983, Vol. 1: 175–84.

In public communication, structures are also closely related to socioeconomic development. Where the development of groups is 'natural', the press, radio and television tend to be created as 'semi-legitimate' dependent associations of the broad (or some of the broad) legitimate groups. Since radio and, even more, television stations are based on more advanced techniques and are more expensive to run than newspapers, only some groups will be in a position to set up their own channels. Where group development is imposed, the media are used in the same way as other dependent associations, although because it is obvious that the media provide leaders with means of influencing the people most easily, more attention is given to the control of the press, radio and television than to the control of other organizations. Yet it is not at all proved that they are the means which enable these leaders to exercise most influence on the polity. Moreover, like other associations, the public communication structures may gradually become somewhat autonomous and disengage from the organization on which they originally fully depended.

### Political systems and processes of communication

Third, *processes* of communication take place within the context of these structures, but the analysis of processes is most difficult to undertake. Neither in theory nor in practice is the distinction between processes, structures and techniques always clear. With respect to the mass media, there is a choice of three types of process. These media can be *wholly independent* associations: their relationship with the political parties is then random, and they have complete freedom. They can be *controlled by each major political party*, and thus be 'dependent' associations of these parties: this means in effect only limited freedom. Finally, there can be *only one national organization*, which may be controlled in an entirely imposed or in a pluralistic manner: the amount of freedom varies according to the way in which the controlling bodies are composed. Since technical complexity increases as we move from the press through radio to television, a solution has sometimes been for the press to be organized on the basis of independent associations, and for radio and television to be organized on the basis of a 'single national institution'. The United States has been at one extreme; fully authoritarian systems in the communist world and elsewhere have been at the other; most western European countries have tended to adopt an intermediate model.

**Table 8.2**  Examples of legal arrangements relating to press, radio and television

|  | Press | Radio | Television |
|---|---|---|---|
| (1) Pluralistic and wholly based on commercial arrangements | USA<br>Japan<br>Brazil<br>Britain<br>France<br>Italy | USA<br>Japan<br>Brazil | USA<br>Japan<br>Brazil |
| (2) Intermediate: partly state, partly private |  | Britain<br>France<br>Germany<br>Italy | Germany<br>Italy |
| (3) Monopoly | China | Sweden | Sweden |

If one keeps in mind the ranking – press, radio, television – one can have an impression of patterns of processes throughout the world. First, costs will play a major part in countries of low socioeconomic development: not only television and radio, but also the press will tend to come under a 'single national plan' in countries where the income per head is very low, unless, as in the case of some ex-colonial countries, capital costs for newspapers and even radio and television are met by 'newspaper chains' from the ex-mother country. Second, authoritarian political systems will allow the creation of one national organization only, and they will impose this organization on all the mass media.

In effect, cost considerations combine with authoritarian tendencies to make it easier for imposition to succeed where socioeconomic development is low; for the same reasons, success will be greater with respect to radio and television than with respect to the press. Where the level of socioeconomic development is truly very low, even the press is likely to be controlled with ease, since few can afford a printing press. Where socioeconomic development is relatively high, the national authorities will encounter more difficulties in relation to the press than in relation to radio and television. This is probably true of the richer authoritarian countries; in many eastern European communist states, an underground press existed.

## The effect of public communication

### Problems of measurement

The measurement of the effect of public communication poses a number of problems. First, the absolute effects are almost impossible to assess: they are too embedded in the society to be disentangled from it. What can be measured are changes in the effects of communication media over time, and indeed over a short time period. This can be referred to as the *disturbance* in the communication patterns resulting from the introduction of new communication media.

Second, the measurement of a very small disturbance taking place over a long period is also difficult. The effect of communication media which do not grow rapidly, or which grow scarcely at all, and which are therefore likely to lead to a small disturbance over small units of time is rarely observed.

This means that the comparative analysis of the role of the media is complex. The rates of growth of the various forms of public communication – public meetings, the press, radio, television – have been widely different, and only the last two, and indeed in many countries only television, have had marked rates of growth. It is therefore inappropriate to compare the (apparently large) effects of television to those (apparently smaller) of the press or public meetings at present. Comparisons over time may be valuable, but the empirical evidence may be lacking for the earlier period. Cross-national studies must therefore concentrate on countries in which particular media, such as television, developed at roughly the same rate throughout the period of investigation (McQuail, 1977: 73–6; De Fleur and Ball-Rokeach, 1982: 232–50).

### Limits on the effects of communication structures and processes

A number of conclusions can none the less be drawn about the role of the media, and of television in particular. They all suggest that the impact is less striking than had originally been thought. 'The scope of early media studies was primarily concerned with a search for direct, immediate, and deterministic "effects"' (Zukin, 1981: 362; Bruhn Jensen and Jankowski, 1991: 147–8). It is now clear that these effects are more indirect and less determinant.

First, there is more influence on information than on values and norms. In particular, television increases knowledge but does not significantly modify the norms, at least in the short run. Indeed, even if the medium is very biased, the effect is likely to remain limited because the psychological barriers of the pre-existing forms of communication, and in particular of private communication, will buttress existing norms. Evidence for

---

**BOX 8.1**
**The press, radio and television: are they a responsible Fourth Estate?**

The late eighteenth and early nineteenth centuries knew major political battles, in Europe at least, in order to achieve the freedom of the press. The 'Fourth Estate', as the press came to be known, began to exercise considerable power over politicians, and, in the eyes of some, too much power.

The problem arose with the advent of 'press barons' controlling newspapers with large circulations and deemed able to influence large sections of the public and, consequently, to blackmail many politicians into accepting their views. These 'barons' were particularly influential, to begin with at least, in Britain and the United States, prominent examples being Beaverbrook and Hearst (the 'hero' of Orson Welles' *Citizen Kane*).

That issue has not been solved. It was thought that at least a solution had been found for radio and television, since these new media were to be politically 'neutral' and pluralistic, but this solution could not be extended to the press. Moreover, in the context of 'neutral' radio and television, the way news items are selected and presented has raised questions about the nature of the appeal of these media.

The Fourth Estate has thus never ceased to be under criticism from politicians worried about their reputation and their career, as well as from sections of the public concerned about the extent to which the media are the watchdogs that they often claim to be. After 200 years of press freedom in the West, there is still no agreement as to how the media should fulfil their role. There is even less agreement as to how this role can best be fulfilled in the rest of the world.

---

this conclusion has tended to be drawn from developed societies, and especially from election campaigns; but the effect of television and radio seems to be of the same type in new countries. In all cases, the only significant changes which can be observed relate to information (Halloran, 1970; De Fleur and Ball-Rokeach, 1982: 232–55).

Second, where the norms expressed by the new media go in the same direction as those of the polity, the media reinforce these norms. Studies of the disturbance resulting from television at election times show that party supporters are reinforced in their views by the campaign conducted on television. This reinforcement also results from other media of public (and presumably private) communication. But where the disturbance is large, as a result of the appearance of new media coinciding, for instance, with an election, the reinforcement is substantial. This is not surprising: media of political communication are typically not divorced from the cultural characteristics of the polity. Private communication is structured around and within the groups which exist in the polity; the newer mass media are not different in this respect. They are related to the norms of the polity: they are appendages (sometimes, as we saw, legal appendages) of the groups, political or otherwise, which exist in the polity. Their main effect is therefore reinforcement (De Fleur and Ball-Rokeach, 1982: 240–50).

Third, if new media are used in order to change norms, other aspects of the communication process have also to be altered; specifically, private communication patterns have to be modified. The impact of media of public communication is greater on opinion leaders than on the population as a whole. This has been shown to be the case in relation to television, but the point seems general. Meetings, the press and radio as well as television are all primarily used by opinion leaders, since these attend or listen to them more frequently. Moreover, opinion leaders are better able to understand the messages which are emitted by the political leaders (Lazarsfeld and Katz, 1955: 31–42). As a result, only by a combination of public communication and private communication media can changes in norms permeate throughout the population.

If norms are to be altered, the structure of private communication has also to be altered. Since this is not normally possible, at least in the short run, all that can be done is to alter somewhat the content of the messages exchanged by opinion leaders. The change in the political norms which the mass media can achieve is therefore small in the short run. It may be greater in the long run, but any change which then occurs has to be related to other variations in the society as a whole. There is a systemic relationship between communication structures and processes and the political and social system: this systemic relationship determines the limits of what can be changed by using communication media.

## Effects of the mass media

The new communication media have a substantial effect in two ways, however, in both cases because they may reduce sectionalism. First, they increase information. This impact has been shown to exist in developed societies – largely, of course, because more research has been done in these countries. This is particularly the case in connection with television, mostly, it is submitted, because, of all the media, television is the one which caused most 'disturbance' recently. Were it possible to analyze the effect of the press in the nineteenth century, the same finding might emerge. Television helps citizens to acquire information of a general character which private communication networks cannot impart because they function in a narrower framework. There is no consequential change in norms, however, at any rate so long as there is no trend in the society for norms to be modified (McQuail, 1977: 80–2; De Fleur and Ball-Rokeach, 1982: 247).

Second, public communication media appear able to close the gap between norms and policies where this gap becomes apparent. Where the norms of members of the polity (or of an important fraction of its members) are not implemented or cannot be implemented by existing policies or existing political leaders – when, therefore, there is a gap between norms and policies – the media of public communication (and particularly the new media which can create a large disturbance) seem able to fill this gap: for instance, by building the reputation of someone whose views appear to correspond to the norms of members of the polity. In doing so, the communication media do not change the norms; an attempt is simply made to implement them.

If we combine this point with the fact that the media help to increase knowledge, and if we concentrate on the situation in developing countries in which means of private communication are essentially clustered around tribal or other closed communities, the consequences may be or appear dramatic. This is why it is often stated – and in this sense rightly – that media of public communication, especially television and radio, have contributed markedly to the development of the 'rising expectations' of the citizens of Third World countries. It is not that demands have been engineered, but that there was a gap between norms and policies (Lerner, 1958: 19–107; Frey, 1973: 337–418). The 'disturbance' may appear large, and it may well be large in some countries, by comparison with the fact that traditional private communication operated only within the clusters of tribes or other communal groups. But new norms have not been engineered in this way; the media of public communication fill a gap between norms and policies which emerged in many countries of the Third World from a combination of the imitation of practices of developed countries and from limited, and indeed patchy, socioeconomic development.

## Overview

Communication is the *mechanism by which political life takes place*. It determines the way in which relationships develop within and between groups and institutions. The field of political communication therefore goes much beyond the analysis of the mass media alone.

Political communication, like other forms of communication, is *imperfect* in that its area is limited, there are misunderstandings and errors of transmission and interpretation, and it is not full time. These imperfections give some (leaders among others) means of exercising influence.

Political communication is *both private and public*. Both forms have always existed, even if the mass media have markedly opened up opportunities for public communication.

Both private and public communication vary *according to the type of political system*. For instance, types of private communication tend to be clustered within each communal group where these prevail; public communication structures and processes are even more markedly influenced by the type of political system. Because of costs, these media and in particular radio and television can be controlled relatively easily by public authorities in poorer authoritarian countries.

The effect of communication processes tends to be limited to *increasing knowledge and reinforcing existing norms*. This is true even of the mass media, which have to rely to a substantial extent on private communication mechanisms to reach the broad mass of citizens.

Thus a truly comprehensive empirical theory of political communication will emerge only when it becomes possible to relate private and public media in countries where both types are relatively 'primitive', in those where public media are 'in advance' of the private media, and in those where both are relatively 'developed'.

## Further reading

The idea of applying a communication model to political life was pioneered by K. Deutsch, whose *Nerves of Government* (1963) opened up a whole new direction of political analysis.

On the role of the mass media in political and social life, see J. Curran *et al.*, eds., *Mass Communication and Society* (1977) and M.L. De Fleur and S. Ball-Rokeach, *Theories of Mass Communication* (4th edn, 1982). For an earlier view about the large part played by the mass media, see R. Williams, *Communications* (1962), and for a more recent approach, see J. Lichtenberg, ed., *Democracy and the Mass Media* (1990). On the influence of television, see J.D. Halloran, ed., *The Effects of Television* (1970).

For a general analysis of the different aspects of influence, see P.F. Lazarsfeld and E. Katz, *Personal Influence* (1955). See also J. Dennis, ed., *Socialisation to Politics* (1973).

For an examination of the general characteristics of mass communication, see D.D. Nimmo and K.R. Sanders, eds., *Handbook of Political Communication* (1981), J. Curran *et al.*, eds., *Mass Communication and Society* (1977) and K. Bruhn Jensen and N.W. Jankowski, eds., *A Handbook of Qualitative Methodologies of Mass Communication Research* (1991).

**Part III**

# Political parties and elections

# 9

# Political parties: origins, nature and structure

## Introduction

Political parties are one of the major developments of the nineteenth and twentieth centuries. They are an invention of modern political systems, an invention which, at first sight curiously, has served and even truly made effective both liberal democratic political systems and many types of coercive regime. Although some contemporary dictatorships also attempt to operate without political parties, they usually do so for short periods only and with difficulty.

Parties are fundamental to modern society because they are the main means by which political conflicts are domesticated. They do this in two ways: on the one hand, they legitimize conflicts, by giving them a voice in the public debate; on the other, they reduce and even at the limit repress conflict.

- Before examining later in this chapter the anatomy of parties (their structure), and in Chapter 10 their physiology (how they combine and fight each other in the form of party systems), we need to consider *why parties are particularly associated with modern polities*. We shall do this in the first section of this chapter.
- In the second section, we shall examine the *social bases of parties*, and how these organizations resemble and differ from other groups in society and thus are pre-eminently political groupings, through which and by which both representation and at times imposition occurs. We shall also look at the goals of parties.
- Finally, in the third section, we shall analyze the *structure of parties*. We shall see, in particular, how they relate directly and indirectly, through groups, to the population.

## Political parties in the world today

### The widespread presence of parties

Political parties are one of the main features of contemporary political life. Various types of *faction* existed earlier, which were sometimes well organized and durable, as

---

## BOX 9.1
## From factions to parties

The word 'party' has a bad reputation. Many parties perpetuate this negative feeling and exploit it by calling themselves 'movements', 'rallies' or 'unions' rather than parties. The negative expression 'partitocracy' is in much use on the Continent of Europe: it suggests that the parties band together to exercise power, not by and for the people, but for themselves.

The fact that the word 'party' has such a bad name has much to do with some of the early scholarly literature on parties which appeared towards the end of the nineteenth and at the beginning of the twentieth centuries, and especially with the works of Ostrogorski and Michels, who both viewed parties as organizations which, almost inevitably, frustrate the will of the people. Their attacks, in particular that of Michels, surely contributed to the fact that entire party systems collapsed in Europe in the 1920s and 1930s.

Yet one has to go further back to understand why the concept of party is viewed so negatively. Parties were attacked because they were the successors of *factions*, and factions were regarded as dividing polities unnecessarily, as if total consensus would otherwise have been the norm.

Far from being regarded as normal, parties were almost always considered, before the nineteenth century, as somewhat unhealthy developments which tended to emerge and thrive when countries were in some difficulty. They seemed to be symbols of the decline of polities, as if the arrival of factions was a sign that the country was bordering on civil war. Factions and parties were synonymous with battles in the real sense of the word: this was how the Roman Republic ended, and it was how Italian city-states came to fall prey to monarchs who ruled nearby.

What is perhaps surprising, therefore, is that Europe gradually came to accept in the course of the nineteenth century that parties had come to stay, and that they were indeed an inevitable feature of a modern liberal democracy. Thus the attacks against parties voiced by some, including by scholars, in the last decades before the First World War should be regarded more as rearguard actions than as new observations about the characteristics of the world at the time.

---

in Ancient Rome or in Italian cities of the Renaissance. But only since the later part of the nineteenth century have parties come to be recognized as the normal means by which to fight political battles. We noted in Chapter 7 the dislike for factions of late eighteenth-century political theorists; this changed gradually, as parties developed and became strong, first in Europe and North America, and gradually throughout most of the world.

In this process, parties emerged not just in liberal polities but also in authoritarian or totalitarian societies. First by accident, and later consciously, the single-party system came to be used as a means of imposing regimes; it was more effective in doing so than other structures, such as the military or the bureaucracy. It has been suggested that parties in single-party systems are different in kind from the parties which emerge in pluralistic political systems (Sartori, 1976: 42–7). In reality, as we shall see later in this chapter, there is no clear-cut difference; nor is the role of parties in single- and pluralistic party systems altogether dissimilar.

Parties are not present everywhere, however. Throughout most of the second half of the twentieth century, as many as a fifth to a quarter of the countries of the world (admittedly, mostly not the same ones) have lived under regimes which excluded parties. These are of two types, traditional and military, only the first of these being truly non-party, as we shall see in Chapter 10.

Yet if parties prevail in the large majority of countries in the contemporary world, they do not have the same importance everywhere. Their 'weight' in the polity varies markedly: in some cases, parties are strong and well established; in others, they are weak. This weight also changes over time: it increased globally in Europe in the course of the nineteenth century; it may now be diminishing in many countries.

## Why parties are widespread

Why, then, are parties so widespread in the contemporary world, while they were rare in the past? This cannot be only because of the spread of liberal democracy, since many authoritarian governments are also based on parties. The reasons have to be found in three characteristics of the modern world: namely, the perception of the existence of conflicts in society; the need for the government to be linked to the population, and the belief that 'unity means strength'.

First, parties emerge when members of the polity begin to recognize the existence of conflicts, which may relate to the overall structure of the society, to aspects of its organization, or to policies. These problems may be openly discussed or suppressed (as in many single-party systems), but the perception of the existence of conflicts is an indispensable condition. It is because, in traditional societies, such conflicts are not perceived that these polities can be true 'no-party' states (Huntington, 1968: 407).

Second, parties exist where the national authorities have to be linked to the population and cannot rely on traditional sources of legitimacy, such as the divine right to rule. Parties can provide links with the people – for instance, by developing networks of regional and local branches. The fact that the government has to be linked to the people is a characteristic of the modern world.

Third, for parties to exist, the belief has to be widespread that union means strength. This belief is widely held in the contemporary world, although some may not share it and prefer tiny conspiracies. By and large, better results are expected to be achieved if a large organization is built. The relationship between 'union' and 'strength' has consequences for party life, since it means that a divided party is often felt not to be effective. Yet such a view clashes necessarily with the suggestion that parties should allow for 'internal democracy'. Parties often experience tension as a result.

Parties are therefore characteristic organizations of modern political life, even if they do not exist everywhere, or if their weight varies from polity to polity. The potential importance of parties has been so widely recognized that it is not surprising that imitation should play a large part in the process. Thus socialist parties and, but less so, Christian parties spread throughout Europe in the late nineteenth and early part of the twentieth century; thus, too, the single-party arrangement, which emerged after the First World War in the Soviet Union and elsewhere (in Turkey and Mexico for instance) was adopted in many parts of the world after the Second World War, and especially in the newly independent states. This imitation often created problems, for the imported institutions may have been alien to the society and, like transplants in physical bodies, have been quickly rejected as a result.

## Definition

Parties are groups, but groups of a particular kind. What, then, is this particular character? They are truly political groups, in that they are in existence in order to affect the political process. It is sometimes said that they aim at taking power, while other groups aim only at influencing decisions which are taken by others (Neumann, 1955: 395–400; Lawson, 1976: 1–26). This distinction is valid, though more as a rough-and-ready rule than as a truly conceptual contrast; it is based on a contrast between decision-makers and mere influentials which is somewhat oversimplified; it leads also to taking into account wholly unrealistic aspirations – for instance, among small parties; and it is unsatisfactory when considering change.

To arrive at a truly satisfactory definition, it is better to look at what parties are and at their goals; we can then see how they differ from other groups. Parties are associations, not communal groups. They have aims, but these aims are of their own kind, both because they cover all types of social question and because they relate to all sections of society.

There are two exceptions to these general characteristics. One is constituted by minority parties, which exist to defend a particular section of the polity and therefore resemble protective groups; the other is constituted by single-issue parties, set up to put forward a particular cause and resembling promotional groups. These are borderline cases, however; moreover, in the course of time, changes tend to occur within them. Minority parties often attempt to appeal to other sections to increase their influence – for instance, through alliances – unless they obtain independence for their country and, in the process, cease to become minority parties. Single-issue parties are in effect gradually obliged to concern themselves with all types of social question. Green parties are a case in point: they have moved from being concerned merely with ecology to having an overall programme.

Thus we shall define political parties as groups whose membership is open and which are concerned with the whole spectrum of matters which the polity faces.

## Functions of political parties

From this definition follow the main functions of parties (Neumann, 1955: 395–400). These are at three levels: those of the society as a whole, of the political system, and of daily political life.

First, at the level of the society as a whole, political parties are general mechanisms by which conflicts are handled. They are one of the main means by which rulers exercise influence and endeavour to induce the population to accept their policies, while, conversely, they are the means by which the population (or at least its most active part) attempts to exercise influence. Conflicts thus both arise through parties and are solved (by compromise or repression) through parties. Parties are the institutions by which the people are both represented and mobilized, as they are a two-way means of communication of influence between rulers and population. Some parties 'aggregate' or, to adopt Apter's expression, 'reconcile' more than others; they can be used more or less as instruments enabling the rulers to exercise influence and control (Apter, 1965: 182–7; 206–12).

Second, at the level of the political system, parties are the institutions within which policies can be formulated; or, if the parties themselves do not formulate the policies, they are the points at which and on which other bodies, principally interest groups, put pressure in order to see their own policies adopted. Groups also often bypass parties and put pressure directly on governments and bureaucracies. In general, however, parties can be regarded as key intermediaries in the policy-making process.

Finally, at the level of daily political life, parties play a major part in recruitment of the 'political class'. They are the main mechanism by which such a recruitment takes place continuously and smoothly. Although other groups, such as the bureaucracy or the army, may play a part as well, parties are the best training ground where the skills of politics are learnt. Indeed, this recruitment function is even sometimes viewed as the most important which political parties fulfil.

## Social bases and goals of parties

### The notion of the legitimate party

Parties, like other groups, need support to be effective. This support has to be acquired and, given the breadth of the aims and of the activities of parties, acquiring support can be a difficult and slow process. In fact some, indeed many, parties never become large, and fail. Thus one of the key problems for a new party is to obtain a substantial amount of support relatively quickly. Not surprisingly, given what we saw in Chapter 7, one of the fastest ways of achieving this aim is by means of *legitimacy transfer*. Many parties therefore emerge from pre-existing groups, either communal or associational. One of the groups supporting the parties can be the polity itself, the nation, in the same way as the polity can support, as we saw in Chapter 7, institutional groups such as bureaucracies or the army. In this way, many parties gradually *become* legitimate when the transfer of support from the 'parent' group has lasted long enough to lead to a situation in which the supporters of the party no longer refer to that group in order to support the party. The support for the party ceases to be indirect (through the group) and becomes direct.

Such a process of legitimization of parties can be said to be *natural* if and when the parties emerge from a parent group whose goals are accepted by the polity or by large sections of the polity; this has been the case with most western parties of the right or left. On the other hand, the process of legitimization can be said to be *imposed* if the party aims at maintaining or promoting goals against the wishes of the population or of its main groups. Such an imposed development can succeed only when the parent group is, or at least includes, the state itself, since this alone possesses the coercive powers which will maintain the party's dominance. But the coercive power of the state can be associated with the influence of some communal groups, especially tribes or clans and ethnic groups.

The process of legitimization of parties can thus result from one or another of two types of development. On the one hand, groups which have wide support in the polity may set up party organizations when the need arises – a need which is likely to arise when the society becomes modern. Thus many socialist parties were supported by trade unions, or religious parties by churches. On the other hand, national leaders who have a relatively shaky hold on power may use the state apparatus to back parties which they create. There are parties of this kind of both the right (authoritarian conservative parties) and the left (populist and communist parties). However, this process is difficult and often unsuccessful: these parties may not be truly accepted by the polity, as was shown by the fall of communist systems and of many Third World parties.

## Legitimization by natural development

Let us look at these processes more closely. First, the process of legitimization of parties by natural development takes place with the help of one or more of the four types of broad group (tribal, ethnic, religious and class based), which we examined in Chapter 7, though of course not by all of them in every society. Conversely, the same broad group may give rise to more than one party.

### Tribal or clientele parties

Tribal or clientele groups helped the development of many parties in the past: for instance, in England in the eighteenth century and, more recently, in some developing areas, such as Latin America. These parties can be truly tribal or 'clientelistic'; they can even be geographically based, as they tend more and more to be – the association is then not with a clan, but with a given region which is to be defended. Modern nationalistic parties can be said to have this origin.

This origin characterizes the oldest parties, and in particular the oldest European parties. The English Tories and Whigs, for instance, were based on clientelism, from which they emerged in the course of the nineteenth century; they acquired a legitimacy of their own at that point. A similar evolution characterized the oldest conservative and liberal parties of other western European countries, whatever ideological differences emerged gradually among them.

Parties of this kind are, and indeed were particularly in the past, associated with the hold of individual chiefs and chieftains. There tended to be a pyramid, almost feudal, of personal allegiance. This has become rarer at present, although in parts of the Third World, including in parts of Latin America, this type of party 'vassalage' does remain; traces of it also remain in western Europe, especially in more peripheral areas. Expressions borrowed from the army are often used to describe the relationships. Thus one speaks of 'lieutenants' of various kinds who exercise influence on behalf of the main chief (a 'colonel'). Clientele parties therefore tend to have a personalized rather than a well-developed bureaucratic structure.

### Ethnic parties

Ethnic groups also give rise to parties, although in some cases the basis of the party combines bonds of clientele and race. They often but not always give rise to minority parties. Indeed, some of the oldest parties of the world, the American parties, combined important ethnic elements with a more traditional local group basis: thus the Democratic Party has long been a 'federation' of ethnic groups. Ethnic minorities – or a combination of tribal and ethnic minorities – have also contributed to the emergence of many parties in Europe and in the developing world (Lipset and Rokkan, 1967: 23–30).

### Religious parties

Churches often set up parties. The more hierarchical they are, the more they are likely to do so. Thus Roman Catholic, Muslim, or indeed Jewish parties, as in Israel, are more likely to emerge than parties based on other churches. Moreover, churches will tend to set up parties where they are strong enough, but not dominating. They therefore did so in Germany or Italy rather than in Ireland. When it is dominant, the church does not have to defend its position. When they do not feel strong enough to form a party alone, on the other hand, churches may combine to do so, as was the case in Germany after the Second World War, and in the Netherlands in the 1970s.

Church-based parties tend to develop where other communal groups have not already set up strong parties: for instance, if there is no well-established conservative party or if such a party is strongly antagonistic to church interests. Thus Christian parties gained a larger foothold in many continental countries than in Britain or Scandinavia, partly because the Catholic Church is stronger on the Continent, partly because it has been under attack at times, and partly because traditional conservative parties have tended to be weaker.

### Class-based parties

Class-based parties are perhaps the best known of the parties which developed naturally, at least in western Europe and in various European outposts (Australia, New Zealand), where the political system is characterized by the presence of large Labour or socialist parties allied to and often supported by the trade union movement. Class-based parties are less conspicuous elsewhere in the world, although in the United States and some parts of Latin America class has played a part, with other components, in the process by which other parties acquired support.

The development of class-based parties in Europe is clearly connected to the expansion of the working class resulting from industrialization. Conversely, where this 'objective' base did not exist, class-based parties scarcely developed naturally. Socialist (and communist) parties thus emerge in a particular type of social structure; elsewhere clientele, ethnic cleavages and churches are the groups which generate parties. Moreover, class-based parties are unlikely to become strong where other communal groups formed the basis of strongly implanted parties. In Canada and the United States, ethnic allegiances (often combined with religious allegiances) have been strong, thus undermining the potential class cleavage and accounting in large part for the failure of socialist parties to succeed in North America. In western Europe, too, there are examples of relatively weak socialist parties: for instance, because religious groups were strong (as in Ireland) or because ethnic or clientelistic cleavages were prominent (as in Switzerland) (Epstein, 1967: 138–45).

When parties do not have the backing of one of the large communal groups which we just described to acquire support, they tend to remain small; they may alternatively be 'satellites' of larger parties which keep them in being for tactical reasons. Their fate varies: some maintain themselves in existence for a long period; others have successes for a while and then disappear. For many of them the temptation to strengthen their hold by means of imposition does exist, although the opportunity may not be there.

## Legitimization by imposed development

Parties are often used by governments in order to maintain or press for goals and policies which members of the society find difficult to accept. Yet these parties need external support to be implanted and to be able in turn to act as an 'occupation army' in favour of the national authorities. Such parties typically need to be strengthened at the level of the state by means of coercion; they are also helped by the national leaders who created them, especially when these are 'charismatic', a type of leadership to which we shall return later in this chapter as well as in Chapter 17. The leader hopes to be able to induce the population to support the party and thus in turn to support the regime.

Leadership is not necessarily the only base of these parties. They are often associated with an 'idea', national or ethnic, religious or even class based. Such a frame of reference is particularly evident in populist or authoritarian-egalitarian parties of a communist type. This explains in particular why a major emphasis has been placed on nationalism in many Third World countries. As a matter of fact, some groups, often relatively small, do support imposed parties. Communist parties in eastern Europe have been sustained to an extent by the industrial working class; in China, on the other hand, the difficulties in implementing the communist regime led to the development of a new form of 'rural' communism ostensibly more adapted to the country, although even this system cannot be said to have been entirely successful. Authoritarian-inegalitarian parties are more likely to succeed where traditional groups (tribal, ethnic) still have some strength. Populist parties have received the support of new institutional groups, especially the bureaucracy, and occasionally religious groups, particularly in the Middle East, where the Muslim religion is institutionalized and was associated with nationalism during the pre-independence period.

In all these cases – though, of course, more among communist and populist than among authoritarian conservative parties – the long-term aim is to be able to 'educate' the population to support the goals put forward by the regime: the aim is to mobilize the people, not aggregate demands. But the strategy rarely succeeds because popular attitudes are rarely changed, at any rate profoundly. The more the leaders want to move away from the existing norms of the polity and the more, consequently, they oppose existing communal groups, the more they experience difficulties in strengthening the party. Some imposed parties have seemed to be more effective than others in achieving this aim and in strengthening the regime as a result. But even these may not succeed in the long run, as the collapse of the communist systems has shown. The same can be said about many populist parties. The most famous example is that of the Mexican Party of the Institutional Revolution (PRI), which succeeded in dominating politics for decades, but which has come to be confronted with major problems in its attempt to maintain authoritarian practices (Alexander, 1973: 263–79; Philip, 1988: 99–112).

## Goals of political parties

### *The importance of party ideology*

An important aspect of the activity of most parties is constituted by the elaboration and implementation of policies. Admittedly, some parties exist only for the benefit of leaders, while others claim to be purely pragmatic and not to adopt an ideology, which they view as a 'doctrinaire' posture. A total absence of policy direction is rare, however. Pragmatism is an ideological attitude, both in the negative sense that it rejects the suggestion that countries can be better run if there are general guidelines in the determination of policy, and in the positive sense that it sees the current situation as broadly satisfactory. Pragmatic parties basically accept the tenets of the existing system.

Ideology plays a significant part in the life of most parties, both symbolically and concretely, although that ideology may change over time, or the policies proposed may not be consistent with the ideology. Moreover, it is sometimes, perhaps even often, difficult to define what the goals are. The goals of the leaders are not necessarily identical with those of the followers and intermediate leaders; indeed, there is a high probability that there will be disagreements among them (Esptein, 1967; 290–300). These ideologies can be divided into five clusters within the three-dimensional space of norms in the same way as political systems (Day and Degenhardt, 1980; Janda, 1980; Randall, 1988; Szajkowski, 1991).

### Liberal democratic parties in western Europe and North America

In western Europe and North America, the bulk of parties occupy the same liberal democratic position as the political system; indeed, the goals of the parties have become increasingly close to each other during the last decades of the twentieth century. Most parties, and nearly all the significant ones, can therefore be labelled 'liberal democratic'. The exceptions are or were mainly constituted by the few extreme-right parties which have existed since the Second World War, and by communist parties, which have been more widespread, but have declined markedly.

### Eastern communist and ex-communist countries

Liberal democratic parties have emerged in eastern Europe while communist parties, where they remained relatively strong, have typically found it necessary to change their name. Little remains in eastern Europe and in most of what was the Soviet Union of the strong, indeed massive, constructions which communist parties had built. Meanwhile, however, communist parties remain dominant in much of Asia (China, North Korea, Vietnam), although their ideology has been appreciably altered. The authoritarian features are typically maintained, but changes in economic and social policies have been such in the 1990s that these parties have come close to holding a populist ideology. This is also true of some parties in what was the Soviet Union, especially in central Asia, though a few more 'classical' communist parties have also remained in existence.

### Types of party in the Third World

In the rest of the world (Latin America, Africa and the southern half of Asia), parties are more varied in character. Some countries have or have had parties of a liberal democratic type: this is true of several Latin American countries and of Costa Rica in particular, while India has long been the largest liberal democracy in the world. Moreover, parties in some other countries of the new Commonwealth, such as those in the Caribbean, closely resemble North American or western European parties. Some countries also have or have had parties closely resembling the traditional communist model: this is especially the case in Cuba, which has been communist-run from the 1960s under Castro; it was also true of a substantial number of ex-Portuguese colonies in Africa, such as Angola or Mozambique, but a change occurred when communism collapsed in the Soviet Union and eastern Europe.

By and large, however, parties of the 'developing world' have tended to adopt different ideologies from those of western or eastern parties. To a limited extent, this is because *traditional parties* still exist, although they have diminished markedly in number. Among them can be included the traditional Colombian parties and some parties in some central American republics, in a few African countries such as Lesotho, in some south-east Asian states such as Malaysia, and in the smaller countries of Central and Western Asia. These parties have conservative goals and wish to maintain an inegalitarian status quo, in which the members of an oligarchy (and sometimes a monarchy) control the wealth of the country and are truly above the rest of the citizens in status. Levels of participation in these parties are also low.

While traditional conservative parties have declined, they have been replaced by populist and authoritarian conservative parties. The first examples of *populist parties* were found in Mexico and Turkey after the First World War: the PRI survived for decades, while the Turkish Republican Party lasted only until the 1950s. A party of the same type was set up by Nasser in Egypt in the 1950s; it did last for decades, but its characteristics changed. The model then spread primarily to Africa, although some examples can also be found in the Middle East, Latin America and south-east Asia. As a result, by the 1970s, the majority of Third World parties could be defined as belonging to this type, although there were larger variations among them than between the liberal democratic, authoritarian-egalitarian or traditional parties, one of the prominent examples being that of the Tanzania African National Union (TANU). In all these cases, the emphasis has been on 'development' and on popular participation, essentially of the 'mobilizing' type; these parties have also often been led (indeed set up) by 'charismatic' leaders. In the 1990s, some of these parties have turned to being liberal democratic, or have been replaced by parties which, on the surface at least, are liberal democratic: this has been the case in Zambia, for instance. This change has been accompanied by a move, also often of a superficial character, from the single-party to the multiparty system.

While populist parties spread across Third World countries, especially immediately after they gained independence, they have often been subsequently supplanted by regimes based on an *inegalitarian-authoritarian* ideology, in many cases led by the military, the parties being banned altogether. Sometimes, however, a single or dominant party has been set up; indeed, in a number of instances, the leader's goals – and those of the party – moved from being populist to being authoritarian-inegalitarian, as in Malawi under the long rule of Banda. These parties are the Third World replicas of the interwar European fascist parties. They wish to maintain rather than reduce inequalities of wealth and status; they are also authoritarian and oligarchical, the people's place in decision making being almost negligible.

The spread of parties in the contemporary world has thus been diverse as well as rapid. Their characteristic bases and their goals differ widely, both because of the nature of the society and because of the 'will' of rulers (who often benefited from favourable circumstances, and in particular from independence movements, to put forward their ideology). The variety of arrangements has therefore to be examined in order to assess whether, behind the façade of substantial strength, parties have a strong organization and are indeed able to represent or mobilize the population whose support they claim to have.

## The structure of political parties

The 'weight' of parties markedly depends on organization and structure. A poorly organized party is manifestly not likely to achieve either representation or mobilization, and therefore to fulfil its basic role.

Questions of structure have been the first which students of political parties have investigated, the conclusions being generally pessimistic. It has been argued that, despite many appearances to the contrary, parties tended to be run in an autocratic or oligarchical manner, whether they were ostensibly 'democratic' or not. These were the views of both Ostrogorski and Michels, the latter claiming that there was an 'iron law of oligarchy' under which all parties were said to operate (Ostrogorski, 1902; Michels, 1968). The top leadership – the executives and the secretaries – were viewed as perpetuating themselves in office and as running the parties as they wished, this being particularly true of socialist parties.

These views have since been toned down (Duverger, 1954); moreover, the emphasis has been placed increasingly on the decline of organizations (Daalder and Mair, 1983). This decline has been due to two developments: one is the result of the larger part played by the population in political life, and in particular the part played by a variety of local interest groups – at least in the West, but to an extent also elsewhere – with referendums having an increasing role (see Chapter 11); the other element is constituted by the increased personalization of the leadership, in the Third World, in the communist world and in the West. As a result, the 'bureaucratic' organization of parties has tended to take second place in a game in which leaders often appeal directly to the people or at least to party supporters. At the limit, it even becomes difficult to decide whether or not parties are oligarchical. To an extent at least, the views of the people – if not necessarily of the party rank and file – are taken into account; indeed, sometimes against those of the party rank and file.

Three aspects of the structure of parties need to be considered (Epstein, 1967; Daalder and Mair, 1983):

- The internal arrangements on which the party is based.
- Problems of relationships between parties and supporters, whether individually or in groups.
- Patterns of leadership – in particular, whether rulers are, according to the traditional Weberian distinction, traditional, bureaucratic-legalistic or charismatic (Weber, 1968).

## Internal structure of parties

The internal structure of parties raises two connected problems. One is technical and relates to the 'extent' of organization, while the other is ideological and is concerned with the degree to which parties are more or less democratic, and more or less representative. Both questions are connected at the level of a third problem, which is that of centralization: the implantation of a party will have a more or less centralized character depending on the views of founders and leaders about the extent to which the party has to be responsive to the rank and file.

## *Extensiveness*

The extent of implantation of political parties across countries is somewhat technical, but it is a key question, if parties are to provide links between government and people. An extensive party is one which is present all over the country; an inextensive party is one which does not aim at or does not succeed in being present at the periphery. This may be because the party is very small; it may also be because it does not need to cover the country as a result of the clientelistic structure on which it is based. Traditional parties do not have 'branches' or 'sections': landowners and their subordinates *are* the articulation of the party at the local level. Similarly, a party can be inextensive if it relies heavily on a parent group, ethnic or religious, and even, at least in the early years, on a trade union.

There are substantial differences among extensive parties. Communist parties have always been the most extensive of all; Christian and socialist parties are usually more extensive than conservative parties in western countries, although in northern and central Europe all parties have tended to be very extensive. In France and in North America, on the other hand, parties have always been less extensive (Frears, 1977). In general, authoritarian conservative parties are less extensive than populist and other left-wing parties, often because they can rely on the social structure. Generally speaking, the more a party challenges the goals of the society, the more it will tend to be extensive. Finally, extensiveness varies from area to area: a party may have the support of a particular group in some areas while trying to implant itself elsewhere.

## *Centralization and decentralization*

Party centralization relates to the extent to which decision making takes place at different levels. Parties which have at least a minimum of extensiveness have at least two levels of activity: central and local. More generally, many parties have four levels of activity: national, regional (provincial or 'state' in a federation), local (town, constituency or district), and precinct, branch, section or cell. The lowest level is usually not very important from the point of view of decision making. Thus the question of centralization relates principally to the second (regional) and third (local) levels. Although systematic empirical evidence is still lacking, parties endowed with a strong second (regional) level seem to be more decentralized than parties not so endowed. Where the provincial (or regional) element is weak and the local element is the stronger of the two, the party is likely to be centralized: American, German and Swiss parties are more decentralized than British or French parties, for instance.

The question of centralization and of decentralization does not have a territorial dimension only: functional decentralization commonly exists and takes the form of special organizations for women, young people, trade unionists, students, etc. However, functionally decentralized organs are typically weaker than territorial organs of decentralization, probably because so much of political life (in particular, elections) is territorial. Functional organs thus tend to be ancillary and peripheral, and may even exist only on paper. This appears to be the case even when the party makes a special effort to implant its functional organs: for instance, in communist parties, 'factory cells' were set up, but they were not, despite many efforts, as strong as territorial units.

Parties can be ranked along a dimension of centralization–decentralization:

- Authoritarian parties (of the right or left) are more likely to be centralised than liberal democratic parties, whatever formal structure each of them adopts: western European parties, for instance, are rather decentralized compared to parties in populist or communist countries.
- Centralization increases with the programmatic character of the party within each of the categories.
- Centralization is affected by the type of broad communal group on which the party is based: parties based on clientele or ethnic groups are likely to be less centralized than parties based on churches or class. Thus parties which started from ethnic organizations, like American parties, are more decentralized than parties such as socialist parties which were based, originally at least, on trade unions; parties based on churches, such as Christian Democratic parties, constitute intermediate cases.

### Ideological aspects of structure

The organization of parties raises the question of the extent of democracy, which is itself connected to the extent of centralization, since decentralization might be regarded as a means of enabling the rank and file to exercise some influence. However, a traditional conservative party may be decentralized and yet be undemocratic, since decisions taken at the intermediate echelons are likely to be taken by small oligarchies.

Moreover, paradoxically, democratic goals in a party may militate against a democratic structure because this will result in more demands coming from the rank and file, and therefore in more representativeness. Thus a party with programmatic aims – one which wishes to mobilize the population – may well experience internal difficulties. In order to appear to resolve the contradiction, parties of the left, and primarily parties of the authoritarian left (populist and communist), but even to an extent social democratic parties, have developed a theory of representation which has been known in the Communist world as *democratic centralism*. Policies are presented to the lower echelons for discussion before the decision is taken, but decisions arrived at (presumably on a majority basis) must not only be obeyed, but must be actively and positively accepted by all. This was felt to have the effect of preserving the principle of democracy in the context of a mobilizing ideology, although the reality may be different, and has been in communist systems.

Overall, taking together questions of extensiveness, of centralization and of internal democracy, the main characteristics of structure, over time, are the following:

- The extensiveness of parties is in part related to the type of social environment in which the party developed, and the extent of centralization is also related to the type of social structure.

- As the society and the political system change over time, parties which have remained in existence over a long period tend to see their structure modified.
- Among liberal democratic parties, the more conservative and the more progressive have become more alike, in that the former have spread their tentacles and become more centralized, while the latter have become less characterized by 'democratic centralism'.
- The very inextensive parties of traditional countries have, more often than not, been replaced by more extensive populist parties, but in some cases, they have themselves become more extensive in the same way as many western conservative parties did in the early part of the twentieth century.
- Meanwhile, among populist parties, those which have remained in existence for long periods, such as the Mexican PRI, have also become more decentralized and probably also more representative.

## External aspects of party structures

### Members and supporters

Parties wish to affect the environment: they therefore need to be related to the rest of the society. This takes place through various circles of supporters. The large majority of parties now have 'members' in the strict sense of the word – that is, persons who are legally within the party – while supporters are only psychologically tied to the organization. Although this distinction is often more apparent than real, it was previously given considerable prominence. For instance, Duverger defined as 'mass parties' those based on members, while 'cadre parties' were clientelistic, this contrast being viewed as explaining the difference between modern and non-modern parties, both in modern and in non-modern societies (Duverger, 1954: 62–90; Blondel, 1969: 117–26).

The distinction is too rigid. An index of 'massness' based on the percentage of card-carrying members among the electors of a party is of little significance, since some parties which do not define members in this way, such as American parties, do not then qualify as mass parties (Epstein, 1967: 98–129). The distinction also exaggerates the importance given to members, most of whom play a small, if not almost wholly insignificant part. Membership is not a sign of participation; it means an association of a tenuous kind. It reflects attitudes more than behaviour, while it also measures the ability of the organization to attract sums of money by putting canvassers and other helpers in the field (Bartolini, 1983: 182–91).

As a matter of fact, membership should be understood as being part of the broader linkage between parties and their supporters. It is a legal manifestation of a wider notion of *party identification*. This concept suggests that there exists a natural and perhaps permanent allegiance to the political party, like the adhesion to a church, an adhesion which is part of the socialization process. This adhesion will indeed be natural and long lasting if the party is legitimate: that is to say, if its supporters are directly related to it. Thus, rather than look at proportions of members, it is more critical to

## BOX 9.2
## The ambiguity of the concept of party membership

There has always been a major ambiguity about the concept of party membership. Socialist parties gave considerable weight to the idea at the end of the nineteenth century; other parties did not, or followed more or less reluctantly. Hence many difficulties which have continued to this day about what party members are supposed to be.

For socialists, membership was regarded as central to the concept of party. A democratic party should have large numbers of members; indeed, ideally, everyone who voted for the party should be a member. This was not only in order to increase party funds; it was also, and even more, because party programmes should be given a seal of 'democratic authenticity' by being approved by those who formed the party, if not directly, at least by their representatives at party congresses. For socialists, a party which had few members and a large electoral following was therefore likely to be an oligarchical body of a traditional kind.

Communist leaders quickly saw that this socialist vision was utopian. Most people were 'unconscious'; they did not realize that they should join the party. Communists therefore took the opposite view and claimed that only an élite could be members of the party. One became a party member after having proved one's worth. This enabled communist leaders to maintain their hold on their party and avoid conflicts within it.

Meanwhile, other western parties, especially conservative and liberal parties, but also Christian parties, continued to have a small or at least a limited membership. This did not diminish their electoral successes. As a matter of fact, they seemed more in tune with general feelings, since they seemed to consider that the function of elections was to choose among contenders. Citizens were viewed essentially as observers of the political game. In this interpretation, membership is somewhat redundant.

The ambiguity is not resolved. There are party members in socialist parties as well as in many other parties of the centre and right, especially in Scandinavia and some continental countries. These, however, are far from constituting a majority of the voters of these parties; most of them are also generally rather inactive. They are *identifiers* rather than genuine activists. In other parties, there are few members, but many identifiers: in the United States, there are no members at all, although identifiers are numerous. The ambiguity is not likely to be resolved soon, except by a gradual and sometimes rapid decline in the number of party members.

find the proportion of *identifiers* in the party (Campbell *et al.*, 1960: 120–67; Budge *et al.*, 1976).

One can return at this point to the distinction made by Duverger between 'cadre' and 'mass' parties. When a party draws support from the population indirectly, through the allegiance that members have to the groups which have helped to constitute the party, there is no 'massness' at the basis of party support. Such a party may not be unstable if the group – tribal, ethnic, religious or even class based – on which the party is based is legitimate; but it does not have legitimacy as such and, more specifically, 'mass legitimacy'. What is therefore crucial is whether the party has direct mass support or whether a group is the link in the chain: on this, and not on the existence or non-existence of legal membership, rests the distinction between mass parties and other parties.

A party is of a legitimate mass type if it does not need to rely on one or more communal groups for support. This legitimate mass character develops gradually, as more and more supporters identify with the party directly and cease to use the 'parent' communal group as their reference point. As a result, the development of legitimate mass parties is a sign that political life is increasingly autonomous, and probably also increasingly national in character.

Legitimate mass parties emerge typically in a context of natural party development. Attempts are often made to develop party identification in order to strengthen the party and the regime in the context of imposed parties. This process is obviously slow: the basic lack of legitimacy of the political system as a whole makes for a limited insertion of the party members into the community. Thus such parties are rarely of a true 'mass' type, even if membership figures are high. Communist parties had large memberships; yet they collapsed. Some African populist parties had extremely high numbers of members; yet they were often shown to have little support. Indeed, membership is sometimes high in order to help the party to proselytize among the population. As a result, in these parties, one can sharply distinguish members from supporters. Basic party organizations (the 'cells' of communist parties) are also more closed than the branches or sections of legitimate mass parties. Gradually, the party may become legitimate mass, but for this to occur the distance between members and supporters needs to be reduced, and, in reality, the concept of membership needs to lose its clear and sharp character.

## Associated groups

Socialist parties are sometimes singled out as being closely linked with groups and associations. Duverger does indeed feel the distinction to be of sufficient importance to warrant the dichotomy between 'direct' and 'indirect' parties being applied to parties on the basis of whether their membership comes from individual members only or from groups, such as trade unions and co-operatives – a good example being that of the British Labour Party (Duverger, 1954: 5–17). In reality, the association with groups is general and it is a two-way process, from groups to parties and from parties to groups:

- We know that parties become legitimate by being supported by a broad group of a communal character, but that the association gradually becomes less close and that, at the limit, wholly legitimate parties cease to have any 'special' relationship with any group.

- Conversely, imposed political systems often create parties and groups in order to spread their goals and increase the support which they enjoy, the function of general propaganda being mainly exercised by the party, while the (dependent) groups deal, for instance, with special sections of the population, such as women and the young. If the party (and the political system) become more open, these subsidiary groups also become less dependent on the party.
- Meanwhile, dependent associations may also be created by a party which wishes to free itself from the broad communal group from which it emerged: this occurred in western socialist and Christian parties, for instance. There is then a double linkage – between communal group and party (which declines) and between party and dependent associations (which may be strong for at least a period).

This criss-crossing of associations and of patterns of allegiance has to be related to the extent of conflict in the society, which, as we saw, is one of the reasons why parties exist. Overall, as parties become more legitimate, they become more independent from the broad communal groups, but the associations dependent on the parties also tend to acquire more autonomy. However, when there is no, or little, conflict of goals in the political system, the dependence of groups on political parties and of parties on groups is small. Where the conflict of goals is sharper, parties are likely to be based at least to an extent on broad communal groups, while they will also create dependent associations, especially if they want to proselytize and mobilize the population.

We can then now describe the relationship between groups and parties in the five types of polity which were identified in the course of Chapter 8.

Traditional conservative parties are dependent upon broad communal groups, mainly of the clientele or ethnic types (though perhaps in some cases on religious groups as well). Only if a conflict of goals emerges will they set up dependent associations; by then the parties may well have become legitimate. In practice, they are more likely to have been superseded by populist or authoritarian inegalitarian parties. This has been the fate of many traditional conservative parties in Latin America: for instance, in Brazil in the early postwar period.

Liberal democratic parties grow through a process of legitimization which places them near the legitimate mass end of the dimension. They may have developed in a context in which conflicts of goals are relatively low; in this case, dependent organizations are not set up. They may alternatively have developed in a context in which conflicts are higher; in such a case, dependent organizations are likely to be created. The first situation corresponds to that of the American parties and of those conservative and liberal parties which became legitimate before class-based groups succeeded in becoming important (Britain in particular). The second corresponds to that of most western European parties. One can see why not only socialist parties, but also Christian parties depend on the broad communal groups which helped to make them legitimate. Moreover, the higher the conflict, the more there will be a criss-crossing of group–party special relationships. When conflicts over long-term goals diminish (as is at present the case in western Europe), these special relationships also tend to diminish. The ties between socialist parties or Christian parties and the communal groups from which they originated, as well as the dependent associations which they created, become looser.

The three groups of authoritarian parties vary depending on the extent to which they propose to introduce new goals and on the extent to which they are legitimate. A populist party such as the Mexican PRI is more legitimate than, for instance, most African parties, and the various associations which are linked to it are also relatively less dependent on it. In general, the more 'progressive' the party goals, the higher the dependence of associations, as the need to proselytize and to mobilize is strongly felt, provided levels of legitimacy are about the same.

## Leadership patterns

Party leaders are, or may be in the future, national leaders; more exceptionally, they were national leaders in the past. Thus, not surprisingly, there are relationships and there is often mutual reinforcement between party leadership and national leadership. But there are also relationships between party leadership and party structure. Indeed, they influence each other in a number of complex ways.

Classifications of leadership have been based, for many decades, on Weber's distinction among three types of authority – traditional, bureaucratic-legalistic and charismatic – the latter being more properly referred to, in the reality of political life, as personalized leadership (Weber, 1968: vol. I, 215–16). These are, of course, ideal-types and, in political situations and especially in modern political and party situations, mixed types are most frequent.

### *Traditional leadership*

Given the decline of traditional party structures in the contemporary world, traditional leadership has also declined; it has not disappeared altogether, however. Many leaders, including those of political parties, owe part of their political power to the traditional influence they hold: for instance, to the status of their family in their district. Even at present, the influence of aristocratic leaders is substantial in some Third World and in some western parties. More widespread, however, is the occurrence of a relatively limited local following embedded in the social structure. Thus doctors, lawyers, middle-sized farmers or industrialists enjoy an advantage in standing for political office in the West, especially in the less industrialized areas or where the population is less mobile. The same is true, and indeed to an even greater extent, in many countries of the Third World, and not only in those which are conservative. However, only in about a dozen countries, mostly located in Central America and in western and south-eastern Asia, does the *top* leadership rely primarily on the authority given by traditional social relationships; and this number is slowly declining.

### *Bureaucratic-legalistic leadership*

Leaders are said to be of a bureaucratic-legalistic type when they are professional politicians who have moved gradually within the party hierarchy on the basis of their talent. This type is widespread in the contemporary world in western liberal democracies; it has been characteristic of communist parties; and it does exist to an extent in the Third World.

In most western countries, and in the other parts of the world where socioeconomic developments have followed western lines (Japan, Australasia and Israel), most parties have been established for long periods – usually for at least half a century and sometimes longer. In these cases, the person or persons holding the position of leader, chairman, president or secretary-general have typically made their career in the party: their appointment to the top crowns that career, and the position gives the recipient the authority to act and be followed.

The situation is or was somewhat similar in communist parties. The vastness of the party organization entailed that those in charge at the various echelons of the party be endowed with an authority stemming from the position which these leaders held.

In the Third World, there is bureaucratic-legalistic leadership where parties have existed for a substantial period. It is therefore in the better-established parties of the Commonwealth, particularly in the West Indies, east Africa and southern Asia, as well as in some Latin American parties (for instance, in the Mexican PRI), that one finds most instances of this type of leadership.

### Charismatic leadership

The idea of charismatic leadership has been typically associated with parties in the developing countries, as well as to an extent with those of communist states. In the West, on the other hand, it seems to occur less frequently and indeed almost exclusively in periods of major political, social or economic upheaval.

In the West, therefore, the depression of the 1930s and the Second World War did create situations of this kind, as did decolonization in the 1940s and 1950s in France: forms of personalized leadership have thus emerged in Italy, Germany and France. To a lesser extent, a similar development took place in Britain when Churchill came to power more as a personalized leader than as a loyal member of the Conservative Party. On the other hand, in general, since politics in western countries is typically stable and parties, too, remain stable, pure personalized leadership usually plays a minor part.

Admittedly, less marked forms of personalization are often present. Indeed, it is sometimes claimed that this element is increasing, in particular as a result of media influence; firm evidence to sustain this view is lacking, however. Reagan and Thatcher had a personal following, for instance, but so did F.D. Roosevelt and Lloyd George earlier in the twentieth century, and Disraeli and Gladstone in the nineteenth century. Moreover, even when western leaders have a personal following, their power may not be increased as a result: despite his relative 'charisma', President Kennedy was less successful in policy making than President Johnson, who was not so endowed.

Personalized leadership is or was widespread in communist states, although this may not seem consistent with communist ideology, since Marxism is based on the primacy of the 'underlying forces' in society and denies the strength of personalities as real engines of history. Despite repeated assertions that 'collective leadership' was to be established, communist leadership in Europe and Asia was often markedly highly personalized, as the cases of Lenin, Stalin, Khrushchev, Tito, Mao Tse-tung and many others indicate. This is due in part, but only in part, to the fact that many communist regimes were installed after successful resistance against an enemy or after victory in an internal war. However, the dictatorial character of the regime also had a significant part to play.

In the Third World, personalized leadership has also been widespread as a result of wars of, or at least struggles for, independence. This has been especially the case in Africa (Jackson and Rosberg, 1982). The development of charismatic leadership has also been helped by the spread of presidential systems, especially in Latin America. Moreover, military rule has been a way of building up forms of personal following. Yet personalized leadership has often been unstable, while in some Third World countries, especially in the Commonwealth, and in a number of Latin American countries, such as Venezuela, Colombia and Costa Rica, party leadership has been bureaucratic-legalistic rather than charismatic.

### Leaders and the strengthening of political parties

Throughout the Third World, though to a greater extent in Africa and Asia than in Latin America, strong leaders have created political parties. In perhaps a third of the countries of the world, political life in general, and the party system in particular, would be different if parties had not been created by a powerful leader. This has been the case in Egypt, Zaire, Tanzania, Zambia, Kenya and the Ivory Coast, for example.

However, it is sometimes difficult to disentangle party strength from leader strength. First, the extent and effectiveness of many of these leader-based parties is often in doubt, as the collapse of such parties in many countries, especially in Africa south of the Sahara, shows. But it is also the case that, in these countries, not just the parties but also the state are recent creations. Overall, one can gauge this strength at least to an extent by examining the respective fates of parties created in the postwar period. Out of 64 countries where a party was created by the deliberate action of a leader, usually in the late 1950s or early 1960s, the leader and his party had been toppled by a coup in 21 cases by 1990. In 18, the leader was still in power in 1990, while in the remaining 25, the disappearance of the leader (by death or succession) was followed by the maintenance of the party at least as an important force in the community. Assuming that leaders who remained in office were somewhat stronger than those who were deposed, we may conclude that the contribution of leaders to the creation of effective political parties has been significant in a substantial number of countries of the Third World.

The setting-up of new states can be regarded as exceptional, however, although this process has been continuing throughout the whole of the second half of the twentieth century. If we consider the more 'normal' case of older states, those of western Europe and Latin America in particular, we do find that some new parties have been set up with the help of a highly personalized leader. In Western Europe, the main examples are those of France (the Gaullist Party in the 1950s), Adenauer's Germany (the Christlich-Demokratische Union (CDU) in the late 1940s) and De Gasperi's Italy (Christian Democracy in 1945), although one might also wish to add Greece, Spain and Portugal to the list. In Latin America, at least four parties (the Peronist Party in Argentina, the Venezuelan Accion Democratica, Alianza Popular Revolucionaria Americana (APRA) in Peru, and Movimiento Nacionalista Revolucionario (MNR) in Bolivia) owe their existence to a leader and have survived that leader, despite military coups. This does suggest that a small, but significant number of parties are successfully created in every generation by the action of leaders.

Leaders can also help to strengthen an existing party, although this, too, is difficult to ascertain. In the West and in the Third World, a number of these leaders markedly helped the fate of the parties which they led, Brandt in the case of the German Socialist Party, Mrs Thatcher in the case of the British Conservative Party, Mitterrand in the case of the French Socialist Party, Mrs Gandhi in the case of the Indian Congress Party (despite its splits) being among the best-known examples. On the other hand, there are also numerous examples of leaders who weakened a rather strong party. Overall, therefore, the influence of party leaders on party development is significant, though, as Weber would have suggested, it is in periods of upheaval that such an influence is most pronounced.

## Overview

Political parties are a key feature of modern societies. They are associational groups with goals covering all aspects of social life and potentially open to all citizens.

They have three main functions, those of articulating societal conflicts by creating links (in both directions) between people and government, of formulating policies or helping to transmit policies to the government, and of recruiting the bulk of the political élite.

Parties need *legitimacy* to make an impact. They can acquire it *naturally* from a communal group, tribal, ethnic, religious or class based. They can also be *imposed* on the society with the help of the power of the state also, thanks to the popularity of their leaders.

In the West, liberal democratic parties prevail, despite ideological differences. These parties have remained stable, in the main, at least during most of the second half of the twentieth century. Large communist parties in eastern Europe and part of Asia have turned out to be markedly less strong than they had been said to be for a long time. In the Third World, liberal democratic parties exist in some countries, but the majority of States have had authoritarian, populist or near-communist parties; these have typically not been able to remain in existence for substantial periods.

Party *structure* varies markedly, from being *extensive* to being tiny, from being *centralized* to being highly decentralized, and from being relatively *democratic* to being highly autocratic (as several early theorists of parties had claimed). Liberal democratic parties tend to be relatively extensive and somewhat decentralized, while practising some degree of internal democracy. These last two characteristics are markedly less common in other types of party.

The strength of parties is given not so much by the proportion of members, but by the extent to which there is widespread *party identification*.

The relationship between parties and *associated groups* is important. Nascent or less-established parties need groups to support them (and in the case of imposed parties, they need the state itself). Better-established parties are more autonomous. Both types can and do also set up dependent associations.

The *leadership* of well-established parties has tended to be of a *professional and bureaucratic-legalistic* type. *Personalized* or even *charismatic* leadership is more characteristic of new or of imposed parties.

The problem of the 'weight' and maintenance of parties in political systems is manifestly serious in new countries, and in imposed systems in general. It has also become more serious in western countries than in the 1960s and 1970s. This is due in part to the fact that societal constraints on parties appear to have increased, while many party systems at least are in a state of flux. We therefore need to examine parties in the context of the systems in which they operate before attempting to assess their strength and, therefore, their future.

## Further reading

The number of studies on political parties is vast, although there is still no general world-wide classic on these organizations. There was perhaps even more general interest at earlier periods than recently. The three 'classics' on political parties are those of M. Ostrogorski, *Democracy and the Organization of Political Parties* (1902), R. Michels, *Political Parties* (1968) and M. Duverger, *Political Parties*, first published in French in 1951 and in English in 1954. Duverger's is the only truly cross-national, though within the context of Atlantic and communist countries only (with occasional references to Latin America, Turkey and Israel). A massive cross-national study of party ideology can be found in K. Janda, *Political Parties: A Cross-National Survey* (1980). A more recent presentation of the role of parties and the relationship between structure and role can be found in A. Panebianco, *Political Parties* (1988).

The basic characteristics of parties across the world, as they were in the late 1970s, are given in A.J. Day and H.W. Degenhardt, *Political Parties of the World* (1980). Comparisons about party structures in the West can be found in L. Epstein, *Political Parties in Western Democracies* (1967). A massive compendium on the organization of western parties can be found in R.S. Katz and P. Mair, *Party Organisations: A Data Handbook on Party Organisations in Western Democracies, 1960–90* (1992).

On Christian democracy, see R.E.M. Irving, *The Christian Democratic Parties of Western Europe* (1979); on social democratic parties, see W.E. Patterson and A.H. Thomas, eds., *The Future of Social Democracy* (1986). On the main parties in the Third World, see V. Randall, ed. *Political Parties in the Third World* (1988). On Latin America, see R.J. Alexander, *Latin American Political Parties* (1973) and *Political Parties in the Americas: Canada, Latin America, and the West Indies* (1982). On current developments in eastern Europe and the successor states of the Soviet Union, see B. Szajkowski, *New Political Parties of Eastern Europe and the Soviet Union* (1991).

No comprehensive study of party members and of the liveliness of party organizations, even relating only to western Europe, has so far been published. Some evidence about trends can be found from national monographs. A systematic examination of membership of socialist parties was undertaken by S. Bartolini, 'The membership of mass parties: the social democratic experience, 1889–1978', in H. Daalder and P. Mair, eds., *Western European Party Systems* (1983). For an examination of party identification, see A. Campbell *et al.*, *The American Voter* (1960). The concept has been used since in connection with European countries. See in particular, I. Budge *et al.*, eds., *Party Identification and Beyond* (1976).

Weber's main concern has been with leadership, and not directly with parties; his presentation of three types of leadership has been seminal for subsequent studies on parties. See, in particular, *The Theory of Social and Economic Organisation* (1947) and *Basic Concepts in Sociology* (1962). For a typology of leadership in the Third World, see T.H. Jackson and C.G. Rosberg, *Personal Rule in Black Africa* (1982).

# 10

# Party systems

## Introduction

Parties do not exist in isolation: they are parts and thus relate to each other (Sartori, 1976: 4–11). The character and strength of each part cannot be fully understood without taking into account the character and strength of other parts. This is obvious in the case of systems of more than one party, but it is even true in single-party systems: although only one party officially exists or at least dominates, alongside this 'single' party, there are other parties. Sometimes they are forgotten because they are small and insignificant; but sometimes they have a large following and are repressed because they constitute a threat to those who are in power.

The basic distinction to be made among party systems therefore seems to be that between single-party systems and systems of more than one party, the first type being characterized by the repression of competition, the second by the recognition of competition. This contrast is indeed broadly valid, but it needs to be looked at more closely, since the extent to which competition is repressed or recognised may vary sharply. Moreover, there are also polities without parties. In some of these, parties are totally prohibited; in others, parties have not yet emerged – they are *pre-party* systems rather than regimes in which parties are repressed.

The second half of the twentieth century has been a period of political upheaval. This is in part because the number of independent states has more than doubled in 50 years; it is also because most of the older countries – in Latin America and eastern Europe in particular – have undergone major regime changes, sometimes more than once. In the process, party systems have been markedly affected in several ways:

- The number of 'pre-party' systems has diminished, both in absolute terms and even more in proportion.
- Single-party systems have been popular for a while, not just in eastern Europe and in what was the Soviet Union, but also in the Third World, especially in Africa south of the Sahara, in the Middle East and in north Africa.

- Especially from the late 1960s, the military took over the government in many countries.
- This meant that systems of more than one party were in decline during much of the period, since they were regarded as too western and as unable to bring about societal change. However, they have made a comeback since the mid-1980s, first in Latin America, then in eastern Europe, Asia and Africa, at the expense both of military regimes which prohibited parties altogether and of single-party systems.

In the course of this chapter, we shall analyze types of party system and the dynamics of these systems.

- First, we shall briefly consider the cases in which *no parties* exist or are allowed.
- Second, we shall turn to *single-party systems*. We shall assess the extent to which repression varies in these systems, and examine their likely future in the light of their decline in both communist and non-communist regimes.
- Third, we shall discuss the *characteristics of competition* in systems of more than one party.
- Fourth, we shall examine *stable systems* of more than one party: that is to say, principally those of western Europe and of North America.
- Fifth, we shall consider the past development and the prospects of the large number of *unstable or new systems* of more than one party.

In undertaking this examination, we need to remember that the *number* of parties is not the only element to be taken into consideration in order to describe party systems: we already pointed out that repression can be more or less severe in single-party systems, for instance. This is because the elements which we analyzed in Chapter 9 – social bases, ideology and structure – play an important part in shaping the character of party systems. We shall therefore refer to these elements throughout this chapter.

## Systems without parties

Some countries *never had any parties at all*. These regimes have become exceptional, since they require that traditional communal groups, such as tribes or clans, are still strong enough to control the whole of political life. By the end of the twentieth century this is hardly likely, except in small or isolated polities. There were about a dozen countries in this category in the mid-1990s, half of which were rich Gulf States, Saudi Arabia being by far the largest in the group. In other countries belonging previously to this category, such as Ethiopia, Afghanistan and Libya, the traditional regime was toppled and a party system, typically a single-party system, was introduced.

Meanwhile, *military regimes* which officially abolished parties were established in many countries of the Third World. Typically, there were about two dozen of them at any one time in the 1970s and early 1980s, mostly in Africa, Latin America and the Middle East. But these regimes have been unstable: after a few years they have tended to be toppled in turn, or have had to be 'civilianized': for instance, by setting up parties. From the late 1980s, their decline became so rapid that only about half a dozen were

**Table 10.1** Party systems across the world in 1994

| | No party | | Fully one party | One party dominant | More than one party | Civil war | Total |
|---|---|---|---|---|---|---|---|
| | Traditional | Military | | | | | |
| Atlantic | – | – | – | – | 23 | – | 23 |
| Eastern Europe and northern Asia | – | – | 8 | 6 | 18 | 1 | 33 |
| Middle East and northern Africa | 7 | – | 2 | 4 | 7 | 1 | 21 |
| South and south-east Asia | 5 | 1 | 1 | 1 | 16 | – | 24 |
| Africa south of Sahara | 1 | 4 | 7 | 18 | 14 | 4 | 48 |
| Caribbean, Central and South America | – | 1 | 1 | 4 | 27 | – | 33 |
| Total | 13 | 6 | 19 | 33 | 105 | 6 | 182 |
| Percentage 1994 | 7 | 3 | 10 | 19 | 57 | 3 | 99 |
| 1989 | 9 | 7 | 39 | | 45 | – | ·00 |

left by the mid-1990s, most of which were in Africa south of the Sahara. This may be a temporary fall, however, as previous experience showed the ups and downs of such regimes to be cyclical.

## Single-party systems

### Panorama of single-party systems

Single-party systems have also declined markedly in number in the 1990s. In the late 1980s, two-fifths of the world polities were single-party systems; by the mid-1990s, this proportion had been reduced to under a third. Thus a 30-year trend was reversed, the proportion of single-party systems having increased steadily over the postwar period, especially in the early decades.

Of the 77 countries which existed in 1945, 23 were single-party systems (just under 30 per cent) in the late 1940s (including six eastern European countries in which the single-party system was introduced between 1945 and 1949); between 1950 and 1989 the net growth of single-party systems was 41 countries or 10 per cent.

However, this growth coincided with a change in the character of single-party systems during the intervening period. In the late 1940s, single-party systems were either communist – 13 out of 23 – or authoritarian conservative, as in Spain, Portugal and Taiwan; a populist system such as that of Mexico was exceptional. Two decades later, the number of populist single-party systems became large, especially in Africa south of the Sahara. There were ups and downs: many single-party systems were toppled by the military from the mid-1960s onwards. A coup in Ghana in 1966 started the trend, with coups subsequently taking place in Uganda, Burkina Faso, Mali, Niger, Mauritania, Rwanda, Equatorial Guinea, Burundi and Guinea. There were also returns to single-party rule, however, often prompted by military leaders who were themselves anxious to acquire legitimacy.

Single-party systems have been found essentially in central and northern Asia, where they are what remains of the large 'communist bloc' of the postwar period, in Africa south of the Sahara, where up to two-thirds of the states were single-party systems in the 1980s, and in the Middle East and northern Africa, where the proportion of single-party systems is smaller but has changed little in the 1980s and 1990s. On the other hand, there are no single-party systems in the Atlantic area (Portugal and Spain became systems of more than one party in the mid-1970s) and very few in south and south-east Asia, in the Caribbean and Latin America (Mexico and Cuba being the two main cases in that area).

Thus communist regimes have constituted typically only a minority of the single-party systems, even if one includes among them countries such as Ethiopia or the ex-Portuguese colonies (Angola and Mozambique, for instance), which adopted a Marxist ideology for a period. Single-party systems are none the less often regarded as being essentially a communist country phenomenon. There is some justification in this impression, since communist systems are those which both elaborated the theory and implemented the practice of single-party rule most systematically. The nature of the communist ideology, combined with the concept of the 'vanguard of the proletariat', placed the (single) party at the centre of the political system, while the organs of the state (government, legislature, local bodies) were reduced to a dependent position. Such a 'total' conception of the single-party system has given communist regimes a special character.

However, communist systems were not alone in 'inventing' the model of the single-party system in the early part of the twentieth century. The conservative inegalitarian version was developed and indeed implemented by Italian fascism and German Nazism in the interwar period; these were imitated in turn by a number of European rulers, especially in Portugal and Spain where a fascist-type single-party system remained in existence until the 1970s. Meanwhile, Turkey had a 'populist' single-party system after the First World War, and this example was followed by Mexico, which was to have the most successful single-party system of the non-communist world. Thus, although the communist ideology was a crucial element in the development of the theory and practice of single-party systems, both that theory and that practice were also developed on the basis of different ideologies (Sartori, 1976: 39–51; Holmes, 1986: 96–118; Philip, 1988: 99–112).

## What is a single-party system?

The distinction between systems without parties, single-party systems, and systems of more than one party is important; however, it is not altogether clear-cut. First, there is a gradation between a full and complete single-party system, and a system in which one party is so dominant that the other organizations are, for practical purposes, irrelevant, although they exist. Indeed, the 'border area' is or has been occupied by a substantial number of countries, from Mexico to Egypt, from Nicaragua to Taiwan, and from Madagascar to Singapore. Second, the distinction between single-party systems and systems without parties is also somewhat imprecise. The extent to which a system can be defined as 'single party' depends on the *effective part* which that party plays in political and social life. In a number of cases – in Africa south of the Sahara, for instance – the single party is little more than a formal organization set up by a national leader and designed to give some credibility to a regime. Not surprisingly, a party of this kind is rather shaky and can easily be abolished if the military intervenes.

Thus, even if we have to describe these systems as single party for practical purposes, we must recognize that the lines which are drawn are somewhat arbitrary, both between single-party systems and systems without parties, and between single-party systems and systems of more than one party. On this understanding, we shall define as single party, systems in which one party exists alone or dominates the country in terms of votes or of seats in the legislature, a realistic cut-off point being 80 per cent of the votes or of the seats in at least two elections. This will exclude freak results, such as that of 1986 in Jamaica when one of the two main parties did not contest the election at all. A forced coalition of a number of parties obtaining 80 per cent of the votes or of the seats, as was the case for decades in some communist states, such as East Germany,

Poland and Czechoslovakia, should also be regarded as constituting a single-party system.

## Types of single-party systems

Given this definition, one can distinguish among three types of single-party system. There are single-party systems by *constitutional or legal rule*. This was the case of the Soviet Union and of the large majority of communist states, from Yugoslavia to North Korea and from Cuba to Vietnam, where the party had (and sometimes still has) a formal *monopoly* of representation and mobilization of the population: other political organizations are prohibited. Technically, this situation contrasted with the enforced coalition arrangements which, as we noted, existed in some communist states; in practice, the communist party controlled these countries effectively alone and rigidly. These cases have none the less sometimes been described as 'hegemonic' rather than 'monocentrist' (Wiatr, 1964: 281–90).

Legally enforced single-party systems did not exist only in communist or near-communist states, such as Ethiopia or the ex-Portuguese colonies, which adopted for a while a fully Marxist system of government. They were also set up in some other African countries, conservative and 'progressive', such as Zaire and Malawi. In these cases, the conception of the party was in some cases very different from that prevailing in communist countries: in Malawi and Zaire every citizen was obliged to be a member of the party.

Second, single-party systems arise as a result of *extra-constitutional repression of the opposition*. This form of single-party system has been widespread, and has often been the prelude to the introduction of a legal prohibition, as in Kenya, Zambia and Zimbabwe. The opposition is repressed and forced party mergers may occur, as in East Germany in the late 1940s between the socialist and communist parties, and in some African states. The most successful example of a single-party system by extra-constitutional means is that of the PRI of Mexico, which managed to remain the overwhelmingly dominant force for half a century without the country ever being, legally, single party: the other parties simply happened to have little chance at the polls, at least until the 1990s (P. Smith, 1979: 49–62; Philip, 1988: 99–112).

The third type of single-party system has a *natural character*, when, without any repression, a party is the dominant force in the country, and the pressure that is exercised is of a 'cultural' rather than of a political or legal kind. This type of natural single-party system was common in parts of Latin America in the past; it has become rare, except in small states, such as in the Caribbean or in the Pacific. The 'natural' type of single-party system still exists at the sub-national level, however, including in western countries: the large dominance of the Democratic party in some of the southern states of the United States had this character, as did the dominance of conservative or socialist parties respectively in some remote and in some traditional industrial areas of Europe. Gradually, however, a more competitive system tends to develop in these areas (Polsby, 1962: 144–68).

## Differences among single-party systems

### Differences in policy goals

There are major differences in the policy goals put forward by the single party in single-party systems, as is suggested by the fact that Nazi Germany, fascist Italy and communist states were all single-party systems. If one refers to the three dimensions of goals which were described in Chapter 3 (participation, means of intervention and socioeconomic aims), single-party systems correspond to almost every goal, except true fully fledged liberalism – although, even in this respect, the extent of repression which takes place in single-party systems varies appreciably.

As we noted, the best-known single-party systems of the postwar period have been the communist systems. Their goals are or were authoritarian, relatively participationist and egalitarian, although there have been differences both among eastern European countries before the collapse of communism in 1989 and in Asia since that point, with China having moved appreciably in the direction of a market economy.

Alongside communist countries, the majority of single-party systems propounded a variety of other goals, specifically traditional conservative, authoritarian-inegalitarian and populist, this last category being the largest of the three.

Traditional conservative single-party systems have become relatively rare, both because there is widespread emphasis on development in the contemporary world, and because such single-party systems are unlikely to be able, over time, to prevent the emergence of opposition parties unless they increase repression and thus in part change their goals. The best examples are dominant single-party systems in small and isolated countries, or at a sub-national level (as in Nigerian regions in the early 1960s, shortly after independence).

Traditional single-party systems of the dominant variety have thus tended often to become authoritarian-inegalitarian. This group is appreciably smaller than in the interwar period, when fascist and Nazi regimes were in the ascendant, or from the 1940s to the 1960s: a number of Central American and South American republics (El Salvador, Honduras, Nicaragua, Paraguay) were then ruled by authoritarian-inegalitarian single-party systems for long periods. By the 1980s, the group included primarily remnants of the past, such as the fully fledged single-party system of Malawi or the dominant authoritarian-inegalitarian single-party systems of Paraguay and Taiwan, although, even in these cases, there has been a move away from the very repressive form of single-party system since the second half of the 1980s.

Thus the largest group of single-party systems is constituted by populist regimes, although these, too, declined in number from the second half of the 1980s. There are still a substantial number of them in Africa south of the Sahara (where almost exactly half the single-party systems can be found). 'Populism' is an umbrella expression, however: the goals of populist single-party systems vary appreciably within the broad framework of development. Some, such as those of the Côte d'Ivoire and Kenya, have come to espouse a 'free enterprise' philosophy; the PRI in Mexico gradually came to have the same aims. Others have stressed their belief in a mixed economy with private business alongside state enterprises: Tunisia has been in this category. Yet others have had more marked 'socialist' goals, though there has been a retreat from these positions since the 1980s: this has been the case with Algeria, Zambia and Tanzania. Finally, a number of regimes are – or claimed for a while to be – Marxist, such as Benin, the Congo and Ethiopia, but these experiments have typically lasted a few years only.

These single-party systems are or were populist because of the stress placed on development; they are or were also populist because importance is given to participation, albeit to a varying degree. Some countries, such as Tanzania, have allowed a multiplicity of candidatures from which electors could choose, though within the party; others have not. The level of repression has also varied: it has been appreciably less severe in some countries (Mexico, Tunisia) than in others (Zaire). There is everywhere a limit to the extent to which opposition is tolerated, however: even in the mildest of populist single-party systems, indeed in the mildest of single-party systems as a whole, some degree of repression does take place. Single-party systems can come relatively close to liberalism, but they cannot practise fully fledged liberalism.

## Differences in bases of support

Single-party systems often lack natural bases of support. This is true even when a tribal or other communal group is behind the party, since other groups may be opposed. Rarely does the territory of a broad communal group coincide exactly with that of the state: this will occur mainly in small countries. When the state is physically larger, there may be a 'regionalization' of party support; but this situation has led to conflicts and even occasionally resulted in secession attempts, as occurred in Zaire and Nigeria in the 1960s. Not surprisingly, traditional single-party systems have been weakened as a result.

Moreover, as we noted, single-party systems have often been set up in order to emphasize development, and have therefore come into conflict with at least some of the pre-existing traditional groups. Thus single-party systems are faced with a dilemma. Either they forge ahead in the direction in which they wish to go, attempt to modify the social structure, and hope to undermine the traditional groups after a period; this will mean relying to an extent on repression. Or they try to accommodate these traditional groups, in which case they will have to modify their policy goals and may even be unable to build a united nation (Apter, 1965: 199–212).

Communist single-party systems are those which pushed furthest in the direction of social change. They endeavoured to break traditional groups; some of them even claimed that they wished to create a 'new man'. These efforts have had to be buttressed by considerable repression; in the eastern European states, occupation by the Soviet Union was, to say the least, a considerable help to regimes which otherwise might not have emerged at all (even in Czechoslovakia, where the Communist Party was strong in free elections in the late 1940s), and which almost certainly would not have lasted. Moreover, communist regimes in Europe and Asia did not have to face the issue of nation building (except in East Germany); indeed, they could bank in some cases on support of a nationalistic character, as in Romania. Nor were they confronted with strong tribal or ethnic groups; only in Poland did they face the organized resistance of the church – a resistance which the United Polish Workers' (i.e. Communist) Party did not succeed in breaking, and which indeed formed the basis of the independent trade union 'Solidarity'. Yet, despite these relative advantages, communist single-party systems did not succeed in achieving the transformations which they hoped for: the 'new man' did not emerge. As liberalization took place, changes in policy goals resulted in a move away from socioeconomic egalitarianism in most cases, the real exception being North Korea, while China oscillated over the period and eventually moved firmly into the 'reformist' camp.

Single-party systems which adopted similar radical aims in Africa south of the Sahara (such as the ex-Portuguese colonies and Ethiopia) have been highly repressive and have even had to fight civil wars, partly at least because the base of support of these regimes was very limited. Yet even the populist systems which adopted less 'progressive' goals have also had major problems of support. Indeed, the opposition of the tribal groups, or at least of some of them, was so strong in some countries that it led to the overthrow of the single party – one of the first and best-known cases of such an overthrow being that of the Convention People's Party of Nkrumah in Ghana in 1966. Several other cases followed: in Burundi, tensions have periodically resulted in major tribal violence; in Uganda, violence was also substantial; even in Zimbabwe and in Zambia, tribal oppositions led to severe repression.

Populist single-party systems which wish to avoid these conflicts have attempted to increase the base of their support by practising a policy of overall 'accommodation'. There is less repression and the nation-building process may be less impeded; but this may also mean that the party becomes gradually dominated by traditional tribal groups and thus loses sight of its modernizing aims. This has been to an extent the history of the Côte d'Ivoire.

Thus single-party systems have considerable difficulty in establishing a support base, even when they emerge from a strong traditional group, unless the society remains static – an unlikely occurrence in the contemporary world. Efforts made to extend this base either lead to major conflicts or entail a degree of 'accommodation' of these groups, which result in modernizing policies being toned down and the goals of the party severely curtailed. The problem of support in single-party systems cannot be avoided: sooner or later, all of them are confronted with it.

## Differences in the structure of parties

The structure of parties in single-party systems is as varied as are the goals and the bases of these parties. Moreover, the reality of the structure also differs markedly from formal arrangements, in part because claims are often exaggerated, in turn because the resources required to build an extensive party structure are not available.

In traditional single-party systems, the party has almost no structure at all; it depends entirely on the social groups on which it is based, tribal or clientelistic, to recruit its leaders and run the country. It is merely a loose confederacy of local and regional notables who remain unchallenged because of the strength of their hold on the population. This was the case, for instance, in the Northern People's Congress in the early years of independent Nigeria after 1960.

What could be labelled the 'modern' single-party system is based, on the contrary, on the model of organization epitomized by the structure of communist parties. The aim is to mobilize the population towards new goals by creating a dedicated élite whose main function is to proselytize, not to represent. This is done by building an extensive party across the country and by giving to an 'élite' the function of running that party: there has therefore to be a degree of restriction in the size of the membership. Indeed, the extensive character of the party is further helped by setting up a large number of dependent associations covering specific sections of the population and various types of activity. The dominance of the centre is ensured by the technique of 'democratic centralism', which was described in Chapter 9. Restrictions on membership are relative rather than absolute. With a membership of over 17 million at the peak of its strength, the membership of the Communist Party of the Soviet Union was not small: it constituted about 10 per cent of the adult population of the country. The Chinese Communist Party claims 35 million members and, although this constitutes only about 6 per cent of the adult population, this figure is impressive. Yet the basic principle in communist single-party systems was always that membership should be obtained with some difficulty, after a time of apprenticeship, during which the proselytizing capabilities of the 'cadres' was being tested.

The communist model has been imitated in the case of populist single-party systems in the Third World, although almost always with variations. A number of relatively well-structured parties were established, as in the Côte d'Ivoire, Kenya, Guinea, Zambia and Tanzania during the pre-independence struggle, in Syria and Iraq (the Baath Party) against what were viewed as reactionary regimes, and in Egypt (the Arab Socialist Union) by Nasser after a military coup in 1952. However, the structure of these parties was less developed than that of communist parties. Perhaps the best example is that of the Mexican PRI, since this did set up an elaborate network of component bodies covering the various productive forces in the nation (workers, peasants, etc.). Yet, even in this case, there has been a marked decline of the organization since the 1970s.

What happened to the PRI over several decades occurred more rapidly with respect to many other Third World single-party systems. In some cases, as in Syria and Iraq, the party formally ruled, but this was more in name than in reality, since very strong leaders gave a highly personalized character to these regimes. In Ghana, the leader who created the party used it increasingly as a personal tool, and the party collapsed as the leader was overthrown. The party remained in existence – and survived changes of leadership – in Egypt and, in a different manner, in Kenya and Tanzania; it also survived, under the same leader, in the Côte d'Ivoire and Zambia. However, in these countries, too, party organization was gradually markedly weakened.

Yet these earlier single-party systems 'resisted' better than those which were set up in the 1960s and 1970s, often by military leaders feeling the need to strengthen their hold on the population after a few years in power. Whether these parties were or claimed to be Marxist (as in Congo or Benin), populist or authoritarian-inegalitarian, they were rarely significantly more than machines designed to help their leaders. They did not have the extensive organization or the dedicated 'cadres' of communist parties. They were therefore even less able to mobilize the population than populist parties of the immediate post-independence period, than the PRI, or than the communist parties, though even among these, despite their long experience, many none the less also fell.

## The dynamics of single-party systems

For several decades, it seemed that the form of the single-party system was both 'popular' – in the sense that it satisfied the needs of at least substantial numbers of political élites – and relatively effective. With their substantial decline since the 1980s, the question arises as to whether such systems constitute in essence a transitional phase of political life. There seems, indeed, to be some evidence for this conclusion. We pointed out that truly traditional single-party systems were a thing of the past. Those which were conservative authoritarian have experienced difficulties from the early postwar period onwards, almost certainly as a long-term consequence of the defeat of fascism and Nazism. These regimes have gradually been replaced by systems of more than one party, by military regimes, or by another form of single-party system. Populist single-party systems seemed for a period to be more stable and suitable models of postwar development for the Third World. But their maintenance has depended markedly on their leaders being able to steer a middle course between tradition and modernity, while building a strong party structure. It does not seem possible to be indefinitely successful along such a narrow path. Finally, communist single-party systems seemed the strongest of all and they lasted for a long period. However, the collapse of the whole European part of the communist edifice showed that a longevity of half a century and a good organization accompanied by repression did not suffice. A large base of support appears necessary to build a truly stable political system.

Thus single-party systems seem to suffer from fundamental weaknesses. Yet it must be remembered that, however transitional they may appear to be, these systems have provided with varying degrees of success a political 'formula' of considerable significance. They have made it possible to build some linkages, however fragile, between population and rulers; they have made some forms of development possible, even if it has been with difficulty. They cannot be written off as spent forces, especially since systems of more than one party are often weak and lack the mixture of determination and tolerance which is needed for them to be viable. In the turmoil following the collapse of eastern European communism, many single-party systems have disappeared; but many have survived. Single-party systems existed before communist regimes appeared on the stage: they will remain on the scene even if communist single-party systems were eventually to disappear.

**Table 10.2**   Stable and unstable single-party systems

|  | Total | Number one party ever | Stable one party | Percentage one party | Percentage stable one party |
|---|---|---|---|---|---|
| Atlantic | 23 | 2 | – | 9 | – |
| Eastern Europe and northern Asia | 33 | 33 | 15 | 100 | 45 |
| Middle East and northern Africa | 21 | 10 | 1 | 48 | 10 |
| South and south-east Asia | 24 | 6 | 3 | 25 | 50 |
| Africa south of Sahara | 48 | 43 | 10 | 90 | 23 |
| Caribbean, Central and South America | 33 | 10 | 2 | 30 | 20 |
| Total | 182 | 104 | 31 | 57 | 30 |

# Systems of more than one party

## Characteristics of competition

In principle at least, unlike single-party systems, systems of more than one party are based on open competition among political groups in society. This competition normally takes place in particular through elections. While, in single-party systems, elections have a symbolic role and do not provide any opportunity for choice, they play a crucial part in systems of more than one party; they are the apex or the end-product of the competitive process among the parties. Yet neither in elections nor more generally is competition always entirely open in systems of more than one party. There are marked differences in this respect: differences which, as in single-party systems, are due to variations in the ideology, social base, and structure of the parties.

At one extreme, competition can be so restricted that the regime appears almost to be imposed. This occurs when a social group – based on class or race, for instance – denies the rest of the population the opportunity to participate in political life, as was the case in South Africa for decades. In a somewhat parallel manner, literacy requirements have resulted in substantial proportions of the inhabitants being disfranchised in a number of Latin American countries. Severe restrictions are sometimes introduced by military leaders who wish to maintain an appearance of pluralism: thus in Brazil a two-party system was imposed for two decades, between 1964 and 1984. More commonly, one or more parties are not allowed to be constituted or reconstituted, as occurred in Argentina with the Peronist Party for long periods, or in Turkey with the Democratic Party.

## Problems of party competition

Systems of more than one party can therefore develop in a context of restricted and even contrived competition. More generally, competition poses in these systems three interrelated but analytically distinct questions. There is, first, that of the *extent of competition*. Are societal conflicts freely reflected in the party system, or are there some legal or actual barriers? We just mentioned some extreme cases, but competition can be limited by more subtle means: there can be pressure put on electors; there may be outright electoral fraud; or, and indeed very commonly, as we shall see in Chapter 11, the electoral system may have the effect of making it difficult – at the limit, impossible – for some standpoints to be represented. In practice, there are always some limitations to the 'transparency' of conflicts in all systems of more than one party.

Second, the *nature of the competition* characterizing the system can vary and range between two extremes. Competition can be at the level of groups or at the level of individuals, or, more commonly, it can result from a combination of both types. It is at the level of groups when, as we saw in Chapter 7, parties are closely dependent on a 'parent' organization – tribal or geographical, ethnic, religious or class based. There is then a war between well-defined camps, a 'war' which is waged (normally) by electoral means. Elections determine the strength of each group by calling on the loyalty of group members. From time to time, there can be a truce and parties can come to some arrangement: this type of arrangement between the 'pillars' of the society has been labelled 'consociationalism' (Lijphart, 1977: 25–52).

When parties cease to be dependent on a 'parent' body and can call directly on the support of those who identify with them, some change gradually occurs. Parties then begin to look for new 'identifiers' from outside the groups which supported them originally, since they can increase in this manner their share of the electorate – although they may also lose some of their original supporters as others become involved in similar forms of 'poaching'. The purpose of elections changes profoundly in the process: from being essentially means of expressing old loyalties, elections become markets at which parties attempt to 'sell' their programmes. Traditional loyalties break down as the independence of electors grows. Meanwhile, the competition between the parties becomes close, as each one of them is affected by the actions of the others. There is then a party *system* in the strong sense of the word (Downs, 1957).

Legitimate mass parties play a key part in this evolution, since they are not directly tied to a social group and are, on the contrary, autonomous organizations. As parties take time to become legitimate mass, the evolution from group-based to individual competition also takes a long time. Thus, by and large, countries in which the system of more than one party is new are likely to experience a 'group-based' type of competition, while countries in which it has lasted for a long period will experience forms of competition closer to a 'market'. This happens in particular when electors are 'independent' from the parties, as in the United States and, increasingly, in western Europe (Wolfinger, 1985: 277–96; Beck, 1984: 240–66).

Yet this development may be prolonged or made more complex as a result of a third element: *the type of party configuration.* Systems of more than one party differ markedly in terms of the number and relative strength of the significant parties, often because, originally, tribal, ethnic, religious, or class-based groups emerge in the different polities in varying numbers and with varying strengths. There can therefore be as a result two, three, four, or more significant parties, which may be more or less equal, or differ considerably in the size of their support. This configuration is unlikely to change markedly, or at any rate quickly, even when the party system ceases to be 'group based' and becomes progressively 'market based'.

## Panorama of systems of more than one party

By the mid-1990s, 105 countries out of 182 (57 per cent) were ruled by a system of more than one party. These included all the Atlantic, four-fifths of the Latin American and two-thirds of the south and east Asian states; but only a third of the polities of the Middle East and Africa were among them. The success of systems of more than one party is thus uneven in the Third World, while it is large in the Atlantic area and, since the late 1980s, in eastern Europe as well.

As a matter of fact, truly continuous systems of more than one party are drawn mainly from the Atlantic area. Of the 105 countries which were ruled by a system of more than one party in 1994, only 50 – or half – had been ruled continuously in this way since the end of the Second World War or since independence. Twenty of these 50 countries are in the Atlantic area, 12 in the Caribbean and Latin America, 10 in south and east Asia and the other 8 in the Middle East and Africa south of the Sahara. While Atlantic countries formed less than one-fifth of the countries ruled by a system of more than one party in the mid-1990s, they formed two-fifths of the group of countries which were continuously ruled in that way. They even account for two-thirds of the countries which have had an uninterrupted system of more than one party for four decades or more. Newer systems of more than one party include many countries of the Commonwealth, where, as we already noted, liberal traditions have been by and large stronger than in the rest of the Third World (Blondel, 1987: 311–37). On the other hand, the older Latin American countries have tended to oscillate between military regimes and systems of more than one party during the postwar period, and very few have been ruled by a system of more than one party continuously for more than two decades.

Systems of more than one party have thus tended to be durable primarily in the Atlantic area. This corresponds to the view, discussed in Chapter 6, according to which liberal democracy is significantly associated with economic wealth. Given that, as we pointed out earlier, systems of more than one party tend to change their character over time, it follows that one should first examine Atlantic countries and only afterwards turn to the examination of systems of more than one party in the rest of the world.

**Table 10.3** Stable and unstable systems of more than one party

|  | Total | Number more than one party ever | Number of stable more than one party | Percentage more than one party | Percentage stable more than one party |
|---|---|---|---|---|---|
| Atlantic | 23 | 23 | 20 | 100 | 87 |
| Eastern Europe and northern Asia | 33 | 18 | – | 55 | – |
| Middle East and northern Africa | 21 | 8 | 4 | 38 | 50 |
| South and south-east Asia | 24 | 17 | 10 | 71 | 59 |
| Africa south of Sahara | 48 | 31 | 4 | 65 | 12 |
| Caribbean, Central and South America | 33 | 28 | 12 | 85 | 43 |
| Total | 182 | 125 | 50 | 69 | 40 |

# Atlantic party systems

The large majority of Atlantic countries have been ruled by a system of more than one party continuously from the 1940s to the 1990s (19 out of 23 polities). These systems display substantial differences, however, primarily in terms of the configuration of the parties – from two-party to multiparty systems – but also, though to a lesser extent, in terms of their social base, their organization and their goals.

By and large, the parties of the Atlantic area are liberal democratic; they have an autonomous and relatively well-structured organization; and they are (and indeed often were before 1945) of a legitimate mass character – the support which they receive from the electorate takes the form of a direct identification with the party.

## Similarities and differences among Atlantic party systems

### Social base

The groups from which Atlantic party systems originally emanated are no longer critical to the maintenance of these parties. This suggests that competition among them has been undergoing the type of evolution which was described earlier. Indeed, the second half of the twentieth century has been a period during which most parties of the Atlantic area have moved progressively away from a 'group-based' appeal to an appeal to electors on a 'market' basis. This has had an effect on the solidity of many of the parties and, consequently, on the stability of the party configurations in many of the countries.

Admittedly, in some countries, some of the parties are closely tied to an ethnic or national minority, as to a greater or lesser degree in the case of Britain, Finland, Belgium, Spain and Switzerland; only in Belgium do such parties constitute a true basis for potential separation. There are also, within the larger parties, remnants of communal loyalties of the personal or territorial types, but these are of little electoral significance. Since these pockets of 'communalism' are found mainly in rural areas of difficult access, they have declined in importance with the marked decline of the rural population everywhere. They used to be relatively strong especially in France before 1958, but the advent of the Gaullist Party and its perpetuation since the 1960s reduced communalism to insignificance in that country as well, although parties are still not solidly established in France, especially parties of the centre (Frears, 1977: 58–83).

Ethnic groups had been the basis of party support in America in the past, while religious groups, principally Roman Catholic, and class-based groups had provided support for parties in western Europe in the nineteenth and early twentieth centuries. Gradually, however, as with personal and territorial communalism, only traces of the phenomenon can be found in contemporary Europe and North America. There are some exceptions in scattered areas throughout the various countries, but in general, direct legitimate identification with parties has superseded indirect allegiance taking place through 'parent' groups.

Personalized leadership is of considerable significance, but within parties, rather than in order to build a party. Only in the case of the French Gaullists did a leader both create and sustain a large party. In Germany and Italy after the Second World War, Christian democracy was strongly helped, but not truly created by Adenauer and De Gasperi respectively. A similar phenomenon occurred with the French Socialist Party, which was remarkably boosted by Mitterrand in the 1970s and 1980s. Indeed, even the development of the Gaullist Party can be said to have corresponded to deeper changes in the society: the need to replace the old communal factions which had existed in the past and to set up a large conservative organization.

Thus it is truly the case that legitimate mass parties have spread generally throughout the Atlantic area, although, in doing so, they have become increasingly distinct from their original social base. The 'independence' of the electors has increased and, as a result, western European parties have become less stable than in the past. The extreme case has been that of Italy in 1992–3 where one of the main parties all but disappeared (the Socialist Party), the major party was markedly reduced in size (Christian Democracy) and much of the space on the right and centre of the political spectrum was taken by a new party, in a move somewhat resembling what occurred in France in 1958 with the advent of the Fifth Republic (Budge and Farlie, 1983: 115–28; Pedersen, 1983: 29–65; Dalton et al., 1984: 240–66; Crewe and Denver, 1985).

### Structure

There are more differences in structure among parties of the Atlantic area than differences in their social base, but these, too, are rather limited compared to the differences which can be found between systems of more than one party in the Atlantic area and those which can be found elsewhere. We noted in Chapter 9 that there can be substantial variations in the extent of decentralization, in the relationship between parties and particular groups (even among socialist parties in western Europe, for instance), and in the concept of membership itself. However, because the large majority of Atlantic parties are of the legitimate mass type, these differences are dwarfed by the fact that one of the key elements – the direct relationship between electors and party – is common to all or practically all organizations. Thus it does not seem to be of considerable significance, ostensibly at least, whether the proportion of members is larger among social democrats in Sweden or Austria than among socialists in Germany or France (Bartolini, 1983: 139–75); by and large, policy making appears to be in all cases markedly constrained by the need to appeal to the electorate, while retaining as many as possible of the ideological traditions of the party.

### *Ideology*

There are also some ideological differences among Atlantic parties, but the truly large variations are at the margin, among 'extremist' parties, which indeed have a rather small and often only intermittent following. These ideological differences are of two types, macro and micro.

The *macro differences* are constituted by the fact that some parties are not truly liberal democratic. On the one hand, there are organizations of the 'radical right', typically small and often ephemeral. They are apparently often triggered by outbursts of racism, as in France since the 1980s with the National Front, but the spread of their influence remains limited, even at their peak (about 10 per cent of the votes).

On the other hand, and traditionally more important, some countries have had significant communist parties. These declined in the 1980s, but they were previously large (about 20 per cent of the votes) in six (but only six) of the 19 countries of western Europe (France, Finland, Iceland, Greece, Portugal and Italy). In Italy alone did the Communist Party remain truly a force, although it did begin a decline. Possibly to avert a further decline, it changed its name to become the Party of the Democratic Left and adopted a social democratic stance, while a small minority broke away and formed a renamed Communist Party.

No single explanation has satisfactorily accounted for the long period of strength of Communist parties in these countries. The socioeconomic argument is scarcely valid, given the wealth of some of these societies. The cultural argument, suggesting that 'Latin' or Mediterranean countries are more susceptible to communism than others, has some validity, but Finland and Iceland have to be explained. Overall, what seems critical is whether the party succeeds in building a sub-culture of its own, as a result of some circumstances, such as the resistance to an occupier or to a dictatorship. Once it has reached middle-sized strength, the party can remain for long periods at the same level, since it is able to sustain a large network of dependent associations which in turn help to maintain it. This has been the case in particular with the Italian Communist Party's network of co-operatives and other dependent bodies.

More widespread than the macro differences in ideology are the *micro differences*. These may sometimes loom large on particular issues, although they are relatively small by comparison with ideological differences among other parties elsewhere. Differences between socialists or social democrats on the left and some of the 'centre' parties, such as the Christian democrats, are not, or are no longer, very clear (Irving, 1979). Some conservative parties have moved to the right in the 1980s, like the British Conservative party under Mrs Thatcher, in particular on economic issues. But others have not, and even those which did continued to accept most aspects of the welfare state. The liberals tend to be on the left of the Christian democrats on religious issues, but to the right of these parties on economic and social matters: indeed, the Austrian Liberals are markedly on the right. There are also agrarian parties, principally in Scandinavia, but the shrinking of the rural vote led these parties to rename themselves and to adopt the label of 'centre', which places them fairly close to socialists and to liberals.

Ideological differences between the significant Atlantic parties are thus relatively small; they are probably also declining. Both conservative and socialist or Labour parties have tended to move together on programmes: the New Zealand Labour Party thus pioneered a 'right-wing' economic programme. Moreover, Atlantic parties have picked issues as they have come up, often on the basis of the pressure of interest groups. Some of these issues have also given rise to new parties and in particular to 'green' or ecological parties, which have become a small, but permanent feature in many countries (Muller-Rommel, 1989).

## Configurations of Atlantic party systems

The most important difference among Atlantic parties is therefore their *configuration*. This configuration often still reflects the origins of the parties, but it is also affected by electoral systems, as we shall see in Chapter 11. Yet the gradual move towards a 'market' basis has affected party configurations as well, with the result that party systems, which remained stable throughout the 1950s and 1960s in most of the Atlantic area, have tended to vary appreciably in the 1970s and 1980s.

### Traditional configurations

From the 1950s to the 1970s, Atlantic party systems of western Europe could be classified neatly into four categories:

- *Two-party systems*, in which the two significant parties obtained close to 50 per cent of the votes and where any third party which might have existed was very small and politically insignificant. These were the systems of the United States, New Zealand, Australia, Britain and Austria.
- *Two-and-a-half party systems*, in West Germany, Luxembourg, Canada, Belgium and Ireland, where one party obtained 40 to 45 per cent of the votes, another around 35 per cent, and the third about 15 per cent. These systems were therefore 'unbalanced', in that the second party was smaller than the first and the third was

markedly smaller than the other two. It should be noted that there were no true three-party systems.

- *Multiparty systems with a dominant party*, where the first party also obtained 40 to 45 per cent of the votes, and where three or even four other parties shared rather evenly the rest of the votes. This was the case in most of Scandinavia (Denmark, Sweden, Norway, Iceland) as well as in Italy the situation in the Netherlands also approximating this model.
- *Multiparty systems without a dominant party*, as in France before the 1962 election, Finland and Switzerland, where no party obtained more than 25 per cent of the votes, and where four or five parties shared fairly evenly the votes of the electors (Blondel, 1968: 180–200).

Thus in the large majority of countries at least one party was close to obtaining a majority of the votes; the multiparty system in the strict sense of the term was exceptional. In particular, in large countries in which such a system had prevailed in the past, it simply no longer existed after the Second World War (Germany or Italy) or by the 1960s (France).

### Changes in configurations since the 1970s

Atlantic party systems can no longer be characterized as neatly since the 1980s. The four broad types of party system have remained, but substantial movements have also taken place. Moreover, the percentage of votes obtained by the main parties has tended to decline. Changes have been most noticeable in Britain, Luxembourg, Belgium and Denmark, this last country having effectively become a multiparty system without a dominant party. Changes have also occurred, especially in the second half of the 1980s, in New Zealand, Austria, Germany, Iceland and Norway, as well as even in Finland and Switzerland, which were already multiparty systems. In the 1990s, the movements which occurred in Canada (to the benefit of the provincial parties), Austria, France, Germany and, above all, Italy have been striking. On the other hand, Britain returned to a more 'normal' pattern and, in the United States, Australia and New Zealand, the traditional party system remained broadly unchanged.

Two types of explanation can be given for these movements. One type of explanation concentrates on individual countries. In Britain, for instance, the polarization of the two parties, and in particular the move to the left of the Labour Party in the 1970s, alienated a segment of the electorate which preferred to cast their votes for the Liberal Party. The creation of a Social Democratic Party in 1980 was also an indication of this alienation. When Labour became moderate again, there was a return to the more traditional pattern of the two-party system.

The second type of explanation focuses on more general trends. It is noted that the proportion of 'independent' electors increased in many countries, while party identification was becoming less strong. Evidence for this development has been accumulated in the United States, but there are also indications of the same phenomenon elsewhere in the Atlantic area (Beck, 1984: 240–66; Wolfinger, 1985: 277–96). Party systems in the Atlantic area, especially in western Europe, appear to be in a state of transformation. Legitimate mass parties are still central to these party systems, but they appear to be increasingly treated in an instrumental manner by electors who pass judgement on past policies (*retrospective voting*) or want to obtain specific policy results in the future (Fiorina, 1981: 20–62). However, enough direct allegiance to the parties remains for the change to be taking place slowly, and for the configurations to continue to keep in most countries the shape which they had in the past (Bartolini and Mair, 1990: 96–124; 212–49).

## Other systems of more than one party

Atlantic countries are a small proportion of the polities which are or have been ruled by a system of more than one party. At the end of the 1980s, 82 other states had a pluralistic party system; and a further 20 polities had been governed in this manner at some point after the Second World War. Thus a system of more than one party had been in existence in 125 of the 182 nations of the world.

However, many, indeed most, of the pluralistic party systems which exist or have existed outside the Atlantic area are not fully developed or are relatively fragile, despite the marked successes of the late 1980s and early 1990s, which are sometimes more apparent than real. As we just noted, the pluralistic party system did not survive in 20 polities, presumably because it could not withstand pressures. In a further 32, the system of more than one party was not in continuous existence since the Second World War or since independence, and in several cases there had been more than one successful attempt at overthrowing it. Furthermore, 19 of the remaining 30 Third World countries which had been ruled continuously by a system of more than one party were relatively new states, and in a number of cases were very new. Only in 11 countries, therefore, beyond the Atlantic area, had the system of more than one party lasted since the 1940s. Yet even in this group serious difficulties arose in a number of polities.

We should leave aside the 18 ex-communist countries (out of 33) which became pluralistic in the 1990s, as experience is short: while some are likely to remain pluralistic, this is not as clear for others. On the other hand, it is worth examining in some detail the characteristics of systems of more than one party in the 84 Third World countries in which this type of rule has existed at least for a period, and assessing in what ways and in which countries pluralistic party systems have proved more resistant and more durable (O'Donnell *et al.*, 1986; Randall, 1988).

### Long and continuous systems

In eleven countries, a system of more than one party has existed continuously since the 1940s. Yet serious problems have arisen in about half of these polities, and competition has been severely restricted in some. These eleven countries are Israel and Lebanon in the Middle East, India, Indonesia, Japan, South Korea and Sri Lanka in south and east Asia, South Africa in Africa south of the Sahara, and Brazil, Colombia

---

## BOX 10.1
## The slow build-up of party systems in eastern Europe

Western European party systems are old. They mostly started in the nineteenth century; in Britain, the party system started even earlier. As a result, the relationship between electors and parties has had time to 'mature'. Even if a degree of instability is noticeable since the 1980s, most large parties in most countries continue to keep their hold on the electorate.

The case of eastern Europe is different. In 1989–90, the countries of the area were suddenly confronted with the task of building a party system. This was rendered difficult for three main reasons:

- Not only had a party system to be set up suddenly, but in most cases, there had literally never before been a party system. At best, a party system had existed for a few years only, often after the First World War, but the parties had not been very active, their membership had been small, and they usually did not operate under conditions of complete freedom. This had been true even in the Austro-Hungarian empire before 1914. There was therefore almost no tradition to renew.
- The social cleavages on which parties are based in the West were less strong in eastern Europe, except, in some cases, ethno-nationalism. The class cleavage or the religious divisions which helped to form western parties had been systematically weakened or destroyed by the long period of communist rule.
- An entirely new political class had to be created while the members of the old political class – composed of the ex-leaders of the communist party – wished to retain some influence. The new men and women had too little political experience, the old had much.

Not surprisingly, many members of the old communist élite – those who were least tainted with the previous regime – have returned to power. Not surprisingly, the new parties are weak, and their electoral base lacks firm support and fluctuates markedly. Thus the surprise is more that, in these circumstances, the party systems of eastern Europe should nevertheless have developed relatively smoothly.

---

and Costa Rica in Latin America. Of these, only Israel, India, Japan, Sri Lanka and Costa Rica have had a truly working and continuous system of more than one party, although Colombia comes very close to qualifying, since, from the end of the 1950s, after the fall of the dictatorship of Odria, its two-party system has been almost fully unimpeded (it was based for a substantial period on a power-sharing arrangement over time between the two parties).

In the other five countries, restrictions have been severe. The war in Lebanon almost led to the disintegration of that country. While there was still theoretically a system of more than one party, indeed a multiparty system (highly based on communal ethnic groups) at the end of the 1980s, its operation was seriously hampered by the absence of elections and the dependence of the country on its immediate neighbours. Indonesia and South Korea have been technically ruled by systems of more than one party, but they have been so dominated by the government party that they come close to having a single-party system, though changes which occurred at the end of the 1980s, especially in Korea, suggest a move towards a more regular operation of the system. A similar conclusion can be drawn in the case of Brazil for the period 1964–84, during which a two-party system was imposed by the military rulers. Finally, the two-party system was oligarchical in South Africa so long as the white minority dominated.

Thus only five or at most six countries, outside the Atlantic area, can be said to have had a truly working pluralistic party system throughout the period from the 1940s to the 1990s. This suggests the conclusion that, so far at least, systems of more than one party are primarily a characteristic of Atlantic countries. The presence of Israel and Japan in the group is not surprising, given the similarities between these countries and Atlantic polities. Israel's party system has been successively of the multi-dominant and of the two-and-a-half party variety; Japan's began as multiparty, then became two-and-a-half party and finally multiparty with a dominant party. The presence of India, Sri Lanka and Costa Rica is more surprising. Costa Rica's balanced two-party system has functioned effectively throughout the period. Sri Lanka and India experienced greater difficulties: in India, the 'emergency' of the mid-1970s seemed to suggest a move towards a one-party system, from which Mrs Gandhi retreated; Sri Lanka has known considerable tension arising from communal strife, and its constitution was altered in a semi-presidential and somewhat authoritarian direction. Yet, overall, these two south Asian countries remained consistently under pluralistic party rule, an undeniable but also somewhat unusual success.

## Continuous systems among newer countries

Nineteen other Third World countries and one Atlantic country (Malta), which gained independence during or since the 1950s, have been ruled continuously by a system of more than one party. Two of these 19 are in the Middle East and north Africa (Cyprus and Morocco), three are in Africa south of the Sahara (Gambia, Mauritius, and Namibia), five are in Asia and the Pacific, and nine are in the Caribbean.

In general, the systems of more than one party functioned regularly in these countries. There were major difficulties in only four of them. Cyprus split into two states, Greek and Turkish, but remained pluralistic on both sides of the communal divide. In Guyana, considerable pressure on the system and a degree of imposition was introduced by its long-time president, Burnham, towards the end of his rule. In Jamaica, elections were boycotted by the opposition in 1986, but the system remained broadly pluralistic. It is in Morocco that the greatest amount of manipulation and imposition took place, with elections being postponed on more than one occasion by royal action.

In the other 16 countries of the group, on the other hand, the pluralistic party system prevailed and was generally fully effective. As a matter of fact, overall, the majority of these countries had a working two-party system throughout their independent period (thirteen countries), while there was a two-and-a-half party system in two (Mauritius and St Christopher), a multi-dominant party system in a further two (Papua New Guinea and Cyprus) and a multiparty system without a dominant party in two (Morocco and the Solomon Islands). Only in one country (Malaysia) was there strong dominance of one party, but in this case the dominance was that of an alliance based on a permanent arrangement between Malay and Chinese organizations.

The fact that these systems have operated in general satisfactorily since independence may be ascribed to the peculiar characteristics of most of the countries of the group:

- Seven of these polities are very new, being creations of the late 1970s or early 1980s, while only two (Malaysia and Morocco) date from the 1950s.
- The large majority of these countries have a very small population – less than a million in a number of cases. In fact, only Malaysia and Morocco have a sizeable population.
- The large majority of these countries are islands or groups of islands (13 out of 20), in which there is a high degree of cultural identity.
- A large majority are members of the Commonwealth and were given substantial autonomy before independence (some even became independent reluctantly). Not only has a tradition of parliamentarism been established for many years by way of imitation of Britain in these countries; again in imitation of Britain, a two-party system was successfully implanted. This has been the case in both the Pacific and Caribbean countries of the group, although in some the party system is based on a variety of ethnic groups, as in Mauritius and Guyana.

These countries are therefore not representative of the countries of the world. Only Morocco and Malaysia appear to resemble an 'average' polity, and only Malaysia can be regarded as a truly successful working pluralistic party system. We may note that Malaysia belongs to the same geographical group as India and Sri Lanka, and that it is part of the Commonwealth.

## Relatively recent returns

In 34 Third World countries, a system of more than one party was in existence in 1994, but this was after periods in which a single-party system or a system without parties had prevailed. While the group of continuous, but recent, systems of more than one party is predominantly drawn from the Commonwealth, almost half (15) of the relatively recent returns are in Central and South America; and 10 are in Africa south of the Sahara, almost all of them having become pluralistic again after the collapse of communist systems in eastern Europe.

Beyond the Third World and outside the communist countries, pluralistic party systems returned to three western European countries: Greece, Portugal and Spain. The party system of these countries has become stable and indeed highly effective, the Greek system being of the two-and-a-half party variety, while Portugal has oscillated between a multi-dominant party and a multiparty system; in Spain the Socialist Party has been in a position of dominance for a decade with a centre-right party having slowly gained ground.

Overall, apart from these three western European countries and perhaps Turkey, the extent to which the system of more than one party is truly consolidated is somewhat doubtful. In Spanish America, there are signs in several polities that it is better established than it was previously. Yet, given the economic difficulties which in turn led to social tensions, as well as in several cases to outright violence bordering on civil war in Peru, Colombia and even Venezuela, as well as in some Central America states, the possibility of a return of the military to power cannot be ruled out – any more than it can be ruled out in the Asian or African countries which have opted in the 1990s for a system of more than one party.

## Casualties

If Spanish America is the region where pluralistic party systems are perhaps revitalized, if not truly strong, Africa south of the Sahara remains the region where these systems have collapsed: 16 of the 20 countries belonging to this group come from that area, the four others being Burma, Iran, Syria and Cuba.

While a pluralistic party system might be re-established in at least some of these four countries, this is not likely to be the case in a substantial number of the African polities belonging to the group. Most of these had only had a short and very unsuccessful period of pluralistic rule immediately after independence: this has even been the case in Nigeria, Ghana and the Sudan, let alone in Burkina Faso, Rwanda, Somalia, Togo and Zaire. The Nigerian case is one of the most surprising, as one might have expected a pluralistic party system to take root in that country. In Sudan, the military took over power for the third time in 1989, partly because of the divisions among the parties (as had been the case in Sudan previously as well as in Somalia before 1970), and partly because of the apparently never-ending civil war in the south of the country.

In some other cases, as in Chad (before the military eventually took over), Zambia and Zimbabwe, the pluralistic party system, also based on tribal or ethnic divisions, was replaced by a single-party system as a result of the action of the head of state. A merger was obtained in some cases, while in others the opposition was repressed. There are also cases where both experiences were combined, as in Sierra Leone, where the pluralistic party system led to the arrival of the opposition party in power, the subsequent establishment of a single-party system, and a military takeover; or in Ghana, where the military first helped to install a pluralistic party system after the fall of Nkrumah in 1966, but was subsequently instrumental in the rapid abolition of this system on two successive occasions.

Overall, the system of more than one party has clearly fragile roots in Africa south of the Sahara. In that area, the fact that it has re-emerged in some countries is due more to the prevailing world environment after the fall of communism in eastern Europe than to a genuine change in patterns of political behaviour. Evidence for this conclusion can be found in the fact that the process of change is often extremely slow and chequered in many countries of Africa. Indeed, in several cases the move towards pluralism has been stopped at a dominant single-party system, rather than at a full pluralistic form. In particular, presidents in office have allowed some opposition at the time of their re-election, but in most cases with little chance of success. The system of more than one party does not appear to have strong roots in much of the Middle East and north Africa either. Moves in that direction have been limited, in contrast to what happened in Latin America or, with a number of major exceptions, in south and south-east Asia. None the less, however uncertain these changes might be, the fact that a move towards a pluralistic party system is taking place is clearly a major development which may, in time, alter markedly the nature of political competition throughout the world.

## Overview

The *extent of competition* is naturally the key distinguishing feature of party systems, but the *nature of support, the ideology and the structure* of the parties have to be taken into account in drawing this distinction, since these elements affect both the nature of the competition among the parties and the general patterns of party behaviour.

The main divide is between *single-party systems* and *systems of more than one party*, with a small number of systems having no parties at all, either because they are still ruled by a traditional élite or because parties are banned (typically temporarily) by the military. This last category has declined in numbers, perhaps temporarily, since the 1980s.

The boundaries between these systems without parties, single-party systems and systems of more than one party are not clear-cut, however. While in some countries only one party exists or is allowed, in others there is a degree of openness to limited competition. These are the *single-party dominant* systems.

Single-party systems have often been equated with communist systems. In reality these have typically been in a minority, although they have been the best organized, if not, as it turned out, truly solid. It is in Africa south of the Sahara that the large majority of single-party systems have been found, but these have also often been replaced by non-party military regimes.

Single-party systems have been in decline since the early 1990s, after a long period of relative success. The decline is only relative, however, since in the mid-1990s they still constitute a quarter of the countries of the world.

Systems of more than one party are associated with *substantial competition*, although this competition can be partly limited by traditions and by the operation of the electoral system.

There are two main types of competition. one which is based on the opposition between *established communal groups* (for instance, ethnic, religious or class based); and the other, the *market-type* competition, which is primarily based on interests and issues. Only the latter can be regarded as 'true' or 'full' competition.

Competition which has strong communal characteristics occurs in the earlier phases of development of parties; market-type competition occurs in later phases when parties are legitimate mass.

Established systems of more than one party tend to be found in the Atlantic area, where they have developed over a number of decades. They are only a small minority of all systems of more than one party. These systems are traditionally of four types: *two-party, two-and-a-half party, multiparty with a dominant party, and multiparty.* This last group is small.

There has been some erosion of party support in a number of Atlantic countries, among the larger parties in particular, and a degree of volatility.

There has been a marked resurgence of systems of more than one party outside the Atlantic area in the 1980s (principally in Latin America) and 1990s (in eastern Europe and to an extent in Africa south of the Sahara). In the case of this last group of countries, the pluralistic party system appears particularly fragile.

In general, stable systems of more than one party outside the Atlantic area are found primarily in relatively small countries and/or among nations belonging to the Commonwealth, India being the most outstanding example.

Single-party systems and systems without parties are thus likely to remain features of the panorama of political life. In the end, systems of more than one party flourish when full and open competition among social groups is allowed to last for a substantial period, a situation which, so far, has not been characteristic of many countries outside the Atlantic area, although there are signs of change.

## Further reading

Studies of party systems have become numerous, although they are still typically confined to western and especially western European party systems. The only general study is that of G. Sartori, *Parties and Party Systems* (1976), but it also refers rather more to western European party systems than to other party systems.

On single-party systems, see for instance L. Holmes, *Politics in the Communist World* (1986) for communist systems; as an example of Third World single-party systems, see L. Cliffe, *One-Party Democracy: Tanzania* (1967).

The literature on western European party systems is large. See in particular H. Daalder and P. Mair, *Western European Party Systems* (1983). On electoral change in western Europe, see R.J. Dalton *et al.*, eds., *Electoral Change in Advanced Industrial Democracies* (1984), I. Budge and D.J. Farlie, *Explaining and Predicting Elections* (1983), I. Crewe and D.M. Denver, eds., *Electoral Change in Western Democracies* (1985), and S. Bartolini and P. Mair, *Identity, Competition, and Electoral Availability: The Stabilisation of European Electorates 1885–1985* (1990). On the effect of new parties on party systems, see F. Muller Rommel, ed., *New Politics in Western Europe* (1989).

There has not been so far any systematic study of party systems in the Third World. A number of studies have considered the 'return to democracy' in Latin America; see G. O'Donnell, P. Schmitter, and L. Whitehead, eds., *Transition from Authoritarian Rule* (1986). There are also specific studies of African and Asian parties related to particular parties or to particular countries: see V. Randall, ed., *Political Parties in the Third World* (1988) for an examination of a number of important cases.

# 11

# Parties, elections and direct democracy

## Introduction

Parties are the main link between people and government in the contemporary world. Elections are the key mechanism of this link: they are the only way in which the bulk of the population can express its support for a party rather than another. They are therefore perhaps the most fundamental and the most distinguishing feature of modern governments. Indeed, they are given prominence even where governments leave no choice to electors, since they are designed to appear to give legitimacy to regimes which are basically maintained by imposition.

Yet, even where competition is open and pluralism recognized, the extent to which elections reflect the electorate's attitudes can vary appreciably. As a matter of fact, there is no way in which the best electoral system could provide an entirely accurate picture: there is always an element of distortion. As a result, as soon as elections started to play a part in the political process, discussions on the effect of electoral systems began to take place. Moreover, beyond what might be regarded as fraudulent manipulation, electoral systems are powerful instruments of political engineering: indeed, they have often been regarded as being able to shape the nature of party systems. Thus, not unnaturally, controversies about the impact of electoral systems on party systems have been numerous.

If elections are the channel through which the people can express their support for parties and thus shape the characteristics of party systems, parties and party systems are also affected importantly, even though less directly, by what are typically called *mechanisms of direct democracy* and in particular by *referendums*. These mechanisms are means of increasing popular participation; but this increase often takes place at the expense of parties, which have therefore tended to manifest opposition to the introduction of these procedures in many countries.

We shall examine four issues in the course of this chapter:

- First, we shall look at the *general arrangements* according to which voters and candidates are to act, in order to ensure that the electoral process is as fair as possible.

- Second, we shall consider *electoral systems* from the point of view of the different mechanisms by which seats in legislatures are distributed in relation to popular votes.
- Third, we shall analyze the extent to which *party systems* may be influenced by electoral systems.
- Finally, we shall turn to *direct democracy* and in particular to *referendums* to see to what extent they constitute an alternative channel relating people and governments.

## Arrangements to ensure fair electoral practices

### Electoral rules and the voter

Electoral systems affect the extent and nature of party competition by determining who is entitled to vote, and by providing various types of protection to electors. The question of the *extension of the suffrage to all* has been historically the main issue raised by voter entitlement. By and large, restrictions based on property, literacy or sex have been abandoned. One of the last very serious restrictions to be abolished took place in the early 1990s when the white South African government agreed to grant voting rights to blacks.

The main development of the 1970s and 1980s has been to bring the voting age down to 18 in many countries. Nationality is still almost everywhere a requirement, but that restriction is being slowly eroded in favour of a condition of residence only, thus enabling immigrants to have a vote in some countries, at least in local elections. Such an extension has gradually occurred in particular within the European Union.

Overall, there are nine possible types of restrictions: namely, age, nationality, criminal record, residence, the holding of some office, sex, literacy, property and race. In general, the first four types can be found within a universal suffrage context, though the manipulation of the residence qualification can seriously limit the franchise and has sometimes been used to this effect. The next type of restriction, about holding some offices, constitutes a borderline case. Finally, if any of the last four obtains, the suffrage is clearly not universal.

Entitlement to vote does not mean the effective ability to vote: a procedure has to be devised, in particular to avoid fraud, by which electors are *registered*. In practice, this procedure can constitute a barrier to voting if it is administered bureaucratically – at least, there will always be some delay. This is why permanent registers, amended at periodic intervals or at prescribed periods (for instance, before elections) are more efficient and ultimately less costly than registers periodically created from scratch. European countries tend to have permanent registers, but in the United States, since registration periods are felt to have a mobilizing effect, the periodic register has been maintained.

The existence of a register imposes a place of voting, specifically a polling station. This introduces some rigidity, which can be alleviated by means of *postal or proxy arrangements*, but these entail obvious administrative costs, and opportunities for fraud are increased. A truly comprehensive system of postal voting requires both a highly developed administrative structure and a low level of fraud. In practice, the demand for postal vote facilities increases as the population becomes more mobile – that is to say, with socioeconomic development. Not surprisingly, these arrangements have become more common in the Atlantic area in the second half of the twentieth century.

Overall, whatever the system, a substantial number of potential electors are likely not to be registered – probably at least 5 to 10 per cent, and in many cases more. Absence, illness or pressing business result in some registered voters being unable to cast their ballot on polling day, or being unwilling to take the trouble to do so, especially where a postal or proxy vote is difficult to obtain. Compulsory voting has been introduced in some countries (Australia, Austria, Belgium, Italy and some Latin American states) in order to remedy this problem, but the requirement is somewhat ineffective as the fines incurred are usually small and may not even be collected.

## Electoral rules, candidates and parties

### Negative requirements

Traditionally, electoral systems were concerned almost exclusively with what might be called formal or *negative equality*: that is, with the task of ensuring that there was no impediment against any of the candidates. The most important advance in this context was achieved by the *secret ballot*, a requirement which is sometimes reinforced (as in Britain and Belgium) by the legal requirement that votes should be counted not at the level of the polling station, but at that of a larger unit. The secrecy requirement has been both simple and successful; once rejected by the authorities of the Soviet Union on the grounds that it was a 'bourgeois' practice, it has probably come to be recognized everywhere as the supreme protection of electors and candidates.

Other 'negative' requirements relate to the *repression of fraud*. Permanent registers aim at stamping out impersonation and double voting, for instance. Other forms, such as bribery, threats or blackmail, are more difficult to eradicate, partly because some of these practices cannot easily be defined with precision: for instance, the rumour that some threats may be carried out may lead electors to vote in a certain way. In rural areas in particular, citizens who are in a condition of dependence and on whom employers can exercise influence may be too frightened to consider voting for an opposition candidate. Fraud can also take place at the count: for instance, by spoiling ballots of the opposition, or by secretly introducing piles of ballots of favoured candidates. It is therefore typically required that boxes be opened before the vote begins to show that they are empty, and that they be opened at the end of the process in the presence of representatives of various parties. Voting machines, which are in use in the United States, are of considerable value, since they can be less easily tampered with than ballot papers; elsewhere, there has been resistance to the introduction of these devices, probably on grounds of tradition.

### Positive requirements

In Atlantic countries in particular, the focus of attention has moved more recently to positive requirements designed to achieve *real equality*. In a first phase, mainly

---

## BOX 11.1
## The problems posed by party finance

The problems posed by party finance have become a major issue in almost all western countries. They seem to be more intractable than any other problems posed by political parties. They have led and continue to lead to serious difficulties in France, Spain, Belgium and even Britain. In Italy, the political system has been in turmoil as a result of what has been regarded as corruption on a massive scale.

The problem is unquestionably more serious than in the past. This is in part because the costs of campaigning have markedly increased (television and other media, cavalcades of leaders across the country). It is also in part because the basic sources of funding have diminished as a result of the decline in membership which has affected many, if not most western parties. It is above all because of the regulation of party financing which has taken place almost everywhere in the west, in order to 'clean up' the field and to equalize the chances of candidates, and as a trade-off for the financing of parties by the state.

Two points are clear: first, it is almost impossible for the law to make its prohibitions watertight; second, politicians hold power or are expected to hold power after the election, and they can therefore help citizens in many ways, whether they want jobs, permits or other facilities.

On the first matter, the imagination of all concerned is obviously fertile. If one is not allowed to give more than a certain sum oneself, one can ask relatives to give money: can this fraud be easily proved? If one is not allowed to give money from one's firm, one can set up another firm which can render 'services': can this fraud be easily proved?

Yet the more serious question relates to the very notion of 'fraud' or 'illicit services'. When does 'help' become 'corrupt'? Politicians are supposed to help citizens to solve their problems: is it wrong that the citizens should give some money to the party in return? Is the magnitude of the sum involved the key criterion? If so, at what sum should one draw the line?

None of these problems can be easily solved, and they have not been solved so far. The question of party finance will therefore remain a key issue, one which will poison party debates and one which will lead to an almost infinite number of judicial inquiries, if not necessarily to an infinite number of court cases.

---

immediately following the Second World War in western Europe, an attempt was made to *limit expenditure* by candidates and to provide a number of services in kind, such as the mailing of election addresses and, more importantly, access to radio and television on an equal footing, a requirement which raises problems of apportionment of time among the candidates. In a second phase, which started in the late 1950s, it became suggested that campaigns and political parties should be directly financed out of public funds, in order to offset the increased costs incurred and the consequential inequalities among candidates. Despite criticisms that such developments might lead (and perhaps do lead) to a decline in party mobilizing efforts as the need to obtain funds from individual citizens is reduced, public funding of campaigns and parties has spread widely across the western world in the 1970s and 1980s (Heidenheimer, 1970; Alexander, 1989).

Electoral systems thus include a vast panoply of devices designed to ensure that campaigning and voting take place in conditions of fairness for candidates and electors. Some of these techniques are well established, although they are far from being universally adopted, in part because many governments are not particularly anxious, to say the least, to abolish fraud; other arrangements are in a process of development. In the West, matters of electoral fairness, except perhaps the question of party finance, are no longer regarded as sufficiently controversial or as raising sufficiently large theoretical issues to deserve detailed study. Yet they are manifestly fundamental, as they determine the framework without which matters of seat allocation, to which we are now coming, do not even have occasion to arise.

## Electoral systems and seat allocation

Much has been written about the mechanics of allocation of seats and about techniques designed to improve them (Mackenzie, 1958; Bogdanor and Butler, 1983; Bogdanor, 1984). Originally, this allocation was conceived as stemming directly from the *majority principle*: seats were allocated to candidates having the most votes. Later, however, it became felt that this allocation should be made on a proportional basis and *proportional representation* (PR) thus became an alternative to (and felt by many to be a better alternative than) the majority system (Mill, 1910). But this development led to the recognition that another matter was at stake: namely, the question of the number of seats to be allocated within each area. This question is also of major importance, although it is still sometimes not given prominence in assessing the fairness of electoral systems (Rae, 1967: 19–21).

Proportional representation was adopted gradually throughout most of Europe before the Second World War; various forms of proportional representation are also in use in Latin America. Commonwealth countries on the whole kept the majority system (with some exceptions, such as Guyana); so did the countries which adopted the single-party system: the Soviet Union, for instance, traditionally adopted the single member majority system. With the introduction of pluralistic systems in some communist states, proportional representation has been introduced either instead of or alongside the majority system in some of these countries.

### Method of allocation

#### *Majority systems*

The method of allocation of seats is based in broad terms on the distinction between majority and proportional systems. There are, however, a number of subdivisions of both techniques which lead to appreciably different results. The first method is the simplest: candidates are elected on a *simple majority* basis. This is the 'first-past-the-post' system, widely used in Anglo-Saxon countries, specifically in Britain, the USA, Canada and many new Commonwealth countries, but it has been abandoned in New Zealand in favour of PR; it has been introduced in Italy in 1993 alongside proportional representation.

As this system is often felt to be too harsh on minorities, it can be modified in four different ways. One consists in deciding that there shall be *two ballots* and that, at the first, only those candidates who obtained at least 50 per cent of the votes will be elected. There is then a second ballot for those seats not filled at the first, but at that point, only the top two candidates can stand, or some other arrangements are devised to limit the number of candidates. This system has been in use in France at most general elections since 1870 (in the Third and Fifth Republics), while it was also widely used on the Continent of Europe before 1914. It has been adopted fully or partially in much of post-communist eastern Europe and it is also in use in some 'run-off' American primaries.

Another method, known as the *alternative vote*, which is in force in Australia, consists in avoiding the second ballot by asking electors to express an order of preference among the candidates. The bottom candidate or candidates are then eliminated at the count, and preferences are redistributed until an absolute majority is obtained for the top candidates.

In districts which have at least two seats, two other methods can be used. One consists in deciding that, though the districts have more than one seat, electors will have only one vote. Medium-sized minorities are thus represented, although complex strategies have to be devised by the parties in order to decide how many candidates they need to field to maximize their chances. Despite these difficulties, this system, which is known as the *single non-transferable vote*, is far from unworkable: it has operated for decades in Japan; it has been criticized there for encouraging heavy electoral expenditure and even corruption.

Finally, it may be decided that no party can present more than a *limited number of candidates* (less than there are seats): minorities are therefore necessarily represented. This system was in force in Britain in some districts during part of the nineteenth century, and is currently in use in some American local elections and at the national level in Mexico.

## PR systems

Proportional representation systems can also be divided into a number of categories, which display different degrees of proportionality. A system is perfectly proportional if no vote is wasted, a requirement which is obviously difficult to satisfy, first because there will be 'remainders' when the votes cast for the parties are translated into the much smaller number of seats to be filled in the legislature, and second, because some candidates will have more votes than are needed for election: if three seats have to be filled in a given district, for instance, a candidate who obtains more than $33\frac{1}{3}$ of the votes has 'excess' votes.

These difficulties can be overcome, however, by adopting a method analogous to the one used in the alternative vote, that is to say by redistributing to other candidates both the votes which are in excess and those which result from the elimination of candidates who receive very few 'first preferences'. To simplify the process, which could be long if every preference in every ballot was taken into account, a quota, known as the *Droop quota* from the name of the author who proposed it, has been calculated: it states the minimum necessary to ensure that there are not more candidates elected than there are seats. This is given by the formula $(V/S + 1) + 1$, where $V$ is the number of votes and $S$ the number of seats, since this gives the smallest figure necessary to produce a number of candidates equal to and not larger than the quota. If there are 120,000 votes and three seats to be filled, it is not necessary to redistribute every vote; one can stop at the point when three candidates obtain 30,001 votes, since no other candidate can obtain more than 29,997. The determination of the elected candidates is thus more rapid, but in the process, nearly a quarter of the votes, in this case, are wasted. Contrary to what is sometimes suggested, this system, which is known as the *single transferable vote* (STV) and is in use in Ireland, is thus not fully proportional; but it is 'very' proportional and it also has the advantage of enabling electors to express preferences, even against party wishes.

The other broad method of proportional representation has given rise to the *list systems* which, on the contrary, are in large part based on a pre-ordering of candidates by the parties, although preferential voting may help to introduce some flexibility, as in Belgium or in the past in Italy. Such systems are in force in most countries of western Europe, in Israel and in Latin America (Hand *et al.*, 1979; Lijphart, 1984a: 150–68). They are known as 'list' systems because the candidates are presented on party lists. A *quotient* is calculated ($V/S$), which a list must reach to be allocated seats. However, as the totals obtained by the lists are not normally exact multiples of the quotient, there are unfilled seats and there are 'remainders': these seats are then attributed on the basis of the *largest remainders*, a rough-and-ready method which is scarcely proportional.

In order to improve proportionality, an alternative technique for allocating seats is that of the *highest average* (or *D'Hondt system*, from the name of the author who proposed this arrangement), whereby lists are compared – and given seats – by dividing the totals of their votes by the series of integers. Thus a list will be given seats if the average number of votes, divided by the number of the seats which it is obtaining, is higher than the average obtained in the same manner by the other lists. This system is closer to proportionality than the system of the largest remainder, but it does favour large parties because, as the number of votes of a large party is divided successively by the series of integers, the absolute distance tends mechanically to diminish: the number of extra votes needed to obtain a fifth or sixth seat is therefore less than the number needed to obtain a second or third seat.

To remedy this situation, Scandinavian countries have tended to adopt a variation on the D'Hondt system, known as the *Sainte-Lague system*, which consists in using as divisers, not the series of integers, but numbers which come nearer to producing a proportional result; these numbers are not necessarily integers.

As it is often felt that the representation of very small parties – of 1, 2 or 3 per cent of the votes – should be discouraged, it is sometimes decided to introduce a minimum below which parties will not be allocated seats: the hurdle is 2 per cent in Denmark, 4 per cent in Italy and Sweden, and 5 per cent in West Germany. The introduction of such a clause can reduce substantially the proportionality of the system, especially where there are a number of small parties.

Finally, some systems are mixed and include elements of both proportional representation and majority systems. One may wish to give a boost to a large party or an alliance of parties which agree in advance to be related (*apparentes*) to each other: this was devised in France and Italy in the 1950s, with limited success. Sometimes, as in West Germany, Italy or Russia, a proportion of the seats are allocated on a majority basis, while the others are allocated on a proportional basis. The extent to which the system is proportional overall then depends on whether the seats given to parties on a majority basis are fully, partly, or not at all deducted from the totals to which parties are entitled after the allocation of PR seats is made.

The distinction between PR and majority systems thus covers a complex set of arrangements which lead to different levels of proportionality. In fact, the eleven types which we have just described can be ranked in increasing order of proportionality, although this ranking is given only as an indication. Minimum percentage clauses can have different effects depending on the size of the minimum percentage, for instance. The Sainte-Lague system can come very close to proportionality, but only provided the 'divisors' are adjusted with respect to the particular type of party distribution. The ranking is, from the least proportional to the most proportional:

1. First-past-the-post.
2. Two-ballot.
3. Alternative vote.
4. Single non-transferable vote.
5. Limited vote.
6. Mixed *apparentement* systems.
7. Minimum percentage clauses.
8. Largest remainder.
9. d'Hondt system.
10. Sainte-Lague system.
11. STV.

## The size of districts and the results

Although the technical method of allocating seats is the aspect which is most often mentioned with respect to electoral systems, the number of seats in each district also plays a major part, both within each district and between districts.

Within each district, the effects of the first-past-the-post system and of STV are the converse of each other: with STV, the larger the number of seats in the district, the more proportional the system, as one can easily understand (Ross, 1959: 3–9); in the first-past-the-post system, on the contrary, since the largest party obtains all the seats, the more seats in a district, the less proportional the result. Other electoral systems have intermediate effects because there can be deals among the parties (two-ballot system), because electors can exercise different preferences (alternative vote), or because the largest remainder system tends to favour smaller parties as the number of seats in each district increases. Between districts, on the other hand, electoral systems have different results if the number of votes per seat varies markedly from one district to another.

Parties which benefit from the arrangements existing at a given point in time are naturally anxious to maintain the status quo. The matter is further complicated by the question of the *gerrymander* (or curiously shaped districts drawn to minimize the chances of opponents), and therefore by the need to find impartial authorities empowered to draw the map of the districts, such as Boundary Commissions in Britain.

Yet there are also administrative and political difficulties in approximating equality, since one may have to cut across local or regional boundaries in the search for equality. Moreover, frequent redrawing of districts creates problems for party organizations, which are therefore often opposed to such changes. The question is particularly serious when the number of seats is small, and is especially difficult to solve with single-member districts. At the opposite extreme, it is completely bypassed when the whole nation is one large district, as in the Netherlands and in Israel, or when the remainders are allocated on a national basis.

Given the large number of electoral systems and the almost infinite permutations which can be obtained by playing both on the allocation of seats and on the number of seats in each district, it is not surprising that the technical problems posed by these systems should have fascinated both political theorists and mathematicians, from the French eighteenth-century scientist Condorcet onwards. The direct effect of these mechanisms on the result in each district and even on the overall result is manifestly large, as we just saw; not surprisingly, the question also arises as to whether there is not an *indirect* effect on the party system as a whole: it is to this matter that we now turn.

## Electoral systems and party systems

### Electoral systems and national party representation

Electoral systems are typically regarded as having an effect on the nature and characteristics of party systems: thus it is said that majority systems lead to two-party systems. The relationship is more complex, however, and it has two dimensions: temporal and geographical. Let us examine the geographical dimension first.

The effect which we described earlier occurs at the level of each district: what needs to be assessed is how this effect is translated at the national level. For a national effect to take place at all, the parties need to be the same throughout the country. Thus the

## BOX 11.2
## District size and proportionality

The debate over the relative merits of proportional representation and majority systems typically relates to the general principles of allocation of seats. Yet this debate may well miss the real point in many cases, since what may be more crucial than the method of allocation of seats is the district size.

Attention to this problem was first drawn in the context of Irish elections. The country has had a working two-and-a-half party system: it seems therefore that the fears that PR would lead to the lack of a majority and to governmental instability were clearly not founded. But this result has been obtained largely because the size of electoral districts in the Republic of Ireland is small: most constituencies have three to five seats only. Indeed, the size of districts has declined from the original period to the 1940s. This situation makes it difficult for candidates to be elected unless they belong to a party which obtains at least 20 per cent of the votes or more, except if these candidates have a local personal following in a given district. This can happen, but it is rare where parties tend to be national.

The same situation has occurred in Spain with the return of democracy in the mid-1970s. Ireland has adopted STV, Spain the list system of proportional representation. Yet the result is similar in that, without having to introduce 'five per cent' clauses, the large parties are markedly favoured. Each province of Spain constitutes a district and only one, however small or however large. Most provinces are entitled to four or five members of the Cortes, only Madrid and Barcelona having more than twenty seats. The system is thus naturally biased in favour of the two large national parties, but it is also quite acceptable to the nationalist or regional parties, which have a strong provincial implantation: thus the Catalan and Basque nationalist parties are well represented in Parliament. On the other hand, smaller parties whose support is spread out, such as the communist and the centre parties, since 1982, are not well represented.

Electoral systems such as the Spanish system have an advantage over majority systems: they are technically proportional and do not therefore suffer from the opprobrium of being 'majoritarian', which, for many, means unjust. However, they have almost the same effect, except that they give more power to the party leadership. In single-member majority systems, seats are rarely entirely safe; at any rate, local élites choose the candidates. With proportional representation systems based on small districts, some seats are safe – those at the top of the lists of the large parties or even of the small parties in the few large districts – and the selection of the candidates is done by party headquarters.

The key to the proportional character or otherwise of an electoral system is thus as much district size as it is the formal labelling of the system.

electoral system can be expected to affect the party system as a whole if the parties are national in character; or, to be more rigorous, the more the parties are national, the greater the potential effect of the electoral system on the party system. It may also be that the electoral system will, in some circumstances, 'nationalize' the party system. However, such a 'nationalizing' effect is even more likely to be the consequence of social and economic development. This is one of the reasons why conclusions on the national impact of electoral systems can therefore be drawn more easily for Atlantic countries than for other polities.

Let us assume, therefore, that the same parties exist across the nation. In proportional representation systems, we know that the result becomes increasingly proportional as the number of seats per district increases. The impact of the electoral system will therefore vary if the number of seats varies from district to district. Parties which are thinly spread throughout the country are at a disadvantage if the average district size is small. They will gain somewhat if some of the districts are large (as sometimes happens with big cities): election results in Spain are a good example of this effect. In general, with districts of three to five seats only, parties which obtain 15 per cent of the votes or less are ill represented. Thus, in a party system in which five or six parties receive a significant share of the votes, districts should have six to eight members at least for the representation to be relatively accurate.

In majority systems, on the other hand, the smaller the number of seats per district, the more accurate the representation. Yet, even with single-member districts, large parties are at a premium, while those whose support is thinly and evenly spread can be grossly underrepresented, a state of affairs from which the British Liberal Party has markedly suffered, given that what counts is the size of the support in each district. On the other hand, for the same reason, a relatively small party whose support is clustered geographically can achieve satisfactory representation, as has periodically been the case in Britain with the Scottish National Party.

Furthermore, even among the major parties, a marked unevenness of the distribution of votes across the country will result in substantial distortions. At the limit, a party which would come second in every district would not obtain a single seat, even if it were to obtain a substantial proportion of the votes, since what counts is the existence of clusters of strength.

Thus, in majority systems, three conditions have to be fulfilled for the representation of the major parties to be relatively accurate:

- The distribution of the support has to be statistically 'normal' across the country. Support is not normal if it is spread in such a way that the second party is *always* or nearly always second in all the districts. This is more likely to happen if there are only few seats to fill. In Britain, for instance, results at the local level, where there are fewer seats to fill than in the national Parliament, sometimes lead to the overwhelming dominance of one party in seats, although differences in the proportion of votes may not be very large.
- The overall strength of the major parties needs to be relatively close since, even if this strength is distributed 'normally', a large imbalance in votes will result in a

much larger imbalance in seats. The disparity has been found empirically to be expressed, both in Britain and in New Zealand, in the form of a *cube law*, by which the ratio of the seats of the two major parties varies like the ratio of the cubes of the votes going to these parties, a ratio which seems independent of the number of 'observations': that is, the number of seats in the legislatures (Butler, 1963: 194–204).

- In single-member majority systems, a relatively accurate translation of votes into seats among the major parties also depends on the absence of any bias with respect to the number of electors per district. This number must be approximately the same across the nation or, at a minimum, the zones of strength and of weakness of the major parties must be distributed at random among these parties. Given a large number of districts and provided the boundaries are drawn by impartial commissions, this condition is likely to be fulfilled.

Single-member majority systems can therefore produce a relatively accurate representation of broad voting patterns if there is a (small) number of relatively equal parties, if their support is spread 'normally' (evenly) across the nation, and if the boundaries of the districts are drawn in an impartial manner. This means in effect *national homogeneity*. It also means that the smaller the number of significant parties the better and, consequently, that a two-party system is preferable. In the real world, opportunities for distortion are substantial: not surprisingly, politicians often prefer proportional representation since by comparison, this system appears to constitute a simpler piece of 'machinery' which is less likely to 'go wrong'.

## Electoral systems and party systems over time

There is an apparent impact of electoral systems on party representation with respect to each election; it seems natural to expect an impact – or at any rate a relationship – over time. Given its importance, this question has long exercised political scientists, although analyses have tended to be limited to the examination of the possible influence of party systems on the number of parties, rather than on their relative strength, their ideology, their structure or their social base.

Almost certainly, there is indeed an impact of electoral systems on party structure and social base, but it has not been fully explored, probably because, as we saw in Chapter 10, systems of more than one party have lasted for only short periods outside the Atlantic area. Moreover, where parties are not of the legitimate mass type, even if they have existed for a long time, the conditions of the competition are such that the mechanical effects of electoral systems over time are likely to be minimized. An example of a possible impact is constituted by the question of the 'nationalization' of parties. It has been argued that, because large or larger districts are a prerequisite of proportional representation, PR is more likely to 'nationalize' the confrontation than the single-member majority system. Indeed, proportional representation was introduced for a time in France as a weapon against sectional electoral politics (Duverger, 1954: 239–44). Where communal politics plays a large part, proportional representation might contribute to the integration of the various communities, although such an effect has not been noticeable in Northern Ireland or in Guyana. Overall, the evidence from countries outside the Atlantic area is still too scattered: the possible long-standing effect on the base and the structure of parties needs further investigation.

On the other hand, there is enough evidence drawn from within the Atlantic area and from a few other countries, to see whether there is a lasting relationship between electoral systems and the number of significant parties. This relationship is said to have existed at least since the beginning of the twentieth century; for a long time it has been presented in the form of the proposition that single-member first-past-the-post systems lead to two-party systems, while proportional representation encourages multiparty systems. This assertion has been put forward most strongly by Duverger in the 1940s; its first really rigorous test was made by Rae in the 1960s (Hermens, 1941; Duverger, 1954: 206–55; Rae, 1967; Lijphart, 1984a: 150–69).

The relationship does indeed appear close: four of the five western two-party systems of the 1950s and 1960s had a first-past-the-post electoral system (the fifth being Austria), while the first-past-the-post system did not coincide with a two-party system in one western country only (Canada) (Rae, 1967: 93–105). Moreover, the large majority of the two-party systems outside the Atlantic area can be found in countries which have adopted the first-past-the-post system.

## Extent and direction of the relationship

The extent and direction of the relationship need to be examined more closely, however. The extent of the relationship has been grossly exaggerated by early studies. For instance, the victory of Nazism in Germany was attributed to proportional representation because it was argued that this electoral system had led to unstable government, a proposition which we shall have occasion to examine in Chapter 16 (Hermens, 1941). The argument was based on the sequence: proportional representation, number of parties, instability of government. In this reasoning, it is because the existence of a large number of parties is attributed to PR that the instability of government is in turn linked to this electoral system. At this stage the only conclusion that can be drawn is that the two-party system and the single-member, first-past-the-post system are related to each other.

In a general manner, to back the view that the extent of influence of electoral systems on party systems is large, it has been claimed (by Duverger) that there is a natural tendency for polities to move towards dualism if they are not 'hampered' by the electoral system (Duverger, 1954: 1915). No evidence was given to support this proposition, however. As a matter of fact, on the contrary, one cannot detect any apparent movement towards the two-party system over time; indeed, we noticed that some polities moved in the other direction, as a result of the erosion of the support of some of the major parties. Moreover, in the nineteenth and early twentieth centuries, countries which had a single-member majority system, such as the Scandinavian countries and Germany, did not move at all towards a two-party system; during the same period, in Belgium, the two-party system lasted for half a century and was broken by the arrival of socialism *before* the introduction of PR. Finally, Duverger's assertion is based in part on the further claim that PR leads to party splits, a development for which there is only scattered and inconclusive evidence, and which is in fact rare. It did occur in the Danish and Norwegian social democratic parties, but this was due not to the electoral system, but to disagreements over membership of the European Community. The same development occurred also for a while in Britain for the same reason, yet Britain has a first-past-the-post system.

Moreover, it is noticeable that both the single-member, first-past-the-post system and the two-party system are widespread primarily among Anglo-American countries. Of these, only Australia and Ireland (as well as Guyana in the Third World) do not have a first-past-the-post system. Conversely, no country outside this group has a pure first-past-the-post system: Italy began to experience the first-past-the-post system only in the 1990s, and even then partially; other countries which have adopted the majority system, such as France, Japan and some eastern European countries have introduced different versions of these systems. The two-party system may not be a preserve of the Anglo-American world – several Commonwealth countries may not have a two-party system – but the relationship is close. The extent of association between two-party systems and single-member, first-past-the-post systems is not higher than the degree of association between two-party systems and Anglo-American political culture, a culture which gives a high premium to a sharp dichotomy between government and opposition and even organizes political life around this dichotomy. There is thus ground for suggesting at least that the 'cause' of the relationship may not be entirely found in the electoral system.

Further, the direction of the relationship may also be in question. As we saw, one of the conditions which have to be fulfilled if the first-past-the-post system is not to introduce unacceptable distortions is that the major parties be relatively equal in strength, at least over a period. Proportional representation, on the other hand, can cater for polities in which the strength of the major parties is unequal and the number of significant parties is large.

It may therefore be not that the single-member, first-past-the-post system 'causes' a two-party system, but rather that only polities in which parties tend naturally to be equal can tolerate this electoral system. In polities in which this is not the case, the single-member, first-past-the-post system is likely to be regarded as profoundly unjust. The only examples of countries which have maintained the single-member, first-past-the-post system without having a party system in which the major parties are rather equal are Canada and India, although Britain itself came close to a similar situation in the 1970s and 1980s. In the Canadian case, the complexity of the party system is compounded by the existence of different configurations at the provincial level: this appears to reduce the call for a change, together with the fact that the fate of the country remains uncertain and that a modification of the electoral system is therefore not likely to take place (Rae, 1967: 94–5). In India, the dominance of Congress has not prevented coalitions of opposition parties from taking place, even if this has occurred relatively rarely. In Britain, pressure for a change in the electoral system increased with the growth of the

Liberal Party after the late 1960s, although it tended to be less marked each time that party fared less well at the polls.

The question of the influence of electoral systems on party systems has probably overoccupied the minds of political scientists in search of 'laws' appearing to account mechanically for the development of party systems. The whole of a country's party system cannot be modified through the operation of a device such as an electoral system. In the first place, opponents of change would be likely to resist such a form of 'engineering', as they have done in Britain. Moreover, when the system is changed by a non-consensual decision, a move to return to the old rules quickly takes place, as occurred on a number of occasions in France, including in the 1980s.

## Referendums and direct democracy

Alongside elections at which electors select those who will represent them and might form the government, there are an increasing number of situations in which citizens are asked to express their views on specific issues by means of referendums or popular initiatives, or to support leaders through plebiscites.

The methods used can give greater or smaller opportunities for the people to participate. There are thus differences in the procedures. With *popular initiatives*, electors may suggest that a matter be submitted to a popular vote to force the legislature to discuss it. With *referendums*, on the other hand, electors can only approve or reject a project which has already been approved by the legislature. In practice, constitutions rarely allow for initiatives. There can also be differences in the opportunity given to the people to make their views felt on specific problems: popular participation can be restricted to some types of proposal and even to constitutional amendments only. The opportunity given to the people to participate may also be increased by means of advisory referendums when the national legislature or local councils consult the people before taking decisions, although they are not bound by the result.

The main reason why more referendums and initiatives do not take place is constituted by the tradition of 'pure' representative government. This tradition has been maintained as a result of the strong opposition to the introduction of techniques of semi-direct democracy on the part of observers and practitioners of politics alike. Two arguments have been traditionally put forward against greater direct popular participation:

- It is claimed that these procedures have often been abused by authoritarian leaders from Napoleon to many contemporary rulers: referendums are turned into plebiscites.
- It is also claimed that referendums tend to be conservative or negative: Australian and Swiss evidence has been provided in support of this claim (Livingston, 1956: 116–28; 183–98).

### Increased use of referendums

Despite these criticisms, the referendum technique has come to be used increasingly in western Europe since the 1950s, including in Britain, which has traditionally been one of the strongest supporters of pure representative government. In western Europe, only Germany, the Netherlands, Luxembourg and Iceland have never consulted the people directly on any issue between 1945 and 1995. Developments are still on a somewhat modest scale, admittedly, as in most countries only one referendum per decade has taken place and as, even in those countries in which they have been more frequent, such as Italy and Denmark, there have been just two or three per decade. Only Switzerland uses the technique truly extensively and regularly; elsewhere, referendums which do not relate to constitutional amendments occur on a haphazard basis, there being a tendency for initiatives or referendums to take place in Italy over matters of personal status (divorce and abortion), while they tend to occur in Denmark on some aspects of social legislation; in Austria and Sweden, referendums were called in order to solve controversies relating to nuclear energy. There have also been referendums in Latin America: for instance, in Chile, where military rule was ended as a result, and in Brazil, where the presidential system was confirmed by this process.

## Decline in criticisms of referendums

Recent experience from western Europe, Latin America, Australia, and a number of states (primarily western) of the United States suggest that referendums and initiatives do not have the effects which had been suggested. Referendums do not necessarily constitute plebiscites: some Third World leaders have used the procedure to boost their power, but they have also used ordinary electoral processes to the same end and with the same effect; De Gaulle used the referendum weapon against his opponents, and especially against those who wished to maintain French presence in Algeria (he did win on this point, but he later lost a referendum aiming at modifying the constitution, and subsequently resigned). Overall, the influence of leaders does not appear to be necessarily larger in the context of referendums than in the context of elections.

Referendums do not seem to be always conservative either. Some of the adopted policies have indeed been conservative, such as Proposition 13 which introduced stringent financial rules in California's budget in the 1980s; the Irish electorate also refused to repeal a constitutional clause forbidding the introduction of divorce laws in the Republic. However, other proposals of a conservative character have been rejected: the Italian people, for instance, refused to repeal a law which had made divorce legal in the country; ultimately, after much controversy, the Irish electorate accepted not to forbid contraception altogether. Moreover, the conservatism of electors may lead them to reject proposals of a 'radical right' character as well as proposals of a progressive nature: a majority of the Swiss electorate thus opposed measures designed to restrict severely the rules regarding the position of immigrants in the country; admittedly, substantial minorities favoured such restrictions, although these had been opposed by the major parties.

## Referendums, party systems and interest groups

The real consequences of referendums and initiatives are different: they relate to the part played by parties and groups in the process. These consequences are complex. Referendums and initiatives have an effect on parties – an effect which the parties themselves sometimes tend to provoke, since referendums have been more than occasionally called by parties which were divided internally on an issue. This was the case with the popular votes which took place on the European Community in Britain, Denmark and Norway in the early 1970s. In reality, these referendums did not solve the difficulties which the parties faced, and in all three cases they were followed by splits in the main Labour or social democratic party.

Meanwhile, groups appear to play a substantial part in provoking and, according to some, manipulating referendums, especially at the local and regional level, as is shown by many proposals put forward in a number of states of the United States; a similar influence can also be felt at the national level, as the case of Switzerland indicates. Some groups, often somewhat marginal to the political decision-making process, use the referendum device as a means of bringing to the fore issues which parties may not want to raise. A similar tactic is also adopted by parties which are either small or outside the government, and which may not otherwise be able to exercise much influence. This has led to the suggestion that referendums may lead to a manipulation of the electorate; it also suggests that the referendum and the initiative may not altogether help to link the people as a whole to the political system.

Such a conclusion is unwarranted: the manipulation by groups and small parties can be effective only if the turnout is truly very low. Moreover, if groups identify problems (such as environmental problems) which traditional parties do not raise, and if, in the process, the population manifests its interest in these issues, the result is a more open debate. Admittedly the danger remains that inconsistencies between results might occur and that it might become difficult to develop an overall policy for the nation.

Overall, the clearest outcome is probably that well-established parties are shaken and lose some of their support as a result. This may diminish the probability that comprehensive programmes will be put forward, and debates may become more sectional. Yet this can be of relatively limited importance in practice, since parties often do not have clearly defined programmes of a mobilizing character.

Finally, referendums frequently take place on large constitutional issues, and the support for the political system can be increased as a result. For instance, this was unquestionably the case in France in the late 1950s and early 1960s when the political system was markedly shaken by anti-democratic elements because of the war in Algeria, in which France was trying (unsuccessfully, as it turned out) to maintain its hold on that country.

## Overview

The direct links between people and government are somewhat limited in scope, even in the West, as elections and referendums are infrequent events. But these events are of major importance and they give to modern political systems a popular base which governments almost never had before.

Perhaps the most fundamental effect of electoral systems is to introduce *fairness* into the competition. They have to ensure that there is no discrimination, on grounds of sex, race, age and income, in particular.

Fairness entails introducing and strictly applying strong measures against *fraud*, which remains widespread in many countries.

Fairness also means giving candidates adequate means of fighting campaigns: hence the widespread development in the West of forms of *public finance* of elections and parties.

There are many techniques of relating seats to votes, under the general umbrella of the distinction between *majority systems* and *proportional (PR) systems*. The latter translate the voting patterns of electors more accurately, but there are many differences within each of the two broad types.

An essential component is constituted by *district size*: that is to say, the number of seats in each district. The larger this number, the more accurate is the relationship between seats and votes in proportional systems, but the less accurate it is in majority systems, especially in the first-past-the-post systems.

There is a broad tendency for single-member majority systems to be associated with two-party systems, and for other party systems to be associated with other electoral systems. However, single-member majority systems are also characteristic of Commonwealth countries, in which political battles take the form of contests between government and opposition.

Conversely, many continental systems have abandoned majority systems in favour of PR out of a desire to ensure the representation of more than two parties and, through these, of more than two broad groups in the society.

*Referendums* and other techniques of giving the people a direct voice on proposals have traditionally been regarded with suspicion by many supporters of liberal democracy. The grounds were that these devices were often used by dictators to manipulate opinion or that they led to decisions of a conservative character. These views are gradually being abandoned.

Although direct democracy techniques have only been adopted to a limited extent outside of Switzerland and some western American states, there is an upward trend, in large part as the criticisms levelled against these techniques are also increasingly being proved to be unjustified or exaggerated.

## Further reading

Although the literature on electoral systems is vast, much is descriptive rather than systematic. A comprehensive description of types of electoral system can be found in W.J.M. Mackenzie, *Free Elections* (1958). For a more recent presentation, see also V. Bogdanor, *What is Proportional Representation?* (1984) and V. Bogdanor and D.E. Butler, eds., *Democracy and Elections* (1983). See also G. Hand, J. Georgel and C. Sasse, *European Electoral Systems Handbook* (1979) and A. Lijphart, *Choosing an Electoral System* (1984).

The question of campaign finance began to be studied in the 1960s. The subject became increasingly popular, both among scholars and among politicians, as a number of proposals were presented and laws were passed. See A.J. Heidenheimer, ed., *Comparative Political Finance* (1970) and H.E. Alexander, ed., *Comparative Political Finance in the 1980s* (1989). For the United States, see H.E. Alexander, *Financing Politics* (1984). On political corruption, see A.J. Heidenheimer, M. Johnston and V.J. Levine, *Political Corruption: A Handbook* (1989).

The main problem which has attracted attention has been the question of the effects of majority and proportional systems on party systems. The controversy in this field has lasted many decades. In the 1930s and early 1940s, it was sometimes argued that proportional representation was responsible for the coming to power of Hitler: see, for example, F.A. Hermens, *Democracy or Anarchy?* (1941). In his classic on *Political Parties*, M. Duverger attempted to develop what he described as the 'law' of the relationship between two-party systems and the single-member single-ballot system on the basis of both psychological assumptions and the examination of a number of cases (*Political Parties*, 1954 edn: 206–55). The question was first truly systematically examined in the late 1960s by D.W. Rae in *The Political Consequences of Electoral Laws* (1967). See also A. Lijphart, *Democracies* (1984: 150–68). On the effect of district size, see J.F.S. Ross, *The Irish Electoral System* (1959). On the 'cube law' and its effect, see D.E. Butler, *The Electoral System in Britain since 1918* (1963).

The literature on referendums is still not comprehensive. See D.E. Butler, ed., *Referendums: A Comparative Study* (1978) and A. Ranney, ed., *The Referendum Device* (1981). The view that referendums are conservative was primarily based on the examination of earlier Australian and Swiss referendums: see W.S. Livingston, *Federalism and Constitutional Change* (1956).

# 12

# Parties in the world today

## Introduction

Most countries have parties, and nearly all countries have had parties at some time in recent decades. These organizations are thus a major feature of contemporary societies. But not all parties are strong and influence markedly the political life of the countries in which they emerge and develop. Party leaders often talk, in a somewhat grandiose manner, about the way parties guide political life: they may not all claim, as in communist states, that parties are at the 'vanguard'; but, in different terms and with a different emphasis, they usually hold the view that their organizations shape society in a significant manner. How far can these claims be sustained and, since the role of parties manifestly varies, how far can one assess the extent of these variations both among countries and over time?

Despite the importance of these questions, it is not possible as yet to give precise answers to them. We have neither the empirical knowledge nor the conceptual tools to undertake such a task fully. Evaluations of the impact of parties have begun to be undertaken, to be sure, especially with reference to western countries, but these analyses are essentially concerned to assess how far governmental policies differ if the parties in power are of the left or of the right (Castles, 1982; Budge *et al.*, 1987). There is only a limited stress on the more general role of parties, and in particular on the question whether they shape the structure of society or, on the contrary, are primarily the product of that society. To be comprehensive, the analysis needs to take into account the three functions listed in Chapter 9: namely, the extent to which parties provide a link between people and government, help to formulate decisions, and contribute significantly to the recruitment of those who rule the country. One needs also to assess general party strength or 'weight' and this can be done by finding out how stable parties have been over a long period.

On this basis, this chapter will be devoted to four issues:

- First, it will investigate the extent of *party stability* as an indicator of both the general and the relative strength of parties in contemporary societies.

- Second, it will examine how far the *political élite is recruited* by and from the political parties.
- Third, it will see whether parties appear to contribute significantly to the *policy-making process* in different types of society.
- Fourth, it will assess whether parties do provide a strong *link between people and government*, and whether this link is directed upwards from people to government, or downwards from government to people, or covers movements in both directions.

# Party stability

### The limited stability of parties

The basic assumption is that parties which remain in existence for long periods have substantial strength or 'weight' in a polity. Some of these long-standing parties may eventually collapse and retrospectively appear to have been weak. This has been the case with the communist parties of eastern Europe, which suddenly disintegrated in the late 1980s. It has also been the case, perhaps even more surprisingly, with two of the largest Italian parties in the mid-1990s, Christian Democracy and the Socialist Party. However, in general, it seems reasonable to move from the fact that parties are stable to the conclusion that they are well-implanted and therefore strong forces in the society.

On this basis, the judgement which has to be passed about parties in the contemporary world is rather negative. Only little more than a third of the polities had stable parties from 1950 or from the moment they were independent to the mid-1990s. Out of 182 countries in existence in 1994, 13 had never had parties, all of these being run by traditional regimes. In 65 countries the parties were stable during the period. In the other 104 there had been some form of party instability, periods without parties, or both, and in some cases more than once.

### The geographical spread of stable and unstable parties

The 65 countries which had stable parties divide unevenly between single-party systems (25) and systems of more than one party (40). They also divide unevenly geographically. Two-thirds (but only two-thirds) of the countries of the Atlantic area had had stable parties, all of them in the context of systems of more than one party. Between two-fifths and half the countries of south and south-east Asia and of the Caribbean and Latin America had had stable parties, most of them also to be found in the context of systems of more than one party. In the case of the Caribbean and of Latin America, however, 10 of the 12 countries with stable parties in the framework of systems of more than one party were English-speaking countries, while only two were Latin American. Finally, in eastern Europe and northern Asia a third, and in the Middle East and northern Africa and in Africa south of the Sahara a quarter or less, of the polities had had stable parties: these are to be found mostly, indeed exclusively in the case of eastern Europe and northern Asia, among single-party systems.

**Table 12.1** Stable and unstable party systems, 1950–94

| | Non party stable | Stable single party | Stable more than one party | Total stable parties | Total countries with parties | Percentage stable parties |
|---|---|---|---|---|---|---|
| Atlantic | – | – | 20 | 20 | 23 | 87 |
| Eastern Europe and northern Asia | – | 15 | – | 15 | 33 | 45 |
| Middle East and northern Africa | 7 | 1 | 4 | 5 | 21 | 24 |
| South and south-east Asia | 5 | 3 | 10 | 13 | 24 | 54 |
| Africa south of Sahara | 1 | 10 | 4 | 14 | 48 | 25 |
| Caribbean, Central and South America | – | 2 | 12 | 14 | 33 | 42 |
| Total | 13 | 31 | 50 | 81 | 182 | 45 |

Three different situations emerge from the examination of the geographical spread of stable and unstable parties:

- In the Atlantic area, south and south-east Asia and the Caribbean, stable parties prevail and they prevail in the context of systems of more than one party.
- In northern Asia and part of what was the Soviet Union as well as in parts of Africa south of the Sahara, the stable parties which developed did so in the context of single-party systems.
- In other parts of Africa south of the Sahara, in the Middle East and northern Africa, in Latin America, as well as since the late 1980s in eastern Europe, many important parties were set up, flourished and disappeared.

## Types of party instability

One can also distinguish among three broad types of instability. One is constituted by movements in and out of parties altogether. This occurs when the military takes over power in a country; the military may in turn subsequently be replaced by a civilian government. This type of move has been widespread in Africa south of the Sahara and in Latin America as well as, though to a lesser extent, in the Middle East and northern Africa. In this last region, a number of traditional non-party regimes among the small and rich countries of the Arabian peninsula have succeeded in avoiding change.

The second type of movement is that from a single-party system to a system of more than one party, or vice versa. Changes to a system of more than one party have taken place in eastern European countries in the late 1980s and early 1990s as well as (and in large part as a consequence of events in eastern Europe) among countries of Africa south of the Sahara. But movements of the same kind had occurred earlier: for instance, in Turkey in 1950 and in Spain and Portugal in the mid-1970s. Changes in the other direction – namely, from a system of more than one party to a single-party system – have also been frequent, especially in the late 1940s in eastern Europe, under the pressure of the Soviet Union, in the 1950s in the Middle East and northern Africa (as in the cases of Syria and Egypt) and in the 1960s in Africa south of the Sahara. Movements away from the system of more than one party to the single-party system are likely to continue to occur, as will movements from a system of more than one party or from a single-party system to a non-party military regime. Sudan has been a case in point in the late 1980s.

Third, party change does occur within single-party systems and within systems of more than one party. Some countries have moved from a conservative to a 'progressive' single-party system, Cuba being an example. The converse movement from a 'progressive' to a conservative single-party system has also occurred: for instance, in some of the successor states of the Soviet Union. Substantial changes within systems of more than one party are taking place periodically. The collapse of the Italian Christian Democracy and of the Italian Socialist Party in 1994 is only the most remarkable example of such movements. In the 1950s, the first Gaullist Party and the Christian Democratic Party collapsed in France; so did the Spanish Union of the Democratic Centre in the early 1980s.

## The erosion of party strength

As a matter of fact, even those countries which can be regarded as having had stable party systems have not been immune from some party changes. Indeed, by and large, there seems to be a general erosion of the strength of many and perhaps of the majority of these parties. In systems of more than one party, there is often some decline of the larger parties; in single-party systems, the move has been from a full to a dominant single-party system. Yet this erosion is typically valued differently in the case of single-party systems and in that of systems of more than one party.

Examples of the erosion of large parties in systems of more than one party were given in Chapter 10: clear cases are those of Denmark and Austria, but there has also been a decline of the larger parties in other Atlantic countries, such as Germany for instance. An erosion of support within the context of what still constitutes a stable set of parties might be regarded as a milder form of the large changes which have affected some parties in other Atlantic countries, such as France, Italy, Belgium, Canada and the Netherlands. By and large, however, this erosion is less pronounced in most Scandinavian countries and in the Anglo-American world. If we consider jointly all 40 countries in which parties remained stable among systems of more than one party, a majority (23) are English-speaking and the large majority of these belong to the Commonwealth. However, as was noted in Chapter 10, this group of Commonwealth countries includes many newly independent and small island countries of the Caribbean, the Indian Ocean and the Pacific. The largest number of older countries with stable parties in the context of systems of more than one party does therefore continue to be found in Western Europe (15 countries).

In systems of more than one party, the erosion of support experienced by the major parties seems to suggest that countries are moving towards a new situation in which political forces are atomized and national decision making becomes very complex as a result. Among single-party systems, on the contrary, the erosion of support of the controlling party tends to be regarded as the beginning of an opening towards pluralism, and therefore as an improvement in decision-making processes in these polities. The number of full single-party systems is indeed declining sharply: by the mid-1990s, out of the 25 single-party systems in which the controlling party remained stable, over half had allowed some opposition to manifest itself legally, and had therefore become dominant single-party systems. Such changes occurred primarily in the two regions of the world in which single-party systems are numerous, eastern Europe and northern Asia, on the one hand, and Africa south of the Sahara, on the other. The trend is general, however: Mexico and Taiwan also moved away from the almost complete dominance of the main party to a configuration which begins to resemble that of a system of more than one party.

Yet, even if this type of movement suggests a gain for political liberalization, it also means a possible increase in political instability as a result of the reduction of the strength of the dominant party, unless the emerging new parties are strong enough to form a truly organized alternative. This is rather unlikely, however, as the strategy of dominant single parties consists in undermining the potential strength of the forces which might constitute the opposition. Turkey is a case in point: after decades of single-party rule, the dominant Republican Party allowed a free election to take place in 1950 and was defeated; but that defeat was never wholly accepted, and much of the subsequent political instability in the country can be attributed to the fact that each of the various political forces is never sure that the others will follow the rules of the game. A similar point can be made about postwar Argentina as a result of the dominance of the Peronist Party in the 1940s and 1950s: this created such suspicion among other organizations that the political climate was poisoned for decades. There are other examples of the same type of difficulty experienced by single-party systems in the process of liberalization, in particular in the Middle East and in Africa, from Algeria to Zambia and from Sudan to Gabon.

## Durability of party systems and the 'weight' of parties

Parties and party systems of the contemporary world are thus not truly durable. In most countries, the party systems have been unstable and so have been the parties within these party systems. This instability was first thought to be confined to the Third World; it was seen to extend to the communist area in the late 1980s and early 1990s; it has also affected the parties of the Atlantic area to a substantial extent. The question therefore arises as to whether contemporary parties and party systems are not becoming less strong than they were, even in the Atlantic area. What potential do they have to exercise influence? And does the strength or 'weight' of parties depend on their stability?

There are grounds for doubting that stability and strength are always closely linked. The link probably exists at both extremes, in that very unstable parties are unlikely to have much 'weight' and very stable parties are likely to be rather strong; but the link is almost certainly not as strong at the intermediate points. For instance, ostensibly at least, some parties which collapsed and were never reconstituted, such as Nkrumah's Convention People's Party in Ghana, which was overthrown in 1966, or parties which were reconstituted after a long period during which they were banned, such as the Peronist Party in Argentina, throughout the 1950s, 1960s and 1970s, have had a considerable impact on their country. Conversely, parties which were in existence continuously or at least for long periods, such as those which the military set up and maintained in a number of countries of sub-Saharan Africa, appear to have had little influence. We therefore need to turn to a closer examination of the different aspects of the role of parties to be able to assess realistically what their strength can be.

## Recruitment of national decision-makers

Of the three aspects of the role of parties, recruitment is the easiest to analyze. Although no comprehensive study has as yet examined comparatively the extent to which governmental leaders and ministers are selected through parties, more limited analyses suggest fairly definite conclusions in this respect.

By and large, the role of parties is large because the 'political élite' is widely recruited through and from the parties, both in single-party systems and in systems of more than one party. This has been the case in Atlantic and communist countries as well as in many Third World states. Even parties which have not necessarily lasted very long have contributed significantly to the recruitment of national decision-makers: this has been true in Latin America during periods of civilian rule.

There are three types of limitations to this broad conclusion, however. First, some parties are 'façade' parties: this is the case with those which are set up by military leaders wishing to 'civilianize' their power. In such cases, the parties are typically not able, nor are they even asked, to provide the political élite: the leaders draw their ministers from among loyal military men or from among civil servants. Sometimes these ministers may be subsequently asked to join the party, but this is more to boost the organization than to ensure that the party is a source of recruitment.

Second, in some civilian regimes in which there is a strongly personalized leader, this leader may simply appoint whom he or she wishes without paying much attention to the party élite. There may, for instance, be an appeal to specialists and to technicians whose ties with the party are small or even non-existent. This type of situation occurs primarily in the Third World, but it has been known to exist in some western countries as well, as in France under De Gaulle in the 1950s and 1960s (Blondel, 1985: 55–76).

Third, the institutional framework may provide leaders with some room for manoeuvre outside the party framework. Parties are less likely to be involved in the recruitment of members of the legislature and of the national executive where the head of that executive has acquired legitimacy through a popular election. This is why, in some presidential systems and in the United States in particular, the part played by party in the recruitment of national decision-makers is smaller than in western European parliamentary systems, although, even there, there are differences which arise from the fact that the leader and the government as a whole may be somewhat distant from the legislature (Blondel and Thiebault, 1991).

Thus, even where parties are stable, a section of the political élite may not emerge from the parties. Yet, by and large, the role of parties is important in recruitment: they have almost a monopoly of selection of the members of the legislature and of the executive, both in many single-party systems and in most systems of more than one party; and they have a monopoly of the recruitment of the members of the legislature in those countries in which the executive is at some distance from the legislature. This is true in stable party systems and, for some periods at least, in many unstable parties. Thus parties do play a substantial part in the building of the political élite in contemporary polities.

## National decision making

It is not possible to be as definite with respect to the role of parties in national decision making. To begin with, the measurement of this role is more problematic: if parties are highly decentralized, for instance, their impact is likely to be more diffuse. More generally, party influence on decision making has to be assessed in conjunction with the influence of other bodies, such as interest groups, the bureaucracy and the military; but some of the influence of these bodies also takes place through the parties as well as alongside them. Finally, there are probably variations everywhere according to the fields of governmental activity: parties seem to be less involved, at any rate in a continuous manner, in foreign than in domestic affairs; they may be also more concerned with short-term gains than with long-term developments.

Some general conclusions can be drawn, however. First, parties often play a substantial part in the definition of governmental programmes and even in the solution of conflicts over specific issues. This is especially the case in parliamentary systems, both where the government is controlled by one party and where there is a coalition. Parties tend to exercise greater influence where the party system has been stable for a substantial period, although they may occasionally play a substantial part even if they are in control for short periods only. By and large, the countries in which this type of party influence prevails are in the Atlantic area and in some Commonwealth polities of the Third World (Castles, 1982; Katz, 1986: 31–71; Budge *et al.*, 1987). Moreover, in single-party systems of the communist variety, both in the past and among those which have remained, parties have had an even larger role: they have helped to *implement* policies by exercising substantial control over the bureaucracy (Holmes, 1986: 230–50).

On the other hand, many parties of the Third World are too inchoate to have a significant decision-making impact. This can be because the party has emerged slowly from a large communal group and the leaders of this communal group remain in control of the decision-making process, the party being essentially a façade organization. It can also be because the party is a recent creation of a leader, especially of a military leader: the main national decision-makers are then the leader, the entourage of the leader, and the bureaucracy. Thus, in Africa south of the Sahara, in the Middle East and northern Africa, as well as to a lesser extent in Asia (in South Korea and Taiwan, for instance), the role of the party as such in the national decision-making process appears limited.

These situations are not fixed, however. Parties in which the leader was originally fully in control can gradually acquire some influence with respect to at least some aspects of decision making; conversely, parties which are typically relatively influential can become, sometimes only temporarily, so dominated by a leader that his or her policy may prevail whatever the party may have wished: this has been the case in some western European countries, Mrs Thatcher's Britain being an example. The result is a combination of relatively small areas of party influence and of large areas in which the leaders and their entourage (often with the help of the national bureaucracy) are in charge of decision making. There are also intermediate cases which are more stable, when the institutional arrangements lead to a sharp distinction between party and governmental decision making: this is the case in presidential systems in general and in the United States in particular, where parties appear to play more the part of pressure groups than that of central elements in the elaboration of the policy framework.

Thus parties play a substantial part in decision making in a minority of polities only. Indeed, even in these cases, they often help merely to define broad options within which governments operate, although they sometimes follow through these options at the level of specific decisions, which can be very contentious – for instance, in coalition governments. It is primarily in western Europe and, in a different manner, in communist regimes that parties have played such a part. Elsewhere, parties are more vague and more peripheral: they are unlikely to be closely involved in the solution of national conflicts even if they are often involved in some manner in the presentation of problems or in the setting-up of at least some elements of the public agenda (Randall, 1988).

## The link between rulers and the population

### Tension between representation and mobilization

Perhaps the most important role of parties is to provide a link between people and government. This link can take the form of an upward movement which results in the *representation* of the desires of the population to the political élite. It can take the form of a downward movement and constitute an attempt to 'educate' or mobilize the population in the direction of the goals which leaders wish to pursue. It can also be of both types within the same party.

Western parties are deemed to be of the first type. They operate within a constitutional framework which is based on the representative principle. Yet western parties – at any rate many of them – also aim at mobilizing and educating the population. This has traditionally been the case with parties of the left, which often claim that the status quo is maintained only because large numbers of electors do not realize where their 'true' interests lie; but many parties of the right also wish to mobilize electors, since they sometimes claim that they need to modify the views of electors, who may be misguided – for instance, as a result of what they sometimes describe as 'liberal' or 'socialist' propaganda. There is therefore at least some effort by most western parties to mobilize the electorate even if they are obliged, at election time, to place a strong emphasis on the representative function. This leads to ambiguities and tensions within parties which sometimes emerge when they are defeated, as one side blames the other for being 'overpragmatic' or 'too ideological'.

Communist systems and the more 'progressive' regimes of the Third World traditionally emphasized mobilization rather than representation as their goal. This has been justified by their supporters on the grounds that a wholly representative approach favours forces of conservatism rather than the long-term development of the economy and of the society. Indeed, the mobilizing goal has been given considerable prominence in some cases, such as during the cultural revolution in China. But even when it has not been pressed as strongly, it has remained profoundly embedded in the philosophy of the parties which propose authoritarian-egalitarian and populist ideologies. This stance also enables the leaders of these parties to justify their policy of pressing ahead with their goals irrespective of opposition, and to regard as wholly unacceptable any move designed to 'distract' the population away from these goals.

## Mobilization in communist and Third World countries

It is because of the need to enlist the support of the population in this way that parties have been critically important to authoritarian-egalitarian and populist leaders. Consequently, perhaps, 'charismatic' leaders who set up populist parties have not been overconcerned with other aspects of the role of parties: they have not been anxious to see the organizations they created or inherited from their predecessors being markedly involved, if at all, in decision making. Such an involvement would naturally tend to diminish their influence and can therefore be regarded as leading to representation rather than mobilization. Only in the communist world have parties of a 'progressive' character been sufficiently well structured and sufficiently controlled by a dedicated élite to make it possible for a (limited) degree of rank-and-file involvement to take place within them. The purpose of populist parties of the Third World is essentially to provide an instrument through which the views of the leaders can be communicated to the population in such a forceful and convincing manner that that population is induced to adopt these views.

This last hope has rarely been fulfilled. A goal of this kind can be achieved only through a complete transformation of mentalities, which even the extensive and active organizations of communist parties did not succeed in realizing. In Third World countries, the resources at the disposal of leaders have not been adequate. Thus the experience of the second half of the twentieth century suggests that this type of mobilization effort is not attainable. The failure of the cultural revolution in China provides at least circumstantial evidence of the inability of parties to change mentalities and to mobilize the population fully. Single-party systems which originally had such a goal have come gradually to redefine, deliberately or not, and in an outspoken manner or not, the purpose of the party. This purpose has come closer to the administration of existing arrangements than to a striving towards new structures. Consequently, there has been an element of representation, in effect, in these parties, at least in terms of a part of the membership of the party itself. Parties have become self-contained organizations in which there is greater stress on the placement of colleagues than on the provision of a link designed to influence the population on behalf of the rulers.

## What mobilizing parties can achieve

This means not that no mobilization effort can ever succeed, but that it will succeed only if backed by a strong organization, and if it does not attempt to push the population too far away from its original values. Too much has been expected of parties during the second half of the twentieth century: the amount of change in attitudes and behaviour which can be achieved with the help of parties is clearly markedly smaller than party activists have generally tended to believe. The same conclusion can be drawn by considering the activities of western parties: indeed, these parties have generally come to recognize the limits of their potential for mobilization, particularly since the 1970s. Western socialist and other parties of the left have markedly reduced the scope of their proposals in the course of the postwar period. Few of their leaders, but admittedly more among the rank and file, believe that they can go appreciably beyond limited changes in the status quo. As a matter of fact, contrary to what many activists have claimed, socialist parties have not tended to lose votes to the left to a significant extent by becoming moderate in the 1980s in several western European countries, particularly France and Spain.

## Erosion of the representative role in the West

This self-denying ordinance can be considered to be a victory for the representative model of the political system. Yet, while the mobilizing philosophy has lost ground, both in the reality of party achievements and in the minds of party leaders, the representative capability of parties appears also to have been eroded. By and large, the representative-cum-mobilizing model which some western parties tended to espouse was based on the general assumption that parties were the supreme channel between people and government in the contemporary world. We saw in Chapter 9 why there are grounds for believing that this view could be correct. However, the emergence of many new groups, covering a variety of interests cutting across the traditional divisions between parties, especially in the West, has tended to undermine the representative character of these parties: supporters of these groups often do not seem to believe that parties are able or even willing to defend their interests. This development is in part the consequence of the increased strength of such bodies as feminist, ecological and regional organizations. Some of these groups have set up parties of their own, as the Greens did; other have preferred to operate outside the party framework. All have undermined the supremacy of more traditional parties. They have not altered markedly the configuration of party systems, but they have appreciably reduced the credibility and therefore the strength of the existing parties. To attempt to protect themselves, parties have adopted issues as they came, and have become almost passive intermediaries. American parties are those which have moved furthest in this direction, perhaps because they had long been predisposed to be extremely open. A substantial proportion of the issues raised by the parties or by members of parties in the federal and state legislatures come from interest groups, while relatively few come from within the parties themselves. Indeed, the parties are so decentralized that a uniform policy has little chance of being adopted. In this context, the 'democratic' way in which candidates are selected (through primaries at which many electors participate) militates against the possibility of a uniform 'programme' of the parties.

Thus parties in western countries float somewhat above the population more than they are truly drawn from it and closely tied to it. This state of affairs coincides with the idea that parties compete in a market and attempt to sell their products to an increasingly independent electorate. This means that parties are no longer representative of the population in the true sense of the word. They may be representative in the global sense that the party system as a whole, by way of the operation of the electoral market, provides the population with at least a rough mechanism through which to express their desires; but each party separately does not fulfil a strongly representative role.

The linkage between rulers and ruled is only partly achieved by political parties, whether of the mobilizing or of the representative variety. Some of these organizations are truly artificial; they have few real contacts with the people. Yet even those which are extensive and have many branches locally are psychologically somewhat distant from 'the people', whether because they cannot convince the majority about their goals or because other bodies seem better able to catch the imaginations. Parties do have an impact on society, but this impact is not such that they can be regarded anywhere in the world as providing the deep intellectual and associational link which they had often been expected to provide, and which in many cases they had been set up to provide.

## The overall role of parties today

It could therefore be that parties were characteristic of and well suited for a particular phase of the modernization process, but that they are not equally appropriate to provide the link which is needed when societies acquire a complex but disparate set of needs,

---

## BOX 12.1
## What long-term future for parties, especially in the West?

It is becoming increasingly fashionable to view the future of political parties as bleak. The decline of several large parties in continental Europe is noticeable; it is not as pronounced in the Anglo-American world. It is pointed out that parties do not fulfil their function of programme elaboration in a truly serious manner, and that they prefer to borrow ideas from others. It is also pointed out that the representation of interests and views is increasingly provided by groups, which are closer to the people than parties. The polity may become 'ungovernable' as a result; but the movement cannot be stopped. Parties would therefore seem to be on the path towards extinction.

The way parties have been declining in the United States, especially in the west, is interesting: they have come to have only a symbolic role. They do not propose programmes; they do not even select candidates, since these are in effect chosen by primaries which are outside the control of party leaders. On this basis, however, parties survive.

The evolution is different in continental Europe. The traditional parties attempt to resist, but as large sections of the population are no longer close to them, they lose votes to new parties which seem to make better proposals. The number of significant parties may become so large as a result that no party any longer has a true grip on political life.

Britain and some of the older Commonwealth countries appear to be among the few western polities where parties remain small in number (thanks to the electoral system, unquestionably, but also thanks to the general political culture), while preserving some of their original functions of policy elaboration, policy management and recruitment.

Hence there are three apparently distinct scenarios in the West. In America, parties seem to retain primarily a symbolic role: they remain in existence because people apparently feel that there have to be parties in a democracy. On the Continent of Europe, there is gradual fragmentation: everyone presses for his or her views or his or her cleavages; representation is preferred to policy making. In Britain and some of the Commonwealth countries, what may keep parties alive is the old joy of the battle between government and opposition.

Does this constitute a solid basis for the future of political parties?

and that groups are a better channel in such a situation. Developments in the United States, where parties seem to have declined considerably in strength, especially in California, suggest a possible demise of parties in the future. While such a point has not been reached in western Europe, the reduction in the solidity of traditional parties and the corresponding increase in the volatility of the electorate may constitute a move in the same direction.

Yet the practical way in which parties could be replaced is not clear, not only with respect to the recruitment of the political 'class' or to the process of national decision making, but with respect to the provision of a satisfactory linkage between government and people. This linkage cannot take place through the groups, since these are specialized and are in marked competition; an aggregative element has to emerge if the political process is to function effectively. Parties are therefore probably here to stay, for many decades at least. It is not surprising, however, that there should be periodic worries about the problems which they pose; nor is it surprising that they should be less stable and less effective than they have typically been expected to be by those who have been their faithful supporters (Blondel, 1981).

## Overview

The links between people and parties are not as yet fully known, and many aspects of these links can be described in general terms only.

The majority of parties have not been stable across the world. Only in the Atlantic area and in most countries of the Commonwealth has there been a high degree of stability. The fall of communism in eastern Europe also shattered the view that strong single-party systems were inherently stable.

Parties do play a large part in the *recruitment of the political élite*, both in legislatures and, though to a lesser extent, in national governments.

Parties play less of a part in the *elaboration of policies*, even in western countries. In the Third World, parties often simply endorse and orchestrate policies formulated by leaders: this is the case even in the better established among these parties.

Parties provide *a link between people and government*, but this link is often tenuous. It also often takes more the form of a *downward* attempt by governments to influence the population through the parties than of an upward endeavour to enable the population to be represented.

Downward attempts at *mobilization* are typically far from successful, as has been shown in the case of most 'progressive' and communist parties.

In the West, the *representative function* of parties is often limited by the action of groups. Parties then seem to float above the population rather than to be truly close to its desires and its requirements.

Yet, despite their limitations, parties remain the only mechanism by which a general link is established between people and government. They are therefore unlikely to disappear or to be replaced in the near future.

## Further reading

The question of whether parties 'matter' began to be examined systematically for western Europe in the 1970s and 1980s. See in particular F.G. Castles, ed., *The Impact of Parties* (1982). For a spatial analysis of programmes of western European parties (as well as a few others), see I. Budge, D. Robertson and D. Hearl, eds., *Ideology, Strategy, and Party Change* (1987).

The question of the role of parties in the recruitment of political leaders is examined in J. Blondel, *Government Ministers in the Contemporary World* (1985) and J. Blondel and J.L. Thiebault, eds., *The Profession of Cabinet Minister in Western Europe* (1991).

There is no general study of the role of parties in decision making. In the context of western Europe, see F.G. Castles and R. Wildenmann, eds., *Visions and Realities of Party Government* (1986), and in particular the chapter by R.S. Katz, 'Party government: a rationalistic conception', pp. 31–71. On the role of mobilizing parties, see D. Apter, *The Politics of Modernisation* (1965: 179–222). On the role of parties in communist states, see L. Holmes, *Politics in the Communist World* (1986: especially 96–118 and 230–50).

**Part IV**

# Governmental structures

# 13

# Constitutions

## Introduction

We have so far examined the nature of the relationship between people and government in different types of political system. We must now turn to the structure of governmental institutions and to the processes of public decision making. Such an analysis is rendered complex, however, because it is not sufficient to describe structures of government as they are: one must also take into account the part played by constitutions in prescribing how these structures *should* be organized and how governmental bodies *should* behave. For a long time, the analysis of governmental structures was almost entirely confined to the examination of the constitutional provisions regulating these structures. For the reasons which we discussed in Chapter 1, modern political science has deliberately emphasized the analysis of patterns of behaviour alongside the examination of constitutional arrangements, occasionally at the expense of constitutional arrangements. A truly realistic approach entails that prescription and behaviour be examined in parallel, since the prescriptions put forward by constitutions both influence behaviour and are, in themselves, behavioural statements about the characteristics which governments are expected to embody.

It is difficult to combine the analysis of patterns of governmental organization and the examination of prescriptions of constitutions. The two elements are intertwined, but they are not intertwined to the same extent or in the same manner in every polity.

On the one hand, while governments exist everywhere and are therefore necessarily organized in a certain way, constitutions have introduced ideas and precepts about the organization of governments which have deeply affected both theory and practice, even where there is no formal constitution: Constitutional developments which have occurred since the end of the eighteenth century have resulted in a universal debate about the principles of the organization of governments and about how best to implement these principles.

On the other hand, constitutions have been distorted and even set aside in many parts of the world at many points of time; they are indeed distorted to an extent everywhere. The main difficulty does not stem so much from the fact that some countries have a constitution and others do not. The polities which do not have a constitution now are either a few remaining traditional states (principally located in the Arabian peninsula) or military regimes, where sooner or later the military has to leave office or feels the need to proclaim a new constitution. Nor does the main difficulty stem either from having to distinguish between countries which implement their constitution and those which do not, although many constitutions are deliberately set aside in practice while being extolled in theory. The real problem is that constitutions are implemented to a degree, and to a different degree, in various countries, and that the reasons why constitutions are more or less implemented range from, at one extreme, the existence of customs and traditions which the constitution cannot break to, at the other extreme, a deliberate desire not to implement on the part of the rulers of the day.

Thus the analysis of the structures of government entails looking at these structures as they are, as well as at the extent to which these structures follow the precepts of the constitution. We shall examine the various aspects of the organization of governments in the contemporary world in subsequent chapters; in this chapter, we shall analyze the general characteristics of constitutions and their possible impact.

- In the first section, we shall consider the various ways in which constitutions can affect the *structure of government*.
- In the second section, we shall look at the manner in which constitutions can be and are *modified*.
- Finally, in the third section, we shall outline the main elements of the *content* of constitutions.

# Constitutional rules

All governments are organized in a certain way, resulting from the combination of a number of factors. Constitutional arrangements are only one of these factors; others include traditions and customs, which in turn are the product of the influence exercised by individuals and by groups. This is why constitutions can change patterns of behaviour only with difficulty, with the corollary that they will tend to be most effective if they do not depart markedly from existing practice (Wheare, 1966; Bogdanor, 1988).

## Constitutional and other rules

Constitutions aim at organizing the operation of governments on the basis of a number of principles, but in most cases, if not always, they are introduced against a background of strongly established conventions and customs. Even where there is no constitution in a country, there are rules shaping the organization of the government.

These rules may include statutes which do not have constitutional status, but which in practice play the same part. For example, there is no constitution in Britain, since there is no document with this title in that country, but there are many statutes which have an effective constitutional character because they organize the governmental institutions. There are also conventions and customs which are no less stringent for not being written.

This is the case not only in Britain, but also in other countries. In theory there might be no conventions, no customs, no statutes in a country, meaning that leaders could operate exactly as they wish. In practice, even very authoritarian leaders need typically to organize their mode of operation: only when a country or a regime is being established can a leader have almost complete freedom to act. In other circumstances there are some rules and there are some customs. Constitutions play a part among these rules, although this part may not be the most important.

## Meanings of the word 'constitution'

As a matter of fact, the words 'constitution' and 'constitutional' have three distinct meanings:

- They refer to a series of *prescriptive* arrangements: this is summarized in the expression 'constitutional rule', which tends to refer to a form of government which is liberal, emphasizes restraint in the operation of government, and gives maximum freedom to the citizens.
- The word 'constitution' refers to a *document*, written at a given point in time. This document establishes institutions and procedures, which may or may not be in conformity with the principles of 'constitutional rule', yet it is the document which prevails in practice, not the principles.
- The constitution also relates to the *actual organization* of the polity. To this extent, it is simply a description of the existing institutions (Sartori, 1962; Bogdanor, 1988: 2–7).

In this last sense, all countries have a constitution. The descriptive meaning of the constitution applies to all types of government, since all states are organized in a certain way. It is only by reference to the first two meanings – 'constitutional rule' and the existence of a document – that some states can be said not to have a constitution. In the contemporary world, the large majority of states have a constitutional document, but probably only a minority can be said to be 'constitutional' in the sense that the government abides by truly 'constitutional' rules. Meanwhile, the descriptive meaning is the one which provides an impression of the conventions and customs on the basis of which the government operates. By comparing description and 'constitutional principles', one can see whether the principles are put in practice. Some norms prevailing in a state may not be embodied in the constitutional document at all; others which are prescribed in the document may not be applied. On the other hand, the document may also specify rules which have little to do with the overall organization of the state and are inserted only because most constitutional documents are relatively difficult to amend.

## Types of constitutional principle

Constitutional principles vary noticeably. 'Constitutionalism', as was pointed out earlier, refers to a form of government which is based on restraint. From the end of the eighteenth century and throughout the nineteenth, constitutions were viewed as the main means of combating tyranny and of guaranteeing freedom. These constitutions related primarily to what was defined in Chapter 3 as the *dimension* or *means* of government, rather than to participation, and even less to substantive policies: they emphasized *procedures*. This came subsequently to be regarded as unsatisfactory by those who felt that the state should not merely promote freedom, but also bring about greater equality. Efforts were therefore made to insert statements to this effect in the constitutions which were drafted later.

There are three types of broad principle on which constitutions have been based. In the first type, the emphasis was almost exclusively on *restraints* placed on the executive. This was the case in the earlier constitutions, such as those of the United States, of Latin American countries and of continental Europe in the nineteenth century (though not all French constitutions before 1815 fall in this category).

Second, after the First World War in western Europe, and in some other parts of the world after the Second World War – in the Constitution of Weimar Germany in 1918 or in the French Constitution of 1946, for instance – constitution-makers were less concerned with restraint and placed more emphasis on the need to develop *positive rights*, mainly social and economic, alongside traditional individual rights. These 'positive' rights were even viewed as logical extensions of the liberal protection provided in earlier texts.

Third, in communist states and in some 'progressive' Third World countries, constitutions gave precedence to *egalitarian goals* over liberal restraint, the first example being that of the Soviet Constitution of 1936. Based on the Marxist ideology which emphasizes the primacy of the economic substructure over the political superstructure, these documents called for policies designed to achieve 'positive' freedoms: for instance, by stipulating stringent conditions under which traditional freedoms could be exercised, and by ascribing to the single communist party the task of guiding the nation towards these goals, in theory during a period of transition only. Subsequently, however, communist societies retreated somewhat from these 'orthodox' postures; there was a move towards traditional ('bourgeois') freedoms which were given greater recognition, while matters of state organization were also given greater prominence. The demise of communism in eastern Europe struck a major blow to this 'socioeconomic' approach to constitution making, despite the fact that some states, and in particular China, have continued to follow the principles of communism.

## Constitutional supremacy

If constitutions prescribe the basic principles under which governments are to operate, they must logically be supreme and therefore take precedence over all other rules, written or unwritten. From a juridical standpoint, the case for the supremacy of constitutions is watertight. It is less strong in practice, however, since constitutions relate to the context within which they come into existence (Beard, 1935); with time, this content is likely to change. Moreover, since political life may be governed by customs and conventions which differ widely from the constitutional prescriptions, the scope for constitutional supremacy may be reduced and, at the limit, be limited.

## Constitutional rigidity

Constitutional supremacy tends to lead in practice to the legal principle of constitutional *rigidity*, which means that the constitution can be amended only by complex procedures. This seems to follow logically from the fact that the constitution embodies the most fundamental rules. In practice, however, constitutional rigidity may become in many cases a serious impediment, while being unnecessary in others. Where the political evolution has been gradual, as in Britain, the constitution does not need to be rigid. The situation is paradoxical: where the constitution could be rigid because there is limited challenge to its norms and even its detailed provisions, it is unlikely to be rigid because it does not need to be; where, on the contrary, the constitution is under challenge from sections of the society who do not approve of the norms which it embodies, the constitution is likely to be rigid. This may increase the extent of opposition to the constitutional provisions, and therefore build up tension in the society.

Admittedly, the rigidity of constitutions is not justified only on the legal ground that these documents are supreme; rigidity is also justified on the political ground that only if constitutions are rigid will they be likely to affect behaviour gradually. Yet, since they are difficult to alter if they are rigid, they are also likely to adapt with difficulty to social and political change. The reasons which militate for rigidity in the eyes of framers of constitutions are also those which risk leading to problems as time passes. This is particularly the case where constitutions are detailed, since they may include provisions which are not merely contentious but cumbersome as well. Thus the constitutions of many states of the United States and of a number of Latin American countries describe the organization of governmental institutions in great detail, and include financial and other provisions which may be widely regarded as not being part of the general framework of the organization of the state. The more such topics are introduced in the basic law, the more problems are likely to occur.

## Constitutional change

The question of constitutional change becomes particularly serious where the constitutional amendment process is arduous. This is why, in practice, contrary to what might – and should – be expected, constitutional amendments are not the only way in which constitutional change takes place. Another way is by means of daily customary or indeed judicial practice. A further way is the pure and simple abrogation of the constitution as a result of a coup or revolution.

Constitutional *amendments* have to follow the procedures laid down by the constitution. These vary from maximum 'flexibility', when the constitution can be amended in the same way as any piece of legislation, to maximum rigidity, when no amendment is allowed at all. The constitutions of New Zealand and Israel are wholly flexible; Britain has no constitution, but a number of statutes which can be modified by other statutes. At the other extreme, some constitutions are very rigid indeed.

Constitutions can be rigid 'in bulk' or 'in detail'. The whole constitution may be made rigid by requiring *special majorities* of the legislature (from three-fifths to two-thirds normally), by electing *special conventions* (Belgium and some of the US states), by stipulating that there has to be popular approval by *referendum*, or by combining this last condition with one of the previous two (as is the case in many western countries). There can also be *special rigidity* if some clauses are entrenched and can be amended only if there is concurrence, unanimous or in a majority, of the group or groups which are to be protected. These may be ethnic minorities (as in Lebanon), geographical bodies (typically states in a federation), or even institutions (as in the case of the French Senate, which may not be abolished if it does not concur). Entrenchment can even be total, as was the 'Republican form of government' in the French 1946 Constitution. Levels of rigidity have frequently been imitated from one constitution to another. Constitutional amendments are, on the whole, rather infrequent: for instance, there have been only 15 amendments to the United States Constitution since the Bill of Rights was passed in 1791.

Constitutions are also modified, and indeed are often modified, by *customary practice*, sometimes even formally recognized and even partly helped by *judicial action*. Such changes are strictly 'unconstitutional', but they occur frequently as time passes. The question of customary change is mainly referred to in the context of the English Constitution, which is formally unique, not because it is flexible (as we saw, the New Zealand Constitution is also flexible), but because it is not found in a single document; yet the problem arises everywhere. Thus the American Constitution has in practice been amended with respect to the behaviour of the members of the Electoral College, who, contrary to the document which wished them to be free to decide among presidential candidates, have become pledged to vote for the candidate with whom they associated themselves during the election campaign. Similarly, and even more important, the American Constitution was amended when the Supreme Court declared itself competent, in 1803, to quash federal legislation, a matter which we shall examine again in Chapter 20.

It is because of the incidence of customary change that it is often difficult to decide how far a constitution is being 'truly' implemented. There are slow gradations, ranging from minor twists given to the spirit of the text, or simple abandonment of provisions which thus become a dead letter, to clear and outright flouting of a positive command. No constitution is fully applied; in fact it is probably *because* they are slowly modified by customary change that many constitutions survive. Customary change is one way of bypassing formal provisions, quietly and step by step, and thus a means of reconciling the rule of law and the supremacy of constitutions with the fact of social and political change.

# BOX 13.1
# The relatively short life of constitutions

Constitutions are the most solemn documents which can exist in a nation, yet their life is relatively short. Given that Britain does not have a constitution in the sense of a specific formal document, the American Constitution is by now the oldest of all constitutions in the world, having come in force in 1789 and being therefore over 200 years old. Most other constitutions are not only more recent, but markedly more recent.

Sweden and Belgium both had old constitutions until the 1970s and the 1980s respectively: the Swedish constitution of 1809 was replaced in 1975; the Belgian constitution of 1830, which had established a centralized unitary state was replaced in 1989 by a federal constitution. Switzerland now has the oldest European constitution, which dates from 1874. Only the Netherlands, Denmark and Norway have constitutions dating from before the First World War, while the Finnish Constitution was approved in 1919.

Several western European countries have recent constitutions, dating from after the Second World War. The Italian Constitution was adopted in 1947, and the German Constitution in 1949. France has had two constitutions since the Second World War, in 1946 and 1958. Indeed, France has had over fifteen constitutions since the first revolutionary document of 1791. The Spanish Constitution was adopted in 1977, after the end of the Franco regime. Portugal and Greece also adopted new constitutional documents after the end of the dictatorships in these countries in 1974.

Nor is the longevity of constitutions greater outside western Europe. All communist states naturally had new constitutions when communism was established; a further batch of constitutions have emerged with the end of communism. Most Third World states were postwar creations, admittedly, but Latin American countries date from the early part of the nineteenth century and their constitutions have not fared better than their European counterparts. Much of the problem is the result of the repeated incidence of military regimes, which have typically suspended the implementation of the current constitution. This has sometimes been followed by a return to the previous constitutions: thus Argentina reintroduced the constitution of 1853 on several occasions. Other countries have adopted a number of constitutional documents in succession: Brazil, for instance, adopted a new text in the 1980s. Outside Latin America, the constitutions of states which have a long independent history have typically lasted for short periods: China has had more than one constitution since the beginning of the twentieth century; Japan has had two constitutions, that of 1889 (of the Meiji) being superseded by the 1946 constitution written after the defeat of the country.

Thus constitutions rise and fall, in part because of wars and defeats, in part because of 'peaceful' changes of regimes. Thus, too, while constitutions may be solemn documents in theory, the practice may be different. It is difficult really to revere a constitution which has existed for only a few years and which comes after a list of other, equally solemn documents which proved to have only a rather short life. Whether this situation has an effect on the overall legitimacy of the regime is a matter which would require further investigation.

Finally, constitutions come also relatively often to be abrogated by *revolutionary overthrow*. Despite the 'supremacy' of constitutions, lawyers always recognized, rather realistically, that a coup or a revolution meant the end of the previous constitution and that new rulers could make a fresh start. This view is consistent with the point that a revolution constitutes a major change in the configuration of norms of the polity; but there will be consequences for the political strength of any subsequent constitutional document which the leaders of the new regime may wish to promulgate. A constitution born under these circumstances may have little support and be in turn rapidly overthrown; examples were numerous in nineteenth-century France as well as in several Latin American countries up to the present day.

## The content of constitutions

Constitutions are based on general principles which they attempt to embody. Often the most solemn way in which they do so is by means of 'declarations of rights', typically listed and expounded in the early part of the document, although this is not always the case: the American Bill of Rights took the form of a series of ten amendments to the Constitution. However, constitutions are primarily concerned with the setting-up of the institutions of government which are expected to regulate the operation of the polity in the future. The sections devoted to these institutions are the most practical elements of constitutions.

### Declarations or bills of rights

Many constitutions include declarations or bills of rights, but these pose serious problems of implementation. Such problems have actually increased as the documents have come to include social and economic 'rights' and not only individual liberties (Henkin and Rosenthal, 1990).

Early declarations of rights were almost exclusively concerned with freedoms, as was the case with the French Declaration of Rights of 1789 and with the American Constitutional Amendments of 1791. Rights covered freedoms of speech, religion, press and meetings; they usually also included a reference to property, which was, in Locke's interpretation, the protection of free men. These rights were firmly and clearly expressed as 'natural, sacred and inalienable, in order that this declaration constantly in front of all members of the social body should always remind them of their rights and duties', to use the expression of the French Declaration of Rights of 1789. Rights were 'expounded'; they were 'absolute' (at least in the French version), 'general', and individual.

Modifications arose from criticisms of these characteristics. Marxists suggested that such declarations were formalistic. It was claimed that rights were not absolute, but relative to a particular society, since they existed only where a society existed and in relation to that society. They should not be deemed to be general, but should be given to a degree and an extent appropriate to each individual. They were not truly individual, but affected the community and should be granted appropriately. Finally, they should not be viewed as 'expounded', but conceived dynamically in relation to the structure of the community, to the education of the people and to the general needs (Vyshinsky, 1948).

These criticisms coincided with the affirmation of *new rights*, both in communist and non-communist states, as, for instance, in France (1946 and 1958), Italy (1946) and West Germany (1949). The United Nations Declaration of Rights of 1948 and the European Declaration of Rights of 1955 also mentioned these new rights. They include education, the right to work and the right to strike, social security and restrictions to private property, even in western countries, in the form of suggestions for the nationalization of monopolies. These new rights were placed alongside the old rights, but in communist states, emphasis was also placed on the fact that old rights would not be applicable unless specific policy conditions were met. This was the case with Article 125 of the Soviet Constitution of 1936.

The new rights entail a *positive state function*. This distinguishes them sharply from old rights, which had only to be protected by the courts. New rights involve positive action on the part of the government and the public administration. Services, often expensive, have to be set up: thus such rights cannot be granted quickly, let alone immediately. There is always a danger that they may not be met in full. Constitutions cannot merely 'declare' these rights and expect them to be implemented automatically.

Because of these difficulties, two kinds of limitation have tended to be introduced. Either the right is mentioned, but the same or the following sentence includes a reservation about conditions of implementation: this is the case with the right to strike. Or declarations are given merely a programmatic character, such as the 1946 and 1958 French Declarations, which are classified as 'preambles' and do not have a straightforward constitutional status. These limitations have also been extended to old rights, possibly because constitution drafters became aware that conditions had to be met before these rights could be truly implemented.

### How authoritative are declarations of rights?

These limitations to the direct implementation of declarations of rights have affected their authority. There is a dilemma: should no mention at all be made of rights on the grounds that they cannot easily be implemented, or should they be mentioned with the corresponding danger that discrepancies will occur between ideal and reality? A preamble is perhaps the best way of ensuring that the underlying ideas gradually permeate the polity. Principles are mentioned, but it is also suggested that the declaration of these principles is not fully part of the constitution.

Preambles thus tend to be exercises in socialization as much as legal provisions. By moving into new policy fields, declarations of rights have extended the domain of constitutions. This has meant greater difficulties of implementation, but has also meant a gradual increase in the awareness on the part of citizens about the existence of rights, and of the need to see them implemented. There has been a resurgence of the part played by rights in the 1970s and 1980s, perhaps the most striking case being that of

# BOX 13.2
# The European Convention on Human Rights

Here are some excerpts from the European Convention on Human Rights, which was signed in 1950 and came into force in 1953.

The Governments signatory hereto, being Members of the Council of Europe,

Considering the Universal Declaration of Human Rights proclaimed by the General Assembly of the United Nations on 10th December 1948;

. . .

Being resolved, as the Governments of European countries which are like-minded and have a common heritage of political traditions, ideals, freedom and the rule of law . . .

Have agreed as follows:

. . .

Section 1. Art. 2. 1. Everyone's right to life shall be protected by law . . .

Art. 3. No one shall be subjected to torture or to inhuman or degrading treatment or punishment.

. . .

Art. 5. 1. Everyone has the right to liberty and security of person. No one shall be deprived of his liberty save in the following cases and in accordance with a procedure prescribed by law;

. . .

Art. 9. 1. Everyone has the right to freedom of thought, conscience and religion;

. . .

Art. 10. 1. Everyone has the right to freedom of expression . . .

Art. 11. 1. Everyone has the right to freedom of peaceful assembly and to freedom of association with others, including the right to form and join trade unions for the protection of his interests.

. . .

Art. 13. Everyone whose rights and freedoms are set forth in this Convention shall have an effective remedy before a national authority notwithstanding that the violation has been committed by persons acting in an official capacity.

. . .

Section 2. Art. 19. To ensure the observance of the engagements undertaken by the High Contracting Parties in the present Convention, there shall be set up:

(1) A European Commission of Human Rights . . .

(2) A European Court of Human Rights . . .

the Helsinki Declaration, which led to considerable pressure being put on eastern European communist countries, and which can be regarded as having been indirectly instrumental in the fall of these regimes.

## Organization of governments

Constitutions often 'declare' rights, but their primary function is to organize government. Since the eighteenth century, constitutions have been regarded as the main mechanism by which the ideas of such political theorists as Locke, Montesquieu, Rousseau and others could be translated into specific institutions and procedures. Not surprisingly, however, since there have been differences of opinion among these theorists, there have also been differences among the constitutions about the principles which they embody. There have also been differences, at the practical level, about the way these principles could best be operationalized.

At the level of *principles*, not all constitutions state that power should be given to 'the people'; nor do all constitutions state that considerable power should be devolved to regions and localities. At the level of the *operationalization* of the principles, some constitution-makers might feel that 'popular sovereignty' could be better achieved by separating sharply the executive from the legislature, while others, with the same aims in mind, might come to a different conclusion on this point. It might also be felt by some that the powers of localities would be better preserved in the context of a federal system, while others might believe that it is preferable to maintain a unitary state even if this means fewer powers to the localities (Wheare, 1966).

Differences relating to the operationalization of principles stem primarily from differing views about the effectiveness of given institutions and procedures. Constitution making is a form of political engineering: it attempts to change behaviour by setting up institutions and procedures. There will naturally be different views about the effectiveness of particular pieces of political engineering, especially since constitutions tend to be written without a systematic analysis (often impossible to undertake) of the consequences of certain provisions. Moreover, the effectiveness of provisions is likely to depend not only on the intrinsic value of these institutions and procedures, but also on the extent to which they fit a given context. Constitutional provisions have tended to emerge out of theories which, for the most part, were elaborated in the eighteenth and early nineteenth centuries in western Europe and North America. It is perhaps not surprising that they should often prove somewhat ineffective when they are applied many decades later to societies which are vastly different. It is perhaps more surprising that they should be, by and large, as effective as they are.

### *The main fields of governmental organization*

Constitutions have to cover three main areas of governmental organization, since these are the three areas on which an answer must be given in all governmental systems. If constitutions do not provide an answer, an answer will be provided by the practice of political life.

### *Structure of the executive*

First, they have to specify how the central decision-making body is to be organized. Is the executive to be a pyramid with one person at the top, or is a group to share the overall responsibility? This question is closely related to views about the best way to achieve both reasonable and speedy action; it is also closely connected to the crucial role of *leadership* in political systems. Ideas have differed markedly, both about the principles and about the operationalization. Monarchical rule was based on the principle that the executive should be led by one ruler: some constitutions have inherited this tradition; others have proclaimed that the executive should be collective. The first principle led to a variety of forms of *presidential rule*, while the second resulted in various types of government by committee, the best known and probably the most effective of these types being *cabinet government*. There are also intermediate arrangements. All of these may be determined by the constitution, but they may also emerge in practice, as a result of the action of some leaders or, more simply, by a series of circumstances.

### Representation

The second area with which the organization of government is concerned is that of representation, and specifically the structure and powers of *legislatures or parliaments*. Since constitutions have typically aimed at limiting the powers of executives, at least in principle, they have naturally attempted to introduce (or reinforce) the principle of representation. The characteristics of legislatures and parliaments are therefore a central part of constitutional documents.

Here too, however, both principles and operationalization vary from one basic law to another. Perhaps the most important – and surely the best-known – distinction is that which differentiates between *separation of powers systems* and *parliamentary systems*. In the first type, legislature and executive are elected separately, while in the second, the government needs the confidence of parliament to remain in office, although the government may be allowed to appeal to the people by dissolving the chamber. Some constitutions also proposed a further model, in which the chamber appoints the government but cannot be dissolved by it, but this system so weakened the executive that it proved generally unworkable.

As a matter of fact, executive–legislative relationships have often been different in reality from what the models suggested, both in liberal and in authoritarian countries. In most polities, the role of the legislature came to be markedly reduced, in part because of the influence of strong parties. Although constitutions had a key role in developing the idea of representative government, the forms which constitutional engineering has taken have often led to a marked distortion of the principles: legislatures and parliaments officially designated as sovereign have in reality a less exalted position.

### Centre–periphery relations

The third area in which government has to be organized is that of the relationship between centre and periphery: that is, of the extent to which public decisions are to be taken at a number of different levels and therefore to be *decentralized*. Decentralization is sometimes put forward by constitution-makers in the name of citizens' freedoms; it is often also a necessity because the burden of decision making at the centre would otherwise be very heavy. Experience in the eastern European communist states showed that a degree of decentralization had to take place, whatever communist principles might have suggested.

The question of decentralization is therefore one which every state (and, consequently, every constitution) has to address. In practice, however, in western Europe at least, many constitutions (especially the older ones) say little about the problem, and leave ordinary laws and perhaps traditions free to handle the matter. In other cases, and in the United States to begin with, constitutions have put forward a model of centre–periphery relations based on *federalism*. This stipulates that central and regional bodies must be separated in order to ensure that the regional bodies retain maximum power. In practice, federalism has not always achieved its stated aims and, by design or by accident, the degree of decentralization which has resulted has not matched the ambitions expressed in the constitution.

In the course of the coming chapters, we shall examine central–local relationships, the nature and role of representative bodies, and the characteristics of the executive, as well as the nature and role of leadership, as these are problems which all polities have to face, and which therefore pose universal questions. We shall also see to what extent various types of constitutional arrangement have attempted to modify, and have modified in practice, the ways in which these problems are being tackled in the different political systems of the contemporary world.

## Overview

*Constitutions* are basic documents which, in the contemporary world, organize in the large majority of nations the way in which governments operate as well as 'declare' the rights of citizens.

However, constitutions are more than these documents: they affirm the principles under which nations should be run. They therefore have an essentially *prescriptive character*.

Since constitutions organize basic rules, they are considered to be *legally supreme*. But this legal supremacy may not correspond to the reality: customs may markedly modify the rules.

Since constitutions are regarded as legally supreme, they are often *rigid*, that is, constitutional change is subjected to complex procedures. This may be so cumbersome that changes may be introduced in practice, particularly through judicial interpretation. Sometimes constitutions are even purely and simply abrogated by a coup or a revolution.

Constitutions typically include *declarations or bills of rights*, which have increasingly included socioeconomic rights alongside more traditional individual liberties. Many of these rights are difficult to implement, however, and declarations of rights are sometimes ambiguous about implementation.

Constitutions are perhaps primarily concerned with the *organization of government*, on the basis of principles and distinctions dating for the most part from the eighteenth century.

The organization of governments covers three main areas. These are the *structure of the executive*, hierarchical or collective, the *forms of representation*, based on legislatures and parliaments, and the *relationship between centre and periphery*, which is the extent of centralization or decentralization of public decision making. The latter is sometimes achieved in practice by means of *federalism*.

Even if constitutions have to be considered in context and even if they have often been brutally abrogated or have been implemented only in part, they are an essential aspect of modern government. They shape politics and provide a solemn reference point for the rights of citizens.

## Further reading

Constitutions and constitutional analysis have given rise to an immense literature, especially on a country basis. Comparative work is less abundant. One of the best and clearest presentations of the problems posed by constitutions is to be found in K.C. Wheare, *Modern Constitutions* (1966). See also D.V. Verney, *The Analysis of Political Systems* (1959) and M. Vile, *Constitutionalism and the Separation of Powers* (1967).

For a presentation of constitutions, see S.E. Finer, *Five Constitutions* (1979), which describes and analyzes the constitutions of the United States, France, Germany and the Soviet Union, as well as the British documents which can be described as 'constitutional'. For a presentation of constitutionalism and of a range of constitutions in the contemporary world, see V. Bogdanor, ed., *Constitutions in Democratic Politics* (1988).

On the question of the meanings of the word 'constitution', see G. Sartori, 'Constitutionalism: A Preliminary Discussion', *Am. Pol. Sc. Rev.* (1962: 853–64). An expression of the (earlier) classic communist view on constitutional matters can be found in A. Vyshinski, *The Law of the Soviet State* (1948).

There has been a resurgence of the part played by rights in the 1970s and 1980s. On the part played by rights in constitutions, see L. Henkin and A.J. Rosenthal, *Constitutionalism and Rights* (1990).

# 14

# Centralization and decentralization

## Introduction

No government, even the most authoritarian, can ever take all public decisions at the centre. Some power has therefore to be given to authorities below the national level to take the decisions which the centre cannot take. From this general remark emerges the idea of *decentralization*, an idea which can, of course, take many forms and vary markedly in extent. The concepts of centralization and decentralization can be formulated simply in a general manner: if we list all the decisions taken in a country by all the public bodies, that country tends to be centralized if the proportion of the decisions taken by the central authorities is large to very large, and tends, on the contrary, to be decentralized if the proportion is small to very small (Fleiner Gerster, 1987).

While the concept of centralization is relatively simple to define, it is complex to measure. Indicators of the extent to which decisions are taken at the centre or away from the centre are impressionistic and therefore unsatisfactory. The problem of measurement is further complicated by the fact that the questions of centralization and of decentralization, which relate to the extent to which various agencies are responsible for decision making, are confronted with the concept of *federalism* which, in its various forms, is typically regarded as the constitutional answer to the problem of decentralization. If decentralization is difficult to measure, the relationship between federalism and decentralization is also encumbered by many ambiguities.

This is in part because there are many federalisms – perhaps as many as there are federal states. The words 'federalism' and 'federal' have also become symbols, sometimes empty of real content, and have for this reason attracted both support and criticism. Moreover, since it has many 'faces', federalism is but one of the formulas which can bring about decentralization. There are other formulas, such as confederacies or supranational arrangements, in the context of unions of states, and regionalism or semi-autonomous local authorities, in the context of single states.

The ideas of centralization and decentralization, being truly general, should not be considered merely in the context of individual countries. They should be examined by reference to any relationship between bodies which are in some way either above or below each other. This means that, while a country can become decentralized – for instance, by means of greater powers being devolved to local authorities – there may also be some form of centralization 'above' that country if some powers are exercised 'higher up' by a body covering a number of states. Such *unions of states* can be very loose, but they may be or progressively become tighter, as has been the case with the European Community and European Union as well as with other organizations, such as the United Nations. Thus centralization and decentralization have to be viewed as phenomena affecting all the levels of government which exist in the world: centralization and decentralization within the state are only the best-known and most studied forms of these phenomena.

The aim of this chapter is therefore to look generally at levels of centralization and decentralization in the contemporary world, and to assess how far these levels vary as a result of constitutional and other rules.

- We shall first examine what *criteria* lead to centralization and decentralization, and what forms *central–periphery relationships* can take as a result.
- Second, we shall look at the *federal model* to see how far it meets criteria of decentralization and how far it raises problems which are difficult to overcome.
- Third, we shall look at *concrete differences in the extent of decentralization* between states which are federal and states which are not.
- Finally, we shall analyze the ways in which states have come to form *closer associations*, federalism being one of the formulas by which these closer associations are achieved.

## Centralization and decentralization

The analysis of centralization and decentralization poses two general questions:

- Under what conditions does the problem arise? What are the societal forces which tend to move countries towards more centralization or towards more decentralization?
- How is the problem solved? What are the characteristics by which one can assess whether a state is more or less centralized or decentralized?

It will then be possible to see what rules are most likely to bring about centralization or decentralization, and in particular how satisfactory the federal model is if the desired object is a high degree of decentralization.

### Patterns of centralization and decentralization

In the contemporary world, at least in the older nations, patterns of centralization and decentralization appear to be a legacy of history. Some countries, such as France or

Japan, are regarded as traditionally centralized; the same appears to be true of many Latin American countries, if not of all. On the other hand, countries such as the United States, Britain and Germany are regarded as inherently decentralized. Indeed, although in western Europe in recent years pressure for decentralization has increased, long-standing traditions persist and seem to continue to account for the fact that some states remain centralized while others are decentralized. Thus French centralization appears to be the consequence of the policy of the kings who wished to extend their hold on the country against the local aristocracy centuries ago. American, British and German decentralization also has a long history: no ruler was able to ensure, or at least to ensure for long, that most major decisions were taken in the capital.

History as such, however, does not explain trends towards centralization or decentralization, it merely suggests that what exists cannot easily be modified. Some sociopolitical forces have to account for the existence of these traditions. These forces have usually been regarded as being of two kinds, ideological and structural. In recent years, moreover, centralization and decentralization have been increasingly discussed in terms of a third characteristic, efficiency.

*Ideology* is powerful in that it helps to justify or forces to reject a particular stance on centralization or decentralization. Thus liberalism can be regarded as leading naturally towards decentralization and authoritarianism towards centralization. Thus, too, egalitarianism is likely to lead to centralization because decentralization means the acceptance of differences – of variations from one part of the country to another. Regimes which propose to bring about equality are therefore likely to be uneasy about decentralization, which is why, by and large, the left has tended to centralize more than the right. However, to the extent that it advocates political liberalism, the left has tended to be cross-pressured, in the West at least.

*Structural* forces relate to group conflicts in a society and history plays a substantial part in this context because the longer these conflicts last, the more difficult they are to overcome. The presence of such conflicts accounts for high levels of centralization in France: the battles between monarchists and republicans and between clericals and anti-clericals created such a climate of suspicion in the country that no central government was prepared to allow for a truly large dose of local autonomy. Thus liberals can become champions of centralization – though perhaps more uneasily than supporters of authoritarian systems – when their preferred regime is under attack. Gradually, however, the contradiction between liberalism and centralization accounts for the fact that moves towards decentralization may be made: this was the case in France from the late nineteenth century onwards; it has also been the case in Spain, where in the late 1970s regions were set up and given considerable autonomy. Conversely, while the right can often be comfortable with decentralization, in western democracies at least, those conservatives who wish to stop the 'excessive profligacy' of left-leaning local authorities have been known to increase centralization: this was the case with the British Conservatives in the 1980s.

Overall, therefore, a relationship exists between ideology, the degree to which the regime is accepted, and centralization. Liberal regimes which are well accepted will tend towards decentralization. Authoritarian regimes are likely to promote

---

## BOX 14.1
## Decentralization and the structure of the state

Decentralization has become fashionable in the second half of the twentieth century, in part, probably, because the experience of the communist states showed both the political dangers and the economic inefficiency of hypercentralization. Yet decentralizing efforts have remained relatively limited, both formally and in practice. Much of the difficulty appears to lie in the legal arrangements of the state, in the philosophy which underlies these legal arrangements and, therefore, in the habits of mind of administrators and citizens.

Indeed, the nature of the state is antagonistic to the notion of decentralization, since decentralization means the self-government of lower-level authorities. The state is a self-contained entity: all its elements have to be linked. This means that it is difficult to achieve full autonomy or full self-government for lower-level bodies where there is a fully fledged legal notion of state structures. In such a case, the relationship among the public bodies must be hierarchical – otherwise there is no state, only a 'central government'.

Thus, on the Continent of Europe in particular, decentralization tends to exist only to an extent. On the one hand, local authorities may be given powers, but state agents supervise these authorities directly to see whether they act in conformity with the laws of the state. On the other hand, the state tends to build a large network of agencies at regional and local levels (an arrangement known as *déconcentration* in the French language). These field agencies are supposed to be closer to the population, but they also 'help' and supervise local authorities.

In such cases, the state organization tends to perpetuate itself. State civil servants are not anxious to see their jobs disappear, so any reform which occurs will not touch their jobs. Local authority representatives and even the citizens are accustomed to the state agencies: decision processes have a certain shape which it seems inconvenient to modify.

Only where there is strong pressure, as in the case of the Spanish 'autonomies', and in particular Catalonia, the Basque Country and Galicia, has the umbilical cord between central government and regional authorities been cut. Elsewhere, as in France and Italy, decentralization means only a little more freedom within the context of the state hierarchy.

---

centralization, except if they are so well accepted and so traditional that they do not propose to put a new mark on their polity. Most authoritarian systems and those liberal systems which are not well accepted are likely to veer towards centralization, though to a varying degree and with greater or lesser consistency.

The question of *efficiency* has also come to play a large part in debates over centralization. This is due in particular to the experience of highly centralized economic systems such as the communist systems, as well as some western mixed-economy systems. Previously, criticisms were more often levelled at the opposite extreme – at the inefficiency of decentralized bodies – because they breed duplication. The emphasis then changed and came to be placed on avoiding the inefficiency of centralization. As a matter of fact, the desire to reduce inefficiency has led not just to the introduction of federal institutions, but to other moves towards decentralization taking place in the context of some unitary states.

## Techniques of centralization and decentralization

Assuming that there is a move towards centralization or towards decentralization, some techniques and some instruments must be adopted and implemented to achieve the desired goal. These techniques and instruments are numerous and complex, and it would be difficult to identify them all. But it is possible to survey the domains or areas in which the question of centralization and decentralization occurs. There are seven such domains:

1. There may be more or less centralization with respect to substantive *fields of public decision making*, such as education and housing.
2. There may be *two, three or more levels* of decentralization, such as regions, counties, cities and villages.
3. The question of centralization and decentralization poses that of the nature of the authorities in charge of each field. There can be a *general authority* concerned with the whole of a level of government or, on the contrary, specific or *ad hoc bodies* in charge of a given field each: this is the case with Boards of Education.
4. Decision making in each field may be *wholly given to one level of government* or there may be *power sharing* among the governments of the different levels.
5. Each authority may be entirely free to *appoint its decision-makers* (for instance, elect all its rulers), or other authorities may intervene in these processes.
6. Each authority may be free to *set up its own administration* or there may be *common services* among authorities at the different levels. The central administration may, for instance, collect the taxes for the local authorities and redistribute the sums subsequently.
7. A decision has to be taken on who has '*constituent*' *power*: that is, on who allocates the powers which we just mentioned. This may be done entirely at the central level, at the level of component bodies, or at both jointly.

It is manifestly difficult to assess in every case where a country is to be located with respect to each of these domains, but one can at least have an impression of the extent of centralization or decentralization by taking these questions into account. This is also the way in which it is possible to assess, first, what federalism aims at and, second, whether federal states are truly decentralized.

## The federal model

Federalism is widely regarded as the pre-eminent means of achieving decentralization within a state, as well as a means of unifying states without destroying the identity of each of them. As a result, as well as in part because of the success of the United States as a polity, there has been an 'aura' around federalism, and the word has tended to be used in many different cases to cover different realities.

Federalism was therefore conceived partly through *logical reasoning* and partly *empirically*. Its characteristics developed gradually in the course of the nineteenth century as the American model itself developed and was imitated in Latin America, Canada and Australia, while different versions of the same idea developed in Switzerland and Germany.

Since the setting-up of the United States as a federal government by the Constitution of 1789, federalism has been presented by some as *the answer* to the question of the relationship between centre and periphery, on the ground that it maximizes decentralization and yet avoids the break-up of the polity: expressions such as 'unity within diversity' have sometimes been used to describe federalism. In practice, however, there have been disagreements as to which institutional arrangements would best achieve the desired aims and thus be 'truly' federal. To be more realistic, discussions should not be so much about whether a given set of arrangements is truly federal or not, but about whether these arrangements lead, if not to the 'maximum' possible amount of decentralization compatible with a coherent polity, since such a 'maximum' cannot be assessed, then at least to a high level of decentralization.

### The basic principle of the classical federal model

What, then, is the main principle on which federalism is based? As there are many types of federal system, no single answer can be given, but one type of federalism, that of the United States, is often regarded as providing the 'classical' model. One should therefore begin by looking at this model and see to what extent it provides satisfactory answers with respect to the various domains of decentralization which were listed earlier.

The basic principle of this classical model lies in the idea that, in order to optimize the two prerequisites of decentralization and of national unity, rule-making authorities should be divided into two sets of authorities independent of each other within their own sphere. The concept that each of the two levels should be independent in their own sphere is *fundamental* (Wheare, 1963: 1–14; Elazar, 1979: 13–57; Burgess, 1986). This is not to say that there are no other levels of government, such as counties or cities; but only two, the central government and the upper level of the component unit, are 'independent'. The names given to these upper-level component units vary: they are called states in the United States, Australia, India and some federal Latin American countries; they are called provinces in Canada, cantons in Switzerland, and *Länder* in Germany and Austria.

If we apply the principle of the classical federal model to the seven domains which we identified earlier, the following conclusions can be drawn:

1. The model gives no precise guidance on the division of the fields of decision making. By and large, however, it is (or, more correctly, was) felt that the central body should deal with foreign affairs and defence, currency and customs, as well as with matters affecting commercial relations among the component units. This list has never been regarded as truly limiting and, by a variety of means, the powers of the component units in economic and even social matters have been in part reduced.
2. The model states that two levels of government, but two only, should be independent. There might be more, but federalism stops at two levels.
3. The model states that each of these two levels should be organized on the basis of one authority only: federalism is not 'functional'. It is based not on *ad hoc* authorities covering specific fields of government, but on general authorities.
4. The model states that each authority has to have all the power, or none at all, in each sphere. There is no power sharing between the central government and the component bodies.
5. The model states that each of these two levels should be completely independent in the appointment of its decision-makers.
6. The model states that administrative agencies of the two levels should be entirely distinct.
7. Finally, the model gives no clear guidance as to who should have the 'constituent' power to decide how powers are to be allocated between the two levels of authorities.

Thus the classical federal model gives precise answers with respect to five of the seven domains, but, with respect to the other two, there are uncertainties and there is no real guidance. The model is thus partly successful and partly unsuccessful.

It is partly successful in that it articulates a number of clearly defined characteristics which make it possible to give a precise content to a 'half-way house' position between the two extremes of the unitary state and of the confederacy. In a unitary state, only the central body is legally independent, and the other authorities are subordinated to the central government. In a confederacy, the central government exists only because member-states are prepared to keep it in existence. Thus the British Parliament is 'sovereign' and can regulate absolutely the division of labour between authorities within the United Kingdom. On the contrary, the United Nations and the Organization for African Unity can only do those things which the individual polities are prepared to let them do, and as long as those polities concur in letting them do those things. Historically, the concept of the 'half-way house' represented by federalism emerged at a time when earlier confederacies seemed to have been ineffective. This view was exaggerated because not only the Swiss Confederacy but also the Dutch United Provinces (which were a confederacy until the French Revolution) were successful arrangements. However, the view that confederacies were unsuccessful was apparently strengthened by the fact that the United States was a confederacy before becoming federal, and by the fact that the same development occurred in Switzerland (although it remained a confederacy in name) and in Germany.

The classical model is also unsuccessful in part, in that it leaves open two critical questions: the authority which is in charge of the constituent power; and the determination of the fields of government to be given to the federal body and to the component agencies. As a result of the inability of the model to give clear answers in both these domains, substantial differences are likely to exist among federal countries and a ranking will be found among them. There are an almost infinite variety of solutions with respect to the distribution of fields of government between centre and component bodies; there can also be many different formulas with respect to the constituent power.

## The federal model and the constituent power

With respect to the constituent power, the problems faced by the federal model are particularly serious. Ideally, centre and component bodies should be independent of each other: neither should be able to destroy the other. In practice, this is a recipe for deadlock, and mechanisms have therefore to be found to overcome the difficulty. These mechanisms, which fall broadly within three areas, are all somewhat unsatisfactory: they leave some problems unsolved; they also result in substantial differences in the power of the centre and of the component bodies.

- *Constitutional change itself is to be made difficult.* The majorities required for amendments are to be large; in particular, there should be a requirement that at least a majority of the component bodies should concur for constitutional amendments to pass. Yet even if there is such a rule, the component bodies are not wholly safeguarded, since a minority of them can be overruled.
- The supervision of the division of powers between the two levels of government is to be given to a *Supreme Court*. But this means giving enormous powers to judges, who may effectively modify the constitution in a centralizing or decentralizing direction if they are so inclined. The question of who appoints them is therefore crucial: we shall see in Chapter 20 the difficulties which have arisen in this respect.
- Component bodies are to be represented at the central government level in a *Second Chamber*. However, the composition of that body can vary sharply: for instance, each component body may or may not have an equal number of representatives in the Second Chamber; the powers of that Chamber may also vary.

## The federal model and fields of policy making

To these problems with respect to the allocation of the constituent power, one must add the difficulties which emerge with respect to the allocation of policy fields between the two levels. In this respect, the constitution may be more or less precise. If it is vague, the scope for variations in decentralization is large; if it is precise, the question of what is to happen to *new fields* (new forms of communication, environmental problems, etc.) is open. The centre is in practice likely to fill the gap. Furthermore, the constitution may simply state that the centre or the component bodies, or both, will have the right to intervene in some fields or in the fields which are not listed. This is a recipe for conflict and, almost certainly, a recipe for centralization.

## Federal states and decentralization

The consequence of these difficulties is that it may not be altogether as important in reality as it seems in theory to declare solemnly that each level is 'independent' with respect to appointments or to administrative services. If the central government can take control of large, new and important fields, if it can play a major part in constitutional amendments or in the customary change of the constitution, it can be by far the most influential body, and the level of decentralization in the nation can become rather low. This is indeed what occurs in many federal states, and is one of the reasons why it has been said of several Latin American federal states that they are not 'truly' federal (Wheare, 1963: 21–3).

There were sixteen federations in the mid-1990s. Nearly half (seven) were in the 'Atlantic area' (the United States, Canada, Australia, Belgium, Switzerland, Germany and Austria), one only in eastern Europe (Russia, since Yugoslavia and Czechoslovakia had split), four in Latin America (Mexico, Venezuela, Brazil and Argentina), two in Asia (India and Malaysia), one in the Middle East (the United Arab Emirates) and one in Africa south of the Sahara (Nigeria). Two of the three most populous countries of the world are federal (the USA and India, the third country of the group being China). As a result, while under 10 per cent of the world's polities are federations, over a third of the world's population live under a federal form of government.

There are marked variations in the extent to which these federal states are decentralized. Many of these have been classified as *quasi-federal* because they do not apply rigidly the principles which have been stated earlier, such as India, Venezuela, Argentina and Mexico, and even Germany and Austria (Wheare, 1963: 21–3; 26–9).

If we look at the three mechanisms relating to constituent powers which we described, and which aim at organizing in practice the relationship between centre and component bodies, there are substantial differences from one federal state to another. The procedure by which constitutional amendments are passed is more or less strict: in the United States, three-quarters of the state legislatures must approve a constitutional amendment if it is to become law; in Australia and Switzerland, amendments need the approval by referendum of the majority of the population in a majority of the component units if they are to pass. However, such stringent conditions are not in force in all federal states.

Supreme courts do not all have the power to intervene in disputes between the two levels of government and among the component bodies. Thus the powers of the Swiss Constitutional Court are more limited than those of a 'full' Supreme Court.

Finally, while second chambers always exist, there is not equality in the representation of the component bodies everywhere. It does exist in the United States, Australia and

Switzerland, but in Canada, despite the fact that the country is usually regarded as a 'true' federal state, the second chamber is not organized on the basis of the idea of representation of the component bodies. Elsewhere, there is sometimes a weighting in favour of the larger component units; this is the case in practically all the new federations, in particular in Germany.

Meanwhile, in some federal states, the constitution itself gives the federal government powers of 'intervention' or of veto. The centre may thus interfere in decisions of component bodies and in the election of officials. In some cases, it also specifies that there shall not be separate administrative services. If one adds the fact that the area of competence of the component bodies can be gradually reduced on the basis of the legal rule, which exists in some federal states, according to which 'federal law breaks state law', there are serious doubts about the ability of the federal model to ensure that decentralization is really maintained.

## Comparison of federal and unitary states

As there are such variations in the extent to which decentralization is achieved through federalism, the question arises as to whether unitary states may not be as decentralized as federal states. Is not a unitary state like Britain as decentralized as a federal state like Venezuela? It is difficult to provide a general answer in view of the point made at the outset, that the measurement of decentralization is complex and has so far not been satisfactorily achieved. However, at least a partial answer can be given by considering the following issues.

### Centralization and decentralization in unitary and federal states

There is indeed a general tendency for unitary states to be, as a group, more centralized than federal states. A substantial number of unitary states are very centralized, while even the most centralized federal state achieves at least a moderate degree of decentralization.

Unitary states are often highly centralized by design. France was highly centralized for centuries as a result of the deliberate policy of monarchs – a policy which was maintained, even reinforced, by Napoleon at the beginning of the nineteenth century. What France was under Napoleon is replicated in many countries of the contemporary world, particularly in the Third World. This is or was also the case in communist states as a result of the dominance of the single party in these countries. Thus, in general, a substantial number of the nearly 170 states which are not federal are highly centralized, often as a result of the very authoritarian character of the regimes under which they are run, or simply because there is little or no *tradition of local autonomy*. There are no decentralized local authorities in many African and Middle Eastern polities, for instance, although this is more frequently the case in countries which were dependencies of France or Portugal than in countries which were dependencies of

Britain. These states are therefore clearly more centralized than even the least decentralized federal or quasi-federal state.

Centralization is not always due to authoritarianism and/or to a colonial past, however. It can also occur naturally, where the country is very small in population and/or area. The question of decentralization does not arise in the same terms in a country with a population of one million or less and in a country which has 50 or 100 million inhabitants.

Conversely, federal states tend to be large in both population and area. Only Switzerland and in general the European federal states are geographically small countries, and except for Germany, their population is also relatively small, although not as small as that of the 30 or so states which have fewer than one million inhabitants. The federal state with the smallest population is Switzerland, which has six million inhabitants; it is also larger in territory than many states, often islands, which are found in the Caribbean, the Indian Ocean and the Pacific.

*Wealth* is also a factor. If, as was noted in the first section of this chapter, decentralization is somewhat inefficient and wasteful, one would expect richer countries to be more decentralized than poorer countries. Indeed, by and large, western countries as a group, whether unitary or federal, are more decentralized than Third World countries. Characteristically, over two-fifths of the federal states (7 out of 16) are to be found among western countries although these constituted only 23 or 12.5 per cent of the 182 polities of the world in the mid-1990s.

## Overlap between unitary and federal countries

Although, as a group, unitary states are more centralized than federal states, in part because of the existence of a large number of highly centralized states, there is also an overlap between federal and unitary states in terms of the extent of decentralization. This overlap is found especially among western and to an extent among Latin American countries.

While *component bodies are protected* in federal states, a similar effect is also achieved in some unitary states. The second chamber may thus represent the component bodies in some unitary states, as is the case in France and in several non-federal Latin American countries. Moreover, some courts – often administrative courts – also guarantee, to an extent at least, the powers of component bodies in unitary states. The result is that there is in practice a real protection of the existence and powers of component bodies in some, typically western but also Latin American, unitary states, while some federal states, often also Latin American, do not give greater protection to component bodies.

Moreover, the *appointment of rule-makers* in the component units of federal states is sometimes subjected to forms of control, at least of a negative kind, by the central government, while this may not be the case in some unitary states. In India, there is a power of federal intervention in cases of emergency, while in some Latin American federal states the centre may veto appointments of governors or other executive agents of federations as well. In Britain, France and the Scandinavian countries, on the other hand, local bodies have complete autonomy with respect to the appointment of decision-makers: the central government has no control over the appointment of the personnel.

Finally, *administrative authorities* are combined rather than separated in a number of federations, while this is not the case in all unitary states. The best-known example is that of Germany. In sharp contrast to the United States and Switzerland, but also in contrast to a unitary state such as Britain, which has wholly separate administrative structures, there is only one administrative structure for both levels of government in Germany, this provision having been inserted in the Constitution of 1949 in order to avoid duplication. Admittedly, this administration is controlled by the component bodies, the *Länder*. However, as this situation might mean that the German federal government could be in the hands of the *Länder* authorities if these refused to comply, the constitution gives the central government a power of intervention known as 'federal execution' which, were it often used, might result in close supervision and detailed control of the action of regional administrations. The separation of authorities is one of the principal ways in which the federal system can be regarded as costly and inefficient, as we have seen; but this also means that there is overlap between federal and unitary systems of government and that federal systems cannot be regarded as uniformly more decentralized than unitary states.

## Partnership and the centralization of powers in federal states

Federal states are gradually becoming more centralized. The upper level of government has increased its influence, and has even come to supervise the activities of component bodies. This is typically achieved by means of a *partnership*, a type of arrangement which goes against the ideas of separation at the root of the federal model. What we just noted about the structure of administrative authorities in Germany constitutes a form of partnership between two sets of authorities. But partnership extends further, especially in the area in which the federal model is the vaguest – namely, the allocation of powers – precisely because the model is vague in this respect.

First, sometimes by constitutional amendment and more often by customary change, including as a result of judicial action, the scope of the powers of federal authorities has increased. In the economic field, a 'liberal' interpretation of clauses such as those on interstate commerce in the United States enables the federal government to legislate widely. Rearguard battles did take place in this respect, especially in the United States in the mid-1930s, when a number of texts were quashed by the American Supreme Court, one of the grounds being that the federal authorities were interfering in matters which came within the jurisdiction of the states. Eventually, however, these battles were lost. In various social fields, changes have also gradually increased the scope of federal activity in all federations, so that social security, housing and education are covered by federal legislation, even in those polities, such as the United States, where federal legislation is still relatively less developed.

Differences still exist, not so much between all federal states and all unitary countries, but between the older federal states and unitary states, even those which are decentralized. However, these differences are being reduced to an increasingly narrow front. Less energy is now required on the part of the 'centralizers' in federal states: for example, a constitutional amendment was needed to introduce federal income tax in the United States; but the Supreme Court later desisted from its role of defender of the States after its effort against the 'New Deal' legislation in the 1930s. As central intervention in socioeconomic affairs is now no longer seriously challenged, differences are sometimes more pronounced in matters pertaining to private law (especially in the United States), although, in this respect, too, differences have decreased. Systems of private law may be different within unitary states as well: for instance, Scottish private law differs from English private law, despite the fact that the United Kingdom is a unitary state.

Second, a spirit of 'partnership' has emerged between federal authorities and the authorities of the component bodies as well as, in some cases, between federal authorities and cities or counties, with the result that the authorities of the component bodies are bypassed. By a number of means, whether financial (through grants-in-aid), administrative (through the issuing of circulars, model by-laws and even model laws) or sociopsychological (through meetings of technical experts), federal authorities succeed in inducing component bodies to adopt policies conforming to those of the federal government. The success is not universal – authorities of component bodies in federal states may be better placed than those of unitary states to resist central encroachments of this type – but these moves have taken place on a wide scale. Federal authorities do what the governments of unitary states do: they cajole, press and, where they are not obeyed, warn or use sanctions. In order to avoid having to use sanctions, however, they engage in partnership activities, whether with decentralized units in a unitary state or with the component bodies of a federal polity.

The basic principle of the division between the two types of authority is thus flouted. While the classical model stresses the need for two sets of bureaucracies and two distinct 'power structures', the practice in all federations amounts to a situation which is little different from the one which the German Constitution recognizes, and which is practised in unitary states in which local authorities are powerful: namely, a partnership between authorities (Beer, 1974).

## Decentralization In unitary states

Federal states have therefore moved towards greater centralization in a number of ways – a process which has also taken place to an extent in unitary states. Centralization can thus be regarded as somewhat characteristic of contemporary societies. Meanwhile, however, at least in some unitary states, a movement towards decentralization has started to occur. To begin with, in the West at least, the extent of centralization of a number of unitary states has come to be regarded as being above the level which complex societies can tolerate. We noted earlier that the use of sanctions against local authorities is often politically inadequate, although more when the authority is large than when it is small. Administrative sanctions are also inadequate because the system can be clogged and the machine may then not render the services for which it was created. Centralization cannot therefore go beyond a certain point without considerable costs. The administrative problems of the Soviet Union and other communist states have repeatedly pointed to the difficulties resulting from the centralizing ideology of these regimes; various decentralizing techniques were adopted in many of them before they collapsed.

However, evidence for the existence of such maximum levels of centralization can be found not just in communist states but in other polities, particularly western. The movement towards *regionalism* which characterized western Europe after the 1960s, most strikingly in Spain, but also in France and in Italy, was not merely ideological; it was also the consequence of the increasing difficulties experienced by central governments in coping with the management of public decision making. One could argue that the regionalism which has been introduced in these countries constitutes an imitation of federalism – indeed, is federalism in all but name. Such a conclusion would not be valid for the French or Italian cases up to the mid-1990s, but where it was valid, as it might be in the Spanish case, it would mean that the difference between federal and unitary states is becoming smaller, not only in practice but formally as well.

## Unions of states

So far we have discussed federalism in terms of its role *within* polities; but the idea and the technique were conceived as means of associating hitherto independent states. In practice, as few as four or as many as six polities among the 16 federal states (the United States, Switzerland, Germany, the United Arab Emirates and, arguably, Canada and Australia) were established as a means of bringing together independent countries. Indeed, as the list of these countries shows, the majority of the federal states which were created from independent units included countries which had very strong historical cultural reasons for being closely associated; Switzerland and Canada are the only multicultural countries among them. In four cases a common colonial origin accounts for the setting-up of the federal link, and in three of these countries, Australia, Canada and Germany, the federal link was effectively forced on the component units by an outside power (Britain in the first two cases) or by the most powerful component unit (Prussia in the German case). Whatever those who had developed the idea of federalism may have wanted to achieve, federal states mostly originated from existing states wishing to increase decentralization, and not primarily in order to bring together independent states.

In the cases in which independent states form a federal association, this association is regarded as a *centralizing formula*, in contrast to what federalism is considered to be when it is introduced to replace a unitary system in an existing polity. This probably explains why associations among independent states have tended to take looser forms than that of the federal state, the European Community or European Union being a case in point. Despite the fact that federal states are described as 'half-way houses', and despite the idea, expressed for instance by Laski, that federalism is transitional and constitutes an intermediate step between the confederacy and the unitary state, there have been only three or at most four countries in which the first move – to a federal arrangement – has taken place (and none where the second move, towards a unitary system, took place). These cases are those of the United States, Switzerland, Germany and perhaps Canada (Laski, 1940). Since no such development has taken place anywhere else, the question of the 'true' value of the confederal link needs to be discussed, as does the 'true' value of models which are intermediate between confederal and federal arrangements.

## Confederal arrangements

While the confederal arrangement is often regarded as unsatisfactory, a survey of the contemporary world shows that there are in reality many *confederacies*, the archetype being the United Nations. The United Nations groups polities which retain their power of decision and which give to the organization as much or as little power as they wish to give. Some aspects of the United Nations have begun to go a little beyond the pure confederal model, however, particularly inasmuch as many decisions taken by a majority of states or by the Security Council are, at least in practice, binding on the other members.

Other types of confederal arrangement are constituted by the *regional organizations*, often of an economic character, which have been set up in the last decades of the twentieth century. Many of these are highly specialized, but some are not and aim at covering, for instance, all the trade relations between the member-states. This is the case with the European Free Trade Area (EFTA), with Mercosur, which groups a number of countries of South America, and with the North American Free Trade Area (NAFTA), which groups the United States, Canada and Mexico.

Other regional organizations have primarily a political and/or a defence dimension, such as the North Atlantic Treaty Organization (NATO) and the South-East Asia Treaty Organization (SEATO). In both these cases, the high degree of joint activities among the member-states indicates that these organizations are more than conventional alliances: they link together the member-states over a wide variety of policy fields. Appreciably weaker and often very divided, but none the less aspiring to have a large political role, are the Arab League, the Organization of African Unity and the Commonwealth. The sense of common purpose is rare in these bodies, especially the last two: they can be viewed as being at an intermediate point between the confederal model and what are little more than forums for discussions.

## Supranationalism and the European Community or Union

Largely because many European leaders have been aware of the difficulty of establishing a federal link, the European Community or European Union, which has been the most

---

**BOX 14.2**
**The European Union, Switzerland and the idea of 'gradual'**
**federalism**

Switzerland is officially a confederacy. The country went through a long process of gradual centralization, starting after the Congress of Vienna of 1815 and going through the traumas of a civil war in the 1870s. At the time, Switzerland was a true confederacy, much of the power remaining at the level of the cantons and even of the communes.

When thinking of a closer union among the states to which they belong, Europeans normally think of the United States: the expression 'United States of Europe' is often used in this context. This seems to suggest that Europe should follow the model of America and begin by elaborating a 'compact' analogous to the compact among the American states in order to progress towards unity. However, more than the United States, Switzerland is the microcosm of what Europe at large consists of, for three main reasons:

- Europe, like Switzerland, is culturally diverse. There was diversity among the American immigrants, but they wished to forget their past and join the new common venture which America was. This is not so in Europe.
- Cultural diversity implies that European institutions be based, like those of Switzerland, on 'consociationalism': that is to say, on consensual government. The institutional and practical arrangements of the European Union are indeed developing in this way.
- The move of the European Union towards closer unity has to be slow, as has been the move of Switzerland towards its unity. Unity was also slow to come in the case of the United States; but, from the start, US federal institutions had an authority which the Swiss executive, the Federal Council, did not have. One should not be surprised or worried if the executive of the European Union, the Commission, should also have relatively limited popular support. The contrary would be surprising.

---

ambitious effort so far at building a permanent link among neighbouring states, has also stopped short of becoming a federal state while attempting to be more than a confederacy. Although some at least of its supporters wish to move eventually towards a federal link, the steps taken so far are more limited, the technique invented having been labelled *supranationalism*. This consists in moving by stages and in attempting to cover some fields of decision making only. These fields are typically different from those which go to the central government in the classical federal model, since they include primarily economic and social fields. The states belonging to the supranational unit remain 'independent' for other aspects of public decision making. Only a few powers are fully transferred (often slowly) to the central authority and these transfers are accompanied by safeguards for the member-states, such as the representation of the member-states in Councils of Ministers, special majority requirements, and even vetoes in some cases. Supranationalism is therefore a 'half-way house', but this time between the confederal and the federal models.

Meanwhile, the European Community or European Union has a highly developed set of institutions which in many ways imitate federal institutions, although more those of Switzerland than those of the United States. There is a Commission, which has a consociational character and is in some ways the executive, a Council of Ministers representing the member-states, a popularly elected Parliament, and a Court of Justice; there are also advisory councils representing local authorities and economic and social interests.

The European Community or European Union is also innovative in that it is openly and consciously based on the idea that it evolves continually. Both the fields which are covered by the Union and the structures set up to handle these fields are regarded as not being truly fixed. Nor is the membership fixed, since it increased from the original six states (France, Germany, Italy, Belgium, Luxembourg and the Netherlands) to nine states (Britain, Denmark, Ireland), then to ten (Greece), to twelve (Portugal and Spain) and to fifteen (Austria, Finland and Sweden); it is also confronted with the matter of the accession of several polities from eastern Europe. The enlargement to new members has a manifest impact on the scope of the Union and on its institutional structure: the more members join the Union, the greater are the decision-making problems and the greater also are the differences, cultural, social and economic, between the member-states.

The examples of the European Community and the confederal or near-confederal bodies which have multiplied in the second half of the twentieth century show that federal arrangements remain exceptional, because the ties are too strong. They also show that there is a need to find formulas which can provide a degree of association without going as far as a full federal structure. As many such models are being experimented and seem to succeed, one can surely conclude that, in this respect at least, the world and its leaders have shown imagination (Wallace, 1992; Dinan, 1994).

## Overview

The questions of *centralization* and *decentralization* arise in every polity. The constitution or the practice, or both, have to settle how much of policy making is to be decided by the central government and by component bodies.

By and large, *liberalism* and *decentralization* tend to go together, while *authoritarianism* tends to be associated with *centralization*.

The constitutional model which is generally regarded as bringing about the largest amount of decentralization is *federalism*. This is said to constitute a 'half-way house' between confederacies (where component units dominate) and unitary states (where the centre dominates).

In its 'classical' form at least, federalism stipulates that there have to be *two 'independent' levels of government* (the centre and upper-level component bodies (often named 'states'). Each of these levels has the right to decide on matters falling within its own sphere. There are difficulties in practice, especially with respect to the *constituent power* and to the *fields* allocated to each level.

Federalism must be based on a *rigid constitution*; there has to be a *supreme court* protecting the 'independence' of the two levels of government; there has to be a *second chamber* defending the rights of the component bodies at the central level. Yet there are variations in the extent to which the component bodies are protected and, generally, in the extent to which there is decentralization.

On the one hand, federal states are becoming more centralized; on the other, centralization cannot go beyond a given point without leading to gross inefficiency and perhaps to a break-up of the regime, as the communist experience showed. Partly for this reason, there is a *degree of convergence* between federal and unitary states.

Federalism is also associated with efforts to *bring together independent states*, but this has occurred in a small number of polities only. Attempts at achieving closer co-operation between states has led more commonly to confederacies, such as the United Nations.

The *European Community or European Union* has innovated by forming a type of association, labelled *supranational*, which is intermediate between the confederal and the federal models. There is innovation in that developments take place gradually, with new fields being progressively covered, new structures being set up, and new member-states joining.

The problems of centralization and decentralization have exercised the minds of many in relation to many types of organization: both efficiency and freedom appear to be at stake. Federalism succeeded in a number of contexts, but it is not the panacea which some suggest it is; it is also so diverse that one has to refer to 'federalisms' rather than to 'federalism'. What is at stake is the need to find an equilibrium between the two extremes of overcentralization and break-up. Given the large number of situations in the contemporary world, one should look for a variety of solutions and for a continuous evolution of the models which have hitherto been proposed.

## Further reading

The literature on federalism is large, although much of it tends to be juridical. Moreover, the problem is not normally related to and discussed in terms of decentralization: one author who does so is T. Fleiner Gerster in *Federalism and Decentralisation* (1987).

A classic description of the characteristics of federalism can be found in K.C. Wheare, *Federal Government* (1963). Two older presentations of the nature of federalism across the world are those of W.S. Livingston, *Federalism and Constitutional Change* (1956) and A.Q. MacMahon, *Federalism, Mature and Emergent* (1955). More recent works have to a large extent built on these studies. The most important are those by D.J. Elazar, ed., *The Federal Polity* (1974) and *Federalism and Political Integration* (1979) and M. Burgess, *Federalism and Federation* (1986).

A comprehensive coverage of the (full as well as near or nearly) federal states can be found in D.J. Elazar, ed., *Federal Systems of the World: A Handbook* (1991). For a historical vision of the development of federalism, see M. Forsyth, *Unions of States* (1981: especially 17–72).

The problems posed by federalism are analyzed in T.M. Franck, *Why Federations Fail* (1968), R.T. Golembiewski and A. Widavsky, eds., *The Costs of Federalism* (1984) and W.H. Riker, ed., *The Development of American Federalism* (1987). See also S. H. Beer, 'The modernisation of American federalism' in D.J. Elazar, ed., *The Federal Polity* (1974: 49–95).

Books on the European Union have also become very numerous. Among the more recent, see W. Wallace, *The Transformation of Western Europe* (1992) and D. Dinan, *Ever Closer Union* (1994).

# 15

# Representation: legislatures and parliaments

## Introduction

No country is fully centralized: the question of the extent of centralization and of decentralization thus arises everywhere. In parallel, the question of *representation* also arises everywhere, even if the extent of representation varies markedly from country to country, and if, where representative institutions formally exist, their role also varies markedly. No government can make rules *wholly* in isolation from the sentiments and even the pressure of at least some segments of the polity: a degree of representation, however limited, has therefore to exist.

The forms which representation takes obviously vary, however, and as with respect to decentralization, constitutions have provided different formulas. Indeed, it is on representative institutions that constitutions have placed the greatest emphasis. Perhaps as a result, it is also in this context that there have been most disappointments about the effectiveness of constitutions. Through constitutions, efforts were made to establish, often for the first time, powerful representative institutions; yet often, authoritarian habits and the need for rapid decision making reduced markedly the role of these bodies. The success has been greatest where, as in the United States, a tradition of representative government preceded the promulgation of the constitution. Where, on the contrary, as in France at the end of the eighteenth century or in Latin America in the course of the nineteenth, parliaments and legislatures were introduced as entirely new institutions and granted major powers at the same time, their development was difficult and gave rise to repeated false starts. The story of the many failures of constitutions with respect to representative assemblies suggests that it is unrealistic to expect these quickly to play a central part in the national decision-making process, if they can ever play such a part.

- In the course of this chapter, we shall therefore look first at the general reasons for *the weaknesses, but also the resilience of legislatures*, and of representative bodies in general.

- Second, we shall examine the *general characteristics* of the structure and composition of contemporary legislatures.
- We will then turn to the *framework of activities of legislatures*, and examine the characteristic ways in which they undertake their tasks.
- Finally, we shall assess the *influence of legislatures*, distinguishing between their influence on detailed questions, on important but limited issues, and on the major problems facing society.

## Formal powers and the effective role of legislatures

### Types of legislature

In the overwhelming majority of countries, constitutions state that the 'legislature', the 'parliament' or the 'congress' is the expression of popular sovereignty, and either that it is the top decision-making body or, at least, that its status is on a par with that of the executive. The reality is different, however: to simplify, one might say that there are four broad types of situation along a continuum:

- In a minority of cases, the legislature is *abolished or suspended*.
- In a substantial number of countries, the legislature is wholly *manipulated*. This type of situation prevails in most authoritarian states.
- There are many cases of legislatures which are *controlled*, more or less tightly, by the executive. This occurs in many liberal countries, including many western European countries, though to a varying degree.
- There are only a few polities in the fourth category, that of legislatures which constitute *an essential element in the national decision-making process*. It is therefore not surprising that the subject of representation should have led to disquiet and pessimism. From the late nineteenth century at least, comments have repeatedly been made about the 'decline of legislatures' (Bryce, 1921: I, 367–77; Blondel, 1973: 5–7).

Admittedly, this is only one aspect of the picture. Almost every year, some legislatures are abolished by military coups, but almost every year, too, some legislatures are established or re-established. Moreover, at a minimum, the existence of national representation has great symbolic value. Many regimes attempt to ensure that the legislature is limited to being a symbol: modern single-party systems have been most sophisticated in this respect. Yet these legislatures do survive and, by surviving, keep alive the idea of representation. When the regime relaxes its domination, the legislature can come to life, as has been the case in most eastern European countries since the late 1980s.

---

## BOX 15.1
## A decline of legislatures?

In what was the first truly empirical study of western governments, *Modern Democracies*, Bryce devoted a chapter to the subject of the 'decline of legislatures' (I: 1921, 367–77). He argued that legislatures were weak and legislators incompetent or even corrupt. The idea of a decline of legislatures seemed confirmed in the twentieth century by the weaknesses of western European parliaments, not to mention those of most Third World countries.

While contemporary legislatures are often weak, there is some doubt as to whether they *declined* in quality and power during the period which preceded Bryce's investigation, let alone in the decades which followed. The view that there was a 'golden age' of legislatures seems at best exaggerated.

There is little which can be said positively about the early development of continental European legislatures. They were weak and in most cases manipulated. For instance, the French legislature of the 1830s and 1840s was dominated by civil servants whom the government controlled. The British Parliament was at times more effective, but its relative strength in the 1860s was preceded by long periods during which it was controlled by the prime minister as well as by the local élites: it was not a sedate and enlightened debating chamber in the early part of the nineteenth century.

Perhaps the American Congress, when it was first set up, approximated more closely the model of the 'ideal legislature'. Yet it certainly did not consistently display a highly rational and dispassionate behaviour. It therefore seems exaggerated to conclude from the few cases in which legislatures have been shown to be 'great' that they were better in the past than subsequently.

Legislatures are generally weak. Their weakness is due to general causes, many of which are structural and are connected with the complexity of matters and the need for urgent decisions. Only on very few occasions did they realize the standards which Bryce, and indeed earlier Locke and Montesquieu, would have wanted them to display.

---

## The relative weakness of most legislatures

Representative assemblies perform at least an important symbolic function, but they rarely exercise to the full the *effective powers* which are granted to them by the constitution. These are typically very large, Including the power to legislate and, in many cases, to oversee and even overthrow the government. It is argued that such parliaments are *sovereign*, or at least embody popular sovereignty. Were it possible to divide legislatures into two groups only – the powerful assemblies of liberal countries and the purely symbolic bodies of authoritarian states – the fate and characteristics of these bodies would be easier to understand. In reality, although legislatures are weaker in authoritarian than in liberal polities, the difference is not sufficiently sharp to allow for a clear-cut division.

Governments of liberal countries allow legislatures to debate major issues and representatives to voice criticisms, but they also generally succeed in ensuring that the policy-making process is not markedly affected as a result. This is largely the consequence of the fact that, in Western European systems at least, governments can normally control the assembly because of strong *party discipline*. As a result, they can see to it that laws are passed in the shape which they wish these to have. In such a case, the effective influence of parliaments is so reduced that they can scarcely be said to exercise the powers which are constitutionally theirs. Indeed, one can go further: when parliaments have exercised a real power of control over the government, as in France before the establishment of the Fifth Republic by De Gaulle in 1958, a period during which the legislature made and unmade governments at a very rapid rate, the effect appears to have been negative. In fact, the legislature seems to undermine the legitimacy of the regime by its inability to pursue a consistent policy line.

Legislatures of western European parliamentary systems are thus often rather docile. Those of presidential systems appear to be less so, because, as is sometimes argued, they are not closely tied to the executive. The Congress of the United States is strong; occasionally at least, the congresses of some Latin American countries appear also to be strong. Yet even the United States Congress is not truly determinant in policy making: its main strength consists in scrutinizing, delaying and from time to time blocking presidential proposals, but its positive role is less obvious. In Latin America, the congresses which have been powerful have sometimes generated such conflicts with the executive branch, as in Chile between 1970 and 1973, that a major trial of strength has ensued, in turn giving rise to opportunities for military takeovers (Shugart and Carey, 1992: 156).

Representative assemblies thus encounter major problems. Dictatorships not only often abolish them, but they also domesticate those which they do not abolish. Many liberal governments not only succeed in markedly limiting the effective powers of legislatures, but when these powers are fully exercised, the result seems to be a considerable loss of prestige for the regime and indeed for the assembly itself. Are the formal powers given to legislatures by constitutions unrealistically large? Are these powers ill suited to the characteristics of modern government? Has representation to be given only limited scope for the machinery of government to be able to function?

## Representative assemblies and legislation

The difficulties experienced by the legislatures of even the most liberal states suggest that these bodies may not be able to deal with the role which is assigned to them. In reality, the main problem relates to the fact that, as the name of these bodies indicates, one of the major functions of legislatures, if not their main function, is that of law making; yet representative assemblies are not well equipped to generate and develop modern legislation. When both Locke and Montesquieu put forward the view that laws should be passed by the legislature, legislation was primarily concerned with personal affairs: they dealt mainly with the family, property and crime. It seemed natural that such laws should be debated by an assembly if the system was to be liberal. The aim was to *protect the citizen*: laws were to 'declare' in a solemn manner, and as long as they were not changed, what the relationships between citizens were to be.

With the development of *state intervention* in the society and the economy, most laws acquired a new and different character. Instead of being primarily designed to regulate private relationships among citizens, their main goal is now to establish services, such as education, housing and social security; these services are highly technical, but also dynamic. Moreover, unlike the traditional 'declarative' laws of the eighteenth and nineteenth centuries, modern laws entail high levels of expenditure as well as the training of large numbers of specialist staff who have to be paid. Economic life is also regulated on a daily basis, and is helped and promoted by a whole series of governmental actions. Locke and Montesquieu realized that the need for continuity and the urgent character of decisions in the realm of foreign affairs made it impossible for an assembly to take key decisions in this field: hence this was to be the province of the executive power. Indeed, Locke suggested that there be a 'federative' power dealing with external relations (from the Latin *foedus*, which means treaty). The current role of governments in economic and social matters stems from similar needs for continuous action and for *urgent decisions*.

It is therefore not surprising that legislatures should have to concede to governments the function of preparing legislation, including that of deciding when this legislation could be prepared. Interestingly, legislatures often continue to exercise substantial influence in the field of private law. In Britain, for instance, many aspects of the personal status of individuals are still dealt with by private members' bills, while MPs have free votes on questions of conscience. Moreover, governments are also markedly constrained with respect to many aspects of modern legislation, since they too have to contend with a situation which results in only some proposals being realistic. Thus, first, it is simply impossible for assemblies to be *sovereign* with respect to modern social and economic legislation: they can only *participate* in a general process of decision making. The real question is therefore how large their influence is in a given country at a given point in time. Second, the constitutional emphasis on the legislative function of assemblies has had the paradoxical effect of leaving aside a number of other ways in which legislatures can – and often do – exercise influence: for instance, with respect to the scrutiny of administration. In these matters too, however, they can only participate in an overall decision-making process.

Such a conception of the role of legislatures has consequences for the structure of these bodies and the attitudes of their members. On the one hand, the procedures designed to pass laws are not equally well adapted to the other types of activity which legislatures undertake. On the other hand, members of parliament cannot fulfil their tasks adequately if they are generalists: they need to *specialize* if they are to grasp the intricacies of social and economic problems, and thus exercise influence. With the conception that the law was general, members could be 'amateurs'; this is no longer appropriate with complex social and economic legislation, and with the need to scrutinize the activities of the civil service.

Only within this framework does it become possible to assess the real 'weight' of legislatures in the contemporary world. Clearly, such a weight will vary from country to country and from period to period: the 'symbolic' legislatures of authoritarian systems are unlikely to exercise the type of generalized influence – even to *consider exercising* the type of influence – which legislatures of more liberal countries can aim at exercising. But the need to examine generally the extent to which legislatures participate in the national decision-making process means that one must consider these activities – and the activities of members individually – in the broadest possible way. One needs to look at the effect of assemblies on bills, to be sure; but one must also look at all the fields in which legislators intervene. This effort has only begun to be undertaken in recent years and it is far from complete (Blondel, 1973: 92–131; Mezey, 1979: 21–44).

## Characteristics of contemporary legislatures

### Number of legislatures

Before considering the modes of influence of legislatures, we need to examine the general framework, structure, powers and composition within which contemporary representative bodies operate. Variations are wide in this respect, especially since, for the first time in the history of mankind, nearly all countries have, or had recently, a representative assembly. Only a few traditional monarchies, mainly located in the Arabian peninsula, have never had an elected legislature.

The exact number of legislatures varies from year to year, however: because of military coups and revolutions, in the 1970s and early 1980s, as many as 20 or even 30 legislatures, typically in Latin America and in Africa, were closed or suspended in any given year. The number of military regimes declined from the mid-1980s, while new states, principally in what used to be the communist area, were set up, most of these being, at least formally, liberal democratic. As a result, the number of legislatures effectively in existence was over 170 out of 182 countries in 1994, the highest number ever achieved. The return to liberal democracy, first, of many Latin American countries, and second, of many Black African countries, accounts in large part for this situation (Blondel, 1973: 7–10).

### Structure

#### One or two chambers

Two aspects of the structure of legislatures are most important. One, which has given rise to a very large literature, is that of the division of representative bodies into two chambers. It has been variously claimed that the possible 'excesses' of lower houses needed to be counterbalanced by the 'wisdom' of more sedate upper houses; and, on the other hand, that if an upper house were different in composition from the lower house, the system would be undemocratic because the popular will could then be frustrated. The debate has lost much of its strength, however, in large part because governments can rely on parties to control the legislature, whether it is based on one or two chambers and also because second chambers have also lost many of their powers; in several countries they can only delay legislation (Britain and France, for instance). They are more powerful in federal countries, for reasons which we discussed in Chapter 14, but even there, they are not always equal to the lower house (Germany, Canada) (Wheare, 1963: 87–90).

There are now about as many legislatures which have one chamber only as there are which have two chambers. It is difficult to detect any major differences between the two situations. Some truly liberal countries – Sweden, Denmark and New Zealand, in particular – abolished their upper chamber without any apparent deleterious effect. On a world-wide basis, the number of two-chamber legislatures is diminishing, but only slowly. Two-chamber legislatures are mostly found in South America and the Caribbean (but not in Central America) and in Atlantic countries. They are rare in Black Africa, and they are or were rare in communist states, unless they were federal. The end of communism led to the re-establishment of second chambers in some countries (such as Poland), but not in all. Apart from federalism, one of the factors which appears to account for the existence of a second chamber is the population size of the country: the most populous countries tend to have a second chamber. Overall, it is therefore questionable as to whether there is any longer a real case for a second chamber, except in countries where there are sharp geographical cleavages (hence their value in a federal context) (Matthews, 1960; Blondel, 1973: 32–5).

## *Size of legislatures*

Perhaps a more important aspect of the structure of representative assemblies is their overall size, although the question is less discussed. There are legislatures of nearly a thousand members (India) and many have five hundred members or more (Britain, France, Italy); at the other extreme, there are legislatures of about fifty members (Costa Rica, Luxembourg, Iceland).

The size of the legislature is related to the size of the country's population, but not proportionately. As a result, there is one representative for one million inhabitants in India, one representative for half a million inhabitants in the United States (and one senator for two million inhabitants), and one Russian deputy for 250,000 inhabitants. In Britain, France, Germany and Italy, there is one member of parliament for about 100,000 inhabitants, in Belgium one for 50,000, in Switzerland and Sweden one for 25,000, and in Ireland and Norway one for 20,000. This means a double advantage for smaller countries: since the legislatures are smaller, representatives have more opportunity to participate in the activities of the chamber; and since each MP represents fewer constituents, the links between people and parliament are closer. Thus the legislatures of smaller countries probably function better, other things being equal, than those of larger countries.

## Powers

### *Parliamentary and presidential systems*

The framework within which legislatures operate is, of course, also characterized by the range of the formal powers of these bodies, although the relationship between formal powers and influence must not be exaggerated. Traditionally, a sharp distinction has been made between *legislatures* (assemblies which do not have the power to force the executive to resign and, as a counterpart, cannot be dissolved) and *parliaments* (which can censure the government, but at least in many cases can be dissolved) (Verney, 1959: 17–97). This distinction remains valid and constitutes the basis of the differentiation, in liberal countries, between *presidential systems* (the United States and most Latin American countries) and *parliamentary systems* (most of western Europe, Japan, Israel and many Commonwealth countries). The parliamentary system has also been introduced in most eastern European countries after the fall of communism, but there are still uncertainties about the final arrangements, as there are uncertainties about the parliamentary character of the liberal democratic systems introduced in the early 1990s in Black Africa.

Meanwhile, the distinction does not apply to those Third World states where there is a more authoritarian form of presidentialism, since the president may dissolve the assembly, while the legislature does not have the right to censure the government. Moreover, in the states which have remained communist, the regime is formally described as 'assembly' government: that is, the chamber can legally force the executive to resign without being threatened by dissolution (Verney, 1959: 57–74). This system so weakens the government that it exists in communist states only because the reality does not conform at all to the theory. Such a system formally exists also in Switzerland, as the members of the national executive (the Federal Council) are elected by the two houses of the legislature for a fixed term; they cannot be dismissed, nor can the chamber be dissolved. Beyond these cases, other polities cannot easily be divided into presidential and parliamentary systems. There are intermediate systems, together with variations within presidential and within parliamentary systems. It is therefore unrealistic to adopt a dichotomous distinction (Shugart and Carey, 1992: 154–65).

One intermediate category which has grown in importance has been labelled *semi-presidential*: France (since 1958) is the best-known example in this group. These systems are labelled semi-presidential because heads of state are sometimes given substantial powers. These heads of state also have substantial authority because they are elected by universal suffrage, as we shall see in Chapter 17 (Frears, 1981: 30–50).

In these cases, as in others, the question of whether the government can be censored by the chamber is an important factor, but the arrangements may vary markedly. The right to censure the government may be subjected to stringent conditions, as in France or Germany; conversely, the right of dissolution may be severely limited (Germany) or not exist at all (Norway). Moreover, since the existence of parties reduces the extent to which the chamber can effectively exercise its power of censure, the distinction between parliamentary and presidential systems has to be regarded as being in the nature of a dimension. It used to be claimed that the existence of a right of dissolution was critical for the successful development of a parliamentary system. The case of pre-1958 France was typically mentioned as an example of the dangers for governmental stability resulting from the absence of a right of dissolution. But this situation has to be seen in the context of the fact that the French party system has traditionally been less well structured than the party system of other western European countries. Meanwhile, neither the absence of a right of dissolution nor the fact that this right is limited appears to lead to instability in Norway and Germany respectively (Blondel, 1973: 38–43; Shugart and Carey, 1992: 106–26).

### Law-making and budgetary powers

Whether they are legislatures or parliaments, representative assemblies have two main formal powers: *making laws* and *voting the budget*. But these are not always given in full, even in theory, let alone in fact. Budgetary powers are restricted, including in some liberal countries: for instance legislatures may not have the right to increase expenditure or reduce income, as in France (as a result of the constitution itself) or in Britain (as a result of the standing orders of the chamber).

The power to legislate can also be restricted. First, there is a slow, but gradual increase in the use of the *referendum*: it is now no longer merely Switzerland, Australia and a number of (primarily western) states of the United States which use this technique, but many other liberal countries. We noted in Chapter 11 that the prejudice against referendums is being gradually overcome, and the power of the legislature to legislate is consequently being reduced. Second, and again even in liberal countries, the executive is sometimes granted legislative powers. Legislatures may be asked to pass 'outline laws' which the government subsequently fills in, as in France, or the government may be entitled to promulgate decrees which are ratified afterwards, as in France and Italy. Furthermore, the constitution (in France) or the standing orders of the chamber (in Britain) may either give the government the power to restrict debates, or allow it to force a vote to achieve this effect. Thus, even in some liberal states, let alone in authoritarian systems, the power of the legislature to pass laws or decide on the finances of the state can be restricted formally at a time when the power of parliaments to censure governments (coupled or not with the right of dissolution) is also sometimes limited (Blondel, 1973: 35–8; Shugart and Carey, 1992: 132–46).

## Social composition

Structure and powers establish the framework within which legislators can exercise their tasks, but legislatures are also naturally affected by the background of their members. An assembly composed of lawyers is not likely to behave in the same way as an assembly composed of manual workers. In general, legislatures tend to be overwhelmingly *male*, though gradually less so, *middle-aged*, and drawn from the *middle class*. Women were a tiny minority (5 or 6 per cent or even less) almost everywhere up to the 1980s: only in Scandinavian countries and in some eastern communist states did they then form a substantially larger group, though not a majority. There is now some redress, but it is still patchy. Legislators are normally middle-aged, though they are younger in African legislatures than in Latin America or in the West. This means that the world's representatives are elected only after having held another job, often for many years (Blondel, 1973: 17–20).

Such a job is likely to have a middle-class character. Farmers are rare, and particularly rare in the Third World, although they are most numerous in the population at large. In western countries, they come closer to the proportion of farmers in the population, but only because the size of the workforce which works on the land has markedly declined. Manual workers are a small minority, even in countries where socialist parties are strong, since in these parties white-collar employees and managers are gradually replacing trade unionists. Only in communist states was or is the proportion of workers in the legislature rather larger, but even there it began to decrease after the early period.

Thus the large majority of legislators are lawyers, teachers, managers or civil servants. In the United States and Canada, lawyers alone form the majority; in western Europe, they are about a quarter of the total. Teachers are more numerous in western Europe, while businesspeople, managers and civil servants often form a third of the legislature. This distribution is fairly close to the one found in the Middle East, in Asia and in Latin America (though two-thirds of Colombian Congresspersons are lawyers). In communist states, on the other hand, alongside manual workers, most representatives are or were teachers and white-collar employees: there have been very few lawyers among them.

There are therefore three types of representation in the contemporary world:

- In North America, the stress is on representation in the *legal* sense. Legislators are spokespersons, and they act 'for' the people.
- In western Europe and most Latin American countries, this view competes with another model, that of *social representation*, especially with respect to socialist, Christian and agrarian parties, in which different groups are represented. This is particularly the case in Scandinavia and central Europe.
- In eastern communist states, while some groups have been represented, the main stress has traditionally been on a third model, that of the *vanguard*, in which an *intelligentsia*, composed mainly of teachers and managers, leads the rest of the population, the aim being to mobilize rather than to represent. A similar model has also been adopted in the more 'progressive' Third World countries, especially in Africa and the Middle East.

## The short career of legislators

Is a legislator part of a *profession* in the strong sense of the word? This is debatable, both because the background of members is diverse and because some of them are part-timers. It is also debatable because their stay in the legislature is usually rather short (less than ten years on average), as a result of a variety of political 'accidents', and of traditions, at least as much as of electoral vicissitudes. In some countries, the military may close the legislature; in others, especially in Latin America, legislators are

---

## BOX 15.2
## Should there be 'career' legislators?

In the early 1990s, the membership of the legislature of the state of California ceased to be open for 'permanent membership': members had to retire after having been legislators for two terms. In some Latin American legislatures, such as Costa Rica, members cannot be immediately re-elected. Such provisions are far from new: the members of the French Constituent Assembly of 1789–91 barred themselves from standing for election to the legislative assembly which was subsequently elected.

The rationale for such provisions is the desire to ensure turnover and to prevent the emergence of a professional class of politicians. The fact that top committee appointments in the United States Congress go to the most 'senior' (i.e. longest-serving) members of the committee is regarded as undemocratic. Citizens should not be controlled by a permanent group of legislators who, because they have an electoral appeal in their district, can manipulate the legislative process. Enforced rotation is regarded as the solution.

Yet such moves have not so far been adopted widely in the legislatures of the polities which consider themselves liberal democratic. This may be because those who are members wish to remain members; but there are also dangers in the principle of rotation. Public policy making is complex: to stipulate that legislators, who are often without adequate experience, should leave at the time when they have acquired some experience seems mistaken.

Furthermore, as the political career is uncertain, given electoral upsets and even nomination upsets, it may not be judicious to add to these hazards the rule that the career is not allowed to last: this might impair the recruitment of good men and women, while those who do choose the career may be primarily looking after their future. A move designed to achieve democracy may result in legislators being even more concerned than now with their own personal problems.

As the majority of members of legislatures tend to leave after having been less than ten years in the elected chamber, it may not be so valuable to insist on making retirement compulsory.

---

not permitted to stand again, at least immediately. In single-party systems, representatives are sometimes not renominated for a variety of reasons: this has been the case, for instance, in Kenya and Tanzania.

American and western European legislators, who remain in the chamber ten years or more on average, tend to be, paradoxically, more secure in their jobs than legislators from many non-competitive systems; indeed, in Atlantic countries, disappointment and frustration with the parliamentary experience lead to many resignations besides electoral defeat. There appears to be a tendency for the average duration to be longer with time passing, as analyses in countries as diverse as the United States, Switzerland and Colombia have shown. However, so far at least, even in these cases, the 'career' in the legislature remains relatively short; it begins as a second job and it is typically followed by a third (or by the return to the original occupation) (Blondel, 1973: 85–91).

## The activities of legislators

### Frequency of meetings

The powers of legislators can be exercised only if the framework of the activities allows members to discuss and debate a large variety of problems. This means, first, that the chamber needs to meet rather frequently. Yet there is a sharp contrast in this respect: some legislatures meet almost every day throughout most of the year (the United States, Britain and Canada, for instance); others scarcely meet at all, resembling party conferences more than debating chambers. Many parliaments of communist states had or still have this character. Before 1989, there had been some changes in Hungary and Poland, where the legislature did debate laws and even pass amendments, but this was not the case in the majority of communist states (Holmes, 1986). The number of days during which chambers meet can thus range from upwards of 150 a year to not more than a handful. In between, many legislatures meet for only two or three weeks in the year. Most western European parliaments meet for about 75 to 100 days a year (Blondel, 1973: 56–62; Interparliamentary Union, 1986).

The fact that the chamber meets frequently does not mean that members can participate often on the floor of the House, especially when the legislature is large. For instance, British MPs can only speak for about an hour and a half a year on average, despite the fact that the House of Commons sits almost every day; a similar situation characterizes other western European countries. Members of African parliaments have even less time to speak from the floor, while those of communist parliaments, except perhaps Polish and Hungarian representatives in the later years of the regime, typically had almost no opportunity at all to do so. Thus individual legislators are unlikely to exercise substantial influence through speeches and debates and, consequently, committees are likely to be a significantly more effective platform.

### Activities on the floor of the chamber

There are four main types of activity on the floor: legislation, the discussion of financial provisions, general debates, and 'questions'. This last activity is widespread mainly in Britain and in a number of Commonwealth countries. The procedure has been spreading to an extent to the Continent of Europe, but it remains more formal there, and has less the character of a pugnacious exchange (Marsh, 1985: 83–5). The discussion of legislation occupies most of the time of most representative assemblies; indeed, some never have general policy debates, probably as a result of government pressure. This has traditionally been the case in many African parliaments, for instance.

## Legislative debates

Even if legislative debates are the main activity on the floor, there may not be much real discussion, and there may be few or even no changes to the government text as a result of these discussions. Moreover, the importance of the bills presented to parliament varies greatly. In the West, parliaments discuss and approve between 50 and 100 bills a year, some of which are truly important and may lead to long debates; this is also the case in several Latin American countries or in India. In many Third World countries, on the other hand, the bills presented by the government appear to relate primarily to matters of private or commercial law. There are opportunities for discussion with respect to these bills, but broader economic and social matters do not come to the legislature and are dealt with by other means. This has been the case in Tunisia, Senegal, Kenya, Madagascar and Singapore, for instance. In communist states, the inner body of the chamber, the Presidium, has everywhere been empowered to approve bills between sessions of parliament. As a result, only very few bills are or were presented to the full house, and debates are or were almost non-existent. Among communist countries, only in Poland, Hungary and Yugoslavia, and in the last years of the communist regime, did more prolonged discussions occur in the legislature (Blondel, 1973: 62–6.)

One can therefore divide legislatures into three broad types from the point of view of the characteristics of the debate on the floor:

- In western Europe, as well as in most Latin American countries and a number of Commonwealth states, much time is devoted to (primarily governmental) legislation, but the final outcome is rarely in doubt. The main exceptions are the United States and, in some cases, Latin American congresses, where government bills are not only debated at length, but frequently rejected or markedly amended.
- In many, probably most, Third World countries, some debates do occur, but they typically concern bills of relatively limited importance.
- In most authoritarian systems in which legislatures exist, such as the Middle East, some African countries and the communist states which remain in existence, legislation does not lead to debates in the real sense of the word: leaders make speeches about broad governmental policy.

With the move towards liberalization which occurred in eastern Europe and in Black Africa in the late 1980s and early 1990s, the third category has become (temporarily perhaps) rather small; but the second category is large. The situation in western countries has not been markedly modified, despite pressure being exercised by some legislators and some (minority) parties to 'open up' legislatures rather more.

## Committees

Since activities on the floor do not give legislators marked opportunities to exercise influence, the major stress has been placed on committees, which being smaller, appear better able to exercise genuine supervision and influence. Legislative committees have increased markedly in number over the last decades in western countries, even where, as in Britain, there was a great reluctance on the part of governments to allow them to develop. France is somewhat exceptional in this group of countries, in having seen its parliamentary committees reduced in number and power by the Constitution of the Fifth Republic of 1958, on the grounds, apparently justified, that the activities of these bodies had contributed to the rather chaotic character of previous French regimes.

On the other hand, outside western countries, the committee system is usually not well developed. In many Third World states, few committees exist and those which do meet infrequently. Interestingly, they had played a part in the legislatures of communist states, where they multiplied after the 1960s: even in that early period and even in the Soviet Union, amendments to legislation were occasionally adopted as a result of committee action.

Committees have two main functions: *examining legislation* and *scrutinizing administration*. Britain is rather exceptional in having established two different types of committee for the two purposes. Elsewhere, the same committees are normally involved in both types of activity partly because, historically, the scrutiny of administration emerged in the context of the examination of bills or of financial discussions. The United States Congress is the legislature in which activities of inquiry are by far the most developed, with representatives of the executive and other witnesses being grilled in the sharpest manner. Major scandals have been uncovered as a result. Moreover, while the United States Congress cannot censure the government as such, the appointment of members of the executive gives rise, in the Senate, to 'confirmation' debates which are also extremely searching. In western Europe, committees are less forceful, although they have gradually been increasingly engaged in more systematic inquiries, especially in Britain, and these have had an impact on governmental policy (Patterson, 1978: 125–77; Lees and Shaw, 1979; Downs, 1985: 48–68).

Committees are thus very important: they give legislatures and their members an opportunity to exercise influence, not just because bills submitted by the government may be modified in the process, but because policies and administrative practices can also be gradually altered. Consequently, committee work has an impact in boosting the morale of legislators who can see that they are not reduced to supporting (or opposing) the government mechanically. However, the influence of members is also a function of the extent to which these become specialized – a move which committee work naturally fosters. While committees do not by themselves shift the initiative in policy making away from the executive (a shift which, as was pointed out earlier, is rather unrealistic given the nature of legislation), legislatures can and probably always do acquire a greater say as a result of the development of committees.

## The influence of legislatures

The influence of legislatures is complex to measure. One needs to take into account the effect which these bodies have in a variety of ways. Alongside their role in the legislature, whether in the whole chamber or in its committees, legislators can also exercise influence individually. This influence can be exercised at three different levels (Blondel, 1973: 92–130; Mezey, 1979: 47–59).

### Influence at the level of specific issues

It can be exercised over *detailed and individual matters*: for instance, over personal requests from electors or sectional demands from groups and associations. This is the nearest to a universal activity of legislators, although the extent of the pressure and of the success of this pressure varies. In many countries, representatives have to open *surgeries*, more or less regularly, to handle requests. Delegations from associations may also come and meet legislators, which occurs primarily in western countries. Most complaints are probably made by correspondence. This is bulky in some countries – 100 letters a day for the average American Congressperson, 15-20 letters a day for the average British MP. It is much lower outside western countries (Blondel, 1973: 94–6; Barker and Rush, 1970).

To deal with these requests, members typically first raise the matter by approaching the appropriate government department. If this is unsuccessful, the legislator may put the matter in the hands of an official in charge of examining complaints (the *ombudsman*). In some countries, such as in Britain, this civil servant can be approached only through an MP, as we shall see in Chapter 18. Alternatively, members may raise the issue more formally, especially if it has general implications, by way of written or oral questions (especially, as we noted, in Britain and Commonwealth countries), and even by way of *private members' bills*. The fact that MPs present private members' bills does not mean that they hope to see these bills passed; indeed, in many legislatures, vast numbers of such bills are presented and quietly buried. In presenting them, MPs may have a variety of aims, ranging from satisfying their constituents to attempting to place an issue on the agenda. In the United States, specialized bills are often drafted by members of Congress. Finally, *budgetary debates* may also provide opportunities to present specific cases.

Although these activities are specific and affect the public policy process only marginally, they are important for citizens. Legislators give them prominence because their personal standing with electors may depend on showing concern for constituency matters. They have to do so, not merely where elections are competitive, but even in single-party systems, since their renomination may be at stake. This has been the case in particular in Tanzania (Hopkins, 1970: 754–71; Barkan and Okumu, 1979: 64–91). The overall impact cannot be measured by the number of successes only, since pressures of this kind may have the effect of forcing the administration to be less casual and more responsive to the public at large. These specific actions therefore affect to a substantial extent the relationship between government and citizens.

### Influence at the intermediate level

More general are the 'intermediate' matters, which are concerned not with the overall aims of a policy, but with some of its aspects. Legislatures may want to modify the list of bodies or groups to which a measure is to be applied, or the fields to be included or excluded in a measure, or the conditions under which the measure will apply. The influence exercised by legislators in this fashion may not be well publicized or even take place in the open; yet it may affect appreciably the characteristics of the law.

*Committees* are the supreme arenas where such an influence can be exercised. This influence is related both to the extent to which legislators have access to information (which they may be able to obtain from groups) and to the extent to which they are specialized. The part played by committees is especially large in relation to bills, though it should not be exaggerated. Even in communist states, as we saw, some amendments have been known to be accepted by the executive, but this has remained relatively rare. Liberal democratic governments – western European governments, for instance – also accept relatively few amendments. Government bills tend to emerge out of committees in their original shape, although there have been some changes in this respect in some western European countries: in Italy, for example, committees have been very influential (Furlong, 1990: 52–67).

However, the influence of legislators in this respect should not be measured only in terms of successful amendments passed, even if these constitute obvious indicators. There may be greater influence resulting from pressures exercised over a period of time, as these may induce the government to modify its views and present different proposals. Influence can also be exercised, normally in committees, by scrutinizing administration. Indeed, legislators can begin a process as a result of which changes may eventually take place by a variety of means: namely, questions, short debates and budgetary debates. They can use these to press points on their colleagues, on the government, and to an extent on the public at large.

The measurement of the influence of legislators over these matters of an 'intermediate' importance is imprecise. However, this influence does exist in all legislatures except those which are truly tightly controlled. As the extent of influence depends in part on the readiness of the government to allow debates to take place and committees to develop, the legislatures of authoritarian states are clearly hampered in this respect, but on some issues at least, even these play some part. In liberal countries, this type of influence remains diffuse and depends significantly on the level of the research support which members can enjoy; it also depends on the size of the government majority and on the standing of the executive in the country. It is because American Congresspersons have substantial research support and the executive can never be sure of enjoying a majority that they are able to exercise greater influence than western European parliamentarians on these matters.

## Influence at the broad policy level

The role of legislatures is normally assessed at the level of broader policy influence. Most pessimistic comments about their role are typically made in this respect as well. Whether on 'grand' social and economic policies or on financial provisions, the large majority of legislatures appear to be little more than ratification bodies. Even the few representative assemblies, such as the United States Congress, which are able to modify appreciably the proposals of the executive do so to a limited extent only and, in most cases, by means of delaying rather than by wholly overturning the requests of the administration. Legislatures do not initiate: they follow. The difference is between those which follow without grumbling and those which follow grudgingly and by dragging their feet.

Yet there is hidden influence in this respect as well. To appreciate it fully, and to be able to distinguish between legislatures from the point of view of their impact at the broad policy level, the activities of legislators need to be considered in a wider context. Two general characteristics must be taken into account. First, legislatures often have an overt and even more a hidden *veto* impact. They may not be able to affect markedly the bills which governments present, but they frequently play a part in preventing governments from launching some policies which might otherwise have been started. One cannot measure precisely the extent to which the executive self-censors itself in this fashion, but some cases are well known, such as in Britain the celebrated instance of the withdrawal of trade union legislation in the late 1960s. This type of legislative power is probably unknown in authoritarian states, where, by and large, policies are accepted on the nod or even implemented without reference to the legislature at all.

Second, legislatures are often able to play a more *positive* part as well. They may not be in a position to initiate, as we saw, in part because they do not have the technical competence required to do the necessary preparatory work which the civil service, advised by a variety of organizations, can undertake. They can none the less exercise influence in starting 'great debates'. This influence is rarely exercised when bills are fully developed and presented to the chamber because, at that point, many discussions are likely to have taken place with interested parties. But legislators who launch suggestions on issues when they are still being discussed can, over time, exercise influence. The executive and the civil service may as a result be obliged to make specific proposals. *Committees of inquiry* can therefore be crucial, especially if they include members of the interested public alongside legislators. The legislature then provides a forum which can play the part fulfilled by Royal Commissions in Britain and by Presidential Commissions in the United States. A development of this kind occurs in Sweden, where members of the legislature are involved in a significant manner in this 'pre-preparatory' phase of policy development.

So far, legislatures are involved in this stage of policy preparation to a relatively limited extent, even in western Europe, partly because the potential of such activities does not seem to have been fully perceived. But involvement is growing as legislatures become more specialized and have better research support. These opportunities are probably open almost exclusively to the legislatures of liberal countries, not merely because in authoritarian states, the pressure of the government is strong, but also because the institutional infrastructure is likely to be unsatisfactory.

While differences among legislatures seem elusive when the only criterion used is that of the origin of the bills which are passed, such differences can be rediscovered by closer examination. Western European representative assemblies may not reach the level of open and apparently direct involvement in policy making of the United States Congress; they can none the less play a 'subterranean' part in determining the *national agenda*. The potential exists, despite the fact that these legislatures do not often use in practice all the opportunities which are offered to them (Norton, 1990).

## Overview

Some form of *representation* exists in every polity, even if many legislatures are strictly controlled and some are abolished, at least for a period.

On the other hand, legislatures, even in liberal states, are not in a position to fulfil the role which constitutions ascribe to them, in large part because of the nature of *modern legislation*, which requires a degree of preparation and development which assemblies are ill equipped to provide.

The real powers of legislatures over *law making* and over the *budget* as well as of parliaments over the *survival of the executive* are therefore appreciably more limited in practice than they are in theory.

Legislatures tend to be composed mainly of *middle-aged men* drawn primarily from among lawyers, teachers and civil servants. Their tenure is relatively short – under ten years on average.

Most legislatures meet for *short to very short periods*, although western chambers sit most weekdays throughout most of the year. It is not so much in full sittings as in *committees*, however, that the real work is done. Committees are most developed in western legislatures.

Legislators often play a substantial part in helping to solve the *problems of their constituents* or of their district. They play a part more rarely in *modifying governmental proposals* or in *scrutinizing administration* and uncovering scandals.

Their role over *broad policy matters* is generally limited, although, if they focus in a specialized manner on some questions and are concerned primarily with raising the problems posed by these questions, legislators in western liberal democracies at least can exercise substantial influence.

Both potentially and in reality, provided they adapt to the conditions of policy development in modern societies, *legislatures can play a part at all levels of policy*, while also being able to scrutinize governmental and administrative action in an effective manner.

## Further reading

The literature on individual legislatures is naturally large; the comparative literature on the subject is markedly more limited. The first major effort at comparing is the work of Lord Bryce, *Modern Democracies* (1921, vol. 1). Since the 1970s, there has been a great surge of interest on the subject, however: not only western legislatures, but communist and Third World legislatures have been studied. See, for instance, J. Blondel, *Comparative Legislatures* (1973), A. Kornberg, ed., *Legislatures in Comparative Perspective* (1973), M.L. Mezey, *Comparative Legislatures* (1979), and G. Loewenberg and S.C. Patterson, *Comparative Legislatures* (1979). A compendium on the legislatures of the world is provided by the publication of the Inter-Parliamentary Union, *Parliaments of the World* (1986) (2 vols.). The role of legislatures in presidential systems is analyzed systematically in M.S. Shugart and J.M. Carey, *Presidents and Assemblies* (1992).

An interesting examination of current developments in a number of western legislatures can be found in P. Norton, ed., *Parliaments in Western Europe* (1990). An earlier study by W. Agor, ed., *Latin American Legislatures* (1971) is highly revealing of the role of these bodies. On the role of legislatures in the Third World, see J. Smith and L.D. Musolf, ed., *Legislatures in Development* (1979). On behaviour in two African legislatures, see J.D. Barkan and J.J. Okumu, eds., *Politics and Public Opinion in Kenya and Tanzania* (1979).

On the role of committees, see J.D. Lees and M. Shaw, eds., *Committees in Legislatures: A Comparative Analysis* (1979). For the United States, among the vast literature on the subject, see S.C. Patterson, 'The semi-sovereign Congress' in A. King, ed., *The New American Political System* (1978: 125–77).

Among the country studies which are highly revealing of one aspect of the life of legislatures, see D.R. Matthews, *US Senators and their World* (1960) for the particular character of the US Senate, as well as the classic on Congress by D.B. Truman, *The Congressional Party* (1959). A. Barker and M. Rush, *The Member of Parliament and his Information*, analyze the knowledge which legislators have of the problems they have to deal with, and see also P. Norton, ed., *Parliament in the 1980s* (1985) on the characteristics of representation in Britain.

# 16

# National executives

## Introduction

National executives are universal. Every country has an executive, a *government* in the strict sense of the word, as indeed does every other social organization, from the most simple to the most complex. There is always a body, normally relatively small, though varying in size, which has the task of running the organization.

The executive is also manifestly a key point, if not *the key point of political life*. This remains true even if doubts are sometimes expressed about the ability of executives to affect markedly the course of events, let alone alter drastically the social and economic structure of their country. They have, more than any other body, an opportunity to *shape society*; indeed, it is their function to do so.

Unlike almost all the institutions which we have examined so far, national executives are rather *compact bodies*, whose views and pronouncements are usually well publicized. Parties and even legislatures are more amorphous, and their 'will' is less clear – if they can be said to have a collective will. National executives are relatively small and very visible, so that it is easier to think of them as groups which have a *common goal* and which act as *teams*. In practice, admittedly, they may well not be united, and their differences may even come out into the open. However, the notion of a united government is not wholly unrealistic, and it is a characteristic to which many executives aspire. The aim is to give an impression of a well-oiled and efficient machine which can lead the country towards its future.

## Types of executive

Governments may exist everywhere and be, on the whole, rather small and compact bodies. Within this framework, however, major distinctions exist between them. They vary in *composition*, in *internal organization*, in *selection mechanisms*, in *duration* and in *powers* – both formal and informal. There are autocratic governments and governments which emanate from the people or from its representatives. There are rather egalitarian governments and rather hierarchical governments. There are governments which seem to last indefinitely and ephemeral governments. There are strong and weak governments. As one examines the characteristics of national executives, therefore, differences among these appear to be as large as among groups, parties and legislatures.

## Circumscribing executives

If one analyzes executives further, even the idea that governments form clearly defined groups is not altogether obvious nor is it very old. The concept of government did not exist in republican Rome; in absolute monarchies, there were individual ministers helping the king, not a government.

Even now, the exact limits of the set of individuals who form part of the government are not always easy to determine. There are often men and women around the government whose status in relation to that body is not well defined. First, there are likely to be undersecretaries or *junior ministers*. From a formal point of view, these belong to the government, as they are appointed when the government is constituted and leave office when it ceases to exist. But they are normally excluded from the process of elaboration of governmental policy, as are sometimes even some of the ministers – especially in hierarchical executives in which leaders take the most important decisions and are free to choose whom they wish to advise them. Second, there are the *personal advisers* of leaders, who may well play an important part in decision making – a more important part than ministers even – although they do not belong to the official structure of the executive. This is the case with many of the counsellors of the American president. Thus, while national executives may have a clearly defined nucleus, composed of the leaders and at least most ministers, a 'grey zone' whose boundaries are not precise forms the outer circle of these governments.

- In the first section of this chapter, we shall define national executives on the basis of the *functions which they fulfil*.
- In the second section, we shall examine the *forms which governments take* to fulfil these functions.
- In the third, we shall describe the *anatomy of these governments* by looking at their composition and at their duration across countries and among political systems.
- Finally, we shall assess the *achievements of governments* and attempt to discover what is their true impact on the life of nations.

## The functions of national executives

### Conversion of inputs into outputs

In a general way, the functions of a government are often said to be to 'run the affairs of the nation'; but this expression simply means that governments are at the top of the pyramid of decision making. It is also a rather formal definition of the functions of national executives. If we look at the matter more closely, we notice that governments are at the junction between two processes which characterize national decision making. They 'convert' inputs into outputs – that is to say, turn demands into policies – as we saw in Chapter 2.

This process of conversion is not mechanical: governments can choose among inputs; they may discard some demands, however strongly supported, and select others for which there is little support. Yet, even when this is the case, governments do have to pay some attention to the demands which are expressed, if only to oppose them. No national executive totally 'invents' the policies which it formulates. Ideas for policies originate in the public, including in the 'entourage' of the government itself. If these demands arise, they have to be handled by the government in some manner. This is true even where the system is authoritarian, although the reactions of the government are then likely to be different from the reactions which characterize a pluralistic system.

## Conception and implementation

Governments have to show imagination in the development of their policies: this imaginative effort is in large part related to the discovery of *practical solutions* to problems with which they are faced. Realistic policies have to be elaborated – realistic both in the sense that they can be technically implemented and in the sense that they are politically acceptable (if necessary by using compulsion). An agricultural, industrial or social policy will have to take into account the perceived 'needs' of the country as well as what the citizens are prepared to 'live with'.

Thus, while the government has a function of *conception*, which is linked in some manner to the demands which exist in the polity, it also has a function of *implementation*, at least insofar as it must find the means by which policies can become reality. It must therefore appoint and supervise a bureaucracy which is able to put the policies into operation. These two functions are therefore crucial for governments.

Tensions are likely to arise in the process, since conception and implementation require different psychological qualities. This is reflected, for instance, in the conflict between those who 'dream' and those who 'manage'. Members of governments are thus expected to combine skills which may not easily be combined. While the function of conception requires creative imagination based on a certain vision of society (this is true even of policies of relatively limited importance), the implementation function requires an ability to manage individuals and groups. The same men and women may well not possess both types of skill. Admittedly, the distinction corresponds in part to the division between 'leaders' and their 'helpers' (the word 'minister' refers etymologically to someone who 'helps'); but the two functions cannot wholly be separated, since it is not very useful to conceive ideas which cannot be implemented. Some links need to exist, and governments are the key place where these links develop.

## Co-ordination

The link between these two functions is strengthened by the existence of a third function, that of *co-ordination*, which may be viewed as intermediate. An important element of the process of elaboration of policies consists in ensuring that these do not go against each other and, ideally, combine harmoniously. Moreover, policy elaboration entails making choices or at least establishing priorities, as a result of both financial and human constraints. Not everything can be done at the same time, and a timetable therefore has to be drawn up. But such a timetable must take into account the interrelationships between policies and the internal logic of policy development.

Co-ordination can be successful only if close ties exist among members of the government both at the level of policy elaboration and at that of policy implementation. For example, housing policy entails a school building policy, not merely in general, but in detail; the same applies to an industrial policy, which must lead to a housing policy, etc. The natural tendency of branches of the public service to operate independently of each other must be corrected in order to ensure that distortions, contradictions, and ultimately policy failures are minimized. This is the role of co-ordination, although there are limits to which it can effectively take place. Administrative and political centralization cannot go beyond a certain point without reducing overall efficiency, as many examples drawn from communist states in the past made abundantly clear. Even where centralization does not go too far, co-ordination remains a major problem. It must be at the centre of the preoccupations of the government if the process of implementation of public policies is to be efficient.

Conception, co-ordination and direction of implementation are therefore the three elements of governmental action. These elements are analytically distinct, and it is the government's duty to combine them. But this combination inevitably raises problems: depending on the circumstances, conception, co-ordination or implementation will be given more emphasis. It is not surprising that the development of governmental structures in the contemporary world should have been the result of a variety of *ad hoc* experiments, not all of which have been successful; not surprisingly, too, conflicts have arisen between the three functions of government and these have not all been solved equally well (Blondel, 1982: 21–9).

# Forms of governmental organization

## Evolution of governmental arrangements

Contemporary governmental arrangements reflect the diversity and increasing complexity of the tasks undertaken by executives. But the variations in the structure of these executives are not a new phenomenon: the oligarchical arrangements of Italian republican cities of the Renaissance were at great variance from those of the absolute monarchies which began to emerge in sixteenth-century Europe, and from those of theocratic and despotic governments which have existed occasionally across the world.

## BOX 16.1
## How governments emerged

The idea of a 'government' or a 'national executive' seems natural. Everyone automatically assumes that, at the head of each country, a body of men and women is in charge of the affairs of that country. Yet the concept of government is in reality relatively recent. It has been inherited almost entirely from the monarchical and even patrimonial concept of political rule. There were no governments in the strict sense of the word in the early partially democratic experiments which emerged in city-states and above all in Rome.

The concept of government is unquestionably linked to an idea of hierarchy or of a pyramid. This may explain why the idea that there should be 'dualism' at the top is alien to the notion of government.

Thus early republican states were ruled by a discrete number of officials, elected separately to accomplish specific tasks. Rome had consuls (war and foreign affairs), praetors (justice) and aediles (public works). These officials were appointed for short periods only (one year in most cases); re-election, at least immediate re-election, was not allowed. Admittedly, there was a Senate which dealt with many aspects of the life of the Republic, but this was too large (and also too divided) to constitute an executive.

Government in the modern sense came to Rome with the Empire and with Augustus. In the Middle Ages and the Renaissance, it emerged out of the patrimonial rule of kings and other monarchs who were slowly expanding their role. 'Ministers' were appointed to look after the Exchequer, after problems of justice, or after the well-being and strength of the army. Subsequently, the rulers who became known as 'enlightened despots' and wished to develop their country economically began appointing ministers in charge of public works.

This led to what should be defined as *bureaucratic* government: that is to say, the governments of the absolute monarchs who ruled much of Europe between the seventeenth and nineteenth centuries. On the other hand, those monarchs who were not able to control their society fully had to rely in large part on the aristocracy, some of whom were included in the governments. This move prefigured the other form of government which Europe came to know, *representative* government. Britain was the country in which this form of government developed earliest: it became a 'council' whose members worked together, if not necessarily as a team, at least in conjunction with each other. From this emerged a form of democratic executive which city-states had never been able to develop.

Nineteenth-century developments endeavoured to 'domesticate' governmental arrangements and to give them a less haphazard and more rational character. Two constitutional systems, which we already encountered in the context of legislatures,

.ve tended to dominate the European and North American scene for a century. On the one hand, the *cabinet system*, which originated in England, but also in Sweden, is based on the notion that the head of the government, the prime minister, has to operate in the context of a collegial system, in which a group of ministers participates in the decision-making process while also being individually in charge of the implementation of the decisions in a particular sector. Cabinet government extended gradually to western European countries, while in central and eastern Europe, the remnants of absolutism were gradually undermined, to the extent that the cabinet system seemed likely at one point to replace everywhere the old absolutist and authoritarian governmental structures (Verney, 1959: 17–97).

In contrast to the cabinet system, the *constitutional or 'limited' presidential system* was first established in the United States and then extended gradually to the whole of Latin America. In this model, the executive is hierarchical and not collective: ministers (often named secretaries in this case) are subordinates of the president and only responsible to him or her. Although this formula is closer to that of the monarchical government than to that of the cabinet system, it also means some demotion both for the head of state (who is elected for a period and often is not permitted to be re-elected at all, let alone be re-elected indefinitely) and for the ministers (since these typically have to be 'confirmed' by the legislature). The only country in which 'limited' presidential government has truly succeeded is the United States. The formula has been rather unsuccessful in Latin America, on the other hand, as many presidents have been uncomfortable with the restrictions to their powers and many coups have taken place, as a result of which authoritarian and even 'absolute' presidential governments have been installed. The difficulties which this system has encountered can be attributed partly to the rigidity with which it sharply distinguishes between legislature and executive (Blondel, 1980: 108–11; Linz, 1990: 51–69; Shugart and Carey, 1992: 36–43).

At least one of the two constitutional formulas was therefore already encountering difficulties before 1914. The problems multiplied after the First World War with the emergence, first, of the communist system in Russia, then, of authoritarian governments of the fascist variety in Italy and later throughout much of southern, central and eastern Europe, and finally, after the Second World War, of a large number of 'absolute' presidential systems, civilian and military, in many parts of the Third World. These developments were characterized by the emergence or re-emergence of the *role of the strong leader*, which constitutional systems had sought to diminish, and the consequential decline of the idea, fostered by cabinet government, of collective or at least collegial government. But the period was also characterized by the 'invention' of a new form of executive structure, which was marked by the intrusion of *parties* and, in authoritarian systems, usually of the *single party* in the core of the national executive.

## The role of parties in government

For the proponents of constitutional systems, whether of the cabinet or of the presidential type, the executive was regarded as the apex of the national decision-making process.

The question of sharing this position with any other body was not even conceived. With the emergence of parties, the recruitment of the governmental personnel and the determination of the broad lines of policy were gradually, but informally, influenced by these organizations. However, this development was not regarded as having profound consequences for the structure and decision-making powers of the government (Castles and Wildenmann, 1986).

## Single and dual governments

A new idea emerged with the arrival of the Communist Party to power in Russia after 1918. It was felt that it was the function of the dominant single party to ensure that the top organs of the state (that is to say, the government) were kept under control. From this view developed the concept of a *dual structure of party and state*, an idea which was partly followed in other authoritarian regimes between the two world wars: for instance, in Germany and Spain. In communist states the distinction was pushed to its limit, and the top party body, the Politburo, achieved a status equal or even superior to that of the government. Such a model was naturally extended from the Soviet Union to eastern European communist states after 1945. It was also adopted in some single-party states of the Third World, particularly in Africa – especially in those states which were of the 'progressive' variety. By a process of imitation, the formula was also used by some military rulers, who established military or revolutionary councils alongside the regular government. It has, of course, lost much of its popularity with the collapse of communism in eastern Europe, not just in those states which abandoned communism, but in the Third World as well.

The notion of a two-level or dual form of governmental structure was not merely the product of an ideology; it also corresponded closely to the functional division between 'conception' and 'implementation', which was outlined earlier. The increased complexity of governmental tasks (particularly in communist and other centralized states, but also in western systems) seemed to justify such an arrangement. Dualism was also affected, to an extent at least, by other developments. For example, the growth of the office of the President since the 1930s suggests a division of the United States government in practice into two layers (Blondel, 1982: 154–8). Moreover, the fact that western European cabinet systems experienced difficulties in maintaining the collegiality of the government is an indication of a degree of inability of executives to operate effectively if all functions are concentrated in the same hands (Smith, 1989: 217–22; Blondel and Muller-Rommel, 1988).

## Governmental structures in the contemporary world

While every state has a government, it is only in the third quarter of the twentieth century that *independent* governments have come to rule practically the whole of the planet. This means that the number of national executives has more than doubled since the 1940s. Meanwhile, as governments became more 'modern' by being increasingly concerned with a large variety of aspects of social and economic life, their size also increased substantially. While national executives had about a dozen ministers on average in 1950, they had on average about 18 posts in the 1980s. Globally, there were fewer than a thousand ministers simultaneously in office immediately after the Second World War; 30 years later there were over 2,500 (Blondel, 1982: 175–7).

However, the rate of increase in the size of governments has not been the same across the world. Atlantic, Latin American and Asian countries have had the smallest rate of increase, while Middle Eastern and African states as well as (to the extent that they remain in existence), communist states have experienced the largest increases. There are also substantial absolute variations. Communist governments have been large, even if one adopts a rather restrictive definition of governments. For example, the Soviet executive, which was the largest of all, had 75 members in the 1980s. Not surprisingly, perhaps, efforts were made in the late 1980s to reduce this number, but the prospects may not be good: the Chinese government increased in size again after having been substantially cut for a while in the 1970s.

The size of communist executives was in large part commanded by the concern of these systems to direct the economy in great detail, making it necessary to establish specialized ministries relating to various industries. The reduction in the number of ministries has thus been dependent on the ability (and desire) of communist governments to diminish their direct intervention in various sectors of the economy. Other governments have also increased in size, in response to various demands or desires for public intervention. For instance, developing countries, especially those of the 'progressive' variety have had rather large governments. Alongside the executives of countries whose population is very small indeed, such as Luxembourg and Iceland, only in those which have been regulated by legal or even constitutional rules has the number of ministries remained relatively small. This is why constitutional presidential executives – and, therefore, Latin American governments as well as the United States government – have relatively few members (12 to 15 as against 20 to 25 in many western European cabinets).

## Single-party governments and coalitions

An essential feature of modern government is constituted by political parties. These naturally play a key part in many, indeed most, executives of the contemporary world, but this role does vary. At one extreme are governments fully dominated by one party in single-party systems, the clearest example being that of communist systems. At the other extreme are the national executives in which parties play a small part, either because they are weak or because the government and its head have sufficient authority to keep parties at bay. This tends to be the case in constitutional monarchies, of which few have remained, and in many if not all presidential systems. In the United States, the president, being elected on his or her own programme and because of his or her own appeal, may be able to pay little attention to party views.

Cabinet systems have often been described as *party governments* because parties are central to these executives: they help to streamline the relationship between executive and parliament; they also help to organize the life of the cabinet. Yet there are also differences among cabinet systems in terms of the influence which parties have (Katz, 1986: 31–71).

One key distinction is that between *single-party governments* and *coalitions*. This distinction applies also to presidential systems, as several Latin American presidential executives have been based on coalitions, for some or even most of the time. This has been the case in Brazil, Chile, Bolivia, Ecuador, Bolivia and Venezuela. However, the distinction is perhaps even more important in cabinet systems because the government needs the support of a majority of parliament if it is to remain in office.

Continental European cabinet governments are nearly always coalition governments, although these coalitions can be small or large, and can include almost all the relevant parties. British and Commonwealth governments tend to be of the one-party variety, on the other hand, while Scandinavian governments oscillate between the two formulas, except in Finland, where coalitions are the rule.

There are also other differences among these governments, as they can be of a *majority* or of a *minority* character. In the latter case, the government depends on the continued support given to it by parties which have not joined the government. This arrangement may not seem viable, but it occurs relatively frequently, especially in Scandinavian countries such as Denmark, and occasionally elsewhere (Britain, France, Italy) (Strom, 1990: 1–22).

The characteristics of cabinet governments thus vary appreciably from being minority or majority single party to small or large coalitions. The reasons why these forms of government exist are also varied. There tends to be a single-party government (though this is not always the case) when one party alone has or is close to having a majority in parliament; there tend to be coalitions in other cases. The existence of small or large coalitions also results from many factors. Some coalitions are 'minimum sized', in that they include only the minimum number of parties required for the government to have a majority in parliament; others include parties which are ideologically close even if the majority is as a result more than minimum sized; yet others include all or nearly all the parties represented in parliament and are thus known as *grand coalitions* (Riker, 1962: 149–68; Lijphart, 1984a: 46–66; Luebbert, 1986: 67–89, 233–47).

## Collegial governments

Cabinet governments are in principle *collective and egalitarian*: decisions have to be taken by the whole cabinet. It is the parliamentary origin and basis of the cabinet which accounts for its collegial characteristics. Bagehot expressed this point in the nineteenth century by stating that the government is a 'board of control chosen by the legislature, out of persons whom it trusts and knows, to rule the nation' (Bagehot, 1963: 67). Neither the prime minister nor any group of ministers is formally entitled to involve the whole government. The counterpart of this provision is *collective responsibility*, which stipulates that all the ministers are bound by cabinet decisions; in its most extreme form, the rule suggests that ministers are also bound to speak in favour of all the decisions.

These principles are markedly eroded in practice in nearly all the countries which operate on the basis of cabinet government: that is to say, in western Europe (except Switzerland), many Commonwealth countries (Canada, Australia, New Zealand, India, Malaysia, Singapore and most ex-British Caribbean and Pacific islands), as well as Japan and Israel. Some ex-communist states, such as Hungary, Poland, the Czech Republic and Slovakia, have also adopted cabinet government.

The erosion of the collective principle is marked first by the fact that, in many of these countries, following British practice, the principle applies only to members of the cabinet *stricto sensu*: the government can be much larger and include substantial numbers of junior ministers. The practice of appointing junior ministers has extended throughout western Europe and indeed to cabinet governments outside western Europe, the British and Italian governments being among those which have appointed the largest number of holders of these positions. They are bound by the principle of collective responsibility, but do not share in the decision-making process.

Second, the number and complexity of decisions are such that the cabinet cannot, during what are normally short meetings of two to three hours a week (or at most twice a week) truly discuss all the issues which have to be decided on. As a result, while the cabinet ratifies formally all the decisions, the elaboration of these decisions is in reality delegated to individual ministers (if they come within the purview of their department), to groups of ministers sitting in committees (the number of these has markedly increased in many cabinet governments), or to the prime minister and some of the ministers (McKie and Hogwood, 1985). Cabinet government is at most collegial government and in some cases it is even hierarchical.

## Types of cabinet government

One can distinguish among three broad types of cabinet arrangement, although there is strictly a continuum between truly collective and egalitarian cabinets (of which there are very few) and hierarchical governments, sometimes labelled 'prime ministerial cabinets'.

The truly *collegial* cabinets are those in which, often because of the existence of a coalition, but also because of political traditions, the prime minister has to rely on a high degree of interchange with colleagues before decisions are taken. As a matter of fact, although (or perhaps because) Switzerland does not have cabinet government, but has ministers elected for a fixed duration on the basis of a permanent coalition of the major parties, its executive probably is the most equal in western Europe; yet, even there, full collective decision making does not occur. Scandinavian cabinets are more collegial than those of central and western Europe, even in cases of single-party governments, which, especially in Sweden, occur rather frequently.

---

## BOX 16.2
### How coalition governments tend to form

There are three main ways in which governments are constituted: (a) from the top, in one go; (b) by the replacement of individual ministers as they retire; or (c) by discussion, often protracted, among a number of partners.

By and large, the first method is used in the case of the governments of countries in which a leader imposes himself or herself, whether in an authoritarian or in a democratic manner. In Britain, for instance, the leader of the party which obtains the majority in parliament constitutes the government, typically a few days after the election.

The second method, that of the slow replacement of ministers, is in use in countries in which there is effectively no break between governments. The clearest examples have been the communist states. Similar developments occur in traditional regimes in which the monarch is the effective head of the government: ministers are appointed individually to replace those who retire.

In both cases the constitution or reconstitution of the government is rapid. The third method is characterized on the contrary, by a substantial period of discussion among the potential partners of the government. This typically occurs primarily in the context of parliamentary systems as well as of some presidential systems, when it is either necessary or useful to form a coalition among two or more parties.

The process normally begins after the election has taken place, although, in some cases, the idea of a future coalition may be discussed by parties which form an electoral alliance and declare that they will govern together if they win. When this does not occur (or when the alliance proves less tight than had been anticipated), the process of government formation begins. It has two stages.

During the first stage, the potential coalition partners have to be found, sometimes by means of what in the Netherlands and Belgium is called a *formateur*. Various permutations may be possible and the successful formula may be difficult to find.

Once the parties have agreed to form a coalition, the second stage opens, during which a detailed governmental programme is elaborated and ministers are chosen. A general outline of the programme may have been agreed to during the first phase, but it must go much further if future conflicts are to be avoided: specific tax increases or cuts in benefits, for instance, will be agreed to. In some countries, the Netherlands and Belgium in particular, the outcome of the discussions results in the drafting of a long document, of perhaps 70 or 80 pages; this document is sometimes referred to as the 'Bible', since it serves as a guide to governmental action and is invoked in case of conflict. Ministers are then selected, typically by each of the parties of the coalition. Thus, sometimes after months, the government is set up.

The second model is that of the *team*, which is more common in single-party governments, such as Commonwealth countries, including Britain. The ministers, who often worked together for a number of years in parliament, have broadly similar goals and even a common approach. Much is delegated to individual ministers, to committees or to the prime minister, but there is a spirit of understanding which results from the relatively long joint experience of government members. While the prime minister appoints and dismisses ministers, the pool from which these are drawn – mostly the parliamentary party – limits drastically the opportunities for selection. In coalition governments, on the other hand, the partners in the coalition have a large say in the appointment of individual office-holders.

There is a third model, sometimes described as *prime ministerial*, in which ministers are noticeably dependent on the head of the government – for instance, because he or she has considerable popularity. This arises from substantial and repeated election victories or from the fact that the head of the government has created the party, the regime or even the country. Such cases have been frequent in the cabinet governments of the Third World (in the Caribbean and India, for example); in western Europe, they have occurred occasionally in West Germany, France and even Britain. In the British case, it has been suggested, somewhat exaggeratedly, that this was what British cabinet government was becoming (Bagehot, 1963; 48–57). In this model, the relationship between ministers and prime minister is then hierarchical and resembles that which prevails in presidential and indeed in traditional monarchical systems (Blondel, 1982: 67–78).

## Hierarchical governments

The large majority of the other governmental arrangements are, formally at least, *hierarchical*, in that ministers – and any other members of the government – are wholly dependent on the head of the government and the head of state. They are appointed and dismissed at will; their decisions are taken by delegation from the head of the government; and they play no part legally in the elaboration of the policies which do not affect their department. These arrangements were traditionally those of monarchical systems, and the constitutional or 'limited' presidential system did not alter this model. The many authoritarian presidential systems which emerged in the Third World after 1945 adopted a similar formula: while perhaps about 50 governments are of the cabinet type, as many as double that number of countries – mainly in the Americas, Africa and the Middle East – have governments which are primarily hierarchical.

However, these presidential governments are not always hierarchical to the same extent. First, some are closer to cabinet systems in terms of their composition, as when the head of the government is not able to select or dismiss ministers at will, or may have to pay attention to their views. For instance, heads of governments may be constrained in their choice of ministers in traditional monarchical regimes, because members of some families are very influential, or in civilian or military presidential regimes, because some individuals may have helped the successful head of government to come to power. Indeed, the American president is freer in this respect than most other presidents, who are more closely dependent on party support to come to power. We noted earlier that some Latin American executives have more of a 'party government' structure than the American executive.

Second, in terms of decision-making processes, members of presidential executives may not be able to act independently. The complexity of issues, especially economic and social, obliges many heads of government to pay attention to the views of the members of their government to such an extent that the latter may exercise influence well beyond their department. Meanwhile, ministers are sometimes closely linked to the officials of the departments of which they are in charge. As a result they acquire some autonomous power and the head of government may have some difficulty in controlling them. Such national executives are more *atomized* than hierarchical.

### The American federal executive

This situation affects particularly the constitutional presidential executive which is the largest of all, that of the United States. The president may have much leeway in choosing members of the cabinet, but there is considerably less opportunity to control the members of the cabinet in their respective departments. Departments are vast and therefore naturally form self-contained empires. Moreover, any vertical relationships which might exist between departmental heads and president are undermined by the horizontal relationships existing between each department and Congress – especially the committees of Congress relevant to the departments, since these want to ensure that they obtain the appropriations which they feel they need and the laws which they promote. Finally, the links which develop between departments and their clientele (the various interest groups which gravitate around each department) tend to reduce further the strength of the hierarchical ties between departments and president (Heclo, 1977: 166–8).

Thus the American government tends naturally to be atomized. To remedy this defect, presidents since F.D. Roosevelt in the 1930s appointed increasingly large personal staffs, whose aim has been to supervise and co-ordinate the activities of the departments in order to ensure that presidential policies are carried out (Campbell, 1983: 19). This has meant, however, that it has become difficult to discover what constitutes the 'real' government of the United States. Beyond the formal hierarchical structure of president and secretaries, the government seems to have two levels: an 'upper level' formed by the White House Office, which has some degree of collegiality, and a 'lower level', which has little unity. By gradually becoming a government at two levels, the American government thus resembles in part the dual arrangements which have prevailed in other countries, particularly in communist states (Blondel, 1982: 80–4).

### Multilevel governments

For the historical reasons which were described earlier, the party structure and the state structure led to the emergence of divided governments, first, in the Soviet Union and then, after the Second World War, in other communist states. This division goes beyond duality: the *Politburos* of the communist parties have been helped by large secretariats, whose heads have constituted the personal staffs of the General or First Secretaries, the latter being generally regarded as the 'true' leaders of their countries. This was obviously the case with such leaders as Stalin, Tito and Mao. Meanwhile, the state 'half' of the governmental structure has tended to be divided into a *Presidium* and a *Council of Ministers* proper, the Presidium being composed of the most important ministers as well as of some representatives of geographical areas, at any rate in the Soviet Union. There could thus be a Politburo primarily in charge of policy elaboration, a Secretariat, a Presidium in charge of co-ordination, and a Council of Ministers dealing with implementation. The links between these bodies have tended to be achieved through some of the more important ministers and the prime minister (normally a different person from the First Secretary of the Party) belonging at the same time to the Politburo, the Presidium and, of course, the Council of Ministers (Holmes, 1986: 126–30, 156–8).

Comparable multilevel executives developed in some non-communist single-party systems and in a number of military regimes. *Supreme Military Councils* or *Committees of National Salvation* have thus been created to ensure that the regular government (often composed of civil servants) carried out the policies of the military rulers. This formula, which started in Burma in 1962, was adopted by many African states, such as Nigeria; it also existed for a period in Portugal after the end of the dictatorship in 1974. These arrangements have had a varying degree of longevity and of apparent success (Blondel, 1982: 78–93, 158–73).

## Members of governments

### Social and career background

During the decades which followed the Second World War, about 20,000 men and women have been members of national governments. These ministers have similar backgrounds to those of members of legislatures: they are mostly *male*, drawn from *middle-class groups*, and *middle-aged*. However, the number of women in government has been growing since the 1970s. In Scandinavia, women have come to be a substantial minority, and in the late 1980s they formed a majority in the Norwegian government. Manual workers, white-collar employees and farmers are also relatively rare in governments: the proportion of manual workers, once substantial in communist governments (about a third) declined markedly in the 1970s and 1980s. Ministers are mostly drawn from among lawyers, teachers, civil servants, managers and, in military regimes, military men, while business leaders are underrepresented, as they are in most parliaments. Public sector managers and civil servants have tended to be numerous not just in communist and Third World states, but in many western countries as well (Blondel, 1985: 29–54; Thiebault, 1991: 19–30).

## Routes to office

Ministers are rarely young and usually join the government in their late forties. *They come to office by one of three main routes*: politics, the civil service and the military. The *political route*, through parliament and a political party, is the most common, especially in western countries (though not in the United States, where the proportion of ministers coming directly from business is large). This route is naturally important in cabinet systems, where a formal link exists between government and legislature. In the Third World, the proportion of politicians among ministers varies appreciably: it is substantial in south-east Asia, where there are a number of cabinet systems, and in Latin American civilian governments. In some Middle Eastern and Black African countries, it is sometimes difficult to distinguish the political from the administrative routes to office, as ministers often have a party background while being also civil servants; the same has tended to occur in the communist states. Lawyers usually come to office through the political route.

Alongside and sometimes combined with the political route, the *civil service route* provides a way of reaching the government for a substantial minority of ministers. This is pre-eminently the traditional route, monarchs having typically chosen from among administrators because they had expert knowledge and because they could be relied upon. Not surprisingly, therefore, the traditional monarchies which remain in existence appoint many civil servants to the government; so do other non-party systems (primarily led by the military) and even some single-party systems. In communist countries, particularly in China and, in the past, the Soviet Union and (though less so) in eastern Europe, a ministerial position has tended to be the apex of a long career in a ministerial department. The civil service route even plays a substantial part in some western European cabinet governments, notably in France, where civil servants (and managers of public enterprises) started to be appointed to the government with the advent of the Fifth Republic in 1958, as well as in Austria, the Netherlands, Finland and Norway.

The third main route to ministerial office is *the military*, although it has declined in importance since the mid-1980s. A military career has led to ministerial office in many parts of the Third World, especially in Central and South America (though not in the Caribbean), in Black Africa (particularly in northern and western Africa) and in the Middle East. However, the extent to which military men come to office varies appreciably among military regimes. Meanwhile, even in civilian governments, ministers in defence departments are still often members of the military, as they were in western Europe in the nineteenth century.

## The ministerial career proper

Although some come to office suddenly – for instance, after a military coup or other brusque change of regime – a long period of waiting has usually to elapse before one becomes a minister; yet one cannot normally expect to remain in office for more than a few years and, in many cases, for more than a year or two. Admittedly, a position in the *cabinet* often follows a post of junior member of the government, which may have been held for four or five years. Even if one adds up all these positions, however, the average duration is low: to the four or five years as junior ministers can be added perhaps three or four years in the cabinet proper (Blondel, 1985: 10ff.; Bakema, 1991: 70–98).

There are appreciable variations around this average. Some are ministers for a decade or more, though usually not in the same post, and often not continuously, while a substantial proportion, indeed almost a third, are in the cabinet for only one year. There are also variations from country to country: the ministerial career has traditionally been longest in communist states (six years on average), especially in the Soviet Union; it is shortest in Latin America and in the Middle East (two years or less); ministerial duration is relatively long in Atlantic countries (about four years), in Black Africa, and in south and south-east Asia (Blondel, 1985: 90–8).

### Institutional and cultural factors

A number of factors are at the origin of these variations in ministerial duration. *Regime instability* in the Third World and, in liberal systems, the *alternation of parties* in power are important contributory elements. Conversely, ministers have tended to stay in office longer in communist states because these characteristics, traditionally at least, did not obtain. These countries had, in a sense, kept the same 'government' in power for decades, and the near-static position of the governmental personnel may have contributed to the collapse of the regimes. Meanwhile, communist states in which there had been instability, such as Poland, had a shorter average ministerial duration. Because there has not been alternation of parties in government in traditional monarchies either, ministerial duration has tended to be relatively long in these states (for instance, in the Arabian peninsula) and in some Black African states in which a 'charismatic' ruler has been in power for long periods (as in the Côte d'Ivoire). For the same reason, ministerial duration is longer in those western countries where the alternation of parties in power has been relatively infrequent (Canada, Sweden) or where at least one of the parties has been in office for many years, if not permanently, in a coalition context (Germany or Austria, for instance). An indirect effect of these factors can be found in the fact that, by and large, ministerial duration is shorter in constitutional or 'limited' presidential systems than in cabinet systems. In the former, newly appointed presidents tend to select new ministers, while in the more collegial cabinets of parliamentary systems, the departure of the prime minister often does not entail that of the ministers.

Variations in ministerial longevity are also due to *cultural factors*. In particular, there appear to be different traditions with respect to the extent to which cabinets are periodically *reshuffled*. The contrast between Sweden and Japan is particularly sharp in this context, since in these two countries the same party was in power for decades and yet differences in average duration are considerable. Swedish ministers of social democratic governments have been in office for over eight years on average, while in Japan, the average duration has been little over a year – many ministers, and almost the entire cabinet, are replaced every year. Cultural characteristics also account in part for variations between Austria and Germany (where reshuffles are rare), on the one hand, and Britain and France (where reshuffles are more frequent), on the other. They also account for variations among other systems, in particular among presidential systems. In Chile, for instance, both during the period of constitutional rule up to 1973 and during the period of military rule of the 1970s and 1980s, the average duration of ministers in office was also scarcely over one year; in Mexico, on the other hand, reshuffles are rare and ministers remain in office on average for about four years (Blondel, 1985: 110–36, 142–8, 156–9).

### One-post ministers and ministers who move from post to post

The averages discussed so far relate to the total longevity of ministers in office, not to their duration in individual posts. For the majority, the figure is the same, since most government ministers only ever have one post; but a substantial minority hold two or more posts in succession. This sometimes occurs after an interruption, although such interruptions have been rare in presidential systems, in military governments and in communist regimes. They tend primarily to occur in cabinet systems, in part as a result of the alternation of parties in government, and in part also because these ministers can be regarded as 'amateurs' and are selected to governmental posts not because of their specialist ability, but because of their political skills. Reshuffles leading to ministers moving from one position to another in succession are also more frequent in cabinet systems.

### Generalists and specialists

The fact that many ministers move from one post to another is sometimes linked to political considerations, since the prime minister may feel that someone who changes positions is less likely to be a danger; it also relates to different conceptions of the role of ministers. Where the emphasis is on implementation, there will be a tendency to appoint *specialists* to head ministerial departments, and consequently to move these ministers to other posts rather less. This practice has been commonly followed in communist states; it has also tended to prevail in many Third World regimes, in many presidential systems, and even in some cabinet systems, especially in central Europe. Where, on the contrary, the emphasis is on office-holders being concerned with policy elaboration and co-ordination in a collegial manner, ministers are regarded as having primarily a political role: they are often described as being 'amateurs' or *generalists* rather than specialists, because they are selected for their political skills. This view is widely held in those cabinet systems which came directly out of the British tradition. The proportion of ministers having held more than one post in succession is naturally largest in this group of countries (Blondel, 1985: 189–212).

The career of ministers is short; it is almost an accident for most ministers – indeed, it is truly an accident for a substantial number of them. It is perhaps surprising that such a career should be sought after, as it seems to be, even in countries where the duration prospects are very low. Admittedly, the rewards are substantial while in office, and there may also be rewards after leaving office (in business and public enterprises, or in international positions), but there are also dangers, including physical dangers, particularly in the Third World (Blondel and Thiebault, 1991: 153–73). In many cases, an attempt is made to marry political skills and administrative skills, but the duration is so short for most and the preparation so limited that the question does arise as to whether governments can truly have a profound impact on the countries which they rule.

## The impact of governments

It is difficult to measure the realizations of governments or even to have a satisfactory impression of their extent. The contrast is sharp between the sweeping comments often made about the potential achievements of executives and the slow progress of systematic analyses designed to determine what governments can and do realize. This is because there are major problems at several levels in assessing what governments achieve.

A distinction has indeed to be drawn between developments which would have occurred 'naturally' as a result of social and economic change and developments which can be said to have occurred because the government decided them. Comparative analysis can help in this respect, since it is possible to discover whether different policies have a different impact. Thus, while unemployment began to be widespread across most of western Europe in the 1980s, it remained low in some countries, such as Sweden, Austria and Switzerland. Yet these national comparisons do not always provide an answer to the question of whether a particular effect should be attributed exclusively or even primarily to governmental action.

### Attributing impact to a particular government

It is often not possible precisely to relate particular outcomes to particular governments. The duration of governments may be too short for valid conclusions to be drawn: little can normally be said about the impact of governments which last a year or less. Yet we noted that many ministers did remain in office for one year or less. Moreover, governments often 'slide' into one another, so to speak, as a result of reshuffles: the British conservative governments of the 1980s were almost entirely reconstructed, although the same leader remained in office; on the other hand, Italian prime ministers have tended to change frequently, but ministers have tended to stay in or return to office after a few years. What constitutes one government in such cases becomes a debatable point: if one takes a narrow definition and considers that a government has to remain truly identical to be genuinely *one*, then almost no national executive remains in office for more than a year or two; if one relaxes the condition and decides, for instance, to discard partial reshuffles, the problem arises as to which cutting point to adopt. One may suggest that a government is the same if it has the same prime minister or president, is composed of the same party or parties, and corresponds to the same parliament. Such a definition may be valid for some purposes (and for countries in which elections matter); but it is clearly a compromise definition, since such a 'government' will have been modified in composition, perhaps markedly, during the period (Lijphart, 1984a: 80–1; 1984b: 265–79; Blondel, 1985; Bakema, 1991: 77–9).

## The duration of coalitions and single-party governments

It is because of these numerous reshuffles as well as because the problem is almost exclusively confined to western Europe that the question of the relative duration of single-party and coalition governments, though technically very interesting, probably does not deserve the prominence which it was once given. As was pointed out in Chapter 11, it has been suggested that proportional representation has the effect of leading to executive instability because it results in greater party fractionalization in parliament. Yet minority governments and coalitions, which are indeed numerous in continental Europe, are not all weak and unstable; the difference in duration between single-party and coalition governments is substantial only if one does not take into account the incidence of reshuffles in single-party governments. Moreover, as we noted earlier, there are many types of coalition: they can be small or 'grand', 'minimum sized' or 'oversized'. Conclusions about the longevity of these different types are not identical. It is at any rate wrong to claim that coalitions (and even minority governments) are necessarily or even generally weak and ineffective, as German, Austrian and Dutch examples indicate, especially when reshuffles need to be taken into account. British ministers last in office less than West German ministers, for instance; Japanese ministers are reshuffled almost every year. It is in any case difficult to use 'governments' or 'cabinets' as a basis for the calculation of duration: the longevity of ministers is a much better indicator (Lijphart, 1984a: 78–84; Blondel, 1985: 129–34).

## The lag between conception and impact

There is a further difficulty, which is particularly serious because governments normally last for short periods: it takes time for governments to elaborate policies and perhaps even more time for these policies to be implemented. There is therefore necessarily a lag between the moment an executive comes to office and the moment policies have an impact. This point is true even if, as is sometimes claimed, new governments and new leaders may benefit from a *state of grace* (Bunce, 1981). Since there is such a lag, and it varies from policy to policy, results should often be attributed to preceding executives rather than to current ones. Moreover, since governments normally have little room for manoeuvre because the large majority of expenditure (90 per cent or more) relates to matters which cannot be altered (salaries, maintenance of existing activities, etc.), the determination of the real impact of a given government is often speculative and is likely to be highly controversial.

## The likely impact of governments

Conclusions have therefore remained rather vague: they concern certain broad characteristics of whole classes of national executives rather than individual cabinets. It has been possible to establish that social democratic governments do have, at least in many respects, an impact on social and economic life, despite the view which is sometimes expressed that no difference could any longer be detected among governmental parties (Castles, 1982; Rose, 1984). It also seems established that, contrary to what some had claimed, Third World military governments do not perform better economically than civilian governments (McKinlay and Cohan, 1975: 1–30). However, other generalizations often made about governments have not so far been confirmed In particular, it is not established that the instability of the ministerial personnel has the negative consequences for social and economic development that it is often said to have (though it may have a negative impact on the regime's legitimacy) (Kellner and Crowther-Hunt, 1980: 211–12).

The conclusions which can be firmly drawn on the impact of governments on economic and social life are therefore limited. However, to consider only this impact is to conceive the role of national executives too narrowly. The broader cultural and ideological values which governments foster may modify the general climate within which political, social and economic life develops, although such an effect is, of course, even more difficult to assess. The nature and extent of a 'change of political climate' cannot usually be measured adequately, let alone be closely related to the activities of a particular government. But such a difficulty does not constitute a ground for excluding any impact, or even less for deciding not to consider impact at all. Only with patient efforts and on the basis of the general hypothesis that governments do matter somewhat, although probably less than is readily assumed (especially by those who wish to criticize particular cabinets), will the assessment of the role of national executives gradually improve.

## Overview

National executives are at the centre of political life as they 'convert' suggestions and proposals into policies. They have to fulfil three functions, those of *policy elaboration*, *co-ordination* and *implementation*.

To fulfil these tasks, executives have taken different forms. They differ essentially in two ways: they can be *hierarchical or collegial*; they can be *single or divided*.

*Presidential systems* tend ɒ be hierarchical, while *cabinet systems* tend to be more collegial. Presidential systems such as the American system may also be relatively divided; communist governments and many Third World governments have often had a *dual structure*.

Members of governments are generally *male*, drawn from the *middle-class*, and *middle-aged*; they come to office after a purely political career (in parliament, for instance), in the civil service or in the military.

Members of governments stay in office on average *only a few years* (three or four) and many (about a third) stay in office one year only.

Members of governments tend to be *generalists* in cabinet systems, although less so than in the past; they tend more often to be *specialists* in other types of government.

The precise impact of governments is difficult to measure, largely because of the short duration of ministers in office. This may seem paradoxical when so much emphasis is placed on national executives by the media, the organized groups and large sections of the public. Yet this paradox is only one of the many contradictory sentiments which governments create. Governments both attract and repel because they are powerful, at least ostensibly, and because they give to those who belong to them an aura of power, of *auctoritas*, which fascinates, tantalizes, but also worries and, in the worst cases, frightens those who are the subjects and the spectators of political life.

## Further reading

Although the literature on national executives is very large, it tends to be essentially on a country basis. Indeed, there is a high concentration of works on the American government, on the British cabinet and on a number of European governments as well as on what was the Soviet Union. Works on other countries exist, but they are more sparse. On the structure of governments themselves, see J. Blondel, *The Organisation of Governments* (1982), J. Blondel and F. Muller-Rommel, eds., *Cabinets in Western Europe* (1988) and *Governing Together* (1993).

Among the texts giving an impression of the nature of government in the USA, one could cite T.E. Cronin, *The State of the Presidency* (1975), H. Heclo, *A Government of Strangers* (1977), A. King, ed., *Both Ends of the Avenue* (1983) and R. Neustadt, *Presidential Power* (1960). Among the numerous studies of the British cabinet, that of J. Mackintosh, *The British Cabinet* (1962) remains most valuable because of the historical account which it gives. On the part played by committees in the cabinets of a number of western countries, see T.T. McKie and B.W. Hogwood, eds., *Unlocking the Cabinet* (1985). On what were the characteristics of communist executives, see L. Holmes, *Politics in the Communist World* (1986). For a view of the nature of governmental rule in Black Africa, see R.H. Jackson and C.G. Rosberg, *Personal Rule in Black Africa* (1982).

On the recruitment and career, as well as the role, of ministers, see J. Blondel, *Government Ministers in the Contemporary World* (1985) and J. Blondel and J.L. Thiebault, *The Profession of Cabinet Minister in Western Europe* (1991) as well as B. Headey, *British Cabinet Ministers* (1974).

On the characteristics of coalitions and on the problems they pose, there is now a considerable literature. The pioneering study is that of W. Riker, *The Theory of Political Coalitions* (1962); see also G.M. Luebbert, Comparative Democracy (1986) and, for a summary, A. Lijphart, *Democracies* (1984: 46–66). See also V. Bogdanor, ed., *Coalition Government in Western Europe* (1983).

On the question of the problems facing contemporary executives, see C. Campbell, *Governments under Stress* (1983) and R. Rose, *Understanding Big Government* (1984). A rather old but interesting comparison of the role of government in America and the Soviet Union, is given in Z. Brzezinski and S.P. Huntington, *Political Power USA/USSR* (1963).

# 17

# Political leadership

## Introduction

Political leadership is highly visible, much talked about, and complex to assess. The visibility of leadership has been markedly enhanced by the mass media, and in particular by television, but it always was large. Great leaders of the Antiquity, of the Renaissance and of the modern period were all well known to their contemporaries, despite the fact that they could only be seen and heard by relatively small numbers. Their qualities and defects were probably the object of many conversations; scholarly work was at any rate devoted to them. Indeed, studies of historians were primarily concerned with the description of their actions, while the concept of leadership began to be analyzed.

Yet the literature on leadership has scarcely led to the development of what might be regarded as an established theory on the subject. It is vast, whether in the form of biographies or autobiographies; and so is the psychological literature on middle-level leaders and on managers. But the comparative literature on political leadership remains limited, although there has been a remarkable increase in interest in the field, especially lin the United States, since the mid-1970s.

Uncertainties litter the academic field as a result. To begin with, there have always been controversies about how to assess leaders from a normative standpoint: qualities and defects coexist to such an extent that little guidance can be provided. There are heroes and there are villains; but many, perhaps most, leaders are both heroes and villains, and their performance can be judged only in a sharply contrasted manner. Except for some mythical rulers, such as Cincinnatus, who returned to live an entirely ordinary life after having shaped Roman society, few are the leaders who have not made citizens suffer and die as well as prosper and live harmoniously. Leadership seems double-edged: on this ground alone, it is difficult to pass straightforward judgements.

The number of villains has been such that many efforts have been made to reduce the powers of leaders. Constitutional developments since the eighteenth century were the clearest manifestation of this trend, although attempts were made earlier, in Greece and in Rome, in Italian cities and in medieval England, to ensure that rulers became unable to abuse their powers and become tyrants. These moves had only limited success, as did many constitutional endeavours of the twentieth century, a period during which emerged some of the most ruthless rulers whom the world had ever known. Thus leadership often had a bad name and analyses have consequently been devoted more often to finding means of reducing the power of leaders than to discovering ways of fostering their positive role.

Meanwhile, it proved difficult to determine the relative role of leaders and of the environment in which they emerged. We encountered similar difficulties with respect to governments and to parties. Do their achievements depend primarily on the efforts of those who run them, or on the environmental conditions in which they develop? Leaders seem ostensibly powerful, but their emergence, their subsequent actions, even their opportunity to remain in power are markedly affected by the context in which they operate. This question led to inconclusive controversies between those who believed in the primacy of social and economic forces, and those who believed in the influence of individuals (Hook, 1955). One part of this paradox is that those regimes which believed most in socioeconomic forces being the engine of history, the communist Marxist regimes, have also been those in which individual leaders have played the most obvious part. It suffices to think of Lenin or Mao and of Stalin or Castro, to mention only the best known among the communist rulers.

As a result of these conceptual and empirical difficulties, the study of leadership remains relatively underdeveloped. There is still no generally agreed framework on the basis of which leaders can be classified and assessed. Despite the obvious importance of the topic, much of what can be said about it has therefore to remain somewhat tentative.

- To undertake this analysis, we shall first examine *ways of classifying types of leadership*.
- Second, we shall consider the *institutional framework* within which constitutions have attempted to 'domesticate' leaders.
- Third, we shall investigate the *personal qualities* which appear to play a part in the development of leadership.
- Finally, we shall look at the conditions which are likely to *maximize the impact of leaders*.

## What is political leadership?

### Definition

Leaders seem to be good or bad, heroes or villains; but leaders seem also to be more or less successful, more or less effective. The distinction has been made, in this respect, between *leaders*, in the strong sense of the word, and mere *power-holders*, or, perhaps more accurately, *office-holders* (Burns, 1978: 5). It seems intuitively correct to claim that many rulers – probably the large majority – are not very influential, as they appear to do little to modify the course of events, while some are great 'stars' who at least ostensibly affect profoundly the destiny of mankind. A distinction has therefore seemingly to be made between those who are leaders and those who are not: this means that, to begin with, a definition of leadership has to be given.

To say that leaders have to be distinguished from office-holders means that leadership does not automatically follow from the holding of certain positions. Leadership may be helped by the holding of positions, such as those of prime minister or president; indeed, efforts made to 'domesticate' leadership have concentrated on attempts to regulate the powers connected with these positions. But leadership operates on a different plane: it relates to the ability to make others do what they presumably would not have done otherwise. It is a form of *power* – a special form of power, admittedly, since it is exercised by one individual over a large group and, in the case of the national political leadership, over a very large group. Leadership is therefore an intrinsically highly inegalitarian relationship. This relationship may be accepted for a number of reasons, ranging from 'natural' recognition by, to pressure and even compulsion on, those who are led. They are thus induced to act in the direction which the leader suggests. One can therefore define national political leadership as *the power exercised by an individual* (or, in some cases, two or a few individuals acting jointly) *to push members of the polity towards action in a particular direction* (Janda, 1972: 45–64; Blondel, 1980: 11–15).

## The scope of leadership

It is thus possible, at any rate theoretically, to distinguish leaders from non-leaders: those position-holders who do not succeed in making others act in the direction which they choose are not leaders. One needs to go further, however, and differentiate among various *categories of leaders*. To do so, specific criteria have to be discovered of which two are particularly important.

One consists in distinguishing among leaders on the basis of their *goals*, as Burns does: on the basis of the type of 'project' which they have in mind. There are 'great' leaders, who shape their society entirely, who *transform* its character; there are other leaders who are primarily concerned with the functioning of the society and who make compromises and *transactions*, while accepting the framework within which economic, social and political life takes place (Burns, 1978: 19–20).

Such a distinction should not be viewed as a dichotomy, but as the two poles of a continuous dimension dealing with the 'extent of change' which leaders wish to bring about, this change being orientated either towards 'progress' or towards a return to the past. One should go further, however, as there are in reality two dimensions. Leaders do not merely exercise their power by attempting to bring about more or less change; they also exercise their power by attempting to achieve more or less change over a *broader* or *narrower* area. One can be a revolutionary in the full sense of the word – Lenin and Mao wished to transform their society completely, for instance. But one can be a revolutionary over a limited area as well, since one may wish to transform the educational system, or the system of central–local relationships, or the system of

| | | DIMENSION I | | |
|---|---|---|---|---|
| | | Maintenance | Moderate change | Large change |
| DIMENSION II | Wide scope | SAVIOURS<br><br>Moses<br>Churchill<br>De Gaulle | PATERNALISTS/<br>POPULISTS<br>Bismarck<br>Stalin<br>Shah of Iran<br>Many Third World leaders | IDEOLOGUES<br><br>Mao<br>Lenin<br>Hitler |
| | Moderate scope (aspect of a system) | COMFORTERS<br>Eisenhower | 'REDEFINERS'<br>Kennedy<br>Reagan<br>Thatcher | REFORMISTS<br>F.D. Roosevelt |
| | Specialized scope (policy area) | MANAGERS<br><br>Administering day-to-day problems | ADJUSTERS/<br>TINKERERS<br>Modifying an aspect of policy | INNOVATORS<br><br>New policy, e.g. land reform |

*Source*: Based on J. Blondel, *Political Leadership* (1987) London and Los Angeles: Sage, p. 97.

▶ **Figure 17.1**  A two-dimensional typology of potential leadership impact

labour relations. The scope of leadership should therefore take into account both the extent to which leaders wish to transform or change the existing system (a change which can be either 'progressive' or 'regressive') and the breadth of the governmental area over which this desire for change is manifested (Blondel, 1987: 87–97).

## The bond between leaders and society

One criterion of classification is thus the scope of leadership. Another criterion is the nature of the bond between leaders and society. This type of classification was primarily explored by Max Weber, who identified three 'ideal-types' of such relationships, based on *tradition*, a *bureaucratic-legalistic ethos* and *charisma*. The idea of charismatic leadership subsequently became widely used, while in his original presentation, Weber had construed it rather narrowly around a religious connotation. As a result, instead of being 'a certain quality of an individual personality . . . endowed with supernatural, superhuman, or exceptional forces or qualities', charisma came to be reduced to an idea of 'personalization' of power (Weber, 1968: I, 214).

It is perhaps not accidental that the notion of charisma should have been 'devalued' in this manner, for like the scope of leadership, the bond between leaders and led should be viewed as based on dimensions, rather than on a number of mutually exclusive, well-defined types. Indeed, Weber's ideal-types can be turned into dimensions. The distinction between traditional and bureaucratic-legalistic leadership can be regarded as identifying two opposite poles of one dimension, ranging from a communal society, in which relationships are based on long-standing loyalties, to an associational society in which relationships are based on contracts. Real-world leaders can be expected to be located in many cases somewhere between these two extreme positions.

Ostensibly at least, charismatic leadership is less susceptible to give rise to a dimension if it is considered in its pure religious form – a form which, in Weber's view, tends to emerge when there is a total breakdown of the social and political institutions. But Weber himself envisaged situations which could give rise to charismatic leadership where there was not such a total breakdown (Blondel, 1987: 54–7). More realistically, there are undoubtedly cases when a degree of personalization of leadership occurs, as a result of which the led associate directly with the leader, even when the society is not breaking down, or indeed even when the system functions regularly. Such a bond may exist at whatever point the leader is located on the dimension of traditionalism versus bureaucratic legalism. Thus leaders should be classified with respect to two dimensions in terms of the bond which links them to the population.

Overall, as we have just seen, there are two main ways in which leaders can be categorized, in both cases on the basis of two dimensions: they can be categorized according to their goals and achievements; and they can be categorized according to the nature of the bond which ties them to the population (Blondel, 1987: 51–7).

## The institutional bases of leadership

While positions do not make leadership, they foster its development by giving those who hold them opportunities to exercise power. This is why those who have wished to restrain leadership have attempted to reduce the opportunities open to position-holders by limiting their ability to use power. These efforts have only been relatively successful. In this respect, as with legislatures and with national executives, constitutions have been often bypassed or set aside; they have sometimes not achieved their desired effect at all. Although there are very few formally wholly unrestrained leaders in the contemporary world, there are many rulers who can act in practice in the way they wish.

### Limitations on rulers' powers

The rulers who are effectively constrained to operate under legal limitations are of two main kinds only: they are the prime ministers of cabinet systems and the constitutional or 'limited' presidents. A third category, the constitutional monarchs, now usually have a purely symbolic role.

## Symbolic monarchs and presidents

The position of prime minister is, ostensibly at least, less prestigious than that of president, since it exists normally in conjunction with that of a *symbolic monarch* (as in Britain, most Scandinavian countries and the Low Countries) or of a *symbolic president* (as in West Germany, Italy and India). Although these heads of state have few real powers, they exercise ceremonial functions which contribute to giving them some authority. The fact that the head of state is purely ceremonial (or mostly ceremonial) in cabinet systems does not mean that he or she plays absolutely no political part. In the British case, for instance, the role of the monarch as head of the Commonwealth is significant. On the other hand, in Sweden, since the 1975 Constitution came into force, the role of the monarch is extremely limited. In some countries (Belgium, the Netherlands), monarchs play some part in the process of selection of the prime minister. The fact that prime ministers have a less prestigious position than presidents explains why a number of Third World prime ministers, in particular in Black Africa, brought about constitutional changes a few years after independence in order to become presidents (for instance, in Kenya, Zambia and the Côte d'Ivoire).

## Prime ministers in cabinet systems

The power of prime ministers in cabinet systems is ostensibly limited because it is exercised in the context of a cabinet which must concur in the decisions. Indeed, prime ministers were traditionally regarded as being only *first among equals*; the role of the leader was 'domesticated' because of the collective character of the policy-making process. However, in the contemporary world, there are considerable variations in this prespect.

In some cases, prime ministers are truly strong leaders, especially in two-party systems, such as Britain and many Commonwealth countries, let alone in single-party systems or near-single-party systems, such as Singapore. These prime ministers control their party and the parliamentary majority, and if electoral support is maintained (or unnecessary, as in single-party systems) they exercise control for long periods. In Canada, Australia, Austria, Sweden and India, some prime ministers have dominated their country's politics for a decade or more, although Mrs Thatcher is the only British prime minister in the twentieth century to have enjoyed a similar record. The same has occurred in coalitions in which one party tends to dominate, as in Germany. In other cases – for instance, where there are coalitions with no dominant party – prime ministers are not markedly superior to their cabinet colleagues. They do not have enough political power or enough longevity in office to dominate the scene; and they are frequently chosen because they are good compromisers and not because they are, in the conventional sense of the word, 'leaders'. Developments in the 1980s in the Netherlands and Belgium, however, suggest that there may be some change in this respect. Finally, there are cases when prime ministers are mere office-holders (as were most of the French before 1958).

In some countries, such as Belgium, Austria and even Britain, there have been alternately 'strong' and 'weak' prime ministers. Thus the model is inherently flexible:

the general political conditions, the specific situation and the qualities of the office-holders are the factors which appear to account, more than the institution itself, for the extent to which prime ministers play a limited part or, on the contrary, are truly great leaders.

### Constitutional presidents and monarchs

Efforts at 'domesticating' leadership are more systematic in those systems in which the constitution strictly limits the powers of the monarch or president. *Constitutional monarchs* rarely still exercise effective functions, since in the large majority of cases these have been transferred to prime ministers. Morocco and Jordan are among the few examples of countries in which the monarch really shares power with the prime minister. *Constitutional presidencies*, on the other hand, are relatively numerous. They tend to be located in the Americas, with Latin American countries having broadly modelled their structure on that of the United States. The powers of such presidents are restricted by the constitution, both because the legislature has an independent base, since it cannot be dissolved, and because the president is elected for a limited period only and may not be re-elected immediately, or, at most, as in the United States, may be re-elected only once. Thus American or constitutional Latin American presidents cannot achieve the longevity achieved by a Swedish or even British prime minister. The duration of the term of constitutional presidents is made rigid in order to ensure that the president does not become too powerful. This has led to difficulties, since in practice it may not always be politically satisfactory for the term to be predetermined in this way.

### Problems posed by constitutional or limited presidential systems

The strength of constitutional limitations on presidential rule have led to many problems. They are successful only in part. The truly successful case has been that of the United States; no other limited presidential system has lasted uninterrupted since the Second World War. Conflicts have arisen between president and congress, and these cannot be solved by forced presidential resignation or by appeal to the people, as in a cabinet system, since the congress cannot dismiss the president or the president dissolve the congress.

Moreover, the fact that the president cannot be re-elected more than once, and often not at all, results in extra-constitutional attempts to remain in power. The scenario which occurred in France in the early 1850s, when the elected president, who was the nephew of Napoleon, maintained himself in office by a coup (and subsequently became the Emperor Napoleon III) was to be repeated in many Latin American countries. On the other hand, since the 1950s, presidential succession has been regular in Costa Rica, Colombia and Venezuela; the 'domestication' of leadership may thus become gradually accepted in the region. In Mexico, a regular handover of power has also taken place for many decades, but because of the near-single-party system in that country, the president has traditionally been subjected to few limitations, and in particular has not been markedly restricted by Congress, which is continuously dominated by the same party.

## Authoritarian presidents and monarchs

In large parts of the Third World, leaders are little constrained, or even not constrained at all, by constitutional rules designed to 'domesticate' their power. This is, of course, the case in absolute monarchies, but as we have seen, these have become rare and their numbers are shrinking. It is also the case in military regimes, but these have diminished in number as well, and they tend to be of short duration only, as we shall see in Chapter 19. In order to prolong their tenure, military rulers often introduce some form of civilian structure of an authoritarian character: such presidents are subjected to few formal or even informal constraints.

Authoritarian presidents often devise constitutions designed to suit their ambitions. They are thus allowed to be re-elected indefinitely (and have even sometimes been appointed for life, as was the case in Malawi and Tunisia). They are also allowed to dissolve the legislature, so the government depends entirely on them. The spread of these *absolute presidencies* has coincided with the achievement in many countries of independence, especially in Africa, while in south-east Asia, on the contrary, leaders have often remained constrained, to an extent at least, by the limitations imposed on prime ministers in cabinet systems. As we saw in Chapter 10, a liberal democratic form of government has been maintained in many Commonwealth countries and in particular in south-east Asia, including India, Malaysia and Sri Lanka.

Many authoritarian presidents of the Third World were the first leaders of their country. They were able to build political institutions and to shape these in the way they wished. Some were close to being 'charismatic' in the full sense of Weber's term. They relied on strong popular support, in the main, as well as on authoritarian practices; they were the 'fathers' of their countries. They often remained in office for two decades or more, thereby forming a disproportionately large number of those leaders who were in power for a very long time in the 1960s and 1970s (Blondel, 1980: 217–18). The successors of these first leaders generally found it more difficult to rule in such a 'paternal' and absolute manner: in many cases (in Tunisia and Senegal, for instance) the result has been a more 'domesticated' presidency, albeit still rather authoritarian.

## Dual leadership

Political leadership is usually regarded as being naturally exercised by one person only: the image is that of the pyramid, with a single leader at the apex. A large majority of states are indeed ruled by a single leader, especially if one does not take into account the symbolic heads of state of cabinet systems who were examined earlier. Yet there are also many cases where single-leader rule does not obtain. There are examples of *government by council*, of which the cabinet system is only a partial example because of the role of the prime minister, but which exists also in a 'purer' form in Switzerland, with the Chairman of the Federal Council rotating every year. This form of government also existed for a long period in the former Yugoslavia and in Uruguay. There are *juntas*, in particular among 'provisional' Latin American governments, in which a small number of military officers (often drawn from the three branches of the services) rule the country for a period. There are, above all, a substantial number of cases of *dual leadership*.

Dual leadership has existed at various moments in history: republican Rome was ruled primarily by two consuls, for example. Its modern development resulted in the first instance from the desire (or need) of kings to shelve a part of their burden on to a 'first' or prime minister. This was not only due to popular pressure, as tended to occur in western Europe in the nineteenth century, following the British example; it also took place in highly authoritarian states, from early seventeenth-century France when Richelieu was prime minister to nineteenth-century Austria with Metternich, and Germany with Bismarck. Thus dual leadership is a widespread phenomenon; it does not occur merely in the context of a transition from 'monarchical' to 'popular' rule. It emerges as a result of legitimacy difficulties, as when the king needs to associate a 'commoner' to his power. It is also the consequence of administrative necessities or of the need to combine national legitimacy, which the head of state embodies, with a more specialized administrative or technocratic legitimacy, which the head of the government represents (Blondel, 1980: 63–73).

The existence of a variety of grounds for dual leadership accounts for its spread in the contemporary world in countries as diverse as France and Finland on the one hand, and communist states on the other; in the relatively conservative kingdoms of Morocco and Jordan at one extreme, and the 'progressive' states of Tanzania, Algeria and Libya at the other. There are both liberal and authoritarian dual leadership systems (though liberal dual leadership systems are rarer), both conservative and 'progressive' dual leadership systems, and both communist and non-communist dual leadership systems.

In communist states, the distinction between party secretary and prime minister has traditionally corresponded to the division between party and state which was analyzed in Chapter 16. Many communist party secretaries were also appointed presidents (sometimes only after a period had elapsed). This made their position identical to that of the presidents or monarchs of other dual systems.

Dual systems are sometimes regarded as temporary arrangements, as if it were more 'natural' for leadership to be held only by one person. There are enough cases of dual leadership having lasted for many decades to raise doubts about such a 'natural' character of single leadership. Dual leadership has existed in communist states, in the many authoritarian African presidencies in which there is a prime minister, in the few monarchies in which the monarch shares with a prime minister the running of the affairs of the state, as well as in a scattering of liberal semi-presidential countries, such as France, Finland and Sri Lanka. This last country introduced a strong presidency system in the 1970s, following the French example of 1958. Only in Latin America has the arrangement been rare, except in the context of military juntas, since Peru is the only country of the area where there is a prime minister alongside the president. Overall, between a quarter and a third of the nations of the world have been ruled by a system of dual leadership, and in most of these the system has operated in a stable manner.

A dual system does not entail that the two leaders be equal; indeed, quite the contrary, as is suggested by the distinction between a leader embodying the national legitimacy (the president or monarch) and a leader embodying the administrative legitimacy (the prime minister). The complexity of the modern state is such that it is far from surprising that leadership should often have to be shared in order to be effective.

# The personal qualities of leaders

The role of the environment in helping or limiting leaders is more than just apparent: it is there for all to see. The role of personal characteristics also appears intuitively to be large; yet it also seems to elude precise measurement and even broader assessment.

## Personality and personality traits

There are, first, difficulties stemming from the relatively underdeveloped character of *studies of personality* in general, and of the personality of leaders in particular. Indeed, there are still many controversies around the concept of personality itself, since personality refers to what is permanent, and yet slowly changing, in the characteristics of an individual (Greenstein, 1969: 1–30). Moreover, there is still no generally accepted list of attributes constituting that personality, let alone any weighting of the way in which each of these attributes 'should' be mixed in order to produce a 'well-balanced' or 'forceful' leader. One can suggest a number of elements which seem important, such as energy, courage or intelligence, but one can scarcely go beyond an enumeration of this kind.

Psychologists and social psychologists have attempted to determine a number of *traits*, but the many studies which have been conducted in a large number of organizations have resulted in widely differing conclusions. As many as 40 elements have been found by scholars to be relevant to leadership, including physical appearance (such as age, but also energy), social background, intelligence, 'personality' in the narrow sense (adaptability, enthusiasm, resourcefulness, self-confidence), task-related characteristics and social characteristics (administrative ability, popularity and tact). While these elements were not found to play the same part everywhere, intelligence, dominance, self-confidence, achievement, drive, sociability and energy have appeared to be positively correlated with leadership in a substantial number of studies undertaken by experimental psychologists (Bass, 1981: 43–96). Overall, therefore, leadership seems associated with many, if not all, the aspects of human personality.

## The role of the social context

The second problem posed by the determination of the personal qualities of leaders stems from the fact that these qualities need to be related to the situation with which the leader is confronted. Psychologists have shown that different types of leadership are appropriate to different situations (Fiedler, 1967). A 'task-oriented' leader will be more efficient where problems are relatively simple, a leader concerned to establish a rapport with the led will be more appropriate where the questions to be solved are complex.

Such a conclusion seems to apply to national political leaders, although the size of the problems which these leaders face is such that it may not be valid to extrapolate from observations relating to leaders supervising small groups engaged in rather simple operations. Some national office-holders seem exaggeratedly concerned with the details of the work: former President Carter of the United States, for instance, was successful as Governor of Georgia, but less effective in the broader context of Washington, largely because of his interest in detail (Fink, 1980). Such leaders appear less effective than those who have a wider vision, and who are concerned with the impact of their actions on both their immediate subordinates and the nation at large (former President Reagan of the United States, for instance).

## The pathology of leadership and of revolutionary leadership

Because of these difficulties, studies of the personal qualities required of national political leaders tend to focus on some types of ruler and on some types of situation. Many earlier analyses concentrated on the *pathology* of leadership, as a result of the extreme worry felt in the 1930s and 1940s at the emergence of leaders whose psychological balance seemed to be in doubt. It is difficult to develop a general model on this basis, however, although it has been claimed by one author that the number of severely mentally disturbed leaders has been extremely large across the centuries (Noland, 1966: 232–3).

Special attention has been paid more recently to another group of leaders, the *revolutionary leaders*, in order to assess whether these can be regarded as forming a class from the point of view of their personal characteristics. The studies of Rejai and Phillips have gone furthest in this direction by examining the personal and situational conditions under which these leaders emerged, although, as there is no control group of non-revolutionary leaders, it is difficult to know how far the characteristics found of the revolutionaries apply exclusively to them. They have been shown to have a number of traits in common, such as vanity, egotism and narcissism, as well as nationalism, a sense of justice and a sense of mission; they are also characterized by relative deprivation and status inconsistency (Rejai with Phillips, 1983: 17). These leaders also had marked verbal and organizational skills. Admittedly, it is also pointed out that 'no single motivation or dynamic is sufficient to explain the formation of all revolutionary personalities' (Rejai with Phillips, 1983: 30). However, the analysis does present a picture of a class of leaders, and identifies elements which are of significance among members of that class.

## Early socialization and its role

Political scientists have also attempted to assess the role of early socialization. If it could be proved that this plays a major part in decisions subsequently taken by leaders, it would appear to follow that *personal elements* are highly significant. Too few studies of this type have been conducted for a general panorama to emerge, but the classic study of President Wilson of the United States did at least provide a clear example of the role of early socialization in explaining subsequent decision-making trends (George and George, 1956).

## Towards a more general categorization

A general model of the characteristics and role of personality will probably need to be simpler, however, if fairly robust conclusions are to be drawn. A step in the direction of simplicity has been provided by Barber, whose analysis of the personal characteristics of American presidents is based on two factors only: *drive or energy* (labelled 'activity' or 'passivity'), and *satisfaction with the job* (a 'positive' or a 'negative' approach) (Barber, 1977: 11–14). 'Active-positives' enjoy what they do, and do it with considerable gusto: F.D. Roosevelt, Truman and Kennedy are classified in this manner. At the opposite extreme, those who are 'passive-negative', such as Eisenhower, 'are in politics because they think they ought to be' (Barber, 1977: 13). There are difficulties with such an approach, since it is not stated why these characteristics, rather than others, are particularly instrumental in helping to describe given leaders. There should also be rankings among leaders within each category: not all the 'active-positives', for instance, are likely to be equally strong or equally successful. However, this categorization has the merit of helping to discover some broad personality types, and of relating these types to the way in which leaders take decisions (Blondel, 1987: 16–18).

## Institutions and structures which strengthen leadership

It is still not possible to state with assurance that leaders behave in the way they do because of their personality; it is even less possible to determine the aspects of personality which are most critical. Meanwhile, leaders can be seemingly helped or hindered by the existence of structures such as groups, parties, legislatures, the government itself and the bureaucracy. These enable leaders, to a varying degree, to elaborate and apply the policies which they favour, and to mobilize the population in support of these policies.

These institutions are not givens, however: leaders can play a part in creating or altering them. For instance, at least in new countries or in those which have been in turmoil, leaders have set up parties and groups, as we saw in Chapter 10. Most leaders are able to appoint to the government men and women of their choice, at least within a certain range. Many leaders can also play some part in shaping or remoulding the bureaucracy. The question is therefore how far leaders can and do set up and modify these structures. The part which they play in this respect is often overshadowed by the durable and even ostensibly permanent character of such bodies. This is one further reason why it is difficult to determine precisely the role of personal factors in the development of leadership (Blondel, 1987: 189–93).

## How much does leadership matter?

Related to the problem of the role of personal factors in leadership, but distinct from it, is the equally complex question of the impact of leaders on political life. Leaders clearly have *some* impact; a few leaders have a very large impact, whatever role the environment may have in accounting for their behaviour. The immense influence of some of these is manifest, whether it is Napoleon or Lenin, Bismarck or Churchill, to quote only from among the dead. It is up to those who deny this influence to sustain their claim (Hook, 1955).

The real difficulty is therefore not so much about the large part played by some leaders, but about the smaller impact of the great majority of leaders. It is also difficult to assess to what extent circumstances do help a number of rulers and frustrate the endeavours of others. 'Great' revolutionaries appear to achieve markedly more than leaders whose actions take place within the context of a political, social and economic system which existed when they came to power. But revolutionaries are also helped by the fact that demands for change in their society are large: they therefore have opportunities which are denied to those who rule a society whose members are satisfied with the status quo. Thus the efforts of Lenin and Mao were helped by the turmoil prevailing in Russia and China at the time. These leaders turned the situation to their benefit and developed policies which were truly their own and which the 'situation' in no sense demanded. They were able to start remoulding their society. Such opportunities are not available to leaders who emerge in countries where levels of discontent are low.

### Assessing personal impact and environmental influence

The impact of leaders must therefore be assessed not only by examining the policies elaborated and implemented by these leaders, but by relating these policies to the demands made by the population and in particular by its most vocal elements (Blondel, 1987: 97–107). Ideally, the impact of leaders should be measured by assessing the extent to which they are able to change the framework within which the population approaches public policy problems, as well as by the concrete reforms which they bring about. One must also take into account the two dimensions of extent of change and scope of change. As a result, one might conclude that some rulers who administer the system as it is, and do not aim at altering policies, are influential if they succeed in thwarting demands for substantial change existing in the polity. One might also conclude that rulers who introduce changes on a relatively narrow front do not necessarily have less impact than those who embark on policies designed to alter their society fundamentally.

---

**BOX 17.1**
**The fear of leadership**

One reason why political leadership has not been systematically analyzed is the *fear* which it has provoked among generations of liberal thinkers.

Alongside a few 'good' leaders, so many have been ruthless in controlling their subjects and in acquiring territories, usually by force, that enthusiasm for leadership has been limited, to say the least. Theorists began to hold the view that what was needed was to find mechanisms to limit leadership, which is what many constitutions were about. There was little interest in analyzing what leaders could be 'good at', except on the part of those, such as Machiavelli, who wanted to see a leader emerge to fulfil a particular task, in that case, to unite Italy. The deeds of many twentieth-century leaders, both before and after the Second World War, did not help to modify the pessimistic view.

Hence the widespread belief that leadership was essentially bad – a belief shared by many among the political élites of democratic countries, especially of those countries, on the Continent of Europe and in Latin America, where the population suffered particularly from the excesses of rulers. Thus it took a century and a hard and protracted colonial war in Algeria, as well as the 'civilized' leadership of De Gaulle, for the French to be able to 'exorcize' their fear of leadership and accept effective leaders. Hence, too, the apparent unwillingness of Italians to become reconciled with strong leadership.

For dispassionate studies to take place, what was therefore needed was a gradual move away from the fear of leadership. What had to be recognized was that leadership was a requirement for all societies, including democratic societies. Leaders could be either good or bad, indeed could range from being very good to being very bad, and most leaders were characterized by some combination of good and bad. The real point was not so much to limit leaders as to educate them to accept democratic values.

Some Third World leaders of the second half of the twentieth century were far from perfect; fortunately, others had remarkable qualities, Nehru of India being one example. In part as a result of these 'positive' rulers, the recognition of the importance and value of leadership is gradually taking place in the contemporary world.

---

The assessment of the impact of leaders thus depends on the extent to which the society is predisposed to undergo change. Such a predisposition often follows a period of great uncertainty and in particular a defeat in war. The new ruler can then point to the failures of the previous regime and proclaim that radically new policies need to be adopted. In such a situation, the collapse of the institutions and of the political system as a whole enables the new leader to emerge as the only fixed element to which the population can refer. Not surprisingly, such a leader is often 'charismatic' in the truly Weberian sense, and can make a major impact on the society.

The role of leadership must therefore be assessed by relating the rulers to the ruled, and the characteristics of personalities to the climate among the population. The role of 'obviously' great leaders is partly reduced as a result, while that of other, less dramatically prominent statesmen and women may appear more substantial. The impact of leaders must also be assessed over time. When examining national executives in Chapter 16, it was noted that there was an often substantial 'lag', between elaboration and implementation in national policy making: a similar lag exists with respect to the role of leaders.

The impact of leaders may never be fully determined, since it may be exercised on generations as yet not born. It can also fluctuate because what has been done by one leader can be undone by his or her successors. Mao's effect on China has thus been substantially modified, even overturned, by those who followed him. Thus the impact of the founder of the communist regime in the world's most populated country may not be as large in the 1990s as it was in the 1970s.

## The need for a ranking of leaders

There is still no means of ranking the impact of various leaders. What is probable is that this impact is larger than is often recognized in the case of many rulers; it is perhaps smaller than is often claimed with respect to the best-known leaders. The difficulty of the measurement is no justification for the extreme view that leaders do not matter, or that they can, on the contrary, achieve what they wish. What needs to be better assessed are the personal qualities which are essential for leadership: here lies the most important key to understanding the link between the rulers and the ruled.

## Overview

Leadership has often been regarded with suspicion; it has also been highly praised. Judgements are typically *extreme* and tend to be based on *dichotomies*.

A much more precise analysis is required, which is in the process of taking place and which will help to characterize better both the *scope of leadership* and the *bond between leaders and led*, including the *charismatic* bond where it exists.

Constitutions tend to limit the powers of leaders, often with little success. *Prime ministers in cabinet systems* and *presidents in limited presidential systems* are those whose powers are typically limited in the contemporary world. *Authoritarian presidents* tend to have broad, indeed sometimes full powers.

The role of leaders depends considerably on *personal qualities*, and in particular on energy. There is still no precise determination of what are the psychological characteristics most required for effective leadership.

The *impact* of leaders also needs better assessment. While great leaders clearly have a major influence, this has to be balanced with the part played by the environmental context. Revolutionary leaders thus emerge only where there is already a large amount of discontent in a polity.

Views about leadership have been very ambiguous. In the past leaders have been regarded, often justifiably, with considerable suspicion. Attitudes have changed somewhat since the Second World War, as a result of a better recognition of the positive (indeed probably unique) part which leaders can play, especially at the time of the birth of nations. Yet leadership is not important only in the context of new nations, or in the context of older nations when these are in turmoil. It plays a part in every situation, even though this part is less obvious by being less dramatic. Thus the problem is not only to contrast a few charismatic leaders with a mass of grey and indistinct office-holders, but to see under what conditions these office-holders can truly become leaders.

## Further reading

The literature on individual leaders is vast, whether in the form of biographies or autobiographies; so is the psychological literature on middle-level leaders and on managers. The comparative literature on political leadership remains limited, however, although there has been a remarkable increase in interest in the field, especially in the United States, since the mid-1970s. Among the most general books are those of S. Hook, *The Hero in History* (1955), G.D. Paige, *Political Leadership* (1972), J.McG. Burns, *Leadership* (1978), J. Blondel, *World Leaders* (1980) and *Political Leadership* (1987), R.C. Tucker, *Politics as Leadership* (1981) and B. Kellerman, ed., *Leadership* (1984).

On the personal qualities required of leaders as well as on the role of the environment, see J.D. Barber, *The Presidential Character* (1977), B.M. Bass, *Stogdill's Handbook on Leadership* (1981), F.E. Fiedler, *A Theory of Leadership Effectiveness* (1967), A.L. George and J.L. George, *Woodrow Wilson and Colonel House: A Personality Study* (1956), F.I. Greenstein, *Personality and Politics* (1969) M. Rejai with K. Phillips, *Leaders of Revolution* (1979) and *World Revolutionary Leaders* (1983). The part played by 'new leaders' and the possible role of the 'state of grace' is analyzed by V. Bunce in *Do New Leaders Make a Difference?* (1981).

On charismatic leadership, apart from the works of M. Weber, *Economy and Society* (1968 edn, Vol. 1), see A. Wildavsky, *The Nursing Father* (1984) and A.R. Willner, *The Spellbinders* (1984).

**Part V**

# Implementation and control

# 18

# Bureaucracies

## Introduction

Legislatures and executives elaborate policies, often under the guidance of parties and the influence of groups. Yet policies are only words and expectations as long as they are not implemented. Legislatures and even executives alone cannot be involved in detailed implementation, particularly day-to-day implementation. This is, in principle at least, the task of the public services and primarily of the civilian bureaucracy.

This is also a task fulfilled in part by two other types of public service, the military and the judiciary. The military are involved because they may have to back up the civilian executive in cases of emergency, or may influence it and even replace it if they feel that it is imperative. The judiciary are involved because they, as the civilian administrators, have to adjudicate on cases and thus have a share of the implementation process. We shall focus on the military and the judiciary in the coming two chapters; in this chapter we shall concentrate on the civilian bureaucracy.

## Implementation of political decisions

In principle, in modern liberal democratic states, legislatures and governments deal with the *elaboration* of laws and other general rules, while the public services are concerned with *implementation*. Indeed, since members of the government are deemed to be in charge of the fundamental decisions, the corollary is that only they are politically responsible, public servants being regarded as acting on their instructions. This view is held particularly strongly in cabinet systems; in presidential systems, such as the United States, there is more of an interpenetration because there are many appointments deemed to be political within the federal public administration. Meanwhile, the view that civil servants should be subordinated to politicians also prevails in many authoritarian states, especially in single-party systems.

## Decision making and management

Whether bureaucracies are or are not deemed to be concerned essentially with implementation, the situation is rather different in practice. First, the distinction between *rule making* and *rule implementation* is far from being clear-cut. This automatically renders less clear-cut the distinction between the role of politicians and that of civil servants. In part this is because a sharp separation does not always exist at the level of the personnel: the same people may fulfil both roles. National executives often include civil servants, as we saw in the previous chapters; and politicians can 'go down' more or less deeply into the hierarchy of ministerial departments, as we just noted for some presidential systems at least. In part, it is also because what constitutes implementation is often obscure, especially in the contemporary world, where bureaucracies are large and have become involved in a vast array of activities. The concept of implementation perhaps has a precise meaning when one is concerned with a set of rather simple rules which have to be enforced; it is less easy to circumscribe when rules are numerous and complex, indeed at times contradictory. To 'implement' therefore no longer means only to ensure that a particular rule is enforced; it means exercising choice and judgement, even discretion, among a number of different rules.

The difficulty is compounded, in the second place, by the fact that members of bureaucracies are not only involved in implementation, even viewed in the broadest possible manner. They also prepare decisions and give advice before these are taken. Politicians, as well as the public at large, have become increasingly aware of the fact that political, social and economic conditions have to be taken into account if laws and regulations are to be effective. This means that evidence has to be collected *before* documents are drafted. Public servants are those to whom one has to turn in order to obtain this evidence. In the process, those particularly at the highest echelons of the hierarchy are naturally closely involved in *decision making*; it becomes difficult to disentangle 'implementation' from 'rule making'.

Third, the wide involvement of the modern state in the life of each country has resulted in public servants also being concerned in a major way with the *management of large organizations*. Such an activity can only vaguely and formally be regarded as a form of implementation. What is at stake is to ensure that a public organization is run as efficiently as possible. This does not mean or does not only mean applying a number of rules; at most what are applied are very general principles, such as the idea of the 'public interest' – itself an elusive concept.

The rather independent action of public sector managers can be regarded as stemming indirectly from a tradition which anteceded liberal democracies. It is connected to the interventionist policies of continental monarchs of the seventeenth and eighteenth centuries, which culminated with enlightened despotism in the late eighteenth century. In this tradition, public servants are the *agents of the state* rather than of the government. They are expected to obey general principles of 'rationality' rather than the desires of politicians (Weber, 1968: 66–77). This view was partly superseded, at least in some countries, by the notion that public servants should be subordinated to democratically elected politicians; it was given a new lease of life in the second half of the twentieth century as governments became increasingly involved in the economic and social sphere.

## BOX 18.1
## Enlightened despotism and administrative behaviour

The development of bureaucracies in the course of the nineteenth and twentieth centuries has been based on a profound ambiguity – an ambiguity which can be related to and indeed stems from differing notions about the nature of government and about the state. Democratic government has tended to view administrators as implementors, perhaps as the best possible implementors, as they specialize in administration and can therefore be regarded as experts on the subject. This view, which has typically characterized Britain and many countries which have followed the British model, can be described as the *minimalist* conception of administration.

The other conception of the role of administrators is much more exalted. It implies that administrators run services for the good of the community and not merely implement the orders of ministers. Such a conception makes sense only if, in the first instance, the state is regarded as having services to run. The British conception of government was traditionally more limited; it was at most a law and order government. On the Continent of Europe, in seventeenth-century France to begin with and in most other countries later, the role of the government was appreciably larger. It was typically characterized by a formula which was to become most fashionable at the end of the eighteenth century, *enlightened despotism*.

There are many reasons why a more 'positive' conception of government should have prevailed on the Continent of Europe. In France, there was originally a desire to unify a nation which was diverse and physically very large. Subsequently, the idea that states should be involved in public works such as roads or land drainage was regarded as indicative of the 'care' which rulers had for their subjects. Despotism was 'enlightened'. The rulers could be said to have acted for the people, the people being regarded as unable to achieve 'progress' by their own devices.

The type of administrative structure and even of administrative philosophy which enlightened despotism fostered continued to play a significant part in the nineteenth century in many parts of Europe, and indeed outside Europe – in Latin America, for instance. The philosophy also made inroads in liberal states as these developed social welfare.

Enlightened despotism can thus be regarded, alongside the concept of the political responsibility of ministers, as one of the principles on which modern public bureaucracies are built, both in the West and in the Third World, with the difficulties which the coexistence of these two principles inevitably raise.

This *managerial conception* of public service activities has thus spread widely. It obviously prevailed in the industrial and commercial enterprises belonging to the public sector, which became numerous, even if their number has been reduced, in some cases drastically, as a result of the privatizations which occurred both in the West and in the Third World in the 1980s and 1990s. The managerial approach also plays a large part in the social services, such as education, health and housing, since these are large, at times huge undertakings. It has its role even in the more traditional aspects of governmental life, both because efficiency has become a key issue in all aspects of the public service, and because the large size of the government departments in many countries means that they have to be administered in a truly professional, i.e. 'managerial', manner.

## The influence of bureaucracies

Many civil servants are deeply involved in management; some play a part in giving 'advice' while bills and regulations are being drafted. Does this not mean that the principle of the subordination of public servants to politicians has in effect ceased to correspond to reality? Are 'bureaucrats' and 'technocrats' gradually replacing or have they even already replaced politicians, directly or indirectly? Can they, in a covert or even an overt manner, dictate decisions and as a result shape the general direction of political life, if only because the duration of ministers in office is typically so short? Rightly or wrongly, these questions have been raised: they therefore need to be examined (Strauss, 1961: 23–92; Riggs, 1963: 120–67; Crozier, 1964: ch. 9; Kellner and Crowther-Hunt, 1980: 203–83).

- In this chapter, we shall analyze first the problems which governments face in attempting to ensure that administrators *implement* their decisions.
- Second, we shall consider the extent to which managerial activities give administrators and technicians *special responsibilities* and even a degree of *independence*.
- Third, we shall turn to a general discussion of the *overall role of bureaucracies* and ask whether it is realistic to suggest that they are taking over the functions of rule making and installing an 'administrative' or 'technocratic' state.

## Governments and administrative 'obedience'

Public services have grown everywhere. They employ a substantial proportion of the workforce in every country, although it is difficult to evaluate their size precisely because the legal and effective status of public industrial and commercial undertakings varies markedly, because the same social institutions may be run by the central government in some countries and by regional or local authorities in others, and because these regional and local authorities may be part of the state public bureaucracy or fully decentralized and autonomous. However, it is safe to say that the services of the central government proper include perhaps 5 per cent of the employed population, while the public sector in the broad sense may employ a quarter or more, even in western countries. Consequently, even if one considers only the civil service strictly defined – namely, the set of bodies which are directly run by the central government – its size is such in most countries that it poses problems of organization and of control which are likely to affect the character of implementation, irrespective of any other activities in which public servants may be involved.

## The structure of the public services

### Personnel competence

Civil servants are likely to implement rules more efficiently if they are competent and well trained. These conditions will be met better where the bureaucracy is small than where it is large, since, when it expands, the state will have increasingly to recruit persons of lesser ability and whose training has been less extensive. Thus the level of competence of the public services will automatically decline with an increase in manpower requirements. In the short run, such a decline can be offset only if the state comes to employ some of the talent which might otherwise have gone into the private sector. But a move of this kind is not without negative effects, since the private sector, being staffed as a result with relatively less skilled employees, is likely to be less effective and indeed to implement less quickly and less well the decisions of the public bodies. In the long run, an improvement can occur, but only provided that education spreads and the competence of the candidates for the civil service increases as a result.

All countries face these difficulties, but those which attempt to expand the public sector rapidly as well as those in which the fund of competent personnel is limited are likely to be most affected. Many developing countries, especially in Africa, suffer from this problem, although, in relative terms, the bureaucracies of these nations are often smaller than those of developed states. Programmes of technical aid of various kinds, such as loans of personnel or training schemes, fill only part of the gap. Conversely, levels of implementation are likely to be higher in countries in which there is less interventionism on the part of the state.

Putting it differently, there are *diminishing returns*, in terms of implementation, as the size of the public sector is increased. No state can escape this general constraint, but those states in which educational levels are low are particularly exposed to the danger of overextending their administrative personnel, especially since, in the contemporary world, these countries have often wished to pursue populist policies which demand continuous pressure by the government if they are to be applied. In practice, these policies may not be implemented because the competent manpower is simply not large enough (La Palombara, 1963: 17–22).

### Size and implementation

Independently of the problem of competence, the extent of implementation of decisions taken at the top – that is to say, by politicians – is affected by the sheer size of the bureaucratic organization itself. Despite some benefits of scale (which tend to relate more to management than to implementation), the greater the distance between the top and the bottom of the pyramid, the greater the likelihood that the intentions of the rule-makers will be distorted. The efficiency of the bureaucratic machine can be improved in various ways, to be sure: modern techniques of organization make for better communication networks, for better relationships between 'staff' and 'line', and for a better span of control of each administrator. But some loss of efficiency will take place as the size of the bureaucratic pyramid increases.

Large organizations reach a point after which rates of implementation are likely to decline. Hence the general development of *delegation* practices, which suggest that a public authority (often local) does the work which another is legally asked to handle. A different arrangement consists in asking private firms to undertake the work under contract, a practice which has long existed in many western countries, although its value has been extolled more recently as a result of the desire to decrease the role of the state. Hence, too, the case for federalism and for other forms of decentralization which we discussed in Chapter 14.

As administrative organizations in developed polities are likely to be larger than in less developed polities, the advantage of developed societies in terms of competence and training of personnel is likely to be somewhat offset by the consequence of size. The measurement of both effects is difficult, however, in particular because processes of decentralization, through federalism or otherwise, have to be taken into account.

## Controlling the administration

### *Problems of control*

Naturally enough, the dangers resulting from poor implementation have been perceived from the early period of development of bureaucratic organizations. Various control mechanisms have therefore been devised. These are confronted with serious problems, however.

First, as control can be operated only through controlling agencies, these are affected by problems of *competence and size*, as are the controlled agencies. In particular, the larger the controlling agency, the less likely it is to exercise its control effectively. It follows that, where the agencies to be controlled are large, control is also likely to be less efficient.

Second, problems posed by the *distance between the controlling and the controlled agency* are serious, and indeed at the limit insoluble. It is not possible to maximize both tightness of control and a good knowledge of the operations of the agencies being controlled. Agents will exercise their controlling function well only if they are somewhat distant from the bodies which they have to control; but they will then not be truly familiar with what these bodies do. Thus, if controllers are to know well what implementing agencies do, they have to remain close to these bodies; but they are then unlikely to exercise their control effectively, since they are too close to the bodies which they control.

In concrete terms, controlling agents must both recognize the authority of their 'political masters' and have a real access to the activities of the implementing agencies. The controllers must not merely be taken round on special occasions; they must be able to discover the real motivations and the real behaviour of the controlled agents. Yet they will do so only if they are 'at one' with the controlled agents. The danger is that, then, they would probably have taken the same decisions. They will tend to punish only those who deviate from the prevailing norms: they are not likely to question the norms themselves. Consequently, if the political masters want to change the modes of behaviour of the public servants, they have to staff controlling bodies with persons who do not originally come from the bodies which are being controlled; but the members of such bodies will be less knowledgeable about what actually goes on. These 'outside' controllers may turn out not to be effective.

### Controlling agencies

Politicians have long been aware of these problems. They have reacted by introducing, sometimes in parallel, a panoply of types of control. There may thus be *inspectors recruited from within* the bodies to be controlled: this maximizes the knowledge of what goes on. There may be *controllers recruited from among politicians* who have no previous experience of the public service: this maximizes loyalty to the political masters. There may also be controllers drawn from different agencies from the ones which are to be controlled: it is presumably hoped to optimize, by using this intermediate formula, loyalty and knowledge of what goes on.

The specific choice of a given form of control, or at least the emphasis given to one or the other of these forms, depends on the extent to which the politicians *trust* the members of the public services to implement their decisions. The more they suspect the public servants not to be loyal, the more they will tend to rely on controllers drawn from outside. Not surprisingly, this view is particularly widespread in new countries, or in older countries after a revolution and even after a government comes to office with the aim of bringing about major policy changes. On the other hand, control will tend to be 'internal' where the political values are widely shared and policy changes are small or slow.

Politicians will often rely on the assumption that these controls will achieve the 'obedience' they need on the part of public servants. This is probably rather mistaken, for the effectiveness of control is not affected only by the characteristics of the controlling agencies and by the background of the controlling agents; it also depends significantly on the *authority of the rulers*. Leaders who impose outside controls may not gain much from such arrangements, unless they also have political authority. It is at this point that the question of the *administrative state* begins to arise, as we shall see later in this chapter.

### Control and political systems

Let us examine the types of controlling mechanism which are likely to be introduced in different political systems. In *developing countries*, the public services are likely to require a large proportion of the skilled personnel existing in the polity, especially

---

### BOX 18.2
### Ministerial cabinets

If ministers mistrust the civil servants who are under them, there seems to be no better solution than that of appointing a number of loyal men and women who will act as their eyes and ears and examine in particular whether their orders are diligently carried out. This is what, in theory, the *ministerial cabinets* which exist in a number of continental European countries are supposed to be doing. Indeed, that this mechanism is valuable seems to follow from the fact that the British civil service resisted (successfully) the introduction of similar arrangements: the claim was made that civil servants could undertake equally well the tasks required.

Ministerial cabinets exist in many countries. They are especially numerous in France, where they originated, in Belgium and in Spain; they have also become large at the Commission of the European Union. They are to ministers what the White House Office is to the President of the United States: they deal with any matter in which the minister is interested.

Defenders of the practice may concede that there has been some inflation in numbers and that the system fosters clientelism; but it is said that, as a result, ministers are more effective and departments better controlled from the top, the disadvantages being a small price to pay for the benefits obtained.

There are doubts, however, about the extent of these benefits. Whether ministers are more effective because of the existence of these cabinets is difficult to assess, but it does not seem that these bodies truly help ministers to exercise genuine control over the departments.

First, ministerial cabinets have increasingly come to be staffed with civil servants, largely because technically competent persons were needed to advise the ministers. These technicians may be the friends of the ministers: they are none the less civil servants. There is therefore little difference between this and the situation in Britain, except that the personal staff is much larger on the Continent.

Second, these cabinets are large because they cover the activities of other government departments, in principle to ensure that nothing is done which would prejudice the department concerned. In other words, ministerial cabinets tend to fight for their patch, rather than for the minister as such. It may be that the system helps to detect potential conflicts early on and solve difficulties before they become large; but some interdepartmental warfare is probably fostered in the process.

The case for ministerial cabinets is thus far from clear-cut.

---

where the government wishes to introduce new goals and new policies (La Palombara, 1963: 17–22). Levels of implementation may therefore be relatively low. A natural tendency is to introduce many controls.

Problems are likely to be less serious in *developed liberal democratic polities*, despite the relatively large size of the bureaucracy in these polities, but there will be differences among countries. Where governmental goals are traditionally accepted, as in Anglo-Saxon countries, problems of control are not regarded as being very serious, and internal controls may be deemed sufficient. Where the acceptance of democratic norms is more recent or less widespread, as in many continental European countries, control tends often to be undertaken both by internal bodies and by outsiders appointed by ministers among their 'loyal' friends. These form part of the *ministerial cabinets* – that is, the personal staff of ministers. Gradually, however, these outside controlling bodies have come also to include civil servants. Conversely, not all controls are internal in a country such as Britain: some intermediate forms of control, such as Treasury control, also play an important part. The combination of the fear of not being obeyed and the worry that there may be behind-the-scenes stonewalling thus leads to some reliance on controllers coming from outside the service which is being controlled.

## Special responsibilities and independence of administrators

Controls may or may not be effective in the context of what can be described as conventional implementation. They are clearly unsatisfactory where what is at stake is the pre-eminence of politicians over top civil servants in charge of giving 'advice', and over managers of enterprises and undertakings which are either formally or in practice autonomous. In such cases, one cannot just send inspectors; the government has to find other means to ensure that these top public servants and managers are at one with the aims of the political masters.

### The position of specialists

The development of administrative bodies in the twentieth century has given prominence once again to characteristics of *enlightened despotism* in state bureaucratic organizations. These characteristics had remained hidden under nineteenth-century concepts of implementation, but with state intervention becoming common, the involvement of officials went markedly beyond the idea of implementation. State intervention implies initiative; it also implies the possession of specialist skills, in engineering, economics, health and social welfare. This means that the training and career profiles of public servants have altered. Rule implementation in the narrow sense entailed placing great stress on a legal background; modern management implies giving prominence to *specialists* or *technicians*. A different 'breed' of public servants therefore tends to come to the top. These do wish to promote the interests of the state, but they do so in a different manner from lawyers or other 'generalists'. Specialists tend to concentrate their interest on the achievements of the *specific service* with which they are concerned, whether this is road building, the development of power stations, or the setting-up of a network of hospitals. Unlike generalists, they are not truly interested in the overall process of governmental life.

Technical services need not be run by specialists, admittedly, but they do need to have specialists close by, even if they are directed by generalists; otherwise, these services may be less efficient and specialists lower down the hierarchy are likely to feel frustrated. Indeed, even where generalists are 'on top' and specialists remain 'on tap', to use a distinction made in the context of the British civil service, the role of the generalists in decision making may be rather formal since, when technical decisions have to be taken, generalists will inevitably have to rely on their specialist 'advisers'. The latter may therefore be the real decision-makers.

There are still cross-national differences in this respect. In some cases, the state as such, in a somewhat impersonal manner, is regarded as having the function of ensuring the development of society. This has been the tradition of many countries of continental Europe, and of France in particular. Specialists tend then to be permanently in charge of services in the name of the state. In other polities, such as Britain and other English-speaking countries, the notion that public servants are concerned primarily with implementation remains vivid, and generalists play a greater part. They are deemed to be closer to the politicians than the specialists. These differences are not as large as they used to be, but they subsist to an extent. The fact that it is periodically suggested in Britain that the civil service should be less 'amateurish' and that little is done about it is a proof that such differences have remained (Kellner and Crowther-Hunt, 1980: 23–45; Drewry and Butcher, 1988: 46–8).

## Shared values

The problem of the control of top advisers, managers and specialists is of great importance for governments, given that these public servants prepare decisions or dominate the services they run and are, in effect, indispensable. Since ordinary forms of control are likely to be insufficient, what are needed are instruments by which or societal conditions in which the values of the ruling politicians become shared by public servants, whether generalists or specialists.

Where the system is liberal, the main underlying political values are based on the doctrine of *democratic accountability* and on the respect for established procedures. By and large, these values are indeed accepted by public servants in the older democracies, especially in English-speaking countries. In these polities, public servants tend to recognize that ministers, and not the experts, have the right to take the basic decisions, even if these experts often feel that many of the decisions are taken too slowly or are even plainly wrong. Thus the principle of *ministerial responsibility*, specifically of individual ministerial responsibility, which exists in particular in parliamentary and cabinet systems helps to reduce somewhat the underlying tendency of top advisers, managers and specialists to exercise power.

In other polities, on the other hand, the values of the ruling political system are often less widely shared. There are then serious problems either because these politicians want to do too little in the direction of development and public servants are frustrated, or, on the contrary, because politicians want to do too much too quickly and public servants are unwilling or even unable to follow. This has been the situation in many Third World countries. In such cases, politicians have often used the tool of the *party* to try and inculcate their values, especially in cases in which they have suspected that public servants were dragging their feet. This practice was particularly developed in communist states, clearly with some success; most, if not nearly all other single-party states have been markedly less successful in achieving these aims through the party.

As a matter of fact, even in the West, an underlying climate of suspicion between politicians and public servants does exist. The sharing of values would therefore probably not be sufficient to ensure that relationships remained satisfactory were it not for the fact that managers and in particular specialists often belong to different organizations, a situation which occurs less frequently in the Third World because these polities are often very centralized. Thus the existence of a private and a public sector, the division of that public sector into nationalized corporations and administrative agencies, and the autonomy of regional and local administrative agencies alongside central agencies are all arrangements which tend to reduce the pressure of managers and specialists on the politicians (La Palombara, 1963: 22–30).

However, two other characteristics tend to have the opposite consequences. First, specialists may acquire a *common outlook* and a sense of solidarity by being trained in prestigious technical schools. These helped development in continental Europe, and especially in France, in the nineteenth century; but they also fostered the influence of specialists. It is significant that the first theories of social and political 'engineering' were developed by men who taught or had been otherwise associated with some of these *grandes écoles* and in particular with the Ecole Polytechnique. Where such schools do not exist, on the contrary, there is less solidarity among managers and specialists. In Britain, the fact that the training of specialists takes place in universities rather than in specialized schools, and the tendency, which universities foster, to create social links cutting across professional disciplines have contributed to a reduction in the status and power of specialists.

Second, specialists are also brought together as a result of the spread and increased role of *professional associations*. These may not foster an *esprit de corps* to the same extent as technical schools, but they unite those who belong to the same profession by enabling them to know each other, and by providing platforms on which common problems are discussed. Common goals and common codes of conduct are defined as a result. Specialists who work in diverse and perhaps competing institutions are thus induced to overcome their divisions and to press for similar policies.

The characteristics of the society in general and of the political institutions can reduce somewhat any desire which top advisers, managers or specialists may have to challenge overtly the political decision-makers; even covert intervention may take place less frequently. Yet there are ostensibly well-known examples of countries in which public servants and notably specialists seem to enjoy great influence. In France, before the Fifth Republic was set up in 1958, this influence was very large, in part because public servants seemed to constitute a pole of stability in a situation in which governmental turnover was high. With the advent of the Fifth Republic, this influence became in a sense recognized formally as public servants were given a share of governmental posts.

France has therefore often been regarded as perhaps the prototype of an *administrative or a technocratic state*, although this description seems to be used less often since alternation in government occurred in the 1980s with the Socialist Party coming to power. Whether the labelling of the French political system in this way is correct or not, a general question arises, and it may arise perhaps rather more in the context of the Third World than in the case of the West: are there nations in which public servants in general and specialists in particular can be said to be fully in control (Marceau, 1980: 48–78)?

## The administrative or technocratic state: myth or reality?

To an extent, all modern polities are administrative states, since many important decisions are in the hands of public servants. To an extent, too, these administrative states are also *technocratic states*, although the distinction needs to be made, since an administrative state would be one where generalists are in control, while a technocratic state would be one where specialists are the key decision-makers. Yet both types can be analysed jointly, since many at least of the conditions leading to either situation are similar, and many of the difficulties which they face are identical.

In both cases, governments have to accept that their decisions are only in part implemented. Furthermore, specialists also have some scope to develop their own ideas of excellence in the context of the industrial and commercial undertakings which they manage. However, an administrative state does more than give generalists and specialists the opportunity to share power: it is a polity in which a very large percentage of decision making is in the hands of the public servants, and in which the authority of these public servants is openly recognized over wide areas of policy. At the limit, such an authority might well extend to all governmental decisions.

### Conditions for the development of an administrative or technocratic state

For the public servants of a country not to be merely influential but to be fully in control, a number of rather special and indeed stringent conditions need to be met:

- The legitimacy of the politicians must be low. This may be because politicians have lost their authority as a result of 'accidental' circumstances (war, defeat or a natural calamity); or because conflicts among leaders or parties are so severe that politicians are unable to take decisions. In the late 1940s and in the 1950s, the Fourth Republic of France was 'accepted', but was unable to generate leaders with genuine authority; it was therefore open to forms of bureaucratic rule.
- The technical and administrative groups in the public service must be large enough to constitute a pole of attraction for citizens. A country which develops slowly and where the number of specialists also increases slowly will not be open to administrative rule.

■ There must be similarity, if not identity, between the ideology of the specialists and the prevailing ideology in the country. This ideology must be one of 'progress' or 'development'. Such an accord will exist only if some progress or development has already taken place in the country and the population recognizes the benefits which development has brought about. This means in practice that the previous political leaders have already pushed successfully for development.

Public servants and specialists will therefore only be in a position to exercise substantial influence if the authority of the politicians, once large, has come to decrease, or if, as was suggested earlier, dissension occurs among leaders within the general framework of a recognized authority (Riggs, 1963).

Specialists are therefore unlikely to take power by themselves at early stages of development of societies; indeed, at that point, they (particularly the indigenous specialists) are probably not numerous enough. In reality, the level of penetration of the public services in these societies is likely to be low. Admittedly, because of the lack of technical skills in new countries, international technical assistance programmes and the governments of developing countries appoint, usually on a temporary basis, public servants from developed nations. But these cannot exercise the same amount of pressure on the political leaders of the states in which they work temporarily as specialists would do in their own country. Countries at early stages of development are therefore unlikely to be able to fall under full administrative or technocratic rule.

## The basic instability of an administrative or technocratic state

Even if public servants, and specialists in particular, were to be in control in a country, this state of affairs would not last long. First, conflicts among the specialists would soon loom large. As we noted, specialists have specific interests: they are concerned primarily with the development of the service in which they work. A political system in which specialists were 'on top' would thus be a 'confederacy' of corps, each of which would want to increase its share of public funds. It is not clear who would have the authority to arbitrate between demands. Problems of *co-ordination* and especially of *resource allocation* would be so severe that the regime would soon collapse.

Second, as co-ordination and resource allocation can ultimately be achieved only by non-specialists, an administrative state might appear more viable than a full technocratic state; but such an administrative state would also suffer from major handicaps. If the ideology is one of 'progress' and 'development', generalists are not as well placed as specialists to satisfy demands. Criticisms can be levelled at administrators in terms of excessive bureaucratic rule, exaggerated caution and lack of drive. Moreover, as sectional demands are likely to be large, the generalists would need to have considerable political authority to be able to cope successfully with these demands. They would need to rely on the support of the population, and such support is unlikely to be forthcoming.

Thus an administrative state is unlikely to be stable if there are many specialists and if the goals of development and progress are prominent. One situation remains, however:

namely, that of a 'pure' administrative state, in which specialists would play relatively little part and where the generalists would be in control. This situation corresponds to the case of a traditional and closed polity. Public servants might indeed rule in such cases: Ancient China approximated such a model; so probably did the systems of the Incas and of the Roman Empire in the second and third centuries AD. As no nation can any longer remain truly closed, this type of political system has become extremely unlikely, to say the least, in the contemporary world.

## The modified administrative or technocratic state

More likely to be found are intermediate situations resulting from a combination of administrative or technocratic rule, on the one hand, and of other forms of authority, on the other. If an administrative or technocratic state is one in which rule making is in the hands of generalists and/or specialists and is recognized to be in their hands, a *modified* or mixed administrative or technocratic state can be defined as one in which *part and only part* of rule making is in the hands of the generalists and/or specialists, and only *some* recognition exists of the authority of the public servants.

The conditions leading to the emergence of a modified administrative or technocratic state are the same as those which would have to obtain for the 'pure' version of such a polity to emerge:

- An ideology of progress must be widespread for technocrats to have some authority among the population.
- Other patterns of political authority need not have completely ceased to exist, but merely have sufficiently diminished for an accommodation to take place between the holders of the formal legitimacy (the politicians) and the technocrats or administrators.

The latter may well occur at early stages of development of societies; it may also occur under military rule, as we shall see in Chapter 19. A similar situation may even be found in more developed societies, if politicians have some (but only some) authority, and if divisions among them are such that they find it difficult to exercise power in a stable or durable manner, as in France before 1958. Such cases are none the less exceptional.

Meanwhile a modified form of administrative or technocratic rule is more likely to occur in a different manner: namely, when the political leaders themselves decide to share power with the civil servants. Some rulers may be uninterested in the details of social and economic development, and may be concerned only with results, while they prefer to devote their activity to other fields, such as foreign affairs. They might then in effect delegate decision making in the economic and social fields to specialists in whom they have confidence.

'Charismatic' leaders have often taken such a stand in the contemporary world, both in developed and developing polities. In postwar western Europe, De Gaulle was the ruler who came closest to this model, although other leaders also left considerable scope for specialists to take initiatives. Such an arrangement is more likely to be stable than that in which a leader does not choose, but is forced to ally himself with the specialists. This is often the case in military regimes, whose rulers sometimes inherit a difficult economic situation combined with strong pressure for development. In the long run, however, all types of modified administrative rule encounter difficulties, either because the leader who made the arrangement is replaced by another, less well disposed towards civil servants, or because specialists do not achieve the kind of economic development which they had hoped to achieve.

## Overview

In most polities, in particular in liberal democratic states, but also in authoritarian single-party systems, public servants are expected to implement the decisions of the politicians. In practice, however, the distinction between *rule making* and *rule implementation* is rather unclear: public servants do not, in fact, merely implement.

Public servants often *prepare decisions* and *advise politicians*. They are also involved in the *management of services*, industrial, social or administrative.

Public service organizations are vast. To exercise effective control over them is difficult. *Internal controls* are often ineffective: controllers may not know those who are controlled well enough; alternatively they may know them too much to be able or willing to impose sanctions on them.

The most effective way in which a better rapport between politicians and public servants can be achieved is by inducing members of the public services to *share the values* of the political leaders.

The role of public servants in general and of specialists in particular is so important that the danger of a complete takeover in the form of an *administrative or technocratic state* has sometimes been raised. This is unlikely to occur, since public servants typically lack the legitimacy to act on their own. More likely to occur is a *mixed* administrative or technocratic state, in which politicians rely on public servants while giving them some of their authority.

Although bureaucracies thus raise problems in almost all types of political system, this tension is probably inevitable, as it stems from the coming together of two distinct groups of people, the politicians and the specialists. What must therefore be done is to find an optimum level of mutual acceptance and understanding. Otherwise all polities, developed or developing, might suffer losses which might reduce appreciably the strides which they make to achieve greater socioeconomic development and greater political participation.

## Further reading

The notion that public administrators are involved in much more than implementation is now well recognized in the literature. See, for instance, P. Self, *Administrative Theory and Politics*

(1977), E.N. Suleiman, ed., *Bureaucrats and Policy-Making* (1984) and J.E. Lane, *Bureaucracy and Public Choice* (1987). The classic on the subject of administration remains H.A. Simon, *Administrative Behaviour* (1957).

The question is indeed an old one, as can be seen for instance from E. Strauss, *The Ruling Servants* (1961) and, especially for the French case, M. Crozier, *The Bureaucratic Phenomenon* (1964). On the characteristics of the British administrators and in particular on the traditional role of the amateur and on some current changes, see P. Kellner and Lord Crowther-Hunt, *The Civil Servants* (1980) and G. Drewry and T. Butcher, *The Civil Service Today* (1988). On the characteristics of French administrators see, alongside Crozier, P.G. Cerny and M.A. Schain, eds., *French Politics and Public Policy* (1980), and in particular the chapter by J. Marceau, 'Power and its Possessors', at pp. 48–78.

On the views and political 'culture' of western public administrators, see J.D. Aberbach, R.D. Putnam and B.A. Rockman, *Bureaucrats and Politicians in Western Democracies* (1981) and J. Richardson, ed., *Policy Styles in Western Europe* (1982).

On the nature, role and control of administrative bodies in the Third World, see J. La Palombara, ed., *Bureaucracy and Political Development* (1963) and F.W. Riggs, ed., *Frontiers of Development Administration* (1971).

# 19

# The role of the military in the political process

## Introduction

While the influence of bureaucracies in government tends to be covert, and therefore remains relatively unnoticed, the participation of the military in politics is a well-documented and often painfully overt experience. Yet the picture which emerges at first sight from this intervention is somewhat confusing.

On the one hand, takeovers of governments by the military – as well as attempts at takeover – appear to occur almost exclusively in Third World countries. Both western democracies and communist states appear to have been protected, by and large, from the phenomenon, although there have been, to limit ourselves to the postwar period, incidents bordering on takeovers or attempted takeovers in France, at the time of the Algerian war in 1958, in Spain, a few years after the re-establishment of democracy in the mid-1970s, and in Portugal, where some members of the military tried to prevent the full return to democracy after the armed forces had overthrown the dictatorship in 1974. There was even an actual takeover in Greece in 1967 and the military regime lasted until 1974. However, these cases affected only a small minority of western countries.

On the other hand, the armed forces have made themselves felt in less obvious ways in all western countries and in communist states. In the United States or in what was the Soviet Union, for instance, the military has been known to exercise various forms of pressure, designed either to prevent the government from carrying out policies which the military did not like, or to induce the policy-makers to pursue some policies more strongly than the civilians might have wished. Thus the role of the military in politics appears to be widespread with respect to some activities and to be by and large concentrated in some types of polity with respect to other activities.

## National values and the values of the military

The picture is thus diverse in terms of the manner in which the military intervene in politics; it is also diverse with respect to the extent to which national values and military values relate to each other. In the past at least, if perhaps not so obviously in recent years, it seemed possible to distinguish between countries which could be regarded as 'militaristic' (such as Germany or Japan) and nations which could be viewed as having a more 'civilian' outlook, and in which the military was not given a prominent position (such as Anglo-Saxon countries). Some countries such as France appeared to stand between these two extremes, with the military and the civilian regime having long been locked in conflict. These differences suggest that levels of military intervention in politics may well be related to and perhaps depend on national and military values or ideologies.

- The first section of this chapter will be devoted to the examination of the *variations in the propensity of the military to intervene in politics*.
- The second section will, on the basis of the analysis of this propensity, analyze the *different levels of military intervention*.
- The third section will then be devoted to the *strongest form of military intervention*, that which results in the establishment of *military regimes*, and to the difficulties which these experience.

## The propensity of military intervention

### The military profession

The military are a part of the public service in the wider sense. Like other branches of the public service, they implement but also 'advise' on policies; and they are involved in managing the huge organizations which the armed forces constitute. They are 'specialists' and act as other specialists do.

They are likely to be even more autonomous from the politicians than other parts of the public service, however, since they exercise a unique function and have *means of coercion* which no one else possesses. The military are entrusted by the state with the role of defending the existence of the nation, and to achieve this aim, they are equipped with a vast array of weapons. Even in the case of small and less developed countries, they can therefore impose their will on the society in a way which no other group can. In fact, they are sometimes called on by the civilian authorities to use this power, not merely to defend the nation externally, but also to quell major outbreaks of internal disorder. Even the police forces do not come close to having the strength of the military; moreover, in many countries, at least a substantial proportion of these political forces are part of the army.

### Values of the military

The military are likely to develop special features as a result of this unique function. Indeed, because of the hard and dangerous character of the tasks which members of the armed forces may be asked to fulfil as part of their duties, they have to receive specialized training. This training naturally develops an *esprit de corps* which is stronger than anywhere else in the public sector. All the branches of the armed forces do not share this spirit to the same extent: technical units of the army and, partly because of the technical character of their job, large sections of the navy or the air force may hold somewhat different attitudes. The cohesion of the armed forces may be reduced as a result. Occasionally, some branches of the navy or of the air force have opposed moves made by the army to oust civilian governments.

By and large, though, members of the armed forces share a number of values, stemming from the nature of the military profession. These values are essentially constituted by an emphasis on *discipline and hierarchy*; a need to prepare for an activity, warfare, which is *almost never undertaken*; and a belief in the magnitude of the *potential dangers* which the polity faces (Huntington, 1957: 1–97).

The first of these three characteristics does not need to be described at length, since discipline ('which is the basis of army strength', according to the French army rule book) and hierarchy are obvious imperatives of military organizations. But these virtues are likely to cause friction between military and civilian power because they are seldom extolled to the same degree outside military establishments. The emphasis on these values is thus likely to lead to a *relative isolation of the military* from the rest of the community; furthermore, this isolation will be deliberately fostered, since the military is unlikely to display the necessary qualities of discipline and hierarchy unless it is at least partly isolated from the society.

Second, the military profession is geared to fighting wars; yet the fulfilment of this ultimate *raison d'être* of the armed forces is conceived as an unlikely occurrence, and indeed one which is expected to be remote because of the very existence of the military. Members of the armed forces tend therefore to have an ambivalent attitude towards war, as can often be detected in the advice given by general staffs to civilian rulers. The military typically feels unprepared and continuously asks for more resources in order to achieve the state of readiness which it feels is required and yet is never achieved (Huntington, 1957: 66). This ambivalence is general. It is especially marked in the contemporary world in relation to nuclear weapons. These are regarded as providing a deterrent: that is, they exist in order not to be used; the defence potential is deployed on such a scale that war becomes impossible. Some of this same ambivalence can also be detected with respect to conventional warfare.

Thus most military men prepare most of the time for an activity which occurs occasionally but may never take place. While other public servants are appointed to fulfil the goals which they are employed to achieve, the military are asked to be ready for an eventuality which is to be avoided rather than pursued. Not surprisingly, this state of affairs creates frustrations and may more than occasionally place the military and civilian government on a collision course.

Third, the need to be prepared derives from the view that external dangers are both very real and very large. This suggests that the military have a conception of society reminiscent of the Hobbesian 'state of nature', where life was 'nasty, brutish and short', rather than a conception of society based on a belief in co-operation and brotherhood among nations. This underlying ideology explains why general staffs are typically cautious when advising about starting a war; but it also leads more broadly to the demand that the nation be prepared, not just from a material, but from a psychological point of view. The military are deeply concerned with the 'morale of the nation', since success against potential enemies depends on citizens and leaders being ready to defend the country. They are consequently likely to support some ideologies and to be suspicious of others; more than the members of other branches of the public service, they tend to believe that it is their duty to look at the possible consequences of governmental policies and to try to stop those policies which are viewed as undermining the moral fibre of the nation (Huntington, 1957: 62–70).

## Conditions favouring military intervention

These characteristics of the military, together with the physical force which the army possesses, are important elements accounting for a general propensity to intervene in politics. 'Instead of asking why the military engage in politics, we ought surely to ask why they ever do otherwise. For at first sight the political advantages of the military *vis-à-vis* other and civilian groupings are overwhelming. The military possess vastly superior organisation. And they possess *arms*' (Finer, 1962: 5).

What makes intervention take place in concrete situations, however, is the combination of the *characteristics of the military* with particular *features of the polity*. Four elements are essential in this respect: the degree of professionalization of the military; the extent of legitimacy of the political system; the level of complexity of the society; and the type of ideology which prevails in the polity.

First, a high degree of *professionalization* fosters military intervention, for, the more the army is composed of professionals, the more it is set apart from the rest of the society and, consequently, the more it tends to develop attitudes which are both idiosyncratic and deeply felt by its members. Hence the case often made for a conscript army by those who want to link the military with the nation. Those who belong to a professional army will have few occasions to meet informally with other groups in society; they will therefore rarely have to defend their ideology or be subjected to the views of others. Their isolation is often reinforced by the tendency of the military to marry within their own group, and thus to belong to families in which particularistic values are passed from generation to generation.

Conversely, the potential for intervention is reduced where the army is drawn broadly from the population at large, and where the bulk of the military have widespread contacts with the rest of the society. The same is true where the technical side of the military is large and powerful, as members of technical corps are likely to have links with colleagues in other walks of life, and may even move from a position in the army to equivalent employment in civilian life. The argument is the same as in relation to sectionalism, which was discussed in Chapter 7: where cross-cutting cleavages are low, subcultures tend to develop; where subcultures tend to develop, tension between the subcultures increases. A high level of military professionalism is a particular instance of subcultural development.

Second, the probability of military intervention increases as the *legitimacy of the political system* decreases. Where legitimacy is low, the military are unlikely to be inhibited in putting pressure on the government or in escalating demands. Moreover, a low level of legitimacy of the political system also indicates to the military that the regime has limited support and, therefore, that the country is unlikely to be morally ready to defend itself with vigour in the event of armed conflict. Finally, a polity in which the legitimacy of the political system is low is likely to be characterized by periodic outbreaks of civil disorder: the army may therefore be called to play a part in internal political life. It may thus already have a foot in the door, and further intervention against a weak government may come to be regarded as a logical next step (Finer, 1962: 72–85).

Third, the probability of military intervention is high when the *political, social and economic system* is simple; it is low when society is complex, as in the case of developed polities. This is due in part to the fact that cross-cutting cleavages tend to increase as the complexity of the society increases. Moreover, direct intervention by the military becomes difficult to bring about in a complex society. Although the army's equipment may be highly sophisticated, the network of state and other public institutions is so vast and so diffuse that military intervention has to take place simultaneously at very many points to be successful. Indeed, in such a society, the military are likely to be incorporated in the governmental machine: for instance, through the interpenetration of civilian and military personnel in the ministry of defence as well as in many other organizations, both central and regional.

Fourth, the probability of military intervention increases if the prevailing *ideologies of the polity* differ sharply from the values which the military characteristically hold. This is why there are underlying problems between military and civilian values in regimes which emphasize, jointly or separately, democratic participation goals, liberal means and egalitarian ends. These values tend to clash with the notions of discipline and of hierarchy which the military uphold. The problem becomes acute when societal norms change abruptly with a new regime or a new government coming to power; on the contrary, slow modifications of norms may be accepted by the military. Potential conflicts between military and civilian authorities are also reduced when a democratic government takes a nationalistic posture. In principle, the values of a democratic regime are associated with an emphasis on universalistic ideas of development rather than on a traditional conception of the national interest. But if the polity is faced with strong opposition from its neighbours because of its policies, the military and the civilian government may come closer to each other, as was the case during both the French and the Russian revolutions.

## Civilian control

There is thus a high probability that the military will intervene in various types of polity. The *theory of civilian control* of the military, which has typically been presented as a model, is therefore likely to be more often a hope than a reality: it is in a sense an application to the military of the theory of ministerial responsibility which was mentioned in Chapter 18 (Huntington, 1957: 80–97). In nineteenth-century Europe it seemed realistic because of a number of societal characteristics which combined then to reduce the opportunity for or the desire of the military to intervene in that part of the world.

The first of these societal characteristics was that the professionalization of the army was slow. The officer class of the traditional European monarchies continued to be drawn from, and to remain closely linked to, the aristocracy, except in France as a result of the revolution of 1789. Not surprisingly, France was one of the countries where problems of civil–military relations were most acute.

In the second place, and again with the exception of France, European countries did not typically experience a regime break in the nineteenth century. Liberalism emerged under the cover of monarchical systems, to which the military remained loyal, because of the traditions embodied by king or emperor. There was a system of *dual legitimacy* not just in Imperial Germany, but also in Belgium, the Netherlands, Italy and even Britain, whereby military men felt that they owed their allegiance directly to the head of state. They could at least have the impression that their traditional status in the nation was protected by the part played by the institution of the monarchy.

Third, in the case of France and, later, of Soviet Russia, potential civil–military conflicts were somewhat reduced as a result of the incidence of international conflicts. The armies of the French Revolution were given the task of defending the regime and nation. Difficulties were not altogether avoided, as the history of nineteenth- and twentieth-century France was to show; but the potential for an army takeover was none the less reduced by the 'nationalistic' tradition of the Republic, as it was later also to be reduced in Soviet Russia for the same reason.

Thus, by and large, the theory of civilian control of the military seemed broadly valid in Europe, at least until 1918. After that date, when many traditional monarchies collapsed, problems began to grow, including in Europe and especially in eastern and southern Europe. Thus military intervention loomed larger. Yet this is not because the theory of civilian control was any less valid after 1918 than it had been before the First World War. Indeed, military coups had taken place frequently in Latin America during the nineteenth century. It is merely that the conditions which had minimized the potential for military intervention in Europe before 1914 ceased to apply to the same extent afterwards.

## Levels of military intervention

The potential for military intervention in politics thus depends on a number of social factors. In practice, this means that it will take a number of forms which will make it more or less severe. Following Finer, these forms can be referred to as influence, blackmail, displacement and supplantment (Finer, 1962: 86–7).

## Influence

At the lowest two levels, the role of the military is not very different from that of an interest group. Influence is used, for instance, when members of the military attempt to increase the resources at their disposal, or to shift policies by lobbying politicians. There is no intention to modify the relationship between, let alone the positions of, the 'players' in the game.

## Blackmail

Blackmail activities are designed to achieve more: for instance, to alter policy on a more general front, especially in foreign affairs or on national unity. The means include a variety of threats, in particular threats of resignation designed to show the civilian authorities that they cannot maintain the line on which they have embarked because they may not find it possible to implement it. A typical blackmail operation was that of some British officers before the First World War, who intimated their opposition to the proposed policy of the Liberal government *vis-à-vis* the whole of Ireland by threatening to resign.

## Displacement

If blackmail does not succeed, the next step which the military may take is to displace the existing government and replace it by one which would be expected to be more amenable to their goals. Displacement can vary in severity. At one end of the continuum, it can merely aim at exchanging one civilian group for another; it is then a form of arbitration, as in the case of the *poder moderador* (moderating power) exercised by the military in some Latin American countries in the past. The military were not supporting any particular political group; they merely believed that their function was to stop the 'excesses' of some civilian governments. The military may want to go further, however. They may want to bring to power a group which they support ideologically, sometimes by revitalizing it. The return of De Gaulle to power in 1958 in France after the army had effectively ceased to obey the Fourth Republic government is an example, since Gaullism had lost practically all of its strength during the preceding years. The intervention of the military on behalf of traditional conservative parties in Latin America also constitutes an instance of the same type of displacement, the electoral strength of these bodies having typically declined appreciably. Perhaps the most extreme case of displacement occurred in Uruguay in the 1970s when the military imposed a civilian president on the country. This was very close to the most severe form of intervention, supplantment.

## Supplantment

Supplantment is overt military rule. The civilian government is replaced by members of the armed forces who act as a group and take the government over. It is a *collective* action of military personnel and not merely the action of the military on behalf of an individual, even if this individual is a soldier. Napoleon's coup of 1799 was not a case of supplantment, but an extreme form of displacement, since it was Bonaparte, rather than the army as such, which came to power. With supplantment, military men become the structure of power: in particular, they typically abolish parties and extend their direct control at the regional level.

## Military intervention and the structure of society

These levels of military intervention need to be related to the four types of societal characteristics (professionalism, lack of legitimacy, simplicity of the society, character of the ideology) which were identified earlier as likely to have an effect on the link between the military and the nation. Influence, being the lowest level, is likely to be characteristic of countries in which the professionalization of the army is low, regime legitimacy and the complexity of the society are high, and the ideology of the civilian government is close to that of the military. A country in which the opposite characteristics prevail is likely to be open to supplantment. Countries where conditions are intermediate between these two extremes will be subjected to blackmail or displacement.

## Military intervention and stages of socioeconomic development

The relationship between levels of military intervention and these societal characteristics can be made more precise if we consider the role of the military at four stages of socioeconomic development: namely, those of underdevelopment, take-off, early development and mature development.

- The *complexity* of the society grows with socioeconomic development. Thus, the more advanced a society is in socioeconomic terms, the more difficult it is for the military to take it over.
- The *professionalization* of the army is likely to be low at the underdeveloped stage and higher at other stages of development, though perhaps not at its highest point at the most advanced stages. The subculture effect of professionalization plays less of a part at the advanced stages of development, so the military is more likely then to be linked to the rest of the population.
- The *ideology* of traditional political systems is likely to be close to that of the military; it is less close at other stages of development, with the added problem that, at the take-off and early development stages, a new democratic or egalitarian ideology may suddenly be pressed on the polity – for instance, at the time of independence.

- *Legitimacy* is likely to be at its highest at the stages of underdevelopment and of mature development, while countries at the take-off and early development stages are characterized by high levels of conflict about regime goals and about the bases of the political institutions, as we saw in Chapter 5.

Countries at the stages of underdevelopment and of mature development are thus likely to be marked by the lowest levels of military intervention. In developed societies, on the whole, the military uses influence and acts as an interest group; where, as in the United States, the legislature is powerful and is able to act either to initiate or at least to veto governmental legislation, the military operate on the legislature as well as on the executive. At the other extreme, in societies which are underdeveloped, such as some traditional monarchies, associational groups are weak and communal groups such as tribes or ethnic groups are strong, as we saw in Chapter 7. The military will also use influence and perhaps blackmail, but the pressure which is exercised takes place through these communal groups.

Gradually, however, as traditional societies start to change, the military begin to acquire a sense of corporate identity: they become, as we noted in Chapter 7, an *institutional group*. At the same time, conflicts over ideology and regime also increase, with some groups supporting modernization while others defend traditional values. The legitimacy of the political system declines, and the military become increasingly concerned with the future of the society and wish to play a part in shaping this future. As a result, the probability of displacement and even of supplantment becomes high, although supplantment is more characteristic of countries at the take-off stage and displacement of countries at the early development stage. This is a stage at which the society begins to be too complex for an army coup to succeed easily, although instances of supplantment can occur and, if they do, can be severe and even brutal, as were the cases of supplantment in Chile and Argentina in the 1970s and 1980s.

The intensity of military intervention is thus related to the development of societies in the form of a bell-shaped curve, with the mildest forms of military action being at both ends of the range, and displacement and supplantment being characteristic of the intermediate positions. Given that, in the postwar period, many countries moved from the traditional to the take-off and early development stages, it is not surprising that there should have been many military coups and many military regimes in the 1960s, 1970s and 1980s.

## Military regimes and their fate

### The spread of military regimes

Military regimes thus tend to occur when societies are at the take-off and developing stages. They occur as a result of the decrease in the legitimacy of the traditional forces, and especially of the communal groups, which exist in undeveloped societies. At that point, a legitimacy vacuum occurs, and the military often embody the hopes of those who are looking for a transformation of the country. As the armed forces have physical

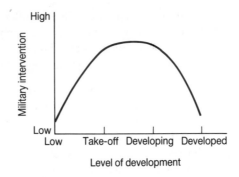

▶ **Figure 19.1**   Military intervention and socioeconomic development

strength, they can carry out a coup successfully, in a context in which state organizations are relatively simple. As they have a hierarchical organization which is likely to extend into the provinces, they can be a substitute for parties and communal groups in providing a chain of command through which decisions at the centre may be implemented at the periphery.

It is therefore not surprising that military regimes should have been established in Latin America on numerous occasions since the early part of the nineteenth century and in eastern Europe between the two world wars; nor is it surprising that half the Third World countries (52 out of 104) in existence before 1970 should have had at least one military regime, together with one western European country, Greece. Indeed, a number of these countries (Ghana, Nigeria, Sudan and Argentina, in particular) had more than one military regime.

**Table 19.1**   Military regimes and military-dominated regimes in 1990

|  | Total countries in region in 1990 | Number of countries which have had military regimes since 1945 | Number of military regimes in 1990 | Number of military-dominated regimes in 1990 |
|---|---|---|---|---|
| Atlantic | 23 | 1 | – | – |
| Eastern Europe and northern Asia | 15 | 1 | – | – |
| Middle East and northern Africa | 22 | 7 | – | 3 |
| South and south-east Asia | 24 | 7 | 1 | 1 |
| Africa south of Sahara | 46 | 22 | 9 | 10 |
| Latin America | 33 | 14 | 2 | 2 |
| Total | 163 | 52 | 12 | 16 |

Although military regimes are numerous, they have not emerged at random throughout the post-1945 period. To begin with, as could be expected, successful coups tend to occur after a few years have elapsed since independence, and not immediately. Thus while most Black African countries became independent in or around 1960, military regimes occurred in that part of the world in the second half of the 1960s, in Ghana, Nigeria, Benin (then Dahomey), Burkina Faso (then Upper Volta), Mali, Mauretania, Zaire and Burundi. Not surprisingly, therefore, countries which only became independent in the late 1980s had not been affected by military takeovers by the early 1990s.

## Decline from the mid-1980s

The number of military regimes has declined sharply since the mid-1980s. The large majority of the Latin American countries which had had military regimes or regimes based on the military from the late 1960s or the 1970s turned to civilian governments in the 1980s. This was the case with Ecuador, Peru, Bolivia, Argentina, Brazil and Uruguay, although various (unsuccessful) attempts at military intervention took place during the presidency of Alfonsin (1983–9) in Argentina. A similar decline in military takeovers can be noticed in the rest of the world, although it is less marked. A coup took place in 1989 in Sudan. Military involvement has more often taken the form of mixed military–civilian regimes than that of pure military rule.

The fall in the number of military regimes in the 1980s has sometimes been regarded as a sign of a long-term decline in the sharpest and most 'naked' forms of military intervention in politics, partly because all societies have become more complex and partly because the military values of hierarchy and discipline have come to be less strictly adhered to. The world as a whole would thus follow a similar evolution to that of southern Europe, where liberal democracy has been regarded as undergoing a process of 'consolidation' (O'Donnell et al., 1986). This may be the case, but there may also be *cyclical trends*. There were earlier periods during which the incidence of military rule was also relatively small: for instance, in the late 1950s and early 1960s when civilian regimes emerged in many countries of Latin America, including Venezuela, Colombia, Ecuador, Peru, Bolivia and Argentina. But civilian regimes survived the 1960s in Venezuela and Colombia only, while even Chile and Uruguay, once regarded as established democracies, joined the list of the countries under military rule. Such cycles of civilian and military regimes seem to correspond to the fact that tensions in developing polities – as well as the ineffectiveness of the bureaucracy in these countries – create conditions for military takeovers, but also create difficulties for military governments which make it difficult for them to maintain themselves in power for long periods.

Some developing countries are able to avoid military takeovers if party and group structures are well implanted, whether these are tribal or associational, such as trade unions. This has been the case especially in the Commonwealth. Only six of these polities among over 30 have experienced successful coups, these six countries being Ghana (where coups occurred three times), Nigeria, Uganda, Pakistan and Sierra Leone (two coups in each of these countries), and Fiji. The extent of legitimacy of the political system tends to be higher where political structures are better implanted: military coups are therefore less frequent.

## Weaknesses and failures of military regimes

While we are accustomed to note the strengths of military regimes – and, to begin with, the fact that they can physically coerce opponents – the weaknesses of these regimes may be less apparent. They are none the less real, and they impede the long-term maintenance of these regimes (Finer, 1962: 14–22). Military rule lasted only six years on average in the post-1945 period, and this average is almost the same for each of the regions of the developing world (Middle East and northern Africa, south and south-east Asia, Black Africa, and Latin America) (Blondel, 1982: 126–7). Only in ten cases did military regimes last more than a decade, the longest being those of Chile (17 years), of Ethiopia and Pakistan (15 years), and of Bolivia and Nigeria (13 years). Conversely, military rule lasted two years or less in 13 cases and between three and four years in 18 cases.

Most military regimes are therefore short-lived, and even those which last for a long period are transient by comparison with civilian regimes, not merely western liberal democratic, but Third World liberal democratic, such as those of India, Malaysia and Sri Lanka. They last less than communist regimes have lasted, and less even than many regimes based on the leadership of a charismatic president, whether or not supported by a single party, such as those of many African states – Senegal, Côte d'Ivoire, Kenya and Zambia.

Military regimes are transient because they suffer from structural weaknesses. These weaknesses counterbalance their strength and affect the ability of the military to run the government effectively. Moreover, the armed forces cannot provide the same kind of linkages between rulers and people as those which parties and groups can provide. Members of the armed forces are not trained to fulfil the functions of party leaders – namely, to elaborate, co-ordinate and supervise the implementation of policies, except with respect to those matters which pertain directly or indirectly to the military (Oyediran, 1979). The military personnel who occupy ministerial positions find themselves quickly in difficulty, both from a technical point of view, since they do not have the specialized answers, and from a broader political point of view, since they uphold rather simple philosophies which are unlikely by themselves to provide a framework for policy making (Odetola, 1982: 23–62).

Military rulers therefore have to rely markedly on the public bureaucracy to give them solutions to the problems which they face. These are usually particularly serious, since coups typically take place in order to speed up social and economic development. However, as was pointed out in Chapter 18, the bureaucracy is handicapped by its sectionalism and its relative lack of legitimacy. Military rulers therefore need to be able to co-ordinate and elaborate policies and also to impose them, occasionally at least, on branches of the bureaucracy (Asiodu, 1979: 73–95).

They are often unable to impose their views. This is in part because they do not have the technical competence required. It is also and most importantly because they cannot acquire and even less maintain sufficient support among the population. The army does have 'tentacles' in the provinces, since it has a territorial structure of garrisons and outposts; but these tentacles do not normally have the 'length' and the flexibility of the local organizations of parties or interest groups. Indeed, such tentacles may not always exist, since the armies of most Third World countries are often very small. The few thousand soldiers who compose them may be able to carry out a successful coup in the capital and subsequently to control that capital and a few urban centres; but their numbers are not adequate to cover the whole country. Members of the military may occasionally engage in activities designed to educate the population, in particular in matters of communication or of land use, especially at times of emergencies; but they are less able to engage in a continuous process of mobilization, since they have to maintain a degree of discipline and hierarchy which results in them remaining somewhat apart from the rest of the nation.

Thus military rulers become confronted after a few years with the emergence of a gap – a zone of silence – between themselves and the people. They then face a dilemma. Either they cannot or do not wish to fill this gap, partly in order to remain relatively 'pure', in which case they soon have to start the process by which they will transfer power back to civilians; or they want to remain in power, in which case they need the help provided by other institutions. They therefore have to start building around themselves a civilian structure, specifically a political party and associations dependent on that party, such as trade unions. In this process, the military regime begins to 'civilianize' itself and becomes transformed into a *mixed military–civilian government* (Finer, 1962: 197–204; Huntington, 1968: 237–63).

## Mixed civilian–military governments

While the number of 'pure' military governments declined appreciably in the course of the 1980s – the peak being in the mid-1970s – there has been a corresponding and substantial increase in the number of mixed civilian–military regimes during the same period (Blondel, 1982: 100). In 1989, over a fifth of all the Third World governments belonged to this category, as against only 10 per cent of pure military regimes.

Mixed military–civilian rule was sometimes in the past the result of the involvement of military personnel in traditional regimes: the Thai government had this character from the 1930s to the 1970s. Since the 1950s, however, military leaders have tended to overthrow regimes of this kind rather than associate with them. This was the case in Egypt in 1952, in Syria and Iraq in 1958, in Libya in 1969, in Afghanistan in 1973, and in Ethiopia in 1974. A new political system had to be created, however, and this new political system was often based on a strong single party (Finer, 1962: 198–204; Huntington, 1968: 237–63). This practice was not entirely new: when Nasser set up a party in Egypt in the 1950s to strengthen his regime, he was in a sense following the lead of Ataturk who had done the same in Turkey after the First World War; and the

## BOX 19.1
## In and out of military rule

Military regimes are relatively transient; but they also recur, at least in some countries. In such cases they almost become the regular 'alternative'. They can be transient in another way, however. After some years, the weight of the military in the political system is likely to diminish; the regime becomes 'mixed' before being 'civilianized'.

In Latin America, military regimes tend to come and go; in the rest of the Third World, the slow civilianization process is more common. However, there are exceptions. Mexico is the textbook case of civilianization by means of the single party; Nigeria is a prime example of the alternation between (rather long) periods of military rule and (shorter) periods of civilian rule.

While Egypt is a straightforward example of a process of civilianization almost as successful as that of Mexico, its neighbour to the south, Sudan, has had the doubtful privilege of combining both methods of military regime. The country had a parliamentary system on three occasions, twice shortly after independence and in the 1980s. All three civilian regimes were terminated by military coups. The first period of military rule was on the 'Latin American' alternation pattern; it lasted a few years and the parliamentary system was re-established. The second military regime adopted the civilianization model: after some years the leader set up a (single) party and hoped to give his regime a more 'acceptable' character in this way. This was not to be, however, largely because of a non-ending civil war in the south of the country: the regime was toppled. After a short parliamentary interlude, the military took over again in 1989. The new regime has been of the 'pure' variety (with a substantial dose of Muslim 'integratism').

Sudan thus experienced different military regime types. The cases of Syria and Iraq are intriguing in another way. In general, a leader who wishes to civilianize the regime sets up a party, which is therefore essentially dependent on the army. In Syria and Iraq, the party (the Baath) preceded the various military coups which took place in its name and within it, until Presidents Assad and Saddam succeeded in establishing their long rule respectively in Syria and Iraq. There is therefore no 'civilianization' in the strict sense: the party is the stage and the military are (at least some of) the actors.

The shape of military regimes is thus increasingly varied as time passes.

Mexican Institutional Revolutionary Party (PRI) had been set up in the 1920s for identical reasons. From the 1960s, a number of military rulers attempted to strengthen their rule in this way in the Middle East, parts of southern Asia and, above all, Africa. This has been the evolution, among others, of Zaire, Sudan (until the 1980s), Somalia, Ethiopia and Burma, as well as, albeit in a different manner, Syria and Iraq.

Single parties set up by military rulers are often highly artificial, especially in the early period; at worst, they may have a symbolic existence only. Yet the situation can change gradually if the leader does have a genuine personal following and is anxious to broaden the base of his power. This effort appears particularly characteristic of military regimes with a 'progressive' ideology, such as those which emerged in the 1970s, especially in Black Africa, in Ethiopia, Benin and Congo. The party is then set up along lines similar to those which characterized communist parties. It may play some part in educating and mobilizing the population, although the extent of this mobilization appears to have often been low and spasmodic (Decalo, 1976: 231–54). However, whatever its success or failure, the party does reduce the military character of the regime. Gradually, as has been the case in Mexico since the 1930s and in Egypt since the 1960s, the civilianization process becomes complete. Mixed civilian–military regimes eventually become civilian regimes.

The fact that pure military regimes last for only relatively short periods does not suggest, however, that the reasons why they emerged have also disappeared. Sometimes the 'civilianization' process is a success, as in Mexico; in many African and Asian countries, on the other hand, this has not been the case. A new cycle then begins, with further takeovers likely to occur in the future, at least as long as the polity does not reach a level of mature development.

## Overview

Military intervention in politics is a universal phenomenon; it is based on the *coercive power of the military* and on the *motivation of armed forces to intervene.*

The motivation to intervene stems from the fact that the *values of the military*, such as discipline and a state of preparedness for war, may not be shared by the bulk of the population.

The conditions favouring military intervention are *high professionalism, low legitimacy* of the existing regime, *limited complexity* of the society, and the wide acceptance of *societal values* which differ from those of the military.

Military intervention can take the form of *pressure, blackmail, displacement of the existing regime, or supplantment.* In the last case, a military regime is installed. The more the conditions facilitating military intervention obtain, the more severe the level of intervention.

Military regimes have been numerous in the 1960s and 1970s, in part because civilian governments in many new countries have lacked the amount of legitimacy required to establish an effective administration, let alone to achieve development.

Military regimes have strengths; they have also weaknesses. They are unlikely to be able to obtain support among large sections of the population.

Military regimes therefore tend to collapse after a few years, or to be replaced by *mixed civilian–military regimes* if the leader succeeds in setting up a party and in establishing a network of ancillary groups.

Military intervention is universal in its mildest forms; in its most manifest expression, it is symptomatic of the profound malaise which some societies experience. Yet military regimes do not provide a cure to the malaise which is at the origin of their existence. Where military personnel take over power, they do not provide more than, at best, a temporary and often illusory solution.

## Further reading

The role of the military in politics has been analyzed systematically since the 1950s. The classics in the field are the works of S.P. Huntington, *The Soldier and the State* (1957), S.E. Finer, *The Man on Horseback* (1962) and M. Janowitz, *The Military in the Development of New Nations* (1964). Characteristics of military regimes and mixed regimes can be found in S.P. Huntington, *Political Order in Changing Societies* (1968) and in J. Blondel, *The Organisation of Governments* (1982).

The problems faced by military governments, in particular in Africa, are analyzed in S. Decalo, *Coups and Army Rule in Africa* (1976), O. Oyediran, ed., *Nigerian Government and Politics under Military Rule* (1979) and O. Odetola, *Military Regimes and Development* (1982).

An examination of trends towards a decline of military rule in the 1980s can be found in G. O'Donnell, P. Schmitter, and L. Whitehead, eds., *Transitions from Authoritarian Rule* (1986). On the complex characteristics of the Baath Party in Iraq and Syria, see M.C. Hudson, *Arab Politics* (1977).

# 20

# Rule adjudication and judges

## Introduction

Bureaucracies (and armies) are the main instruments by which the rules made by legislatures and national executives are implemented, although these institutions are also, as we have seen, more than occasionally involved in rule making as well, even if they encounter difficulties when they attempt too conspicuously to take on the role of the politicians. Yet bureaucracies and armies are not the only bodies whose role is to implement rules: *courts and tribunals* are also engaged in what is in essence rule implementation, albeit of a special nature.

## The notion of rule adjudication

Rule application by courts is special, not just because these bodies have a formally solemn character, are staffed by a personnel whose career is governed by particular rules, and operate on the basis of procedures which are highly distinctive. The activities of courts are special because the *principle of the operation* is different from that of bureaucracies. Administrators typically move from general principles to specific cases; judges, on the contrary, start from specific cases which they then relate to one or a number of principles. This is why the operation has sometimes been described as *rule adjudication* rather than rule implementation (Almond and Powell, 1966: 29, 158–63). Judges 'adjudicate' among the rules which should be (or should have been) taken into account in a particular case. The operation which they conduct is thus the converse of a 'normal' operation of rule application. Yet it is a form of rule application, since the aim is to discover what rule should be implemented in a particular context.

Rule adjudication is special in two ways. First, it has a somewhat *passive* character. It is triggered by an event which has occurred (or has not occurred, but 'should' have occurred); it is therefore normally set in motion after the occurrence. It does not provoke happenings, as does rule application by administrators. Public servants are often concerned with management, as we have seen, but those who are engaged in rule adjudication do not manage situations. They pass 'judgements' (in the ordinary sense of the word) on what has or has not happened.

Second, rule adjudication is necessarily immersed in detail and is concerned with establishing, obviously with various degrees of rigour and precision, what has or has not taken place and why, since the applicability or otherwise of a specific rule will depend considerably on the extent to which it is established that something did indeed occur. Clearly, persons who are professionally engaged in rule adjudication will become interested in the general implications of rules, but they are primarily concerned with the problem of establishing that a particular alleged occurrence did indeed take place.

## Rule adjudication and the norms of political systems

No society can avoid problems of rule adjudication. All societies have norms, whether these are written into laws or customarily passed on from one generation to the next. Whatever governments and the public services may decide and try to implement, there will always be happenings which will not correspond to what should have occurred. Thus all polities need to include bodies which will carry out the operation (or in Almond's terms the 'function') of rule adjudication.

However, societies differ in the extent to which rule adjudication takes place: the judicial process may be more or less sophisticated, for instance. Some happenings may be 'judged' without much care for details; some may even be left 'unjudged' because courts are not allowed to deal with a particular question (of national security, for example). Thus, although the operation of rule adjudication exists everywhere, there will be major variations in its form and extensiveness. This is where the norms of the political system, by way of a written rule or by custom, may have a major impact. An analysis of political life must therefore include an examination of processes of rule adjudication.

The norms of the political system affect all aspects of the rule adjudication process. First, they affect the extent to which the institutions (courts and tribunals) are *autonomous* from the government and from the rest of the public service, not merely formally, but in fact. Liberal systems state that courts should be independent; authoritarian systems, on the other hand, try to control the courts. Second, the norms of the political system also affect rule adjudication in terms of *content*. Not only are the laws likely to be more favourable to the citizen in a liberal state, but in such a state, too, the judiciary may well be given powers to question the validity of the laws themselves. This means that 'constitutionalism' plays a crucial part with respect to rule adjudication, as it does with respect to assemblies and executives. However, third, as with assemblies and governments, the characteristics of courts and of their involvement in the defence of the rights of citizens can *change markedly over time*. This occurs particularly with respect to the scrutiny of the actions of the public services. While the growth of rule-adjudicating institutions – courts, tribunals and other judicial bodies – is closely related to the spread of liberal ideas by way of constitutional

arrangements, it is also related to the development of practices which may extend –
or restrict – the provisions of the constitution.

## Dimensions of rule adjudication

Polities are therefore likely to vary appreciably in terms of the extent to which rule
adjudication is allowed and able to take place. Let us consider the matter in the context
of a concrete case. If plaintiffs try to obtain redress (or alternatively if, being brought
to court by another person or by the state, they attempt to defend themselves), three
basic questions need to be answered:

- To what extent are judges really 'free' or 'independent' in the examination and
  eventual adjudication of the case? This question relates partly, but only partly, to
  the existence of separate juridical institutions: it tends to be assumed that, where
  structures are differentiated, the hearing will be fairer; this assumption has to be
  tested.
- To what extent have judges the legal or constitutional powers to consider the case?
  Is this one of the matters which they are entitled to solve, or will they have to say
  that they have no jurisdiction, not because the plaintiff went to the wrong court,
  but because no court in the country has the right to adjudicate on the matter? This
  occurs if the question is deemed 'discretionary' and the state has the final right to
  decide.
- To what extent is the judge allowed to question the rules? Plaintiffs may complain
  not that they have been wrongly treated according to a specific rule, but that the
  particular rule is wrong, because it does not fit with the provisions of another, more
  general rule, which should have had precedence. However, judges may be constrained
  to say that they have no right to examine whether the specific rule was wrongly
  made, and that they can only examine whether plaintiffs were wrongly treated under
  that rule.

The extent of rule adjudication therefore has thus both a *vertical* and a *horizontal*
meaning. The horizontal meaning relates to the extent to which questions can be
discussed and adjudicated upon. The vertical meaning relates to the extent to which
judges can examine the whole sequence of rules on the basis of which a happening is
being supported or criticized.

These three problems are related to each other, but only to an extent: judges may
be highly independent and yet be severely restricted in the scope of their activities; they
may or may not be empowered to scrutinize any of the rules to see whether they
contradict higher norms and, for instance, the constitution. Thus only by examining
these three distinct aspects of the problem can one assess fully the character and extent
of rule adjudication in a particular polity.

- In the first section of this chapter, we shall therefore see to what extent *judges are
  independent* across the world.

■ In the second section, we shall consider the *depth of rule adjudication*, and in particular the problems posed by the existence of *constitutional courts*.

■ In the third section, we shall analyze the *scope of rule adjudication*, and see to what extent the decisions of public services can be challenged in courts.

## Rule adjudication and the independence of courts

The first question to be considered is whether rule-adjudicating bodies are independent. Independence is a matter of degree: it depends on both formal and informal arrangements; and it cannot go beyond a certain limit. One aspect of this independence is constituted by the existence of separate bodies in charge of rule adjudication. It is obviously important that there should be courts, recognized as such and entrusted with the duty to adjudicate on certain matters. Yet the fact that courts exist does not in itself guarantee independence, while, conversely, some tribunals and even some informal committees of inquiry may operate in a 'judicial' manner, although they do not have the status of courts. Thus what needs to be assessed is not merely whether formal arrangements establish the independence of courts, but whether the methods of selection of the judiciary and the procedures which are in force guarantee the reality of that independence.

### The concept of independence

Such an analysis is difficult to conduct, however, because what is meant by 'independence' is not entirely clear. Independence means lack of imposition, but *from whom* should the courts be independent? Is it just from the political leaders of the day and from their subordinates? This view was taken by the constitutionalists who asked for a separation of the judiciary from the executive and from the legislature. But as we noted in Chapter 16, such a separation cannot be fully implemented. In parliamentary systems, moreover, the 'separation' is far from complete: some autonomy is given to judges, but not a strict separation of powers.

Moreover, independence may mean more than freedom from interference from the politicians of the day: it may mean freedom from the *norms of the political and social system* itself. This is not what the liberal conception of rule adjudication suggests: it claims that courts must protect and indeed uphold the rule of law. Yet some have claimed that this results in the courts being ultimately the defenders of the social order rather than independent bodies striving for justice or equity. By and large, even in the best cases and although there are some exceptions, judges tend to operate within the context of the principles on which the society is based; they are separate from the government rather than fully independent.

## The extent of independence

The extent to which judges are truly free from governmental interference naturally varies from country to country and over time; the precise amount and the exact character of this variation is so far not well known. We know of cases in which judges have been dismissed or harassed (there have been celebrated instances of this type, in Ghana and Nigeria, for instance), but we do not know the degree to which more subtle pressures are being exercised: covert pressure remains largely undocumented. No general investigation has been carried out in order to discover how far courts are able to pass judgements against the government of the day.

Moreover, the question is typically discussed in the context of bodies which are legally defined as *courts*; but there are now a large and increasing number of *semi-judicial institutions* concerned principally with matters affecting the relationship between citizens and public services: for instance, disputes over social benefits, over compensation to be given as a result of accidents, and over compensation in connection with a compulsory purchase of property. These tribunals have grown somewhat haphazard, and the status of their members is less autonomous than that of judges. They must obviously be taken into account when a general picture of rule adjudication in a given country is drawn. For most citizens, 'justice' – at least insofar as it is concerned with the public sector – has more to do with these tribunals than with the more regular courts.

## Legal arrangements designed to ensure independence

Like the constitutional arrangements designed to bring about decentralization, the legal arrangements aimed at ensuring the independence of courts and other rule-adjudicating bodies tend to concentrate on procedural aspects. The main purpose is to see to it that the career of judges is more secure than that of ordinary civil servants. This is being achieved by regulating appointments and promotions.

There are difficulties, however. To begin with, someone has to select the judges. Appointment by the government does occur, but it is naturally regarded as not safeguarding judicial independence. In order to avoid governmental interference altogether, judges are sometimes *elected* directly by the people. This is the case with many state judges in the United States. These may not have the necessary technical competence, however. They may also be anxious to please the majority who elected them or perhaps even more the few who nominated them for election. An alternative is *co-option*, but this has the effect of perpetuating certain traditions or attitudes, and of breeding nepotism.

In practice, most countries have adopted a mixture of co-option and governmental appointment. First, the appointment of the *top* judges is often ultimately in the hands of the government. This might be reduced in practice by a customary form of co-option, even at the top; but this is not always the case, as is shown by the appointment of the United States federal Supreme Court justices. As a matter of fact, although there are strong political considerations in the appointment of these justices, the result is occasionally unexpected: some of those who were appointed by conservative presidents turned out to be liberal on many issues. Second, entry into the corps of judges is often dependent upon passing examinations and therefore showing some general intellectual as well as technical legal competence. Britain is exceptional in appointing judges at superior courts from among barristers: they thus have a second career. What has to be noted, in the end, is that appointment mechanisms never establish, and indeed *cannot establish* a complete separation between judges and executive or legislature.

There are also difficulties with respect to *promotion mechanisms*. Someone has to promote judges, and whoever has such a power can reduce considerably the independence of the more ambitious among them. In this respect as well, the choice has to be made between co-option and governmental decision. Liberal states opt for co-option, with the restriction that, at the very top, the government may be somewhat involved in the process. There is, moreover, the rule that tenure is protected, but this only means that judges can be fully independent provided they are prepared to face the prospects of a promotionless career.

## The independence of judges in practice

These principles are in force in western countries; they are also enshrined in the constitutions of most other states. By and large, they are applied in many parts of Latin America under civilian regimes. There have also been instances when judges have displayed a strongly independent attitude in other Third World countries, particularly in the Commonwealth (for instance, in India when Mrs Gandhi declared a state of emergency in the 1970s and attempted to assume full powers). Even in some communist states, a tradition of judicial independence gradually developed, and differences among these states increased over time in this respect. Only in a minority of countries are there frequent and blatant cases of formal restrictions on the independence of judges.

The question of the separation of judges from ordinary administration arises even more in relation to *tribunals and other quasi-judicial bodies*, which deal with professional matters, with technical questions, and with grievances of citizens against the bureaucracy. The members of these bodies often do not enjoy the type of protection which is given to judges. A classic example is that of the French highest administrative court, the Council of State, whose members have no more security of tenure than other higher civil servants – in theory, very little indeed – and whose career often consists of moving in and out of the court, either into other areas of the public sector or into private enterprise. The paradox of the Council of State is that, despite – some might say, because of – the absence of legal guarantees, members of this body succeeded in being gradually listened to and then 'obeyed' in the same way as the members of an ordinary court.

There is often no or very little security of tenure for members of tribunals and other quasi-judicial committees, which have proliferated in the twentieth century with the growth of social and economic legislation, particularly in western countries. The scope of rule adjudication may have increased, as we shall see in the last section of this

---

## BOX 20.1
## How far do administrative courts protect the citizen?

The question of the extent to which administrative courts protect citizens provoked major debates at the beginning of the twentieth century. The main protagonist against administrative courts was the Oxford law professor Dicey, who claimed that ordinary courts were entirely adequate, and indeed superior to administrative courts on the model of the French Council of State. He deemed these to be dependent on the government and claimed that they therefore tended to defend the state rather than citizens.

This point was probably valid during a large part of the nineteenth century. The Council of State did not formally become a court until the 1870s. As it stated that the conditions under which public bodies operated were different from those applicable to private bodies, it seems that it did indeed tend to favour the state unduly.

Then a change occurred. Administrative courts came instead to be regarded as promoting the interests of the citizen, on the very ground that public bodies operated under special conditions. This idea was interpreted as meaning that public bodies had to act in the public interest (for instance, operate on a continuous basis). It was also noted that the system was cheaper and the procedure simpler than that of ordinary courts.

Moreover, the involvement of the state in so many activities, in particular in the social sphere, meant that special bodies had to be appointed to adjudicate on matters such as pension rights and compensation for the compulsory purchase of land. The bodies set up for these purposes were typically described as 'quasi-judicial' only and officially labelled 'committees' rather than courts. In practice, however, they behaved increasingly like courts.

None the less, the enthusiasm for administrative courts declined somewhat. As they became more numerous, they faced the same problems as other courts: they became slow in rendering judgements; informality and easy access were not universal either. Hence the popularity of ombudsmen's offices, which are even more informal. Is it, then, that the protection given to citizens by administrative courts is not as satisfactory as opponents of Dicey claimed?

---

chapter, but the legal arrangements designed to protect the independence of judges have often not been extended beyond the group of bodies for which these arrangements were originally designed.

However, the limited evidence which can be obtained on new quasi-judicial bodies does not amount to an indictment of these institutions. Attacks were made against specialized administrative courts (for instance by the famous English law professor Dicey before 1914) and later against committees and enquiries (for instance, by Lord

Hewart in the *New Despotism*, 1929): these attacks proved unfounded. The protection given to the citizens by administrative courts and tribunals turned out to be satisfactory, which showed that their members were no less independent than the judges belonging to ordinary courts. Methods of appointment and of promotion are far from constituting always a true indicator of the independence of judges and of members of quasi-judicial bodies.

## The social and political environment

### *Western countries*

A subtle influence can result from the general social and political environment in which judges operate. The *social background* is likely to have an important effect. Studies which have been conducted in a number of western liberal democracies on the origins of judges have shown that members of the judiciary tend to be recruited from the better-off sections of the society. The same obtains often even for juries (or for magistrates in England, who, although they do not legally play the same part as juries, constitute, for relatively small crimes, a lay element which may fulfil an identical social function). Members of juries are likely to come from a wider cross-section of the community than judges, but they are unlikely to be socially representative. If it is assumed that the political and social attitudes of judges and juries correspond to those of the social groups from which these come, they are unlikely to hold views which reflect those of a representative cross-section of the community (Griffith, 1985: 25–31).

Thus, even in the absence of direct political pressure, members of rule-adjudicating bodies in western liberal democracies are more likely to uphold the status quo than to oppose it. This may in part be the reason why the independence of the judiciary is not really seriously questioned in these polities. Only occasionally is there a major clash, and such clashes seem to take place typically (though systematic empirical evidence is lacking) when a government of the left attempts to implement policies which do not appear to coincide with those of the status quo, and which are therefore often regarded by judges as going against the rule of law. Meanwhile, courts have often displayed a tendency to uphold conservative standpoints against more radical policies of governments: the case of the Rooseveltian legislation of 1933–4 is one of the best-known episodes of such a trend, and an episode to which we shall return in the next section. Examples can also be shown in relation to British governments of the left (Griffith, 1985: 207–22). These examples may not be typical, but the fact that members of the judiciary often come from among the well-to-do would appear to constitute a ground for suggesting a built-in tendency towards conservatism among them.

There have been signs of a trend in the opposite direction in some countries, especially in Italy and to a more limited extent in France. Since the 1970s, groups of more 'progressive' judges have been constituted. There has also been, in these two countries in particular, a marked involvement of prosecuting magistrates in political 'affairs' involving either corruption or the illegal financing of political parties.

## *Outside the West*

Political pressures are often blatant outside western democracies, but there are also many cases where the most commonly used pressures are more subtle, even in authoritarian states. The predominant part played by the Communist Party in the Soviet Union and other eastern communist states has constituted the basic framework within which the judiciary has operated in these countries. As a result persons who did not conform to the 'socialist' ideal had little chance of becoming judges. There was therefore little need to use overt weapons of intimidation, at least after Stalin and before the relative opening of some communist countries in the 1980s. The conception of the law put forward traditionally by Soviet analysts excluded the possibility of acceptance of what were regarded as 'bourgeois' rights of dissent; or, more precisely, such rights 'did not need to exist', given the fact that communist states were deemed to embody working-class ideals. However, views in this respect did change towards the end of the communist rule in eastern Europe (White *et al.*, 1982: 222–62).

In the Third World, pressures can come openly from the single party or from the military. Alternatively, they may be more covertly exercised within a more confined political and social élite in order to ensure that judges do not act in ways which would be detrimental to the interests and prestige of that élite. But there are cases of resistance by judges. In Latin America in particular, traditions of a liberal judiciary are strong; they come naturally to the fore principally when civilian governments are in power.

Judicial independence is therefore exercised within limits. In the large majority of countries, a minimum of independence exists: this is necessary if the administration of justice is to be conducted at all in civil, commercial and criminal matters. Yet independence does not go beyond a certain point, not just because courts have to uphold the principles on which the society is based but because they are themselves the products of their society and often of the more conservative parts of that society. This trend is typically reinforced by the recruitment mechanisms in which co-option plays a substantial part.

## The depth of rule adjudication

Even if judges are independent, they may not be entitled to intervene deeply in the rule application process, let alone in rule making, because they may not be allowed to question the validity of the rules which are being applied. The legal system is based on a hierarchy of rules. This means that judges can be asked to state whether a given document conforms to the 'parent' and more general rules on which the document is based. This is one of the principles of the rule of law. If courts are allowed to decide on such a matter, the depth of rule adjudication is obviously greater than if they are not. Moreover, the power of the courts in this respect may be more or less wide. It is truly comprehensive if it entitles judges to go beyond procedures and to examine whether the spirit of the 'dependent' rule is consistent with the spirit of the 'parent' rule.

## Constitutional control as a test case

Judicial supervision is at its deepest if rules can be assessed on grounds of their *constitutionality*, since the constitution is the most general rule which exists in a polity. But this control in depth is not concerned only with the constitutionality of decisions. Judges may be involved in a similar process at a somewhat lower level: namely, to assess if decisions taken by governments and other public bodies are legal – that is, conform with the provisions of statutes. In both cases, the idea is to see whether a (lower) rule is consistent with a (higher) rule. Naturally enough, however, the question of constitutional control has attracted more attention, since the 'will' of the legislator is challenged in such a case. This is why it has been claimed that judges are then involved in rule (un)making. Any assessment of a governmental decision, however detailed, by a court is a form of rule (un)making. But at the level of constitutional control, when the laws passed by legislatures are being questioned, the issue immediately becomes politically truly serious. If courts are allowed to define, interpret and limit the operation of statutes in the name of the constitution, they seem to be *above* all the rule-making agencies rather than merely separated from them.

However, the logic of constitutional control does also appear convincing. If a state operates on the basis of the 'rule of law', it seems to follow that no authority within this state should be allowed to act against principles of the law, even if this authority happens to be the legislative branch of the government. Yet, if courts can do so, this means that they (and, in practice, primarily the supreme courts) can supervise the legislature. Does liberal democracy entail *government by judges?* This worry was voiced at the time of the controversy between Roosevelt and the US Supreme Court, when reference was made to 'nine old men' running the country (the number of justices on the Supreme Court), instead of the Congress and the President (McCloskey, 1960: 220–31; Rostow, 1962: 148–56).

## Constitutional control and the control of legality

This is why there has long been hesitation, in liberal countries, about the extent to which courts should have the right to question the constitutionality of laws. To an extent at least, a similar hesitation has been noticeable with respect to the control by courts of the legality of governmental decisions. This is probably why both constitutional control and the control of legality grew out of practical circumstances rather than out of general principles.

### The development of constitutional control

*Constitutional control* emerged indirectly from the principle of arbitration. Where two or more authorities are in a position to demand the citizen's obedience, a body has to decide which of these authorities is to be obeyed. This problem arises particularly in federal states, since in these systems two types of authority are deemed to be equal in status. Supreme courts have therefore been set up first and foremost to adjudicate in disputes between these authorities, as we saw in Chapter 16. The American Supreme Court in particular was created for this purpose. Nothing in the American Constitution itself suggests that the Supreme Court is more than an arbiter between the component states and the federal government. Indeed, while it quashed legislation for the first time in 1803, it did not do so again until 1857; only from the end of the nineteenth century was the 'customary' practice of constitutional control wholly recognized. Full constitutional control was thus a gradual development which could be said to have resulted from the sharp distinction, made in the constitution, between the jurisdiction of the states and that of the federation – a distinction which the Supreme Court had been set up to protect (McClosky, 1960: 100–6; Wheare, 1963: 68–74; 1966: 100-20).

## The development of the control of legality

The *control of the legality* of governmental decisions developed out of the rather mundane desire to redress errors of judgement which public servants might make. In several continental European countries, councils were set up within the public service structure to examine such errors. Gradually, these councils expanded the type of their control. They were concerned at first only with the regularity of the procedures; they then came to examine the spirit in which public servants had acted; finally, they were prepared to look at the legality of the rules passed by the public agencies. When that point was reached, in some countries at least, the control had become truly general. In the same practical way in which general constitutional control had grown out of the more limited power of arbitration between states and federation, the control of the legality of decisions taken by the executive and the administrative agencies developed out of the more specific idea of ensuring that the public service should function efficiently (Ridley and Blondel, 1964: 154-9).

## Constitutional control in practice

The American Supreme Court's battle with F.D. Roosevelt in the 1930s was the most dramatic example of the limits beyond which a court, albeit endowed with great authority, cannot go without being challenged. After the US Supreme Court deemed unconstitutional part of the New Deal legislation designed to fight the depression of the 1930s, as we saw in Chapter 16, President Roosevelt threatened to ask Congress to pass a law which would have altered the composition of the Court through the appointment of new judges. The independence of the Court was thus at stake (McClosky, 1960: 164–9).

Although the threatened legislation was never formally discussed, the Court did sense the danger and desisted subsequently from quashing the federal legislation presented by Roosevelt. Gradually, it even began to follow another principle, known as the *principle of judicial realism*, according to which the Congress is to be given the 'benefit of the doubt' when it passes a bill. Acts of Congress were therefore quashed only if the breach of the constitution was blatant (McClosky, 1960: 180–7). Moreover, the Court has tended since then to concentrate its action on disputes between states and federation – directly or indirectly, as over matters of racial integration, or the drafting of electoral boundaries – and not on disputes between the federal government and an idealized version of the constitution. The celebrated case of *Brown* v. *Board of Education* (1954), which outlawed racial segregation in schools, is an example of such an action against, on that particular occasion, a local authority.

## Extension of the idea of constitutional control

Supreme courts tend to exist in federal states. Such courts are often, though not always, empowered to decide on the constitutionality of laws as well as to arbitrate between state and federal government. This function of arbitration can be extended beyond federal states to countries in which some separation of powers between various institutions, geographical or not, is stipulated by the constitution. It is thus in the logic of such a 'separation' for a supreme court to exist, even when countries are not federal, but where regions are given considerable autonomy, as happens in Latin America and in Italy, where regional authorities were gradually established after the Second World War. In a parallel manner, it is in the logic of the French Fifth Republic to give a Constitutional Council powers of arbitration between government and parliament, since the President of the Republic and parliament have a separate authority stemming from the fact that they are both elected directly by the people.

On the other hand, when there is not true separation, either on a geographical basis or between the branches of government, there has been considerable reluctance to set up a supreme court or constitutional council. In Britain, the Netherlands and the Scandinavian countries, for instance, the view according to which parliament is sovereign continues to be upheld, and courts cannot question the laws which this sovereign parliament passes.

There has none the less been a gradual tendency for the number of constitutional courts and councils to increase in the second half of the twentieth century. Perhaps the clearest example has been that of the French Constitutional Council, which became truly influential in the 1980s, but the influence of the Italian and Spanish courts has also been noticeable. At the level of the Council of Europe, the European Convention provides the European Court at Strasbourg with powers, in the field of human rights, which are to an extent equivalent to those of a constitutional court. A similar trend has been developing with respect to the Court of Justice of the European Union at Luxembourg in matters within its jurisdiction. The pendulum has thus swung back in the direction of granting judges the power to question the validity of documents issued by bodies of all types, from statutes to detailed orders, on grounds of their constitutionality. This change is almost certainly in part the result of the decline in the trust in politicians which has characterized many western countries in the last quarter of the twentieth century, and which has led to what might be described as the 'judicialization' of political life.

**BOX 20.2**
**The judicialization of political life**

Ever since politics has existed – at any rate, ever since political behaviour has been recorded – politics and law have been closely linked. Typically, the law has been placed at the service of politics. Kings and other rulers used lawyers to justify what they were doing. There have always been lawyers prepared to undertake these activities.

The law has also been placed at the service of democratic politics: liberal politicians invented a legal instrument, the constitution, and made it so solemn that what it prescribed would 'naturally' be obeyed.

Thus, in a sense, the 'judicialization' of politics is almost a natural phenomenon. As a matter of fact, the growth of administrative justice is also a form of judicialization of politics, in that (some, most, perhaps all) actions of public bodies have to be given a seal of judicial approval. The battles over the extension of the role of administrative courts have indeed been battles over whether politics should, or not, be 'judicialized'.

Yet the notion of the judicialization of politics typically goes further. It does not merely relate to the development of administrative courts; it is used in connection with the role of supreme courts when they quash legislation, and with that of those prosecutors and judges who investigate the activities, primarily the financial activities, of politicians.

What makes politicians complain is that the roles appear to be reversed. Traditionally, politicians have called the judicial tune: they have used the law. In what is commonly regarded as the judicialization of politics, judges have the upper hand and assess the actions of politicians.

How far judges can go in this direction without being stopped obviously varies from country to country and from time to time; how far they should go is a delicate matter. It is interesting to note that judges have typically exercised self-restraint in the past, as the episode of the US Supreme Court battle with Roosevelt in the 1930s shows. They may have become more sanguine since then, or perhaps more foolhardy.

## The control of legality in practice

The noticeable gain in favour of the idea of constitutional control, at least in the West, has been paralleled by an increase in the extent to which the control of legality is taking place. In the French case, the Council of State was given the right to examine the legality of all regulations, including the most solemn of these, known as governmental 'decrees'. The scope of the potential intervention of administrative courts was markedly increased as a result. Admittedly, as supreme courts have mostly done, administrative courts have used rather sparingly their power to quash the general regulations issued by governments. These courts tend to sanction principally the less general rules of national executives and the decisions of local bodies, perhaps because these are, indeed, often guilty of breaches of the law, but perhaps also because courts do not relish engaging repeatedly in major clashes with the national government. In France, the relatively limited propensity to sanction general governmental regulations is helped by the requirement that plaintiffs must raise their objections against a decision within two months of that decision being taken. This limitation does not exist in the case of the constitutional control exercised by the US Supreme Court (Ridley and Blondel, 1964: 157–9).

## Constitutional control and the control of legality assessed

Constitutional courts and administrative courts have thus tended to limit to an extent the scope of their intervention in practice. They have in this way avoided confronting legislatures and governments too often. Yet there does remain a difference in the depth of intervention of courts which question the constitutional character of laws or the legal character of governmental regulations, and of courts which merely satisfy themselves that the correct procedures have been followed. It used to be often noted, for instance, that British courts, which had adopted a restrictive view of their role, tended to give less protection to the citizen, perhaps because, being general courts, they were not fully accustomed to deal with administrative matters. The difference may not be as large as it once was, in part because some of the courts which used to be 'timid' in this respect have begun to undertake an active scrutiny of governmental actions, but it still exists (Griffith, 1985: 129–42).

As constitutional control becomes more widespread, an equilibrium seems to be found at an intermediate position, with respect both to constitutional control and to the control of legality. Courts came to realize that they could not extend their scrutiny too far into the governmental process. They did not wish to challenge or could not challenge frontally, the rule-making process of executives and assemblies too often. However, they fostered the development of principles of arbitration between the organs of state, and almost certainly ensured greater respect for legality, particularly at the regional and local levels and generally within the public service. These ideas have extended to a large number of countries in which neither constitutional control nor the judicial control of administration had existed in the past.

## The scope of rule adjudication

### A gradual increase

While traditional liberal theory dealt with the independence of courts and paid some attention to the depth of judicial control, it made practically no effort to extend the scope of rule adjudication. This is partly because the liberal theory of the role of the judiciary emerged before bureaucracies grew appreciably towards the end of the nineteenth century. Although the problem of the possible extension of the scope of rule adjudication did exist before bureaucracies had become large, it was not very salient at the time. Answers to problems were therefore often given haphazardly, and the institutions which were set up varied according to different country traditions. More often than not, these institutions took the form of councils, committees of inquiry, or tribunals, and, more recently, of ombudsmen's offices, rather than of formal courts.

This increase in the scope of rule adjudication with respect to bureaucratic action took place along two dimensions. One dimension concerns the *procedures*, and determines whether the bodies in charge of scrutinizing the bureaucracy have (or are close to having) a judicial character. Four steps can be distinguished:

1. Citizens are allowed to *register complaints* to an administrative authority about a decision. The case is allowed, but only by 'gracious pleasure' of the government.
2. A *specific inquiry* is allowed, but the committee of inquiry can only make a report and the political authority decides.
3. A *general procedure* is set up for future inquiries, though the administration retains the ultimate power.
4. A *committee, tribunal or court* is established which can reverse the decision. Only in this case is a judicial body really set up (D. Foulkes, 1976: 66–83; 107–19).

The second dimension of rule adjudication with respect to bureaucracies concerns the *fields* which these scrutinizing bodies can investigate. Complaints and special inquiries relate naturally to specific matters only; a general procedure of inquiry relates to a whole branch of the administration. Administrative councils and tribunals cover the whole public sector, although in all polities there are some exceptions. These include questions relating to national security or foreign affairs, in part because it is assumed, at least in liberal polities, that the government is responsible politically for such matters. In fact there is a debate over what should be deemed to be political issues and what should be deemed to be judicial issues. One can argue that the government is responsible to parliament for its decisions (for instance, on questions of the compulsory purchase of land) and that courts cannot enter significantly into such fields without effectively reducing the power of parliament. The problem is general: the power of parliament is necessarily reduced as rights given to citizens are increased and courts are set up to ensure that these rights are respected.

The scope of administrative rule adjudication has thus tended to be extended, also by following four steps:

1. *Matters relating to personnel*, in relation both to conditions of service and to dismissals, are being covered.
2. *The acquisition of property by public authorities* (for instance, by compulsory purchase) is open to challenge in administrative courts or tribunals.
3. The broad area of *collective services*, principally local, is also covered.

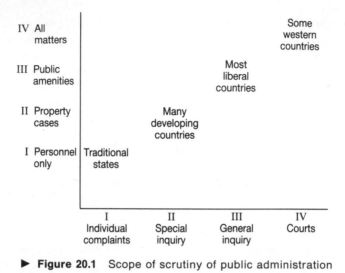

▶ **Figure 20.1**   Scope of scrutiny of public administration

4. The widest form of scrutiny relates to *all other state activities*, but this is almost never achieved. Admittedly, in liberal countries, some development of judicial scrutiny over security matters has begun to take place – for instance, in relation to the deportation of aliens or the granting of passports – but many governments, including in the West, continue to retain substantial discretion in these fields.

## Judicial control of public services

Countries of the contemporary world can be ranked in relation to the extent to which the scope of activities of the bureaucracy is covered by means of procedures ranging from the first type (complaints being made) to the fourth (a court is established). In liberal democratic countries, most of the activities relating to personal matters and to the acquisition of property are covered at least by means of general inquiries. On the other hand, only in a small number of countries do courts cover activities relating to collective services within the scope of general inquiries. Only very few countries, mainly in continental Europe – and in particular those which followed the procedure which gradually evolved in France – have developed a court in the full sense of the word empowered to cover activities relating to personnel, property and collective services. Finally, it is still exceptional for other state activities, and especially those concerned with the security of the nation, to be challengeable in a court.

## Practical difficulties in judicial scrutiny of public services

The gradual development of tribunals and courts dealing with public service matters has been slow. This is not merely because bureaucracies resisted the setting-up of formal processes on the basis of which administrative decisions can be scrutinized; it is also because of the nature of the problems. The control of public services by courts faces the same difficulties as other forms of control of public services. As we saw in Chapter 18, the further a controlling agency is from the body to be controlled, the more independent it is but the less it is able to understand fully the conduct of the public servants. To be effective, inquiries aiming at redressing grievances have therefore to be conducted by agents who are relatively close to those who took the decision. Hence, first, the value of committees of inquiry composed of persons engaged in similar activities and, consequently, the tendency for such committees to be created either *ad hoc* or within the department concerned; hence, second, a general tendency to staff committees with persons previously engaged in 'active' administration and who have a thorough knowledge of administrative processes. The principle of structural differentiation which is at the root of rule adjudication is therefore in part dysfunctional to the redress of administrative grievances.

## Administrative courts and ombudsmen

Such a conclusion goes against the principles of the liberal doctrine, since it seems paradoxical to suggest that redress can be better achieved by setting up institutions which are close to the public services. Yet this is what occurred. It occurred by means of setting up *administrative councils or courts*, of which there are examples in many countries. Some of these courts have a truly general jurisdiction; others have remained specialized 'tribunals' dealing, for instance, with special social benefits. Moreover, the scrutiny of administrative decisions has also been undertaken by other means, the most prominent formula being that of *ombudsmen's offices* on the Scandinavian model. These were first set up in Sweden and Finland, and were charged with the duty of examining the grievances of citizens in a wholly informal manner. From the 1960s onwards, these institutions began to be imitated in western Europe and elsewhere. Unlike judges, ombudsmen only investigate cases and present reports; but their decisions have come to acquire much authority, if not formally, at least in practice. The ombudsman machinery provides a simple, cheap and comprehensive means of redressing most types of grievance against the administration (Rowat, 1968; Caiden, 1983).

The increased scope of rule adjudication is connected to the growth of the bureaucracy. Below a critical level of growth, there is not normally enough scope for the development of full administrative courts. These did emerge in new countries in the 1950s and 1960s, partly because new countries had a larger bureaucracy than western European countries had at a similar state of development, and partly because they could imitate formulas which existed in the West. These courts remain relatively weak, however. This situation resembles to an extent that of France in the early part of the nineteenth century, when the supervision of the public services slowly began to take shape in that country.

The liberal theory of the judiciary was not concerned directly with the question of the control of the public services; it did, however, play some part in the development of this control. It provided a spur and a framework within which this control could take place. It is almost certainly because liberal and democratic values began to prevail that the scope of rule adjudication expanded so widely within the public sector.


# Overview

Courts are part of the *political process*, since governmental decisions and even statutes passed by the legislature may need judicial decisions to be implemented. Courts are also the place where citizens can challenge *decisions of public bodies*.

Courts need to be *independent* in order to provide redress. Yet this independence is difficult to achieve in practice: there is never full independence as far as *appointments* are concerned; and judges cannot be expected to go outside the *norms of the society*.

Courts may or may not be given powers to scrutinize the *constitutionality of laws* and the *legality of governmental decisions*. Constitutional courts have multiplied in the second half of the twentieth century; courts have also come to be more willing to look at the legality of documents. In both cases, however, there is a tendency not to go too far in challenging statutes and national executive decisions.

The *scrutiny of public service bodies* has increased, in terms both of the procedures which have been adopted and of the fields covered. One way in which this scrutiny has taken place is by means of networks of *administrative courts*; another way, more informal, is through the development of *ombudsmen's offices* within or alongside the public services themselves.

The role of judges in the political system is more extensive than in the past, even in authoritarian societies. *Constitutional control* and the *control of legality*, even if they are exercised somewhat sparingly, are important developments. Yet there are dangers in the 'judicialization' of political life going too far: if courts substitute themselves for legislatures and governments, instead of operating at the edges of rule making and of rule implementation, they risk losing some of their authority, and thus may no longer be able to fulfil unimpeded their role in society.


# Further reading

The judiciary is beginning to be recognized as a crucial actor in the political process, not merely in the context of constitutional courts, but generally. The literature on the subject has thus begun to be substantial. The question of the political role of judges, and also of their political biases, is taken up for Britain by J.A.G. Griffith, *The Politics of the Judiciary* (1985).

The role of American courts in politics is mainly viewed in terms of the action of supreme courts in constitutional review. This matter has naturally been analyzed at great length. Among the many works on the subject, see H. McClosky, *The American Supreme Court* (1960), E.V. Rostow, *The Sovereign Prerogative* (1962) and, above all, G. Schubert, *Constitutional Politics* (1960) and *Judicial Decision-Making* (1963).

For a presentation of the conception of the law put forward traditionally by Soviet analysts, see S. White, J. Gardner and G. Schöpflin, *Communist Political Systems* (1981).

On the European Court of Justice, see L.N. Brown and F.G. Jacobs, *The Court of Justice of the European Communities* (1989).

The question of the role of administrative courts has exercised British scholars for a long period, indeed up to the Second World War. As an example of the traditional view, see Lord Hewart, *The New Despotism* (1929). For a contemporary presentation of the problem, see D. Foulkes, *Introduction to Administrative Law* (1976).

On the characteristics and the development of ombudsman services, see D.C. Rowat, *The Ombudsman* (1968) and G.E. Caiden, ed., *The Ombudsman: An International Handbook* (1983).

# 21

# The policy process

## Introduction

Most developments in this volume are about the policy process. Demands are pressed (articulated); they become part of a programme (aggregated) or adopted in other ways by a government and, when required, by a legislature. The various elements of the programme are then turned into policies and subsequently implemented, perhaps only in part and perhaps only after a long time has elapsed. Thus what was originally only an *idea* becomes a *policy*.

Now that we have examined in some detail the ways in which different types of government articulate and aggregate demands, and turn these demands into policies, we can look at these matters the other way: that is, from the point of view of the overall process which these policies undergo. This is not only to summarize the characteristics of the political process from a different angle, but to come to a better appreciation of the effectiveness of political systems. These exist to allocate values in an authoritative manner and policies are the concrete expression of this allocation.

## The current limits of analysis

Serious problems arise as soon as we wish to obtain a precise and detailed picture of the policy process. We need to have at our disposal a large number of cases in order to be able to undertake meaningful comparisons. We also need to be able to analyze these cases on the basis of a common framework. Yet how this is to be done is far from clear. First, we have to determine the contours of what constitutes a policy. Second, the limits of the social constraints under which policy making and implementing take place must be clarified: policy making and implementing mean little if their substance is imposed by the structure of society. Third, assuming that authorities have some choice when they elaborate and develop policies, we have to discover the manner in which they come to their decisions. Do they act on the basis of rational calculations, or are they otherwise motivated? Fourth, we need to assess whether there is a mode of policy making and implementing which is common, for instance, to a country or even to types of country: that is to say, can one identify styles of the policy process?

- In the course of this chapter we shall therefore look first at how the *concept of policy* can be defined operationally, and examine distinctions which can be made among types of policy.
- Second, we shall examine to what extent *social constraints* operate on policy making and implementation, and, as a result, to what extent some policies at least have to be regarded as predetermined and alternatives as unfeasible.
- Third, we shall consider whether policies tend to be based on a *rational assessment* of goals and means, or whether other models of the policy process are more realistic.
- Fourth, we shall analyze the concept of *policy style* and see whether it helps to account for the variations in the way different political systems develop their policies.

## What is the policy process?

### Problems of definition

The expressions 'policy' and 'policy process' are frequently used: they are none the less vague and ambiguous. As a matter of fact, definitions of what a policy is are rare in the literature: Hague *et al.* are among the few who do address the problem. They state that a policy is 'a bundle of decisions [which] involves a general predisposition to respond in a particular way' (Hague *et al.*, 1993: 397). One can thus define policies as sets of decisions taken by one or several authorities and aiming at achieving some result.

What such a definition clearly manifests is that there is no guidance as to how large the set should be to constitute *one* policy and only one, since the term 'policy' can refer to activities pitched at different levels of generality. The scope to be given to the concept is not included in the definition. Thus the word can cover any of the following:

- The whole industrial action of a government over a number of years.
- The action of that government with respect to a given sector (steel or motor cars, for instance) over a more or less circumscribed period.
- The action of the government with respect to a particular firm within a branch of industry.

Could it be that these differences in the scope of what is regarded as being a policy correspond to the fact that what is crucial is *the single common goal* which characterizes that policy? This conclusion is difficult to sustain: there are always disagreements, minor perhaps, but none the less existing, among those who make and implement a given policy. Perhaps the policy might be regarded as having a broad general aim, but this one general aim often covers a multitude of 'secondary' aims about which there may be little unity.

There seems, therefore, no way of defining the scope of policies by logical reasoning. A policy is what one decides to call a policy; the level at which the concept is pitched depends on what the observer finds valuable to adopt. In these circumstances, it does not seem useful to look *systematically* for criteria: as Wildavsky somewhat impatiently said, efforts in such a direction are a waste of time (Wildavsky, 1979: 410).

Yet we cannot let the matter rest entirely at this point. If we cannot find a logical criterion, we must at least find practical solutions. In order to draw comparative conclusions about the different policies analyzed in a study, an understanding of the scope for that study needs to be reached. One can even go a little further: since policy analysis is undertaken to find out what processes of policy making and implementing are followed, the scope given to the concept of policy must not be too broad (i.e. a field of government should probably not be examined entirely); otherwise some of the differences among the processes followed will not be discovered. For example, the government may *impose* an overall structure to the relationship which it has with industry, but it may also be prepared to *negotiate the details* of that policy with those who are involved. If the analysis is conducted at too broad a level, one may conclude that the policy process is characterized by *imposition*; a more detailed examination shows that there is only *partial imposition*. This kind of problem is obviously acute in analyses which are specifically comparative. In such cases, the word 'policy' has to be given the same meaning everywhere: the *scope* at which analyses are pitched must be the same for each element which is being compared.

Since it is so important to have a clearly circumscribed meaning of what constitutes a policy in concrete situations, it is probable that some guidelines will gradually emerge as to what is the level of generality at which policies should best be studied. But this does not mean that, even then, a truly universal definition will be adopted; it means only that political scientists will come gradually to work at fairly similar levels, neither too 'broad' nor too 'narrow', simply because it is convenient to do so if coherent empirical analyses of policy processes are to be undertaken.

## Phases of the policy process

There is a further reason why one cannot easily determine what constitutes a policy: it is that the *phases* which specific policies undergo cannot clearly be distinguished, and that the beginning and end of the process cannot be defined precisely.

We saw in Chapter 18 that it is difficult and perhaps impossible to separate policy making from policy implementation. In particular, those who implement policies also have a hand in elaborating these policies. One reason is that part of the implementation process takes place as the policy is being 'made': it is obviously important to know whether a policy is applicable in practice before one adopts it fully. Policy making and policy implementing can also be intertwined: for instance, if a large margin of discretion is left to those in charge of implementation.

One might feel that it is a matter of secondary importance to be able to distinguish between policy making and policy implementation. What is surely important in assessing the effectiveness of policies is to know when a policy *begins* and when it *ends*. For instance, if we want to find out whether the policy process is slow or rapid, or whether many ideas (demands) are left aside and not handled, we must be able to decide when the process begins. Yet it is sometimes difficult to decide when a suggestion is more than just a suggestion. It is not always permissible to rely exclusively on formal criteria, such as the point in time when a bill or a regulation is drafted; it is not even sufficient to adopt as a criterion the moment when those in authority accept an idea, since they may simply want to 'float' that idea and see what the reactions will be. One has therefore to be content with rather rough distinctions, but efforts have to be made to discover more satisfactory distinguishing mechanisms.

A similar problem arises at the end of the process. We are interested in the *impact* or *outcome* of policies; yet it is often difficult to know exactly when policies are implemented. There may be delays because some time has to elapse during which there is uncertainty about what is to be done. Those in charge of implementation may, for instance, have to contact the bodies on which the policy is to have an impact, in order to examine how implementation is to take place. So long as this has not occurred, the policy is, so to speak, in limbo.

## Types of policy

It is difficult to discover the most appropriate level at which policies should be analyzed; it is also difficult to circumscribe the beginnings and ends of policies. But one can at least ascribe policies to a number of broad types, even if the boundaries between these types are not always precise.

The basis for such a distinction is not constituted by the substantive fields of the policies, although this may seem to be an obvious distinguishing feature. Processes of economic policy making, for instance, differ from processes in the fields of defence or foreign affairs. Yet to distinguish among fields does not provide a basis for a satisfactory classification of policies. The real differences which need to be taken into account stem from the general aims of the policies pursued in these fields. We must therefore determine what these aims are.

Two sets of criteria, which overlap somewhat, have been suggested. One consists in dividing policies into four distinct types: distributive, redistributive, regulatory and constituent (Lowi, 1972). *Distributive* policies promote activities: for instance, by means of grants. *Redistributive* policies aim at modifying the way in which resources are shared among the population, by extracting resources from some groups and allocating them to other groups. Such policies are therefore often regarded as being tantamount to equalizing resources among the population, although this is not always the case: a regressive tax policy is also redistributive, but in the other direction. *Regulatory* policies 'organize' the ways in which activities take place in a polity. Public authorities do not handle these activities themselves; they merely supervise the way they take place. *Constituent* policies, meanwhile, determine the nature and powers of public authorities, at both national and subnational levels.

Despite its merits, this classification leaves some problems unsolved. As Lowi himself recognized, some situations are ambiguous: a policy, especially one which is relatively broad, is likely to have elements of distribution and of regulation, for instance. This is why it may be more valuable to use the *costs and benefits* of policies. For instance and to simplify, one can assess whether these costs and benefits are spread throughout the society or are concentrated on certain groups. One thus determines four types of policy: those in which both costs and benefits are concentrated or, on the contrary, diffuse; those in which costs are concentrated and benefits diffuse; and those in which benefits are concentrated and costs diffuse. Naturally, costs and benefits may not be concentrated on the same groups. This typology has the advantage of distinguishing among redistributive policies and thus of providing rather more precise criteria to characterize the behaviour of public authorities (Dunn, 1994: 294-302).

Both these typologies use the *aims* of the policies as one of the variables. It has therefore to be assumed that these aims are clear and honestly presented, which may not always be the case. Yet one must still use the (presumed) aims of policies, since the determination of the effectiveness of these policies has to be based on a comparison between aims and impact.

## Individuals and socioeconomic forces

Especially in the 1960s and 1970s, a major debate opposed those who viewed western democracies as pluralistic and those who believed that they were dominated by a *power élite*. Ostensibly, this debate was about the *number of persons* involved in the decision-making process and about the extent to which these persons were truly *independent* of each other. The pluralists, among whom Dahl was the most prominent, claimed that decisions were taken by groups which were genuinely distinct (Dahl, 1963a: 3–8); the 'élitists', from Mills to Hunter, claimed that there was an élite dominating political decision making (Hunter, 1953; Mills, 1956).

More fundamentally, however, the debate was really about the role of individuals in society. The power élite was regarded as all-powerful not because of the *personal* role of those who belonged to it, but because the social *structure* (the 'community power structure', to use Hunter's expression) could not be really modified. The members of this élite were only acting the parts which 'society' had written for them.

A deterministic approach was also adopted, albeit in a different way, by those who claimed, broadly during the same period, that *non-decisions* were as important as *decisions* (Bachrach and Baratz, 1963: 641–51; 1970: 44). The emphasis on non-decisions was also based on a structural rather than an individualistic approach, the assumption being that the organization of society makes it difficult, indeed impossible, for certain issues to emerge. Moreover, some potential actors are deterred from proposing policies because they feel that it would be a waste of time, even dangerous, for them to do so; they would be opposed and stopped by the power élite (Ham and Hill, 1993: 69; Bachrach and Baratz, 1970: 46). Finally, the values and preferences of most are so shaped by their early socialization that some matters cannot even be raised. This is described as a form of *latent power* which structures society and may even be the real reason why consensus emerges (Lukes, 1974: 27; Ham and Hill, 1993: 70–1).

While society unquestionably structures both the mentalities (socialization) and the activities (non-decisions) of the members of that society, it seems highly unrealistic to adopt an extreme deterministic position suggesting that structures dominate entirely the action of individuals. What is more realistic is to attempt to determine the extent to which there is scope for the independent action of agents. Dahl did not deny that society was structured to an extent by various socioeconomic forces: his study of power in New Haven is in part a historical survey of the emergence of new social groups reducing the role of the traditional élites (Dahl, 1963b). The concept of *polyarchy* which Dahl elaborated is based on the recognition that liberal democracies are to be defined in terms of a *competition among groups* rather than in terms of *massive popular participation* (Dahl, 1971: 1–9).

While there has been a major theoretical debate about the extent to which individual agents can exercise effective influence in societies, the empirical support for the different standpoints has remained limited. There is still no means of determining whether, and if so to what extent, the influence of individual agents varies over time and space. This means that the debate is not likely to end soon. One must therefore argue, paralleling what Wildavsky said about the problem posed by the definition of the concept of policy, that one simply must go ahead and analyze policy processes. A better understanding of the relative role of individual agents and of social forces will be obtained as empirical studies develop.

## How far is the policy process rational?

The characteristic ways in which individual agents play a part in the policy process have also given rise to debates. For some scholars, the process must be regarded as essentially rational in character; for others, rationality is 'bounded' by substantial limits.

Early thinking on policy analysis centred on an idealized conception of what bureaucratic processes entailed. This conception stemmed directly or indirectly from Weber's approach. Bureaucratic processes meant rational behaviour: decision-makers surveyed both the most desirable goals and the most appropriate means to achieve these goals (Weber, 1968: 66–77).

Such a conception of bureaucratic behaviour soon appeared to correspond only partially to reality; a fully rational process of decision making is not even truly feasible. It is not feasible because the concept of rationality itself is so complex and varied that it is not possible to determine its contours precisely. What is regarded as rational can vary substantially. A fully rational model is also not feasible because of the vast complexities which it entails, especially over time, if decision-makers are to look systematically at alternatives before plumping for one of them.

Thus H. Simon, who founded modern administrative science, can be regarded as having both supported the view that administrative behaviour was based on principles of rationality and sustained the notion that what characterizes the policy process is *bounded rationality* (Simon, 1957: 241; Ham and Hill, 1993: 80). The idea of bounded rationality is based on the recognition that it is too costly, both in time and in financial resources, for decision-makers and implementers to examine all possible alternatives before taking their decisions. Rationality is 'bounded' because it is considered sufficient to look at those alternatives which are 'satisfactory or good enough' (Ham and Hill, 1993: 84).

Once the idea was accepted that bureaucratic processes were not necessarily wholly rational, one naturally went a step further and asked whether, in some cases at least, there was any rationality at all in these processes. This question led to the examination of the part played by 'culture' and by traditions in policy making and implementing. It came to be recognized that the policy process cannot be fully understood independently of the patterns of behaviour, and therefore of the cultural traditions, of the organizations in which these processes take place. Moreover, personal considerations are also at stake: decision-makers and implementers, in all organizations, are motivated by considerations of status and career as well as by the specific characteristics of the case which they are considering. The type of power which some may be able to exercise may thus have a substantial impact on the nature and timing of the decisions (Crozier, 1964: Part IV, Intr.).

Even if one leaves aside the obviously large impact on the policy process of these interpersonal relations within organizations, serious doubts have to be raised about the extent to which this process is or even can be 'rational'. The question of what rationality might mean in particular situations is always difficult, if not impossible, to determine. Once the idea of bounded rationality has been adopted, it is not difficult to go further and to point out that what guides policy-makers and implementers is, more than rationality, the fact that innovation is difficult and costly in terms of effort in convincing others or in changing procedures. It is easier to 'muddle through' or to act on the basis of *incrementalism* (Braybrooke and Lindblom, 1963: 73; Ham and Hill, 1993: 87). It could indeed be viewed as rational to behave in this way, since decisions are then more likely to be implemented because they do not go against prevailing habits.

As a matter of fact, students of policy processes have oscillated between the apparently more admirable model of rationality, even if it is only bounded rationality, and the apparently less intellectually defensible model of 'muddling through', incrementalism being perhaps a way of giving this model a somewhat more acceptable character. What this debate clearly indicates is that it is unrealistic to think of the policy process as having one form only. On the contrary, real-world policy processes are characterized by a wide variety of practices. These range from highly rational and truly systematic analyses of ends and means, to decisions entirely following previous practices because it is simpler and less cumbersome to do so. These variations are likely to be found within the same country; they are even more likely to be found on a cross-national basis. Although there have been no systematic analyses of policy processes across nations

---

**BOX 21.1**
## Policy making and the individual rationality of public servants

The policy process has typically been regarded as being at least potentially rational, although there may be substantial difficulties in the determination of what rationality consists of in particular cases. Rationality tends to be assumed because of the overall conception, indeed ideology, of the public service, whether the public service is deemed to exist primarily to implement the decisions of politicians or to act somewhat autonomously in the 'public interest'. This model of rationality may include 'muddling through', however, since public servants may not have the time to look for a variety of solutions, or the obstacles to other forms of action may be insuperable.

These approaches all have one element in common: namely, that public servants are motivated by the stated object or the purpose of the action. This means not only honesty, but also a lack of personal involvement in the policies which they prepare and implement.

Such a view is rather unrealistic. One may leave aside cases of dishonesty, not because they are non-existent, but because they lie outside the plane of the analysis. One should not, on the other hand, leave aside other forms of personal involvement. Civil servants pursue a career; they relate in different ways to those with whom they work or for whom they work (namely, the public). Such questions must be taken into consideration alongside the more 'noble' aspects of the decision process.

This does not mean abandoning rationality: it means extending it to include the 'individual rationality' of public servants as well as the 'collective rationality' of the stated object of the policy. These individual matters may play only a small part in the process (they may lead to small delays, for instance); but the incidence of these questions may sometimes be large. It is also likely to vary according to circumstances and from country to country: for instance, it is often said, somewhat impressionistically, that personal considerations play a substantial part in some of the new countries.

Another dimension of 'policy styles' may therefore need to be taken into consideration.

---

so far, what is known, admittedly somewhat impressionistically, does suggest that there are marked differences between, say, policy processes in Scandinavian countries and policy processes in large parts of the Third World. As an observer noted of public policy processes in Latin America, 'the growth of public bureaucracies has not yet sufficiently increased rationality in [the] making of public policy' (Sloan, 1984: 151). This seems to be an understatement; the comment would be even more of an understatement if it were made about other parts of the Third World.

## Policy styles and the policy process

These differences in policy processes still need to be clarified, despite the fact that policy analysis developed markedly from the 1960s. Among the reasons why differences are still not systematically surveyed is the fact that most work in the field is concentrated on western countries; but, even within these countries, the substantial variations which exist are also in need of much closer investigation.

One way of characterizing differences in policy processes across countries (or indeed within countries) has been through the concept of *policy style*. Policy styles help to grasp in a synthetic manner the idiosyncrasies of the practices of different polities with respect to the processes which are followed as policies develop. The concept of style assumes that 'policy-makers . . . often try to develop standard operating procedures for handling issues which arise on the political agenda' (Richardson, 1982: 2–3). It is argued that there are characteristic policy styles despite the fact that policy processes may vary from field to field, such differences being known as *sectorization*. Indeed, even if a general style cannot be found for all the policies of a country, one can probably identify styles which are at least characteristic of particular types of policy.

## Dimensions of policy style

To be useful, the concept of policy style must not remain vague: it needs to be operationalized in terms of concrete characteristics which can be found to exist to a different extent in different countries or in different situations. Richardson and his colleagues have suggested that there are indeed two dimensions on the basis of which styles can be defined (Richardson, 1982: 13). One of these measures the extent to which policy making and implementing tends to *react to or anticipate demands*; the other assesses the extent to which policies are *imposed or result from consensus*. There is probably some empirical relationship between positions on the two dimensions, at least to the extent that a liberal government will tend, over time at least, to be reactive; but there are exceptions. 'Transforming leadership' of the type which has been described by Burns and was referred to in Chapter 17 is in essence anticipatory, although it need not be based on imposition. Conversely, authoritarian policy-makers and implementers may well not anticipate demands; they may be content to 'do nothing' and at most react only if pressure becomes strong.

The analysis of policy styles has primarily been conducted with respect to western countries, in part since, as we have seen, policy analysis has also been primarily conducted in the context of these countries. This probably means a greater emphasis on reactive and consensual policy processes than if styles were studied on a world-wide basis. Yet, even in the context of the West, substantial differences are noted, both among countries and among types of policy, although it has also been suggested that policy styles may tend to converge over time.

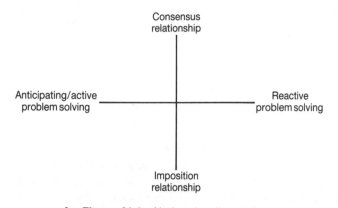

Consensus
relationship

Anticipating/active                                                        Reactive
problem solving                                                        problem solving

Imposition
relationship

▶ **Figure 21.1**  National policy styles
*Source*: J. Richardson, ed., *Policy Styles in Western Europe* (1982), London: Allen and
Unwin, p. 13.

## Policy styles in western countries

In western Europe, at least up to the 1980s, policy styles have been said to be moving towards the reactive and consensual form – a form which has been epitomized by and repeatedly analyzed under the label of *neo-corporatism* (Lehmbruch and Schmitter, 1982: 2–4). It was even suggested that advanced capitalist societies would necessarily move towards this style of policy making and implementing because of the part played by, and indeed the collusion between, groups representing producers in these societies. The smaller European democracies, Scandinavia, the Low Countries and Austria, were indeed shown to be characterized by policy processes in which the main function of governments appeared to consist in responding to demands from organized groups, or in endeavouring to obtain the support of the groups concerned when these governments were developing new policies. Governments and bureaucracies seemed increasingly reduced to being umpires rather than truly active agents in the policy process.

Originally, at least, such a model was less prevalent in Anglo-American polities and in France. The reasons were not the same in the two cases. As Anglo-American countries tended to operate on the basis of 'adversary' politics, there was less of a tendency to build consensus. Meanwhile, the policy-making process was more often reactive than anticipatory: these countries rarely adopted a 'planning approach' to policy. In France, there was also little emphasis on consensus, at least after the advent of the Fifth Republic in 1958, but the tradition of social engineering which had led to an emphasis on planning resulted in an anticipatory rather than a reactive policy style.

These differences decreased gradually in the course of the 1960s and 1970s. By the end of that period, Britain could be said to have moved towards a 'negotiated' policy style in which consensus prevailed, in part because of the failure of imposed policies proposed by governments (for example, on trade union reform and pay settlements). In France, from the mid-1970s onwards, the posture of rejecting negotiation came to be gradually replaced by one in which some place at least was given to discussions among the 'social partners'; meanwhile, government and bureaucracy found it increasingly difficult to maintain an anticipatory approach to policy making and implementing.

Yet, at the very moment when the neo-corporatist, consensual and reactive style seemed on the verge of becoming universally adopted, at least in the West, it started losing its appeal. The multiplication of demands rendered decision making slow and cumbersome when economic competition, especially from the countries of the Pacific rim, made it imperative for European countries to take difficult decisions designed to prevent economic decline. Thus Britain returned with a vengeance to a policy of confrontation in the 1980s, and the apparent success of this policy resulted in a loss of legitimacy of the neo-corporatist approach elsewhere. While the consensual model was not abandoned in all aspects of British policy, it came to be challenged in principle as well as in practice; it no longer seemed to be the only approach which could function effectively in advanced capitalist societies.

This challenge to neo-corporatism did not result in an increase in the anticipatory model of policy making and implementation, however, in part because the challenge to neo-corporatism was accompanied by privatizations and a move away from public intervention in the economy. Thus the policy style of western polities has tended to remain reactive, while moving away from consensus and towards imposition.


## Policy styles outside western countries

Outside western countries, the study of policy styles is embryonic. These styles manifestly vary, although this variety appears to have diminished, perhaps temporarily, as a result of the collapse of communist regimes in eastern European countries. In the preceding period, in principle at least, the style of the policy process was anticipatory and imposed in many authoritarian polities: this was officially stated to be the case both in Communist countries and in those Third World countries in which the ideology was 'progressive' or populist. On the other hand, decision makers in traditional conservative polities were likely to adopt a reactive policy style, although these policies, too, were more often imposed than negotiated.

It is not altogether clear how far the reality corresponded to these principles. In communist states, the anticipatory character of the policy process appeared to have been gradually undermined by the difficulties encountered in implementing a planned process of policy making: the economy was becoming too complex and the society seemed increasingly unwilling to continue being regimented. As the result, the reality of policy implementation probably became much more reactive than it was held to be in principle.

The difficulty in assessing the nature of policy processes in the Third World stems largely from the fact that, there too, the reality of policy styles may often be at great variance from what is being proclaimed about these processes. This is in part because, despite often having the desire to be very active, the bureaucracy of these countries is rarely well equipped to handle the problems which an anticipatory style of policy making and implementing entails – in terms of sophisticated planning, for instance. It is consequently difficult to determine even in broad terms where countries should be located concretely in the two-dimensional framework of policy styles.

What seems clear is that the collapse of eastern European communism in the late 1980s increased support in the Third World for the type of 'liberal' economic policies which had come to prevail in many western countries. Reactive policy styles have probably come to correspond as a result fairly widely to the reality, at least in much of Latin America and in parts of Africa. An anticipatory approach may still prevail in some aspects of the economic policies of the countries of the Pacific rim, perhaps even more, and almost certainly more effectively, than in China and the other Asian countries which have remained communist.

The two dimensions of policy styles can thus be used to categorize decision-making processes across the world. They constitute a means of assessing the nature and the changes in the characteristics of these styles over time as well as a means of assessing differences among countries. A large number of empirical analyses need to be undertaken, however, before it becomes possible to locate polities with some degree of accuracy within the space defined by these dimensions. Only then will it be permissible to determine whether, as a result of the collapse of the planned economies, all polities are moving towards consensual and reactive policy styles.

## Overview

The study of *policy processes* is a key element in the study of comparative government. It should be regarded as complementing the study of governmental processes.

This study is complex because progress in the field depends both on a large number of *case studies* being undertaken and a general *framework of analysis* being developed.

The scope of what constitutes policies remains *arbitrarily determined*, as these can cover a whole field, at one extreme, and a small number of decisions, at the other.

Policies can be distinguished in terms of their *distributive, redistributive, regulatory or structural character*; they can also be distinguished by reference to whether the *costs and benefits* which characterize them are concentrated or diffuse.

There has been a major debate about the extent to which *individual agents* or *socioeconomic forces* are at the origin of policy making and implementation. Empirical evidence is still too limited for a definite conclusion to be drawn.

There has also been a major debate about the extent to which the policy process is based on a fully *rational approach* or on *incrementalism*.

Policy processes can be distinguished by their *style*. These appear to differ according to two dimensions: those of *consensus versus imposition* and of *reaction versus anticipation*.

Up to the 1980s, it seemed that western countries were all moving towards the reactive and consensual policy style. The consensual approach has since declined in importance. Outside the West, variations in policy styles are substantial, but not as yet well monitored, although the anticipatory approach appears to have lost ground.

Given the large number of policies and policy types, one cannot expect a well-grounded theory of policy processes to emerge so long as systematic analyses of these processes are not undertaken. Findings about policy processes will also need to be related to the characteristics of political systems. When this is achieved, it will become possible to understand in a detailed manner the nature of the relationship between people and government in the contemporary world.

## Further reading

The subject of policy analysis has become one of the growth areas of political science, although comparative analyses are still relatively rare. The original classic in the field is the work of H.A. Simon, *Administrative Behaviour* (1957), first published in 1945. An important study is that of A. Wildavsky, *Speaking Truth to Power: The Art and Craft of Policy Analysis* (1979). A small but comprehensive volume is that of C. Ham and M. Hill, *The Policy Process in the Modern Capitalist State* (1993). A larger text is that of W.N. Dunn, *Public Policy Analysis* (1994).

On the debate over pluralism versus the power élite in decision-making processes, see F. Hunter, *Community Power Structure* (1953), C.W. Mills, *The Power Elite* (1956) and R.A. Dahl, *Who Governs?* (1963). On the more specific question of the structural constraints on decision making, see P. Bachrach and M.S. Baratz, *Power and Poverty* (1970).

More detailed aspects of the analysis of policy processes can be found in the volumes of P. Baehr and B. Wittrock, eds., *Policy Analysis and Policy Innovation* (1981), K.E. Portney, *Approaching Public Policy Analysis* (1986) and R. Rose, *Lesson-Drawing in Public Policy* (1993).

An earlier comparative analysis can be found in C. Liske, W. Loehr and J. McCamant *Comparative Public Policy* (1975). Subsequent studies are those of J. Richardson, ed., *Policy Styles in Western Europe* (1982) and A.J. Heidenheimer, H. Heclo and C.T. Adams, *Comparative Public Policy* (3rd edn, 1990).

# 22
# Government and people in contemporary politics

## Introduction

One of the most important questions of political life – perhaps the most important of all – is that of the nature, extent and strength of the relationship between people and government, between the rulers and the ruled. Comparative government analysis is devoted to discovering the many ways in which this relationship *does take place*, while, by and large, works on political theory are devoted to the examination of the manner in which it *should* be established. The institutions and the processes which have been described in the previous chapters can thus be regarded as efforts at providing a solution to the question of the link between people and government.

The question arises even in authoritarian systems, although in this case, much of the effort of the government consists in setting up bodies and establishing practices which attempt to prevent the people from being able to exercise direct influence. There is a relationship between the rulers and the ruled, but the rulers monopolize the communication process and thereby endeavour to press upon the citizens the value of their policies and of their overall goals. Thus the flow of influence goes primarily and, at the limit, exclusively downward.

Conversely, a 'perfect' democratic relationship would privilege upward communication and also, at the limit, exclude any downward communication. This is so unrealistic a scenario that it does not need to be discussed further; indeed, while there is scope for increasing the flow of upward communication and influence everywhere, it is surely valuable, even in a democracy, for leaders to be able to propose programmes and policies to the people. Thus, except in the most extreme authoritarian systems where all or nearly all communication takes place downward, the relationship between the rulers and the ruled consists of a mix of downward and upward influences, with liberal democratic systems including a greater proportion of upward influences, while downward influences prevail in authoritarian and imposed systems.

## Direct and indirect relationships

Whether it is upward or downward, however, the relationship between the rulers and the ruled has another universal characteristic, that of taking place in large part indirectly by means of institutions and of procedures. Political systems, as we have seen, need structures to perform the various operations (or 'functions') of articulation, aggregation, rule making and rule application (Almond and Powell, 1966: 16–33). The people are connected to the rulers – and the rulers to the people – through the structures which we analyzed in this volume: namely, groups, parties, governments and bureaucracies. As a result, all political systems have a 'representative' character, not in the technical constitutional sense that there are necessarily legislative assemblies which embody the sovereignty of the people, but in the more general political sense that the views and proposals of the population are communicated to the government, and vice versa, through intermediate bodies.

Not all relationships are indirect, however. Three types of direct link can and do exist. First, in some countries, and indeed to an increasing extent at least in the West, there are mechanisms by which the people can express their views directly and make their influence felt on specific issues. Admittedly, referendums and other techniques of 'direct' or 'semi-direct' democracy are often regarded as rather unsuccessful and as likely to be manipulated by leaders; but these techniques exist, they are sometimes used, and they are not always manipulated, as we saw in Chapter 11.

A second means of direct communication is provided by the parties themselves. If a party is large, if it is close to the aspirations of at least a majority of the population, and if the government is an emanation of that party, the relationship between government and people can be regarded as direct. This occurs, for instance, in systems of more than one party when a party is given a 'mandate' by the electorate to implement its programme: the election is then almost in the nature of a referendum in favour of the party. Indeed, more than with a referendum, that relationship covers a wide set of issues and can thus serve to sustain a general policy.

A similar conclusion can be drawn in the case of some single-party systems, although the influence tends to go downwards. In such cases, leaders claim generally that the party's standpoints must be supported because the party, by its very nature, constitutes the embodiment of the nation's future, a view which communist rulers in particular often tended to take. Thus an institution which in principle mediates between people and government is elevated to being the means by which a direct relationship is established between the rulers and the ruled, since the party is – or states that it is – the nation itself.

In the third place, at the broadest possible level, albeit in a necessarily vague and diffuse manner, direct links also result from the general support which the people have for some leaders, who, in turn, usually try to benefit directly from this support. The support given to the leaders can then be transferred to the political system, and thereby contribute to the stability of that system. This has occurred in a number of newly independent countries since the Second World War, as we saw in Chapters 5 and 17.

There are therefore three levels at which direct links exist between people and government. These direct links are more or less strong; they appear to an extent to be in competition with the many 'representative' ties which are built by groups of all kinds as well as by parties or by legislatures, for these ties are based on specific interests and issues, and not on global support. Thus the representative links can undermine direct relationships between people and government. This constitutes a danger because direct relationships provide the necessary framework within which groups and other institutions can develop and are able to press efficiently for the policies which they favour.

- In this chapter, we shall look first at the characteristics of *indirect forms* of relationship between people and government.
- In the second place, we shall examine *direct links* and see how far *processes of direct democracy, parties and leaders* combine to achieve a better communication between the rulers and the ruled.

## Indirect relations between people and government

### Group development

In the contemporary world, in many countries at least, the relationship between people and government takes place through *specialized organizations*. The number of these institutions has increased markedly, since one of the characteristics of socioeconomic development is structural differentiation (Almond and Powell, 1966: 48–9; 308ff.). Western societies have tens of thousands of associations dealing with specific issues, and they continue to multiply. The number of groups has also increased in developing countries, in a context in which all-embracing communal groups are declining in strength. Even in communist states, the number of groups increased gradually, although these groups were, by and large, controlled or at least supervised unless they remained clandestine.

While the emergence of more diffuse and broader social movements, such as ecological, pacifist and feminist movements, occasionally give the impression, especially in the West, that 'narrow' interest groups are less dominant, the need to act at a variety of levels and in a number of sectors remains as strong as in the past. Bodies dealing with specific issues and interests are manifestly not in decline.

The web of these intermediate bodies is in reality increasingly large and complex. Not only governments and parliamentarians, but parties and bureaucracies are 'advised' by groups and by their leaders; the larger groups are in turn 'advised' by smaller groups: for instance, trade unions and employers' associations are under significant pressure from specialized bodies. It therefore becomes difficult for the larger organizations and for the parties to develop policies independently. This is particularly true in the United States where parties have mostly abandoned to lobbies their function of policy initiation. But it is true even in many continental European polities where 'peak' organizations – that is, top business and trade union confederations – had dominated the scene in the 1960s and 1970s: groups with a narrow range of interests began to make their voice strongly heard from the late 1970s in these countries. This trend is indeed becoming truly universal: it is occurring in the Third World, though with substantial differences from country to country; it was unquestionably a contributory factor in the fall of eastern communist regimes in the late 1980s. Ecological bodies are prominent among these specialized groups in some of these polities.

## Group increase and participation

These changes can be interpreted as signs that participation is on the increase, and that the relationship between the rulers and the ruled is now developing in favour of the latter and against governmental decisions being dictated to the population from above. The effect would be not only to increase representation in general, but also to enlarge its scope by making it more probable that the views of the members of the public will be considered in some detail.

Such a development alters the traditional conception of representative government. This was based on the principle that the people were to exercise very broad choices only; indeed, the most extreme version of this theory entailed that parliamentarians should remain entirely unconstrained by their constituents, subject only to the condition that these parliamentarians might be defeated at the next election (Burke, 1975: 156–8). The idea became obsolete at the level of each representative with the development of parties, but these, too, tended to provide a general link. In fact they might provide, as we already suggested, a direct link, so long as it is general.

More specialized representation through groups has undermined or rendered more difficult the direct representation by parties. As these and, consequently, the legislatures become constrained by groups, the legal theory of representation is being superseded by one in which the bodies which are deemed to represent the people tend to become the spokesmen of groups or at best the arbiters among groups. This situation is not new; it has even prevailed in some countries for decades, in particular in the United States, where it was criticized on the grounds that special interests played too strong a part in various legislatures (Bryce, 1891: II, 152–7). Yet the model of group representation prevails in western countries; it is also gradually corresponding to the reality in other parts of the world. The conclusion which therefore appears to have to be drawn is that groups provide *real* representation and that citizens only become truly represented as and when the development of groups takes place on a large scale.

Such an interpretation of the role of groups can be regarded as over-optimistic, however. The main reason for the criticism of groups which was traditionally given is that decision making in these bodies has often tended to be in the hands of tiny minorities. This type of difficulty may be currently alleviated: even if most groups are dominated by small oligarchies, the multiplication of these bodies does reduce the strength of each of them, and increase the voice which ordinary people may have.

This is why the main problem may be not so much due to oligarchical tendencies at the top as to the fact that the broad mass of the public are rarely actively involved in the life of groups; at best, they are involved in an intermittent manner only. Participation in groups is low in all liberal democracies, even if there are differences from country to country. Only a small minority are sufficiently interested to be active, at least if one excludes ritualistic or ceremonial events (Verba and Nie, 1972: 25–43).

Admittedly, there are occasions in which a high degree of dissatisfaction against the way in which politics is run seems to lead to marked changes in levels of popular involvement: 'green' parties sometimes had a rapid success in the 1980s in part for that reason. Yet, by and large, these outbursts are typically short-lived and participation quickly returns to what it was previously.

Overall, there is probably none the less a long-term trend towards some increase in participation, not only in western countries, but in the rest of the world as well. One might therefore expect, in perhaps two or three generations, substantially higher levels of participation, possibly triggered by the emergence of even smaller and more specialized groups. Democratization is recent: not surprisingly, popular political involvement is also recent and it has to be learned gradually.

## Atomized societies

A situation in which more participation takes place through specialized groups may be one which has negative consequences for the efficiency of political systems. First, these systems could become 'choked' as a result of the large increase in the number of demands which is being made in the process. Second, the potential for aggregation may diminish, since the presence of a large number of specialised groups may have the effect of *atomizing* the society. By their very existence, these bodies are likely to reduce the support which the larger groups enjoy. Yet it is through the large groups that the aggregation of demands take place. What the society may gain in 'representativeness' may therefore be lost in terms of an increase in the number of cases of conflicts of allegiance among the citizens.

Such a development seems already to be taking place in some polities. For instance, the increase in the number of groups is one of the reasons which accounts for the decline in the allegiance of citizens of western countries to parties, and in particular to the older, broad-based parties. The growth in the number of 'independent' voters in the United States in the second half of the twentieth century, which was referred to in Chapter 11, is one example of a trend which, in various ways, also affects other liberal democracies, both with respect to parties and with respect to such broad-based organizations as trade unions and 'peak' employers' associations.

If the increase in the number of specialized groups results in a decline in the support given to parties and to large groups, the overall problem of representation in the political system is in effect not solved. The result would seem to be, on the contrary, an 'ungovernable' society because of the weakness of the centre and the large number of attacks made from the periphery. Indeed, ungovernability has become a matter of substantial concern, in particular since the 1970s, as we noted in Chapter 16 (Rose, 1980). It is all the more probable as a future development if the decline in support for

---

## BOX 22.1
## Atomization of society and political system

The multiplication of specialized groups, in western societies in particular, has given rise to the fear that these societies might become 'atomized'. Having different sets of goals, groups put pressure on the rule-making bodies in many directions. The rule-making bodies may not be strong enough to be able to resist these demands. The result is likely to be 'overload', lack of decisions and less support.

Thus atomization results from the fact that the aggregative machinery of parties has weakened: parties no longer can or want to elaborate comprehensive programmes; parties are no longer able to set up the dependent associations which link the population to them. The atomized society is composed of a huge number of groups, while parties 'float above' the space in which the groups operate.

The two models, that of the parties closely linked to many groups and that of the parties detached from groups, correspond broadly to the contrast between western European political systems and the American political system, a contrast which has existed for decades. Hence there may not be a universal trend towards the atomization of societies. Groups may become more autonomous in western Europe, but the move remains slow and partial; in America, the autonomy of groups simply perpetuates a situation which has characterized the United States since the setting-up of the country.

Why, then, should there be such a contrast? The difference between the institutional structure of the European and American political systems plays a part. The European cabinet system has a pyramidal structure, governmental parties being domesticated by the executive if the system is to work. The American presidential system is more pluralistic: parties are freer from the executive and so are the legislators, with federalism adding a further dimension of 'freedom'. The fact that groups are also freer may not appear so surprising.

Group tactics and group effectiveness are therefore different in the two systems. In a parliamentary cabinet system, pressure is put on the central government: it can easily be choked. In the United States, groups must attack many points in order to obtain what they wish; they cannot 'besiege' the whole system. The society may be more atomized, but the division of political responsibility among many centres of power means that, in the end, this atomization does not have the same grave consequences as those which it would have in a unitary country run by a cabinet system.

---

the centre of government is added to the technical complexity of modern administration, a complexity which in turn contributes to eroding even more the support which parties and larger groups enjoy among the population.

Since parties and large groups appear destined to become increasingly ineffective while more and more specific demands are made by more and more small groups, it is not surprising that there should be concern for the future stability and effectiveness of political systems. Can direct relationships between people and government still provide sufficiently strong links and thus counterbalance the tendency for society to be atomized as a result of the development of the more specialized groups?

## Direct links between people and government

### Support for liberal democracy in western polities

The image of an impotent political system being besieged by myriads of small groups may be one-sided. Where these groups are most numerous – that is, in western liberal democracies – the general support for the regime is also widespread, and indeed more widespread than it once was. In these societies, the norms of the political system are broadly shared both by the public at large and by the large majority of the political élite. Moreover, the support enjoyed by groups takes place within the broader context of the values of the political system: these are regarded as superior to or more fundamental than the specific goals of particular groups (Almond and Verba, 1979).

The precise effect of this support is difficult to assess. As we saw in Chapter 5, the role of legitimacy in political life is not yet measurable. But one point is clear: while support for the regime is likely to be affected by the multiplication of groups, it is also likely to affect the level of following of these groups. Anti-system groups are likely to find it difficult to obtain a large clientele in regimes which enjoy strong support. Fascist and Nazi parties grew in Italy and Germany at a time when the regimes of these countries had limited legitimacy. Conversely, anti-system parties have been either weak or contained after the Second World War in those and in other western European countries, since the legitimacy of the regimes has been high: for example, terrorist groups had only limited following in Italy and Germany in the 1970s. In those countries or regions in which support for the regime has been relatively low – for instance, on nationalistic grounds – as in Northern Ireland or in the Basque Country, terrorist organizations have survived much longer, as they have survived longer in some Latin American countries and in particular in Colombia and Peru (Gurr, 1970: 22–58; Zimmermann, 1980: 167–237).

Groups do not operate in a vacuum; on the contrary, the detailed demands of these organizations take place in the context of national values which, if broadly and deeply held, markedly constrain the ability of these bodies to press for their demands. This is indeed why western liberal democracies have functioned effectively, by and large, despite the substantial development of groups whose claims are often contradictory; it is, on the contrary, why, in communist states and in the Third World, groups created from above have not proved very effective. Thus, in liberal democracies, the direct link between people and political system seems able to remain strong, even when groups multiply and the society is moving towards associationalism, while it may be weak in imposed systems, even if a complex group structure is organized by the leaders of the political system.

As was pointed out early in this chapter, the direct link between people and government can take one of three different forms. There can be a substantial dose of direct democracy, and in particular a widespread use of referendums; political parties may be receiving a direct 'mandate; and leaders may enjoy a large support. Let us examine in turn the extent to which these may help to unite the polity.

## Direct democracy and referendums

Much has been said about the negative and especially the divisive effects of techniques of direct democracy, and in particular of referendums, on political systems. They are regarded as being manipulated by small groups, which use the fact that turnout tends to be low on technical issues to achieve what they want. The multiplication of referendums is even considered to have the converse result from the one which these procedures aim at producing: abstention increases as a function of the number of referendums.

As we saw in Chapter 11, these criticisms are correct in part only. Meanwhile, referendums have the great value of giving a stamp of legitimacy to some decisions which would otherwise be continuously put in question. This is true of large questions, such as that of the election of the French president by universal suffrage (1962), that of confirming British membership of the European Union (1975), and that of the maintenance of Quebec within Canada (1980). It is true also of more limited questions, such as occur often at the local and regional levels.

More generally, referendums prevent politics from being exercised exclusively at the top. They do so, in particular, by providing an opportunity to appeal from decisions taken by government or legislature to the broader mass of the people. This makes it possible for tensions and frustrations to be reduced. Referendums place the people at the centre, even if this occurs only occasionally and with substantial limitations. They unquestionably contribute to the development of the kind of direct links between rulers and ruled which need to be strengthened if the atomizing effect of specialized groups is to be countered.

## Political parties

Compared to referendums, political parties appear to provide first and foremost an *indirect* link: the views of the people seem mediated by party leaders and by representatives of the parties in the legislature. Yet there are circumstances in which they seem able to provide a *direct* link. This would seem to be true at one extreme with parties which aim at mobilizing the people in the name of an overall goal and, at the other, with competitive parties which succeed in obtaining a 'mandate' from the majority of the people for the policies which they propose to implement. Neither situation probably ever occurs in its purest form; but they both seem to exist in an embryonic manner.

## Mobilizing capabilities of parties

A party system can be described as having a direct mobilizing effect if it enlists the active support of a very large proportion of the population. Many citizens may not be clear about the party's goals or about the ways in which these goals can be achieved; but if large numbers believe that party action will improve society, the result is a close relationship not just between people and party, but between people and government. This occurs rarely: a high degree of congruence has to exist between the party leaders and the population. The birth of a nation may be one of the few moments when such a congruence exists.

Parties rarely have this mobilizing effect because there needs to be at the same time strong leadership at the top and deep party roots at the bottom. While personalized leadership was found to exist frequently in the developing world at the time of independence, the parties which these leaders set up and backed rarely had profound tentacles in the heart of the nation. Many have claimed to enjoy vast support among the population, communist parties in communist states, in particular, as well as numerous parties in single-party systems in developing countries, principally in Black Africa and in parts of Asia. Yet the hold of these parties over the population is usually more apparent than real, as we have seen. Even the well-developed communist parties do not appear to have had a profound effect on 'mentalities'; the single parties set up in African countries are usually so limited in extent that they are likely to touch only a small part of the (mainly rural) population. Thus only in some countries, principally in the Commonwealth, has the model of the mobilizing party been truly successful at least for a few years after independence: the Congress Party of India and the Tanzanian African National Union are perhaps the best examples of organizations having had at that point in time a truly large support among the population of their respective countries.

## Competitive mobilization in the West

The link between party and people can also be direct through competitive parties which succeed in giving the electoral contests a sufficiently tight programmatic character to approximate, in effect, a type of referendum. In this form of *competitive mobilization*, the people are deemed to give the winning party a 'mandate' to put forward a set of policies. The suggestion was made, in particular in Britain, that a mandate was given to the victorious party to carry out the proposals which that party had put forward during the election campaign (Birch, 1964: 16–22). There would be in this way a direct link between people and party, and indeed between people and government. However difficult to sustain empirically, as we are about to see, the 'theory of the mandate' remains widely accepted in British political circles; similar views are held at least in those liberal democratic countries where the 'adversary' rather than the 'consociational' model form of electoral competition tends to prevail.

# BOX 22.2
## Does the theory of the mandate have any value?

A 'responsible party system' has been the ideal towards which liberal democ-racies have been striving: that is, a party system in which the parties act on the basis of programmes which they have elaborated and which the electors have approved at a general election. Such a system functions truly well only with two parties, although a smaller third party may be accommodated. Britain 'invented' the responsible party system and passed on the idea to many countries, principally in the Commonwealth. American scholars have often deplored the fact that such a principle never took root in the United States.

The notion of the responsible party system appears based on a hypothesis: namely, that electors vote for programmes. Voting studies have shown this hypothesis to be false, as voting is more associated with long-standing patterns of 'party identification', which are in turn linked to socialization and to the groups with which electors associate. Issues and programmes enter only to a limited extent in voting decisions.

Moreover, it is simply unrealistic to assume that the electors who vote for a party fully accept the programme of that party. At best they will vote for a party because they prefer, on balance, one programme to another. This may be regarded as good because voters are forced to make a choice. Yet this in turn suggests that electors are unlikely to decide on the basis of programmes: they will avoid problems by following long-standing identifications.

What is rather pompously called the 'theory of the mandate' may therefore have to be rejected. But the idea remains vivid in the minds of politicians and of many members of the public. Is it that they are wholly mistaken and that myths simply die hard?

This may be a correct conclusion from an empirical standpoint, but there is also another view, which suggests that what the theory really means is that a party, having obtained a majority, enters into a contract with the people – the whole people and not just its supporters. The contract stipulates that the winning party can do what it said it would do, but no more and no less. While this view poses problems of implementation – for instance, with respect to emergencies – it has the value of broadly determining the boundaries of what a party in power must and must not do. The theory of the mandate thus becomes a means of restraining the government and of assessing the 'correctness' of its actions, rather than an empirical statement of voting behaviour.

Competitive mobilization occurs rarely, as four conditions have to be fulfilled and these obtain only occasionally in full:

1. Parties must be disciplined. This occurs in most western systems of more than one party, but not in all. It does not even take place in all two-party systems: in the United States, as we know, party discipline in Congress is comparatively low.
2. Voting has to be related to programmes, either on the basis of choices on major issues or through the ranking of issues. As we saw in Chapter 9, voting is often based on broad party identification and on images, rather than on issues.
3. The party battle must be clear-cut. This situation does not obtain in many party systems of the two-and-a-half, multi-dominant, or multiparty varieties. When there are more than two parties or when one of them is at a permanent disadvantage (and is indeed believed to be at a permanent disadvantage), the scope for competitive mobilization is markedly reduced: coalitions mediate the 'will of the people'.
4. Most important, there has to be genuine competition between party programmes. There are times when clear divisions occur, but there are more occasions when this does not take place. The situation which has typically tended to prevail in the United States (except perhaps in the 1930s), in which the two parties do not differ appreciably on broad issues, and in which detailed policies are largely the product of interest group action, has extended to other liberal democracies. From time to time, as in Britain in the 1980s with the arrival of Thatcher to power, or in France in 1981 with the Socialists coming to the government, polarization does occur; but this situation is rare. It takes place in a few countries only and, even there, no more than once or twice in a generation. This is partly because the parties themselves, as Downs pointed out, tend to move to the political centre in order to catch 'marginal' voters (Downs, 1957: 114–42).

Competitive mobilization being the exception, parties tend therefore to be more often vehicles for interest group demands than instruments of a direct link between people and government. But the *potential* for such a link does exist. Indeed, this potential is more important for the viability of the political system than might appear to be the case on the basis of the small number of occasions in which it occurs. Parties can become instruments of direct mobilization if tension is high. The existence of such a reserve opportunity is crucial: it gives the people the chance, in the context of a competitive framework, to use the parties to express their desire for change, and therefore to retain their overall support for the political system.

## The role of leadership

Several parties developed and played a large part because they were set up and 'propelled' by a strong and popular leader. More generally, to be able to move out of their difficulties and achieve some success, nations have had to rely on leaders. This is in part because, as is obvious, it is naturally easier for a population to follow an individual than to act on the basis of abstract values; at least it is easier for populations to support values if these are embodied in the person of a leader. This occurred with monarchs in the past; but, in the past too, generals and other types of usurper have frequently received from the people strong demonstrations of support, even against apparently well-established monarchs. In the conditions which emerged after the Second World War, the role of leaders naturally became large: as an unprecedented number of new nations were set up, and as new values were imposed on some of the older nations, in particular through communism, only strong leaders could hope to begin to 'nationalize' the sentiments of populations against traditional groups, tribal or ethnic, or against traditional values hitherto widely held.

The role of strong leaders has been felt in western countries as well, perhaps even more than in the past. Many leaders of these countries have helped to strengthen the cause of their party. Occasionally they went beyond party and adopted a national posture: for instance, when the political system was reconstructed, as in West Germany in 1949 with Adenauer or in France in 1958 with De Gaulle. Leadership is thus a universal instrument by which links between people and government continue to be direct and are even more direct, than they were in the past in many parts of the world.

Thus leadership, parties and mechanisms of direct democracy combine to maintain direct links between the rulers and the ruled. The tendency towards break-up or atomization which results from the multiplication of groups with specialized goals is thus counterbalanced, to a substantial extent and in many countries at least, by the unifying tendencies provided by these direct links. There is therefore a strong likelihood that aggregation will continue to be high in liberal democratic polities, even if this is likely to be a difficult task which, occasionally, can lead to major tensions.

## Overview

The question of the *relationship between the rulers and the ruled* is the key issue of political analysis and, indeed, of political theory.

The multiplication of groups can lead to a *greater participation* and a *better representation* of the different points of view and interests in political systems.

The multiplication of groups does lead, on the other hand, to a very large number of demands which the political system finds *difficult to aggregate* and therefore to cope with. The political system may become *atomized* as a result.

*Direct links* between people and the political system are needed to counterbalance the multiplication of groups. Such direct links do exist, stemming from direct democracy, parties and leaders.

Despite the problems which they pose in terms of possible manipulation, the mechanisms of *direct democracy*, and *referendums* in particular, help the population to be more closely involved in decision-making processes.

*Parties* can in some cases lead to mobilization, as has occurred occasionally in authoritarian countries, and to competitive mobilization, as occurs sometimes in liberal democracies.

*Leaders* provide everywhere a focus for the population. Many have been dictators and tyrants, but many have also contributed importantly to giving unity to their country and to making the population feel closer to the values which their country stood for.

There is therefore probably only a limited danger that political systems will disintegrate merely because groups multiply in a society. Direct links exist; they will become tenuous only if the political system itself is weak – for instance, because nation building is insufficient or because the regime's goals are too distant from those of the people. It is then not so much that groups undermine the system, but that the system itself does not have enough internal strength. Direct ties between the rulers and the ruled have to be strong for political systems to function effectively. But these can be maintained even where large numbers of groups representing special interests play a significant part in political life.

## Further reading

Most of the reading relating to this chapter has been mentioned in previous chapters, especially in Part I of the book. See in particular Chilcote (1981), Almond and Powell (1966). On the extent of support for political systems, see G.A. Almond and S. Verba, *The Civic Culture Revisited* (1979). On the tendency of parties to move to the centre, see A. Downs, *An Economic Theory of Democracy* (1957: 114–42).

On the characteristics of referendums, see D.E. Butler, ed., *Referendums: A Comparative Study* (1978) and A. Ranney, ed., *The Referendum Device* (1981). See also the further reading at the end of Chapter 11.

On participation, see S. Verba and N.H. Nie, *Participation in America* (1972) and S. Verba, N.H. Nie and Jae-on Kim, *Participation and Political Equality* (1978). On types of 'anti-system' participation, see T.R. Gurr, *Why Men Rebel* (1970) and T.R. Gurr, ed., *Handbook of Political Conflict* (1980).

The traditional view of representation is strongly expressed by Burke, *Letters to the Electors of Bristol* (Copeland, 1950–70). On the theory of the mandate, see A.H. Birch, *Representative and Responsible Government* (1964). For a classical view of the effects of groups on legislatures, see Lord Bryce, *The American Commonwealth* (1891: Part IV).

# 23

# The future of the study of comparative government

## Introduction

In the course of the second half of the twentieth century, the study of comparative government has been transformed out of recognition. This discipline is old: originally, for Aristotle and Montesquieu for instance, it was concerned with the study of the behaviour of all the polities of the world; but with the development of *constitutionalism* in the nineteenth century, analyses came to be devoted almost exclusively to liberal countries, on the assumption that all states would progressively be liberal as constitutionalism spread. This assumption turned out to be false – or at best premature. As a result, a realistic study of comparative government needed to have a broader scope: the aim was to understand the characteristics of all governments and to discover their dynamics.

This was the goal of those who, in the late 1950s and early 1960s, began to rethink the basis of the discipline. *New conceptual frameworks* had to be discovered to replace those which were based on constitutionalism. Not surprisingly, therefore, most of the early developments in this regard were concerned with *model making*, as was particularly the case with the application of structural functionalism and systems analysis to comparative government (Almond and Coleman, 1960; Deutsch, 1963). Gradually, however, there came to be greater interest in the discovery of *detailed findings* and in the search for *general relationships at the middle range*, but these developments are recent and have naturally so far produced only relatively limited results. It is worth examining the progress made and suggesting directions for future inquiries.

- In this concluding chapter, let us recapitulate by first returning to the *general framework*, to the problems which it poses, and in particular to the role played by norms and institutions in structuring behaviour.
- We shall then, second, look at *middle-range analyses* and see where gaps need to be filled in order to obtain a better understanding of the life of political systems.

384

## General theory: norms, structures and behaviour

### Political systems and the three-dimensional space of norms

Perhaps the greatest difficulty to overcome in comparative government results from the fact that behaviour is circumscribed – structured – by institutions and procedures. These in turn are related to the norms and values prevailing in political systems. One must therefore first classify polities according to these norms and, to do so, refer to three dimensions, relating respectively to the extent of *popular participation*, to the *means* on the basis of which political life is conducted, and to the *substantive goals* which the regime attempts to put forward.

Two of these dimensions have long been adopted, indeed were adopted by Aristotle; the third, the one which is concerned with policy goals, was neglected in the past, in large part because constitutionalism stressed liberalism and democracy as the yardsticks according to which political systems should be classified (Dahl, 1971). In the contemporary world, in which much emphasis is placed on socioeconomic development, it is simply unrealistic not to recognize that policy goals are a major element in the categorization of political systems. We therefore need to locate these systems in the space defined by these three dimensions. All three are conceptually clear; there are difficulties of operationalization, however, and so far at least, as we saw in Chapter 3, it has been possible to place regimes only in a broad manner in the three-dimensional space.

### The relationship between norms and structures

The second problem to be solved concerns the relationship between norms and structures. There are major difficulties in this respect, both at the conceptual and at the operational level. All political systems have structures, some of which are defined in detail by laws or constitutions, others having emerged gradually by custom. The way these structures affect the political system is unclear. Each structure can perform different operations or, in Almond's terms, different 'functions' (Almond and Coleman, 1960; Almond and Powell, 1966). These operations have been identified: demands arise from a variety of points in the polity; they are articulated and aggregated before they become policies and are implemented. However, the structures through which the demands are made and the policies elaborated vary markedly. They vary for a number of reasons, not all of which are entirely known, but among these reasons is the fact that traditions differ from polity to polity, and that there is imposition in many regimes.

### Operations performed by structures in political systems

So far at least, there has been little systematic progress in finding means of assessing these variations in detail, but a number of general points can be made in this respect.

First, by and large, the *national executive or government* is the body primarily in charge of rule making; it is subject to limitations, however. These limitations come from *legislatures*, but only to an extent, as most legislatures are unable to influence rule making significantly and few of them truly initiate policies. Yet they may signal ideas and exercise pressure; they are also concerned with rule application, not because they implement rules themselves, but because they attempt to scrutinize and, wherever possible, to modify the implementation of these rules.

*Bureaucracies (and the military)* are also involved in rule making, despite the fact that they exist in principle to apply the policies elaborated by the government: the national executive has therefore to share part of rule making with public servants.

Rule making and rule implementation are not the only operations which bureaucracies and the military perform. On the other hand, the bodies which are often regarded as primarily concerned with pressing demands, *groups and parties*, are sometimes concerned also with rule making and, even more, with rule application. When groups and parties are organized from above to be the means by which governments attempt to strengthen their hold on the country, they do not aggregate demands, or at least do not *only* aggregate demands: they play a major part in implementation. In such cases, articulation and aggregation may be achieved in part secretly, by bodies prohibited by the regime, and in part by the bureaucracy and the military, at least within the context of the range of policies which the leaders tolerate.

Thus the same structures can and do fulfil both an 'upward' or 'input' function and a 'downward' or 'output' function, depending on the characteristics of the political system and in particular of its norms. This is true of parties, of groups, of bureaucracies, of the military, and even of courts; it is indeed probably the case that, everywhere, structures fulfil both input and output functions, but to a different extent. Bureaucracies are concerned with demands as well as with the implementation of policies; parties are involved at least with a modicum of implementation as well as with the aggregation of demands.

The extent of imposition has a substantial part to play in this respect. Where there is little imposition, groups and parties are mainly concerned with articulation and aggregation, while bureaucracies and armies are mainly concerned with rule implementation, as well as, to an extent, with rule making. Where imposition is strong, parties and at least many of the groups are likely to be deliberately set up in order to help rule implementation, while the bureaucracy and even the military can constitute significant channels of articulation and aggregation.

## The nature and characteristics of imposition

The extent to which a regime is liberal or imposed therefore has a major effect, alongside other norms, in determining both the configuration and the characteristics of institutions and procedures. It is therefore essential to understand better the *mechanics of imposition*. We still do not know how much, or for how long, a system can be imposed: dictatorships fall periodically, but some remain in existence for decades. We do not know well the *dynamics of imposition*: we know why governments resort to it; but we do not know under what conditions or to what extent governments can increase their support, in the long run, by using authoritarian means. We do not even know how far charismatic leadership and well-organized parties can help a government to win the hearts of a disaffected population.

After 1945, much was made of the extent to which communist systems on the Soviet model succeeded in introducing new norms; but these regimes have mostly collapsed, not only in eastern Europe and in what was the Soviet Union, but also in the rest of the world. They have not succeeded in imposing the new norms and the structures which had been created to embody these norms. This development suggests that governments have great difficulties in ensuring that wholly new structures take real roots. A better understanding of the dynamics of imposition and of legitimacy building and unbuilding is therefore essential.

## The emergence and development of structures

More fundamentally, the question at stake is that of the conditions of emergence and development of structures. New structures are set up every day, while old structures are also somewhat modified every day. In all political systems, there are therefore large numbers of institutions at different levels of growth and maturity. Some give support to others; some undermine others. There are thus, so to speak, 'baby structures', which need to be upheld and protected, and decaying structures, which are gradually disintegrating. The *rate* at which structures grow and decay is not known: all we know is that this movement is relatively slow, and that it cannot easily be speeded up.

The examination of the development of structures will lead to a better understanding of legitimacy, since the life of institutions provides a history of the support which they enjoy. A better understanding of individual structural development will in turn provide better insights into the life of political systems. This is the type of question with which general theory needs to be concerned in order to make comparative government progress. Only in this way will the problem of the relationship between norms and structures and the problem of the effective role of structures begin to be understood.

## Middle-range theory: the dynamics of structures

In the early 1960s, emphasis tended to be placed on the need to make a theoretical breakthrough and to discover a general model of the political system. What was not sufficiently appreciated at the time was that it was not possible to move easily from a broad descriptive framework to truly causal analyses without an understanding of the dynamics of legitimacy, institution building and normative change. The realization that these problems are prerequisites to the build-up of a systematic theory led to a shift to less ambitious aims and to a greater concentration on *middle-range analyses* (Blondel, 1981: 178–85). The result has been a series of efforts designed to determine the effect of individual structures in different types of political system.

---

## BOX 23.1
## Comparative government and middle-range analyses

The question of the relative value of deduction and induction poses problems in all scientific disciplines at some point of their development. It would be intellectually more satisfactory to be able to proceed by deduction: if we could use mathematical logic to develop the consequences of a small number of axioms and postulates, an elegant theory would emerge. Analyses would be more rigorous.

No scientific discipline has proceeded entirely in this manner, however. In each case (including in the case of a science close to mathematics, such as astronomy), progress has been marked by descriptions. Deduction has tended to come afterwards, to give a retrospective stamp of approval.

The dilemma is not only about the merits of the two approaches, deductive and descriptive; it is also about two types of scholarship, one primarily concerned with rigour, even if little reality is captured in this way, and one concerned to amass facts and curious about discovering what is going on.

This debate has taken place in political science and in comparative government in particular. It has taken the form of the opposition between 'grand theory' and detailed analyses. 'Grand theory' disappointed because it scarcely led to theory at all; its real value was more to develop frameworks than produce propositions. Those who wished to obtain a detailed picture of reality turned away from general theory building. In doing so, they faced another problem, however, that of having to resort to single-country descriptions. To reject grand models seemed also to entail having to reject analysis altogether.

Middle-range studies constitute a significant breakthrough: they allow for descriptions, but within a comparative framework provided by institutions, groups and indeed the patterns of behaviour which fashion political systems. Middle-range studies are more than sheer descriptions. They are even partly deductive in character as they assume the existence of relationships among phenomena: they look, for instance, at the way similar structures (parties, legislatures, etc.) behave in different circumstances. They have led to systematic work and have thus transformed the nature of investigations in comparative government.

---

### Groups and movements

Developments at the middle-range level have been impressive, even if much has still to be undertaken (Blondel, 1982: 162–85). Thus the panorama of *group configurations* in various types of society is better understood. This has led to contrasting those societies in which large communal groups prevail to those in which there is a predominance of 'man-made' administrative institutions, such as the bureaucracy and the military, or dependent associations, such as single parties, or freely developing associations, such as single-issue groups. The break-up of customary bodies is slow, and the move towards *associationalism* is patchy and somewhat uncertain. Indeed, the spread of associationalism carries with it the seeds of serious problems, since associations provide little basis for aggregating demands in societies. There is therefore a need for a careful mapping of the different ways in which polities move from dominance by customary groups to associationalism, as well as of the extent to which, beyond a certain point, social movements may reintroduce feelings of community and indirectly reduce what would otherwise be the excessive societal fragmentation resulting from the existence of many associations.

## Political parties

One of the fields in which cross-analysis is relatively old is that of political parties. Theory started in the late nineteenth and early twentieth centuries with the development of the 'iron law of oligarchy' (Michels, 1949); mass parties and the 'law' relating electoral systems to party systems were discussed from the 1930s onwards (Hermens, 1941; Duverger, 1954; Rae, 1971). These analyses have shaped the direction of the studies in the field. Admittedly, not enough has been done as yet to extend theory beyond competitive party systems; not enough has been done either to understand the dynamics of party organization, particularly in the context of parties whose mass membership is in decline, although this aspect is gradually coming under closer investigation (Panebianco, 1988; Bartolini and Mair, 1990).

What we do not know well is how much 'weight' to attribute to political parties in different polities, and to what extent this weight corresponds to the fact that the parties are engaged in articulation, aggregation, rule making or rule implementation. We know the point at which parties cease to need the support of a broad group and can be said to be in 'orbit' and become legitimate, although we are still rather ignorant of the possible subsequent decline of this legitimacy.

We know much about *party systems* and about their characteristics, as well as about the effect of these party systems on governmental life (Downs, 1957). The way in which parties are inserted in political systems is now well appreciated: what needs to be better understood is why this insertion appears to be diminishing, at least in many countries.

## Bureaucracy and the military

Important studies of bureaucracies and of the military have also taken place. The conditions maximizing *military intervention* have been examined systematically; descriptions stressing the national character of this intervention have been replaced by general propositions linking types of intervention with socioeconomic development. A substantial advance has also been made with respect to *bureaucracies*, in both developed and developing countries. These studies have moved from a description of the general characteristics of administrative structures to the examination of the problems posed by public service culture (particularly in relation to general political culture), and to the difficulties raised by the part which administrative bodies take in rule making.

## Political aspects of the role of courts

Courts played a large part in nineteenth-century liberal institutional theory, as they were viewed as guardians of the constitution. This role has now expanded, although the expansion did not necessarily take place according to the canons of liberal judicial independence. For a while, the new role of courts was not given much prominence in comparative government analysis. This situation changed as the matter of the control of the public services began to raise major problems for rule-makers as well as for citizens. The geographical scope of current studies is still limited, however; there is also a need to introduce all types of rule adjudicating bodies – courts, commissions, tribunals, ombudsmen's offices – into the main body of comparative government analysis, not only in the context of western countries, but on a world-wide basis.

## Legislatures and executives

Where progress needed to be made most was in relation to the core of the political system, since there was little real understanding in the 1950s and 1960s of the role of legislatures and of the modes of behaviour of national executives. A major effort was made in the 1970s to analyze precisely the nature of the activities of *legislatures* in both liberal and authoritarian systems. There was at first considerable scepticism, since it was widely noted that these bodies rarely truly made the rules; but it became gradually recognized that legislatures were important in many ways. One has to go beyond the examination of activities on the floor of these bodies, and even of activities taking place within the physical confines of the assembly building; one then notices that legislatures exercise influence in many aspects of policy, detailed, intermediate and broad (Blondel, 1973; Mezey, 1979). A greater awareness has thus developed of what legislatures can and cannot do, although it still remains rather unclear why some of them, such as the United States Congress, play a much larger part than others in the political life of their country.

The *national executive* has also been an object of systematic investigation. Analyses of the military, of the bureaucracy and of parties first led to the conclusion that the effective scope of governmental action was limited; this view has been gradually modified. Studies of individual leaders have provided a rich descriptive base, alongside works on the politics of individual countries (George and George, 1956; Barber, 1977). Comparative analyses have thus started to examine what governments do in different institutional contexts. The participation of members of governments in decision making is also being examined (Blondel and Thiebault, 1991; Blondel and Muller-Rommel, 1993). There are still many gaps, due in part to the problems of access which naturally surround inquiries at the centre of government; but a comprehensive image of the most sensitive part of the machinery of political systems is beginning to emerge.

All aspects of political life are thus becoming better known. What was previously thought to be too complex to study is being investigated. Middle-range analyses can provide a basis for the development of comparative government, despite the fact that we still lack a general theory of the relationship between norms, structures and behaviour, of legitimacy, and of institutional development. What the evolution of comparative government in the last decades of the twentieth century has shown is that progress depends essentially on a systematic analysis of each *type of institution*, governments and legislatures, military and bureaucracies, parties and groups, before a theory can develop in such fields as legitimacy and institutionalization.


## Overview

Comparative government had come to be concerned almost exclusively with *constitutional structures* before an effort was made to develop *general models* in the 1960s.

General model making proved premature, however, as such fundamental questions as the *relationship between norms and structures* or the *conditions of development of institutions* remained difficult to assess except in a rather vague manner.

What is markedly more fruitful is to concentrate on the *middle range*. Cross-national studies of groups, parties, bureaucracies, the military, legislatures and national executives have become markedly more systematic, thus creating the infrastructure necessary for the build-up of a future general theory.

The study of comparative government will not provide quick pay-offs for those who expect 'recipes' for a new political order. Physics and biology have taken decades to advance, even after the mathematics which they required had been developed to a point which the tools of political science have scarcely begun to reach.

Other social sciences, mainly economics and psychology, have become increasingly successful, though on a rather narrow front. In some aspects of political analysis, pay-offs have also been rather large.

Comparative government poses more complex problems; it needs both a concern for a detailed knowledge of countries and of their institutions and an ability to deal with general models; it needs an interest in concrete situations and a desire to bring these situations within a common mould. Whether comparative government has reached the 'positive' age is a matter of judgement, but there is fervour and tension in the discipline. Tension, as we know, is characteristic of the take-off stage in political life: tension in comparative government may also be an indication that the discipline has now taken off.

# Further reading

For a general survey of the evolution of comparative government, see in particular J. Blondel, *The Discipline of Politics* (1981) and L.C. Mayer, *Comparative Political Inquiry* (1972).

# Bibliography

## General Works on Comparative Government

G.A. Almond and J.S. Coleman, *The Politics of the Developing Areas* (1960) Princeton, NJ: Princeton University Press

G.A. Almond and G.B. Powell, *Comparative Politics: A Developmental Approach* (1966) Boston, Mass: Little, Brown & Co.

G.A. Almond and G.B. Powell, *Comparative Politics* (1976; new edn, 1978) Boston, Mass: Little, Brown & Co.

D.E. Apter, *Ideology and Discontent* (1964) New York, NY: Free Press

D.E. Apter, *The Politics of Modernization* (1965) Chicago, Ill.: Chicago University Press

A. Arblaster and S. Lukes, eds., *The Good Society* (1971) London: Methuen

Aristotle, *The Politics* (1962) Harmondsworth, Middlesex: Penguin

B. Badie, 'Comparative analysis in political science: requiem or resurrection?' *Political Studies* (1989) **37** (3), pp. 340–51

A.H. Birch, *Representative and Responsible Government* (1964) London: Allen and Unwin

J. Blondel, *A Reader in Comparative Government* (1969) London: Macmillan

J. Blondel, *The Discipline of Politics* (1981) London: Butterworth

R. Chilcote, *Theories of Comparative Politics* (1981) Boulder, Colo.: Westview

R.A. Dahl, *Modern Political Analysis* (1963a), Englewood Cliffs, NJ: Prentice Hall

K.W. Deutsch, *The Nerves of Government* (1963) New York, NY: Free Press

M. Dogan and G. Pelassy, *How to Compare Nations* (1984) Chatham, NJ: Chatham House

D. Easton, *The Political System* (1953) New York, NY: Knopf

D. Easton, *A Systems Analysis of Political Life* (1965) New York, NY: Wiley

P. Evans, D. Rueschemeyer and T. Skocpol, eds., *Bringing the State Back In* (1985) Cambridge: Cambridge University Press

R. Hague, M. Harrop and S. Breslin, *Comparative Government and Politics: An Introduction* (3rd edn, 1993) Basingstoke, Hants: Macmillan

T. Hobbes, *Leviathan* (1968 edn) Harmondsworth: Penguin Books

R.T. Holt and J.E. Turner, *The Methodology of Comparative Research* (1970) New York, NY: Free Press

R.J. Jackson and M.B. Stein, eds., *Issues in Comparative Politics* (1971) New York, NY: St Martin's Press

M. Landau, *Political Theory and Political Science* (1979) New Brunswick, NJ: Humanities Press

J. La Palombara, *Politics Within Nations* (1974) Englewood Cliffs, NJ: Prentice Hall

M. Laver, *Invitation to Politics* (1983) Oxford: Blackwell

A. Leftwich, ed., *What is Politics?* (1984) Oxford: Blackwell

S. Lukes, *Power: A Radical View* (1974) London: Macmillan

R.C. Macridis, *The Study of Comparative Government* (1955) New York, NY: Doubleday

J.G. March and J.P. Olsen, 'The new institutionalism', *Am. Pol. Sc. Rev.* (1984), pp. 734–49

J.G. March and J.P. Olsen, *Rediscovering Institutions* (1989) New York, NY: Free Press

L.C. Mayer, *Comparative Political Inquiry* (1972) Homewood, Ill.: Dorsey Press

L.C. Mayer, *Redefining Comparative Politics* (1989) London and Los Angeles, Calif.: Sage

E.J. Meehan, *Explanation in Social Science* (1968) Homewood, Ill.: Dorsey Press

P.H. Merkl, *Modern Comparative Politics* (1970) New York, NY: Holt, Rinehart and Winston

Montesquieu, *The Spirit of Laws* (1949), New York, NY: Hafner

T. Parsons, *The Social System* (1951) New York, NY: Free Press

N.W. Polsby, R.A. Dentler and P.A. Smith, *Politics and Social Life* (1963) Boston, Mass.: Houghton Mifflin

A. Przeworski and H. Teune, *The Logic of Comparative Social Inquiry* (1970) New York, NY: Wiley

C.C. Ragin, *The Comparative Method* (1987) Berkeley, Calif.: University of California Press

J.J. Rousseau, *Social Contract* (1973 edn) London: Dent

D. Rustow and K. Erickson, eds., *Comparative Political Dynamics: Global Research Perspectives* (1991) New York, NY: Collins

G. Sartori, ed., *Social Science Concepts: A Systematic Analysis* (1984) London and Los Angeles, Calif.: Sage

T. Skocpol, 'Bringing the state back in' (1985) in P. Evans, D. Rueschemeyer and T. Skocpol, eds., *Bringing the State Back In* (1985) Cambridge: Cambridge University Press, pp. 3–43

S. de Stael, *De l'Allemagne* (1958–60) 5 vol., Paris: Hachette

R. Trigg, *Understanding Social Science* (1985) Oxford: Blackwell

J.H. Turner, *The Structure of Sociological Theory* (1986) Chicago, Ill.: Dorsey Press

D.V. Verney, *The Analysis of Political Systems* (1959), London: Routledge and Kegan Paul

M. Weber, *On Charisma and Nation-Building* (1968) Chicago, Ill.: Chicago University Press

M. Weber, *The Protestant Ethic and the Spirit of Capitalism* (1976) London: Allen and Unwin

P. Winch, *The Idea of a Social Science* (1958) London: Routledge and Kegan Paul

# Bases of Political Systems, Political Development and Legitimacy

C. Ake, *A Theory of Political Integration* (1967) Homewood, Ill.: Dorsey Press

R.A. Alford, *Party and Society* (1963) New York, NY: Rand McNally

G.A. Almond and S. Verba, *The Civic Culture* (1963) Princeton, NJ: Princeton University Press

G.A. Almond and S. Verba, eds., *The Civic Culture Revisited* (1980) Princeton, NJ: Princeton University Press

D.E. Apter, *Choice and the Politics of Allocation* (1973) New Haven, Conn.: Yale University Press

A.S. Banks and R.B. Textor, *A Cross-Polity Survey* (1963), Cambridge, Mass.: MIT Press

S.I. Benn and R.S. Peters, *Social Principles and the Democratic State* (1959) London: Allen and Unwin

P.L. Berger and T. Luckman, *The Social Construction of Reality* (1966) New York, NY: Praeger

V. Bogdanor and D.E. Butler, *Democracy and Elections* (1983) Cambridge: Cambridge University Press

A. Campbell, P.E. Converse, W.E. Miller and D.E. Stokes, *Elections and the Political Order* (1966), New York, NY: Wiley

H. Carrère d'Encausse, *Decline of Empire* (1981) New York, NY: Harper and Row

J.S. Coleman, *Education and Political Development* (1965) Princeton, NJ: Princeton University Press

W. Connolly, ed., *Legitimacy and the State* (1984) Oxford: Blackwell

P. Cutright, 'National political development', in N.W. Polsby *et al.*, *Politics and Social Life* (1963) Boston, Mass.: Houghton Mifflin, pp. 569–82

R.A. Dahl, *Polyarchy* (1971) New Haven, Conn.: Yale University Press

R. Dahrendorf, *Class and Conflict in Industrial Society* (1959) Stanford, Calif.: Stanford University Press

A. Downs, *An Economic Theory of Democracy* (1957), New York, NY: Harper

E. Durkheim, *The Division of Labour in Society* (1964) New York, NY: Free Press

M. Duverger, *De la dictature* (1961) Paris: Julliard

H. Eckstein, 'A culturalist theory of political change', *Am. Pol. Sc. Rev.* (1988), pp. 789–804

R. Falk, Samuel S. Kim and S.M. Mendlovitz, eds., *Toward a Just World Order* (1982) Boulder, Colo.: Westview

G. Ferrero, *Principles of Power* (New York edn, 1945) New York, NY: Putnam

J.L. Finkle and R.W. Gable, *Political Development and Social Change* (1966) New York, NY: Wiley

C.J. Friedrich and Z. Brzezinski, *Totalitarian Dictatorship and Autocracy* (1965 edn) Cambridge, Mass.: Harvard University Press

F.I. Greenstein, *Personality and Politics* (1969) Chicago, Ill.: Markham

T.R. Gurr, *Why Men Rebel* (1970) Princeton, NJ: Princeton University Press

T.R. Gurr, ed., *Handbook of Political Conflict* (1980) New York, NY: Free Press

M. Harrop and W. Miller, *Elections and Voters: A Comparative Introduction* (1987) Basingstoke, Hants.: Macmillan

G. Hofstede, *Culture's Consequences* (1980) London and Los Angeles, Calif.: Sage

T.K. Hopkins and I. Wallerstein, *World-Systems Analysis* (1982) London and Los Angeles, Calif.: Sage

D.L. Horowitz, *Ethnic Groups in Conflict* (1985) Berkeley, Calif.: University of California Press

S.P. Huntington, *Political Order in Changing Societies* (1968) New Haven, Conn.: Yale University Press

R. Inglehart, *The Silent Revolution* (1977) Princeton, NJ: Princeton University Press

R. Inglehart, *Culture Shift in Advanced Industrial Society* (1990) Princeton, NJ: Princeton University Press

A. Inkeles and D.J. Levinson, 'National character', *Handbook of Social Psychology* (1969), vol. 4, Reading: Addison-Wesley

W. Kornhauser, *The Politics of Mass Society* (1959) New York, NY: Free Press

G.T. Kurian, *The New Book of World Rankings* (1984) New York, NY: Facts on File

R.E. Lane, *Political Ideology* (1962) New York, NY: Free Press

J.J. Linz and A. Stepan, ed., *The Breakdown of Democratic Regimes* (1978) Baltimore, Md: Johns Hopkins University Press

A. Lijphart, *Democracy in Plural Societies* (1977) New Haven, Conn.: Yale University Press

S.M. Lipset, *The First New Nation* (1963) New York, NY: Basic Books

S.M. Lipset, *Political Man* (1983) London: Heinemann

A. Marsh, *Political Action in Europe and the USA* (1990) Basingstoke, Hants.: Macmillan

B. Moore, Jr, *The Origins of Dictatorship and Democracy* (1966) Boston, Mass.: Beacon

D.N. Nelson, *Elite-Mass Relations in Communist Systems* (1988) London: Macmillan

D. Neubauer, 'Some conditions of democracy', *Am. Pol. Sc. Rev.* (1967), pp. 1002–9

G. O'Donnell, P. Schmitter and L. Whitehead, eds., *Transition from Authoritarian Rule* (1986) Baltimore, Md: Johns Hopkins University Press

M. Olson Jr, *The Logic of Collective Action* (1971) Cambridge, Mass.: Harvard University Press

N.W. Polsby, 'The institutionalisation of the House of Representatives', *Am. Pol. Sc. Rev.* (1962), pp. 144–68

L.W. Pye, ed., *Political Culture and Political Development* (1965) Princeton, NJ: Princeton University Press

L.W. Pye, *Aspects of Political Development* (1966) Boston, Mass.: Little, Brown

L.W. Pye and S. Verba, *Political Culture and Political Development* (1965) Princeton, NJ: Princeton University Press

A.A. Rabushka and K.A. Shepsle, *Politics in Plural Societies* (1971) Columbus, Ohio: Merrill

D.W. Rae and M. Taylor, *The Analysis of Political Cleavages* (1970) New Haven, Conn.: Yale University Press

W.S. Robinson, 'Ecological Correlates and the Behavior of Individuals', *Am. Soc. Rev.* (1950) **15** (3), pp. 351–7

R. Rogowski, *Rational Legitimacy* (1974) Princeton, NJ: Princeton University Press

S. Rokkan, *Citizens, Elections, Parties* (1970) Oslo: Universitetsforlaget

R. Rose and G. Peters, *The Political Consequences of Economic Overload* (1977) Glasgow: University of Strathclyde, Centre for the Study of Public Policy

W.W. Rostow, *The Stages of Economic Growth* (1960) Cambridge: Cambridge University Press

T. Skocpol, *States and Social Revolutions* (1979) Cambridge: Cambridge University Press

C.L. Taylor and D.A Jodice, *World Handbook of Political and Social Indicators* (2 vols.) (3rd edn, 1983), New Haven, Conn.: Yale University Press

D. Truman, *The Governmental Process. Political Interests and Public Opinion* (1951) New York: A.A. Knopf

J.H. Turner, *The Structure of Sociological Theory* (1986) Chicago, Ill.: Dorsey Press

S. Verba and H.H. Nie, *Participation in America* (1972) New York, NY: Harper and Row

S. Verba, H.H. Nie and Jae-on Kim, eds., *Participation and Political Equality* (1978) Chicago, Ill.: Chicago University Press

T. Vanhanen, 'The level of democratisation related to socioeconomic variables in 147 states in 1980–85', *Scand. Pol. Stud.* (1989) **12**, (2), pp. 95–127

T. Vanhanen, *The Politics of Ethnic Nepotism* (1991) New Delhi: Stirling

T. Vanhanen, *On the Evolutionary Roots of Politics* (1992a) New Delhi: Stirling

T. Vanhanen, *Strategies of Democratisation* (1992b) Washington: Crane Russak

I. Wallerstein, *The Capitalist World Economy* (1979) Cambridge: Cambridge University Press

M. Weber, *The Theory of Social and Economic Organization* (1947) New York, NY: Free Press

M. Weber, *Basic Concepts in Sociology* (1962) New York, NY: Philosophical Library

M. Weiner and S.P. Huntington, eds., *Understanding Political Development* (1987) Boston, Mass.: Little, Brown

C. Young, *The Politics of Cultural Pluralism* (1976) Madison, Wis.: University of Wisconsin Press

T. Zeldin, *The Political System of Napoleon III* (1958) London: Macmillan

E. Zimmermann, 'Macro-comparative research in political protest', in T.R. Gurr, ed., *Handbook of Political Conflict* (1980) New York, NY: Free Press, pp. 167–237

## Groups

S. Barnes, M. Kaase *et al.*, *Mass Participation in Five Western Democracies* (1979) London and Los Angeles, Calif.: Sage

P.M. Blau, *Exchange and Power in Social Life* (1964) New York, NY: Wiley

A.F. Bentley, *The Process of Government* (1967) Cambridge, Mass.: Harvard University Press

F.G. Castles, *Pressure Groups and Political Culture* (1967) London: Routledge and Kegan Paul

H.W. Ehrman, *Interest Groups in Four Continents* (1958) Pittsburgh, Pa: University of Pittsburgh Press

S.N. Eisenstadt, *The Political Systems of Empires* (1963) New York, NY: Free Press

S.E. Finer, *Anonymous Empire* (1966) London: Pall Mall

M. Fortes and E.E. Evans-Pritchard, *African Political Systems* (1940) Oxford: Oxford University Press

W. Galenson, *Trade Union Democracy in Western Europe* (1962) Berkeley, Calif.: University of California Press

C.B. Hagan, 'The group in political science', in R. Young, ed., *Approaches to the Study of Politics* (1958), New York, NY: New York University Press

B. Klandermans, H. Kriesi and S. Tarrow, eds., *From Structure to Action: Comparing Social Movement Research* (1981) Greenwich, Conn.: JAI

G. Lehmbruch and P. Schmitter, eds., *Patterns of Corporatist Policy-Making* (1982) London and Los Angeles, Calif.: Sage

T. Lowi, *The Politics of Disorder* (1971) New York, NY: Basic Books

D. Rucht, *Research on Social Movements: The State of the Art in Europe and the USA* (1991) Frankfurt: Campus

H.H. Storing, ed., *Essays on the Scientific Study of Politics* (1962) New York, NY: Holt, Rinehart and Winston

A.J. Taylor, *Trade Unions and Politics* (1989) London: Macmillan

F. Toennies, *Community and Association* (London edn, 1955) London: Routledge and Kegan Paul

D. Truman, *The Governmental Process* (1951) New York, NY: Knopf

L. Weinstein, 'The group approach', in H. Storing, ed., *Essays on the Scientific Study of Politics* (1962), pp. 153–224

R. Young, ed., *Approaches to the Study of Politics* (1958) London: Stevens

## Communication

S. Ball-Rokeach and M.G. Cantor, eds., *Media Audience and Social Structure* (1986) London and Los Angeles, Calif.: Sage

K. Bruhn Jensen and N.W. Jankowski, eds., *A Handbook of Qualitative Methodologies of Mass Communication Research* (1991) London and Los Angeles, Calif.: Sage

S.H. Chafree *et al.*, 'Mass communication and political socialisation', in J. Dennis, ed., *Socialisation to Politics* (1973) New York, NY: Wiley, pp. 391–409

J. Curran, M. Gurevitch and J. Woollocott, eds., *Mass Communication and Society* (1977) London: E. Arnold

M.L. De Fleur and S. Ball-Rokeach, *Theories of Mass Communication* (1982) New York, NY: Longman

J. Dennis, ed., *Socialisation to Politics* (1973) New York, NY: Wiley

K.W. Deutsch, *Nationalism and Social Communication* (1953) Cambridge, Mass.: MIT University Press

K. Deutsch, *The Nerves of Government: Models of Political Communication and Control* (1966) New York: Free Press

F.W. Frey, 'Communication and development', in I. De Sola Pool *et al.*, eds., *Handbook of Communication* (1973) Chicago, Ill.: Rand McNally, pp. 337–418

M. Gurevitch and J.G. Blumler, 'Linkages between the media and politics', in J. Curran, M. Gurevitch and J. Woollacott, eds., *Mass Communication and Society* (1977) London: E. Arnold, pp. 270–90

J.D. Halloran, ed., *The Effects of Television* (1970) London: Panther Books

P. Lazarsfeld and E. Katz, *Personal Influence* (1955) Glencoe, Ill.: Free Press

J. Lichtenberg, ed., *Democracy and the Mass Media* (1990) Cambridge: Cambridge University Press

D. McQuail, 'The influence and effects of the mass media', in J. Curran, M. Gurevitch and J. Woollacott, eds., *Mass Communication and Society* (1977) London: E. Arnold, p. 70–94

D.D. Nimmo and K.R. Sanders, eds., *Handbook of Political Communication* (1981) London and Los Angeles, Calif.: Sage

I. De Sola Pool, F.W. Frey, W. Schramm, N. Maccoby and E.B. Parker, eds., *Handbook of Communication* (1973) Chicago, Ill.: Rand McNally

L.W. Pye and S. Verba, *Communications and Political Development* (1963) Princeton, NJ: Princeton University Press

R. Williams, *Communications* (1962) Harmondsworth, Middlesex: Penguin

Windlesham, Lord, *Communication and Political Power* (1966) London: Cape

C. Zukin, 'Mass communication and public opinion', in D.D. Nimmo and K.R. Sanders, eds., *Handbook of Political Communication* (1981) London and Los Angeles, Calif.: Sage, pp. 359–90

## Political Parties, Electoral Systems, Party Systems and Referendums

H.E. Alexander, *Financing Politics* (1984) Washington, DC: Congressional Quarterly

H.E. Alexander, ed., *Comparative Political Finance in the 1980s* (1989) Cambridge: Cambridge University Press

R.J. Alexander, *Latin American Political Parties* (1973) New York, NY: Praeger

R.J. Alexander, *Political Parties in the Americas: Canada, Latin America, and the West Indies* (1982) Westport, Conn.: Greenwood.

E. Allardt and Y. Littunen, *Cleavages, Ideologies and Party Systems* (1964) Helsinki: The Academic Bookstore

S. Bartolini, 'The membership of mass parties: the Social Democratic experience', in H. Daalder and P. Mair, eds., *Western European Party Systems* (1983) London and Los Angeles, Calif.: Sage, pp. 182–91

S. Bartolini and P. Mair, *Identity, Competition, and Electoral Availability: The Stabilisation of European Electorates 1885–1985* (1990) Cambridge: Cambridge University Press

R.A. Beck, 'The dealignment era in America', in R.J. Dalton *et al.*, eds., *Electoral Change in Advanced Industrial Democracies* (1984) Princeton, NJ: Princeton University Press, pp. 240–66

F.P. Belloni and D.C. Beller, eds., *Faction Politics* (1978) Oxford: ABC Clio

J. Bernard, *A Guide to Latin American Parties* (1973) Harmondsworth, Middlesex: Penguin

K. von Beyme, ed., *Right-wing Extremism in Western Europe* (1988), London: Cass

J. Blondel, 'Party systems and patterns of government in western democracies', *Canadian J. of Pol. Sc.* (June 1968), pp. 180–203

J. Blondel, *Political Parties* (1981) London: Wildwood

V. Bogdanor, *What is Proportional Representation?* (1984) Oxford: Robertson

V. Bogdanor and D.E. Butler, eds., *Democracy and Elections* (1983) Cambridge: Cambridge University Press

I. Budge, I. Crewe and D.J. Farlie, eds., *Party Identification and Beyond* (1976) London: Wiley

I. Budge and D.J. Farlie, *Explaining and Predicting Elections* (1983) London: Allen and Unwin

I. Budge, D. Robertson and D. Hearl, *Ideology, Strategy, and Party Change* (1987) Cambridge: Cambridge University Press

D.E. Butler, *The Electoral System in Britain since 1918* (1963) Oxford: Oxford University Press

D.E. Butler, ed., *Referendums: A Comparative Study* (1978) Washington, DC: American Enterprise Institute

A. Campbell, P.E. Converse, W.E. Miller and D.E. Stoker, *The American Voter* (1960) New York: Wiley

F.G. Castles, ed., *The Impact of Parties* (1982) London and Los Angeles, Calif.: Sage

F.G. Castles and R. Wildenmann, eds., *Visions and Realities of Party Government* (1986) Berlin: De Gruyter

J.S. Coleman and C.G. Rosberg, *Political Parties and National Integration in Tropical Africa* (1964) Berkeley, Calif.: University of California Press

I. Crewe and D.M. Denver, eds., *Electoral Change in Western Democracies* (1985) London: Croom Helm

H. Daalder, ed., *Party Systems in Austria, Switzerland, the Netherlands, and Belgium* (1987) London: Frances Pinter

H. Daalder and P. Mair, eds., *Western European Party Systems* (1983) London and Los Angeles, Calif.: Sage

R.J. Dalton, S.C. Flanagen and P.A. Beck, eds., *Electoral Change in Advanced Industrial Democracies* (1984) Princeton, NJ: Princeton University Press

A.J. Day and H.W. Degenhardt, eds., *Political Parties on the World* (3rd edn, 1989) London: Longman

M. Duverger, *Political Parties* (1954) New York, NY: Wiley

L.D. Epstein, *Political Parties in Western Democracies* (1967) New York, NY: Praeger

M.P. Fiorina, *Retrospective Voting in American National Elections* (1981) New Haven, Conn.: Yale University Press

J.R. Frears, *Political Parties and Elections in the French Fifth Republic* (1977) London: Hurst

G. Hand, J. Georgel and C. Sasse, *European Electoral Systems Handbook* (1979) London: Butterworth

A.J. Heidenheimer, ed., *Comparative Political Finance in the 1980s* (1970) Lexington, Mass.: Heath

A.J. Heidenheimer, M. Johnston and V.J. Levine, *Political Corruption: A Handbook* (1989) New York, NY: Transaction Books

F.A. Hermens, *Democracy or Anarchy?* (1941), Notre Dame, Ind.: University of Notre Dame Press

R.L. Hess and G. Loewenberg, 'The Ethiopian no-party state', *Am. Pol. Sc. Rev.* (1964), pp. 947–50

R.E.M. Irving, *The Christian Democratic Parties of Western Europe* (1979) London: Allen and Unwin

K. Janda, *Political Parties: A Cross-National Survey* (1980) New York, NY: Free Press

R.S. Katz, 'Party government: a rationalistic conception', in F.G. Castles and R. Wildenmann, eds., *Visions and Realities of Party Government* (1986) Berlin: De Gruyter, pp. 31–71

R.S. Katz and P. Mair, eds., *Party Organisations: A Data Handbook on Party Organisations in Western Democracies, 1960–90* (1992) London and Los Angeles, Calif.: Sage

V.O. Key, *Southern Politics* (1949) New York, NY: Knopf

E. Kolinsky, ed., *Opposition in Western Europe* (1987) New York, NY: St Martin's Press

E. Lakeman and J.D. Lambert, *Voting in Democracies* (1955) London: Faber

K. Lawson, *The Comparative Study of Political Parties* (1976) New York, NY: St Martin's Press

D.S. Lewis and D.J. Sagar, eds., *Political Parties of Asia and the Pacific* (1992) Harlow, Essex: Longman

A. Lijphart, *Democracies* (1984a) New Haven, Conn.: Yale University Press

A. Lijphart, *Choosing an Electoral System: Issues and Alternatives* (1984b) New York, NY: Praeger

S.M. Lipset and S. Rokkan, eds., *Party Systems and Voter Alignments* (1967) New York, NY: Free Press

W.J.M. Mackenzie, *Free Elections* (1958) London: Allen and Unwin

H. McClosky, H.P. Hoffman and R. O'Hara, 'Issue conflict and consensus among leaders and followers', *Am. Pol. Sc. Rev.*, (1960), pp. 406–27

V.E. McHale, *Political Parties of Europe* (2 vols.) (1983) London: Greenwood.

R.T. McKenzie, *British Political Parties* (1963), London: Heinemann

P.H. Merkl, ed., *Western European Party Systems* (1980) New York, NY: Free Press

R. Michels, *Political Parties* (1968) New York, NY: Free Press

J.S. Mill, *Representative Government* (1910) London: Dent

F. Muller Rommel, ed., *New Politics in Western Europe* (1989) Boulder, Colo.: Westview

S. Neumann, *Modern Political Parties* (1955), Chicago, Ill: Chicago University Press

M. Ostrogorski, *Democracy and the Organization of Political Parties* (1902) New York, NY: Macmillan

A. Panebianco, *Political Parties* (1988) Cambridge: Cambridge University Press

S. Parkin, *Green Parties* (1989) London: Heretic Books

W.E. Patterson and A.H. Thomas, eds., *The Future of Social Democracy* (1986) Oxford: Oxford University Press

M. Pedersen, 'Changing patterns of electoral volatility in European party systems 1948–1977: explorations in explanation', in H. Daalder and P. Mair, eds., *Western European Party Systems* (1983) London and Los Angeles, Calif.: Sage, pp. 29–65

G. Philip, 'The dominant party system in Mexico', in V. Randall, ed., *Political Parties in the Third World* (1988) London and Los Angeles, Calif.: Sage, pp. 99–112

D. Rae, *The Political Consequences of Electoral Laws* (1971), New Haven, Conn.: Yale University Press

V. Randall, ed., *Political Parties in the Third World* (1988) London and Los Angeles, Calif.: Sage

A. Ranney, ed., *The Referendum Device* (1985) Washington, DC: American Enterprise Institute

R. Rose, *Ungovernability: Is there Fire behind the Smoke?* (1978) Glasgow: University of Strathclyde, Centre for the Study of Public Policy

R. Rose, *Do Parties Make a Difference?* (1984) London: Macmillan

J.F.S. Ross, *The Irish Electoral System* (1959) London: Pall Mall

G. Sartori, *Parties and Party Systems* (1976) Cambridge: Cambridge University Press

E.E. Schattschneider, *Party Government* (1942) New York, NY: Holt, Rinehart and Winston

B. Szajkowski, *New Political Parties of Eastern Europe and the Soviet Union* (1991) London: Longman

R.N. Tannahill, *The Communist Parties of Western Europe* (1978) London: Greenwood

J.J. Wiatr, 'One-party systems: the concept and issue for comparative studies', in E. Allardt and

Y. Littunen, *Cleavages, Ideologies and Party Systems* (1964) Helsinki: The Academic Bookstore, pp. 281–90

R.E. Wolfinger, 'Dealignment, realignment and mandates in the 1984 election', in A. Ranney, ed., *The Referendum Device* (1985) Washington, DC: American Enterprise Institute, pp. 277–96

S. Wolinetz, ed., *Parties and Party Systems in Liberal Democracies* (1988) London: Routledge

## Constitutions and Federalism

C.A. Beard, *An Economic Interpretation of the Constitution of the United States* (1935), New York, NY: Macmillan

S.H. Beer, 'The modernisation of American federalism', in D.J. Elazar, ed., *The Federal Polity* (1974) New Brunswick, NJ: Transaction Books

V. Bogdanor, ed., *Constitutions in Democratic Politics* (1988) Aldershot, Hants: Gower

M. Burgess, *Federalism and Federation* (1986) London: Croom Helm

M. Burgess and A.G. Gagon, eds., *Comparative Federalism and Federation* (1993) New York, NY: Harvester Wheatsheaf

D. Dinan, *Ever Closer Union* (1994) Basingstoke, Hants: Macmillan

D.J. Elazar, ed., *The Federal Polity* (1974) New Brunswick, NJ: Transaction Books

D.J. Elazar, *Federalism and Political Integration* (1979) Ramat Gan: Turtledove.

D.J. Elazar, ed., *Federal Systems of the World: A Handbook* (1991) Harlow, Essex: Longman

S.E. Finer, *Five Constitutions* (1979) Harmondsworth, Middlesex: Penguin

T. Fleiner Gerster, *Federalism and Decentralisation* (1987) Fribourg: Editions Universitaires

M. Forsyth, *Unions of States* (1981) New York, NY: Holmes and Meier

T.M. Franck, *Why Federations Fail* (1968) New York, NY: New York University Press

R.T. Golembiewski and A. Wildavsky, eds., *The Costs of Federalism* (1984) New Brunswick, NJ: Transaction Books

L. Henkin and A.J. Rosenthal, *Constitutionalism and Rights* (1990) New York, NY: Columbia University Press

D. Jaensch, ed., *The Politics of the New Federalism* (1977) Adelaide: Australasian Political Science Association

H.J. Laski, *The American Presidency* (1940) London: Allen and Unwin

W.S. Livingston, *Federalism and Constitutional Change* (1956) Oxford: Oxford University Press

A.Q. MacMahon, *Federalism, Mature and Emergent* (1955) New York, NY: Columbia University Press

Merkl, P.H. 'Executive–legislative federalism in West Germany', *Am. Pol. Sc. Rev.* (1959), pp. 732–54

W.H. Riker, ed., *The Development of American Federalism* (1987) Boston, Mass.: Kluwer

G. Sartori, 'Constitutionalism: a preliminary discussion', *Am. Pol. Sc. Rev.* (1962), pp. 853–64

C.G. Strong, *Modern Political Constitutions* (1963) London: Sidgwick and Jackson

M. Vile, *Constitutionalism and the Separation of Powers* (1967) Oxford: Oxford University Press

A. Vyshinsky, *The Law of the Soviet State* (1948) London: Macmillan

W. Wallace, *The Transformation of Western Europe* (1992) London: Frances Pinter

K.C. Wheare, *Federal Government* (1963) London: Oxford University Press

K.C. Wheare, *Modern Constitutions* (1966) London: Oxford University Press

## Legislatures

W. Agor, ed., *Latin American Legislatures* (1971) New York, NY: Praeger

S.K. Bailey, *Congress Makes a Law* (1950) New York, NY: Columbia University Press

J.D. Barber, *The Lawmakers* (1965) New Haven, Conn.: Yale University Press

A. Barker and M. Rush, *The Member of Parliament and his Information* (1970) London: Allen and Unwin

J. Blondel, *Comparative Legislatures* (1973) Englewood Cliffs, NJ: Prentice Hall

S.J. Downs, 'Structural changes', in P. Norton, ed., *Parliament in the 1980s* (1985) Oxford: Blackwell, pp. 48–68

J.R. Frears, *France in the Giscard Presidency* (1981) London: Allen and Unwin

P. Furlong, 'Parliament in Italian politics', in P. Norton, ed., *Parliaments in Western Europe* (1990) London: Cass, pp. 52–67

R.F. Hopkins, 'The tole of the MP in Tanzania' *Am. Pol. Sc. Rev.* (1970), pp. 754–71

Inter-Parliamentary Union, *Parliaments of the World* (1986) (2 vols.) London: Gower

A. Kornberg, ed., *Legislatures in Comparative Perspective* (1973) New York, NY: McKay

J.D. Lees and M. Shaw, eds., *Committees in Legislatures: A Comparative Analysis* (1979) London: Robertson

G. Loewenberg and S.C. Patterson, *Comparative Legislatures* (1979) Boston, Mass.: Little, Brown

D. Macrae, *Parliament, Parties, and Society in France* (1967) New York, NY: Macmillan

J.W. Marsh, 'Representational changes', in P. Norton, ed., *Parliament in the 1980s* (1985) Oxford: Blackwell, pp. 69–93

D.R. Matthews, *US Senators and their World* (1960) Chapel Hill, NC: University of North Carolina Press

D.R. Mayhew, *Party Loyalty among Congressmen* (1966) Cambridge, Mass.: Harvard University Press

M.L. Mezey, *Comparative Legislatures* (1979) Durham, N.C.: Duke University Press

P. Norton, ed., *Parliament in the 1980s* (1985) Oxford: Blackwell

P. Norton, ed., *Parliaments in Western Europe* (1990) London: Cass

S.C. Patterson, 'The semi-sovereign congress', in A. King, ed., *The New American Political System* (1978) Washington DC: American Enterprise Institute, pp. 125–77

J. Smith and L.D. Musolf, eds., *Legislatures in Development* (1979) Durham, NC: Duke University Press

D.B. Truman, *The Congressional Party* (1959) New York, NY: Wiley

## Executives and Leadership

W. Bakema, 'The ministerial career', in J. Blondel and J.L. Thiébault, eds., *The Profession of Cabinet Minister in Western Europe* (1991) Basingstoke, Hants: Macmillan, pp. 70–98

J.D. Barber, *The Presidential Character* (1977) Englewood Cliffs, NJ: Prentice Hall

B.M. Bass, *Stogdill's Handbook on Leadership* (1981) New York, NY: Free Press

J. Blondel, *World Leaders* (1980) London and Los Angeles, Calif.: Sage

J. Blondel, *The Organisation of Governments* (1982) London and Los Angeles, Calif.: Sage

J. Blondel, *Government Ministers in the Contemporary World* (1985) London and Los Angeles, Calif.: Sage

J. Blondel, *Political Leadership* (1987) London and Los Angeles, Calif.: Sage

J. Blondel and F. Muller-Rommel, eds., *Cabinets in Western Europe* (1988) London: Macmillan

J. Blondel and F. Muller-Rommel, eds., *Governing Together* (1993) Basingstoke, Hants: Macmillan

J. Blondel and J.L. Thiébault, eds., *The Profession of Cabinet Minister in Western Europe* (1991) Basingstoke, Hants: Macmillan

V. Bogdanor, ed., *Coalition Government in Western Europe* (1983) London: Heinemann

E.C. Browne and J. Dreijmannis, eds., *Government Coalitions in Western Democracies* (1982) London: Longman

Z. Brzezinski and S.P. Huntington, *Political Power USA/USSR* (1963), London: Chatto and Windus

V. Bunce, *Do New Leaders Make a Difference?* (1981) Princeton, NJ: Princeton University Press

J.McG. Burns, *Leadership* (1978) New York, NY: Harper and Row

C. Campbell, *Governments under Stress* (1983) Toronto: University of Toronto Press

H.D. Clarke and M.M. Czudnowski, eds., *Political Elites in Anglo-American Democracies* (1986) De Kalb, Ill.: Northern Illinois University Press

E.S. Corwin, *The President, Office and Powers* (1957) New York, NY: New York University Press

T.E. Cronin, *The State of the Presidency* (1975) Boston, Mass.: Little, Brown

A. De Swaan, *Coalition Theories and Cabinet Formations* (1973) Amsterdam: Elsevier

F.E. Fiedler, *A Theory of Leadership Effectiveness* (1967) New York, NY: McGraw-Hill

G.M. Fink, *Prelude to the Presidency* (1980) Westport, Conn.: Greenwood

A.L. George and J.L. George, *Woodrow Wilson and Colonel House: A Personality Study* (1956) New York, NY: Dover

F.I. Greenstein, *Personality and Politics* (1969) Chicago, Ill.: Markham

B. Headey, *British Cabinet Ministers* (1974) London: Allen and Unwin

H. Heclo, *A Government of Strangers* (1977) Washington, DC: Brookings Institution

S. Hook, *The Hero in History* (1955) Boston, Mass.: Beacon

R.H. Jackson and C.G. Rosberg, *Personal Rule in Black Africa* (1982) Berkeley, Calif.: University of California Press

K.F. Janda, 'Toward the explication of the concept of leadership in terms of the concept of power', in G.D. Paige, *Political Leaderships* (1972) New York, NY: Free Press, pp. 45–64

B. Kellerman, ed., *Leadership* (1984) Englewood Cliffs, NJ: Prentice Hall

A. King, ed., *Both Ends of the Avenue* (1983) Washington, DC: American Enterprise Institute

H.D. Lasswell, and D. Lerner, *World Revolutionary Elites* (1965) Cambridge, Mass.: MIT University Press

J. Linz, 'The perils of presidentialism', *Journal of Democracy* (1990), pp. 51–69

G.M. Luebbert, *Comparative Democracy* (1986) New York, NY: Columbia University Press

T.T. McKie and B.W. Hogwood, eds., *Unlocking the Cabinet* (1985) London and Los Angeles, Calif.: Sage

R.D. McKinlay and A.S. Cohan, 'A comparative analysis of the political and economic performance of military and civilian regimes', *Comp. Pol.*, October 1975, pp. 1–30

J. Mackintosh, *The British Cabinet* (1962) London: Stevens

R. Neustadt, *Presidential Power* (1960) New York, NY: Wiley

R.L. Noland, 'Presidential disability and the proposed constitutional amendment', *Amer. Psychologist* (1966) pp. 232–3

G.D. Paige, *Political Leadership* (1972) New York, NY: Free Press

M. Rejai with K. Phillips, *Leaders of Revolution* (1979) London and Los Angeles, Calif.: Sage

M. Rejai with K. Phillips, *World Revolutionary Leaders* (1983) London and Los Angeles, Calif.: Sage

W. Riker, *The Theory of Political Coalitions* (1962) New Haven, Conn.: Yale University Press

R. Rose, *Understanding Big Government* (1984) London and Los Angeles, Calif.: Sage

G. Rossiter, *The American Presidency* (1960) New York, NY: Harcourt

M. Rush, *Political Succession in the USSR* (1965) New York, NY: Columbia University Press

M.S. Shugart and J.M. Carey, *Presidents and Assemblies* (1992) New York, NY: Cambridge University Press

G. Smith, *Politics in Western Europe* (1989) Aldershot: Gower

K. Strom, *Minority Government and Majority Rule* (1990) New York, NY: Cambridge University Press

J.L. Thiébault, 'The social background of western Europe cabinet ministers', in J. Blondel and J.L. Thiébault, eds., *The Profession of Cabinet Minister in Western Europe* (1991) Basingstoke, Hants: Macmillan, pp. 19–30

R.C. Tucker, *Politics as Leadership* (1981) Columbia, Mo.: University of Missouri Press

A. Wildavsky, *The Nursing Father* (1984) University, Ala.: University of Alabama Press

A.R. Willner, *The Spellbinders* (1984) New Haven, Conn.: Yale University Press

## Bureaucracies, Policy Studies, the Military and Control

J.D. Aberbach, R.D. Putnam and B.A. Rockman, *Bureaucrats and Politicians in Western Democracies* (1981) Cambridge, Mass.: Harvard University Press

P.C. Asiodu, 'The civil service: an insider's view', in O. Oyediran, ed., *Nigerian Government and Politics under Military Rule (1979)* London: Macmillan, pp. 73–9

P. Bachrach and M.S. Baratz, 'Decisions and non-decisions', *Amer. Pol. Sc. Rev.*, (1963), pp. 641–51

P. Bachrach and M.S. Baratz, *Power and Poverty* (1970) New York, NY: Oxford University Press

P. Baehr and B. Wittrock, eds., *Policy Analysis and Policy Innovation* (1981) London and Los Angeles, Calif.: Sage

E. Burke (1975) *Edmund Burke on Government, Politics and Society* (1975) Hemel Hempstead: Harvester Wheatsheaf

D. Braybrooke and C.E. Lindblom, *A Strategy of Decision* (1963) New York, NY: Free Press

L.N. Brown and F.G. Jacobs, *The Court of Justice of the European Communities* (1989) London: Maxwell and Street

G.E. Caiden, ed., *The Ombudsman: An International Handbook* (1983) Westport, Conn.: Greenwood

R.K. Carr, *The Supreme Court and Judicial Review* (1942) New York, NY: Holt, Rinehart and Winston

P.G. Cerny and M.A. Schain, eds., *French Politics and Public Policy* (1980) London: Methuen

B. Chapman, *The Profession of Government* (1961) London: Allen and Unwin

T.W. Copeland, ed., *The Correspondence of Edmund Burke* (1950–70) Cambridge: Cambridge University Press

M. Crozier, *The Bureaucratic Phenomenon* (1964) London: Tavistock

R.A. Dahl, *Who Governs?* (1963a) New Haven, Conn.: Yale University Press

R.A. Dahl and C.E. Lindblom, *Politics, Economics, and Welfare* (1963) New York, NY: Harper

S. Decalo, *Coups and Army Rule in Africa* (1976) New Haven, Conn.: Yale University Press

G. Drewry and T. Butcher, *The Civil Service Today* (1988) Oxford: Blackwell

Y. Dror, *Ventures in Policy Sciences* (1971) Amsterdam: Elsevier

W.N. Dunn, *Public Policy Analysis* (1994) Englewood Cliffs, NJ: Prentice Hall

S.E. Finer, *The Man on Horseback* (1962) London: Pall Mall

D. Foulkes, *Introduction to Administrative Law* (1976) London: Butterworth

J.A.G. Griffith, *The Politics of the Judiciary* (1985) London: Fontana

C. Ham and M. Hill, *The Policy Process in the Modern Capitalist State* (1993) Hemel Hempstead, Herts: Harvester Wheatsheaf

A.J. Heidenheimer, H. Heclo and C.T. Adams, *Comparative Public Policy* (3rd edn, 1990) Basingstoke, Hants: Macmillan

Lord Hewart, *The New Despotism* (1929) London: Benn

B.W. Hogwood and L.A. Gunn, *Policy Analysis for the Real World* (1984) Oxford: Oxford University Press

F. Hunter, *Community Power Structure* (1953) Chapel Hill, NC: University of North Carolina Press

S.P. Huntington, *The Soldier and the State* (1957) New York, NY: Free Press

M. Janowitz, *The Military in the Development of New Nations* (1964) Chicago, Ill.: University of Chicago Press

W.I. Jenkins, *Policy Analysis* (1978) Oxford: Martin Robertson

P. Kellner and Lord Crowther-Hunt, *The Civil Servants* (1980) London: Macdonald

O. Kirchheimer, *Political Justice* (1961) Princeton, NJ: Princeton University Press

J.E. Lane, *Bureaucracy and Public Choice* (1987) London and Los Angeles, Calif.: Sage

J. La Palombara, ed., *Bureaucracy and Political Development* (1963) Princeton, NJ: Princeton University Press

C.E. Lindblom, *The Policy-Making Process* (1968) Englewood Cliffs, NJ: Prentice Hall

C. Liske, W. Loehr and J. McCamant, *Comparative Public Policy* (1975) New York, NY: Wiley

T.A. Lowi, 'Four styles of policy, politics and choice', *Publ. Admin. Rev.* (1972) 32, pp. 298–310

H. McClosky, *The American Supreme Court* (1960) Chicago, Ill.: University of Chicago Press

J. Marceau, 'Power and its possessors', in P.G. Cerny and M.A. Schain, eds., *French Politics and Public Policy* (1980) London: Methuen, pp. 48–78

C.W. Mills, *The Power Elite* (1956) New York, NY: Oxford University Press

O. Odetola, *Military Regimes and Development* (1982) London: Allen and Unwin

O. Oyediran, ed., *Nigerian Government and Politics under Military Rule* (1979) London: Macmillan

K.E. Portney, *Approaching Public Policy Analysis* (1986) Englewood Cliffs, NJ: Prentice Hall

J. Richardson, ed., *Policy Styles in Western Europe* (1982) London: Allen and Unwin

F. Ridley and J. Blondel, *Public Administration in France* (1964) London: Routledge and Kegan Paul

F.W. Riggs, 'Bureaucrats and political development: a paradoxical view', in J. La Palombara, ed., *Bureaucracies and Political Development* (1963) Princeton, NJ: Princeton University Press, pp. 120–67

F.W. Riggs, ed., *Frontiers of Development Administration* (1971) Raleigh, NC: Duke University Press

R. Rose, *The Challenge of Governance: Studies in Overloaded Politics* (1980) London: Sage

R. Rose, *Lesson-Drawing in Public Policy* (1993) Chatham, NJ: Chatham House

E.V. Rostow, *The Sovereign Prerogative* (1962) New Haven, Conn.: Yale University Press

D.C. Rowat, ed., *The Ombudsman* (1968) London: Allen and Unwin

G. Schubert, *Constitutional Politics* (1960) New York, NY: Holt, Rinehart and Winston

G. Schubert, *Judicial Decision-Making* (1963) New York, NY: Free Press

P. Self, *Administrative Theory and Politics* (1977) London: Allen and Unwin

H.A. Simon, *Administrative Behaviour* (1957) New York, NY: Free Press

J.W. Sloan, *Public Policy in Latin America: A Comparative Survey* (1984) Pittsburgh: University of Pittsburgh Press

E. Strauss, *The Ruling Servants* (1961) London: Allen and Unwin

E.N. Suleiman, ed., *Bureaucrats and Policy-Making* (1984) New York, NY: Meier
A. Wildavsky, *Speaking Truth to Power: The Art and Craft of Policy Analysis* (1979) Boston, Mass.: Little, Brown

# Studies of political life

## General

G.A. Almond, ed., *Comparative Politics* (1974) Boston, Mass.: Little, Brown
M. Curtis, ed., *Comparative Politics* (1990) New York, NY: Harper and Row
S.E. Finer, *Comparative Government* (1970) Harmondsworth, Middlesex: Penguin
R.C. Macridis and R.E. Ward, *Modern Political Systems* (Europe and Asia) (1963) Englewood Cliffs, NJ: Prentice Hall

## Advanced industrial countries

W. Bagehot, *The English Constitution* (1963) London: Fontana
S.B. Beer and A.B. Ulam, *Patterns of Government: The Major Political Systems of Europe* (1973) New York, NY: Random House
Lord Bryce, *The American Commonwealth* (1891) New York, NY: Macmillan
Lord Bryce, *Modern Democracies* (1921) New York, NY: Macmillan
R.A. Dahl, *Political Opposition in Western Democracies* (1966) New Haven, Conn.: Yale University Press
R.A. Dahl, *Pluralist Democracy in the United States* (1967) New York, NY: Rand McNally
A. King, ed., *The New American Political System* (1978) Washington, DC: American Enterprise Institute
J.E. Lane and S.O. Ersson, *Politics and Society in Western Europe* (1991) London and Los Angeles, Calif.: Sage
A.L. Lowell, *Governments and Parties in Continental Europe* (1896) (2 vols.) Cambridge, Mass.: Harvard University Press
G. Smith, *Politics in Western Europe* (1989) Aldershot, Hants: Gower
A. de Tocqueville, *Democracy in America* (1947) Oxford: Oxford University Press
R.E. Ward, *Japan's Political System*, Englewood Cliffs, NJ: Prentice Hall

## Communist countries

F. Barghoorn, *The USSR* (1966) Boston, Mass.: Little, Brown
L. Holmes, *Politics in the Communist World* (1986) London: Allen and Unwin
L. Shapiro, *The Communist Party of the Soviet Union* (1960) London: Eyre and Spottiswoode
R.F. Staar, *Communist Regimes in Eastern Europe* (1982) Stanford, Calif.: Hoover Institution
S. White, J. Gardner and G. Schöpflin, *Communist Political Systems* (1981) London: Macmillan

## Developing countries

J.D. Barkan and J.J. Okumu, eds., *Politics and Public Opinion in Kenya and Tanzania* (1979) New York, NY: Praeger

P. Cammack, D. Pool and W. Tordoff, *Third World Politics* (1988) London: Macmillan

G.M. Carter and P. O'Meara, eds., *African Independence: The First Twenty-five Years* (1985) Bloomington, Ind.: University of Indiana Press

N. Chazan, R. Mortimer, J. Ravenhill and D. Rothchild, *Power and Politics in Contemporary Africa* (1988) Basingstoke, Hants: Macmillan

C. Clapham, *Third World Politics* (1985) London: Croom Helm

L. Cliffe, *One-Party Democracy: Tanzania* (1967) Nairobi: East Africa Publishing House

L.D. Diamond, J.J. Linz and S.M. Lipset, *Democracy in Developing Countries* (4 vols.) (1988–9) Boulder, Colo.: Lynne Rienner

M. Halpern, *The Politics of Change in the Middle East and North Africa* (1963) Princeton, NJ: Princeton University Press

M.C. Hudson, *Arab Politics* (1977) New Haven, Conn.: Yale University Press

K.A. Kemal, *Turkey's Politics: The Transition to a Multi-Party System* (1959) Princeton, NJ: Princeton University Press

J. Lambert, *Latin America* (1967) Berkeley, Calif.: University of California Press

D. Lerner, *The Passing of Traditional Society* (1958) New York, NY: Free Press

R.L. Park and B. Bueno de Mesquita, *India's Political System* (1979) Englewood Cliffs, NJ: Prentice Hall

J. Peeler, *Latin American Democracies* (1982) Chapel Hill, NC: University of North Carolina Press

L.W. Pye, *Politics, Personality, and Nation-Building* (Burma) (1962) Cambridge, Mass.: MIT Press

R.E. Scott, *Mexican Government in Transition* (1964) Chicago, Ill.: University of Illinois Press

P. Smith, *Labyrinths of Power: Political Recruitment in Twentieth Century Mexico* (1979) Princeton, NJ: Princeton University Press

W. Tordoff, *Government and Politics in Africa* (1984) London: Macmillan

R.E. Ward and D. Rustow, *Political Modernization in Japan and Turkey* (1964) Princeton, NJ: Princeton University Press

C. Young, *Ideology and Development in Africa* (1982) New Haven, Conn.: Yale University Press

# Index